Insight Guides

CALIFORNIA

CALIFORNIA
The 31st State

ROCK N ROLL
The 31st State

I ♥ LA
Los Angeles

HOLLYWOOD
The 31st

D1506296

Discovery
CHANNEL

APA PUBLICATIONS   L
Part of the Langenscheidt Publishing Group

ABOUT THIS BOOK

Editorial

Project Editor
Martha Ellen Zenfell
Editorial Director
Brian Bell

Distribution

UK & Ireland
GeoCenter International Ltd
The Viables Centre , Harrow Way
Basingstoke, Hants RG22 4BJ
Fax: (44) 1256-817988

United States
Langenscheidt Publishers, Inc.
46–35 54th Road, Maspeth, NY 11378
Fax: (718) 784-0640

Canada
Prologue Inc.
1650 Lionel Bertrand Blvd., Boisbriand
Québec, Canada J7H 1N7
Tel: (450) 434-0306. Fax: (450) 434-2627

Australia & New Zealand
Hema Maps Pty. Ltd.
24 Allgas Street, Slacks Creek 4127
Brisbane, Australia
Tel: (61) 7 3290 0322. Fax: (61) 7 3290 0478

Worldwide
Apa Publications GmbH & Co.
Verlag KG (Singapore branch)
38 Joo Koon Road, Singapore 628990
Tel: (65) 865-1600. Fax: (65) 861-6438

Printing

Insight Print Services (Pte) Ltd
38 Joo Koon Road, Singapore 628990
Tel: (65) 865-1600. Fax: (65) 861-6438

©2000 Apa Publications GmbH & Co.
Verlag KG (Singapore branch)
All Rights Reserved
First Edition 1984
Seventh Edition (Updated) 2000

CONTACTING THE EDITORS
Although every effort is made to
provide accurate information, we
live in a fast-changing world and
would appreciate it if readers
would call our attention to any
errors or outdated information
that may occur by writing to:
**Insight Guides, P.O. Box 7910,
London SE1 1WE, England.
Fax: (44 171) 403-0290.
e-mail:
insight@apaguide.demon.co.uk**

This guidebook combines the interests and enthusiasms of two of the world's best known information providers: Insight Guides, whose titles have set the standard for visual travel guides since 1970, and Discovery Channel, the world's premier source of nonfiction television programming.

The editors of Insight Guides provide both practical advice and general understanding about a destination's history, culture, institutions and people. Discovery Channel and its Web site, www.discovery.com, help millions of viewers explore their world from the comfort of their own home and also encourage them to explore it firsthand.

How to use this book

Visitors instinctively understand the word "Eureka," California's state motto, when they first discover this rich region. The word means: "I have found it." With its mountains, redwood forests, beaches, cosmopolitan cities and varied lifestyles, California is one of the world's most exciting travel destinations.

How to use this book

Insight guides are structured both to

convey an understanding of the region and its culture, and to guide readers through its best sights and activities:

◆ To truly understand modern California, it's important to know something of the state's past. The first section, therefore, covers California's wide-ranging history and culture in authoritative essays written by experts.

◆ The main Places section, broken down into Northern and Southern California, provides a full run-down of all the attractions and destinations worth seeing. The places of major interest are cross-referenced by number or letter with full-color maps.

◆ The Travel Tips listing section provides a convenient point of reference for recommendations on travel, hotels, restaurants, shops, sports, culture and local festivals. Information may be located quickly by using the index printed on the back cover flap, which can serve as a bookmark.

The contributors

This new edition was supervised by London-based, American-born **Martha Ellen Zenfell**, who looks after Insight's North American titles. This edition builds on the previous version edited on-site in California by **John Wilcock**, a graduate of the *New York Times* travel desk and project editor of several Insight Guides, including *Insight Guide: Los Angeles*. Wilcock updated and contributed substantially to this new-look edition, as did **John Eldan** and **Erika Lenkert**.

Skilled contributors to previous editions include local residents **Jeffrey Davis**, **Sean Wagstaff**, **Tom Cole**, **Joan Talmage Weiss**, **Karen Klabin**, **Dennis Pottenger**, **Jessica Cunningham**, **Howard Rabinowitz** and **Julie Petersen**. A very special thanks must go to **Jon Carroll**, **Tracey Johnston** and **Ben Kalb**, who created such a solid edition back in 1984 that subsequent revamps have been both painless and seamless.

Adding enormously to the look of the book are the photographs of San Francisco-based **Catherine Karnow**, who was also the principal lensperson on *Insight Guide: Los Angeles*, and the contributions of photographers **Doug Traverso**, **Glyn Genin** and **Bret Reed Lundberg**.

Map Legend

Symbol	Meaning
— ‐ —	International Boundary
— — —	State Boundary
⊖	Border Crossing
‐ ● ‐	National Park/ Nature Reserve
— — —	Ferry Route
Ⓜ	Subway
⊕ ✈	Airport
🚌	Bus Station
Ⓟ	Parking
❶	Tourist Information
✉	Post Office
✝ ⚲ ☧	Church/Ruins
⚑ ⚔	Castle/Ruins
∴	Archaeological Site
⋒	Cave
�𝍏	Statue/Monument
★	Place of Interest

The main places of interest in the **Places** section are cross-referenced by letter or number (e.g. ❶), with a full-color map, and a symbol at the top of every right-hand page tells you where to find the specific map.

Insight Guide CALIFORNIA

CONTENTS

Maps

Introduction

History

People and Culture

A golden day
by the bay,
San Francisco

Places

Travel Tips

Insight On...

Information Panels

CALIFORNIA HERE I COME

The California Dream has been described as "a love affair

with an idea and a surrender to a collective fantasy"

For more than a century, since the arrival of the transcontinental railroad, California has been the last stop on the line for Americans heading west in search of a new life. James J. Rawls, author of the above description, said that California's promise raised the expectations of the millions who came to the state hoping that their lives would be better than the one they left behind. "California is to them their best – or perhaps their last – chance for success."

Even if for many longtime residents the dream has soured in the reality of traffic-clogged freeways, social unrest and blue skies too often filtered through man-made clouds, there are always new dreamers arriving – many from lands where a little smog seems a small price to pay for the freedom that goes with it. Truth to tell, California is a highly enticing and fascinating place, America "only more so," as Wallace Stegner put it, "the national culture at its most energetic end. In a prosperous country, we are more prosperous than most… more mobile… more tasteless… more energetically creative… more optimistic… more anxious."

Twenty-five years after writing that, Stegner said he hadn't changed his view, but he was regretful about "the excesses of wide-open opportunities and uncontrollable growth." And mainly over water, he said, referring to the age-old battle between the north and south, it had split itself politically in two.

A curious thing, this split, with Northern California centered around its nominal "capital" of San Francisco, and Southern California beholden to Los Angeles. It's going a bit too far to state that they hate each other, but physically and temperamentally they are very different. From a visitor's point of view that's all to the good: two very different destinations on the same coastline, and both in the same state.

Most trips in this book begin from one or the other, with the dividing line roughly at San Luis Obispo. Although this is about halfway between Los Angeles and San Francisco, it's not, strictly speaking, the halfway point of the state's coastline. California stretches for at least another 300 miles (480 km) beyond the latter, all the way north to the Oregon border. We deal with that in the chapter named "The High North." It's sparsely populated up there, but of course some people prefer that.

Movie stars to the south; majestic solitude to the north. Can you blame anyone for thinking California was their best possible chance for success? ❑

PRECEDING PAGES: the wind-whipped waves of Big Sur; the natural furnace of the Mohave Desert; a San Francisco fog envelops the Golden Gate bridge; Los Angeles by night – one of the world's biggest consumers of electricity.
LEFT: a mad-hatted welcome to San Francisco.

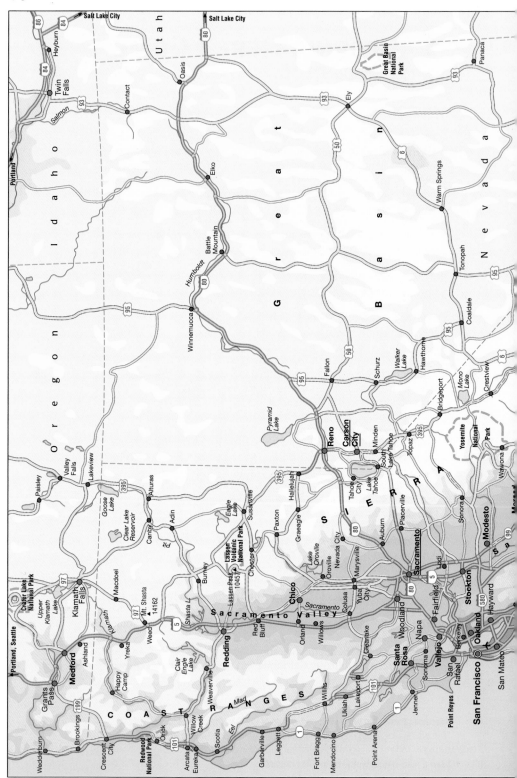

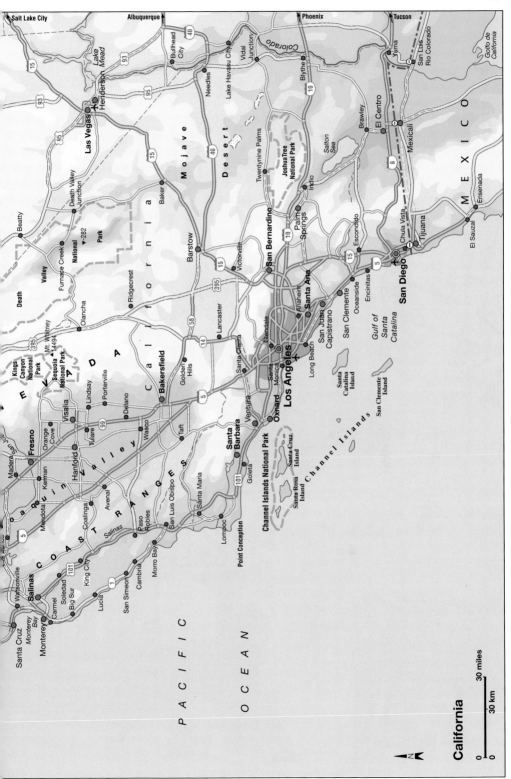

California

N

0   30 miles

0   30 km

History Timeline

Circa **9000 BC** The first nomads reach what is now California.

AD 500 Miwok tribes settle in the San Francisco Bay region.

1579 Sir Francis Drake anchors on the northern coast and leaves behind, near what is now Drake's Bay, a small brass plate, undiscovered until 1936.

1769 Adventurer Gaspar de Portola discovers the small Indian village of Yong-na and renames the settlement Porciuncula.

1770s The Spanish government founds a Presidio (military garrison) and mission near San Francisco Bay.

1781 Don Felipe de Neve marches from the San Gabriel mission with 11 Mexican families to found what is to become Los Angeles.

1769–1823 Spanish padres found 21 missions along the Royal Road (El Camino Real) between San Diego and Sonoma.

1804 The Mexican territory of California is divided into a northern and a southern section, reflecting the land's differences.

1820s Mexico breaks away from Spain.

1846 The US declares war on Mexico and captures California.

1848 Gold is discovered at Sutter's Fort in the Sierra foothills and within three years 200,000 prospectors have flooded Northern California.

1850 September 9, with a constitution already in place, California becomes the 31st state.

1850s Under successive treaties with the Federal government (but never ratified by the Senate) Native Americans sign away up to 90 percent of their lands.

1858 The Butterfield Stage Line delivers Los Angeles' first overland mail.

1859 The discovery of the Comstock Lode turns San Francisco from a frontier town into a prosperous metropolis.

1860s Constructon of railroads to link the East and West Coasts of America begins.

1869 The first transcontinental railroad is completed, with a terminus at Oakland.

1873 The world's first cable car runs between Kearny and Jones Street in San Francisco.

1874 The first navel orange trees are planted at Riverside.

1876 The Southern Pacific Railway arrives in Los Angeles, nine years before the Santa Fe.

1887 Horace W. Wilcox opens a subdivision that his wife, Daeda, names Hollywood.

1893 Edward Doheny and C.A. Canfield strike oil near the site of today's MacArthur Park in downtown Los Angeles.

1905 Abbott Kinney opens his Venetian-style resort with canals and gondolieri near Los Angeles' Santa Monica.

1906 A massive earthquake measuring 8.2 on the Richter scale rocks San Francisco. At least 250,000 people are left homeless, but rebuilding begins immediately.

1908 Ex-Chicago filmmaker William Selig completes *The Count of Monte Cristo,* Southern California's first commercial film.

1911 Hollywood's first movie, *The Law of the Range*, is filmed inside a former tavern in a city gone "dry."

1913 Water from the eastern Sierra Nevada mountains reaches Los Angeles via the Owens Aqueduct.

1915 Thomas Watson, a resident of San Francisco, receives the first transcontinental phone call from Alexander Graham Bell.

1926 Second-string studio Warners adds sound to its feature *Don Juan* and the following year gives Al Jolson some dialogue in *The Jazz Singer* and the sound barrier is truly broken.

1927 The first American Academy of Motion Pictures awards, or, as they are better known, the Oscars, are presented.

1932 The Olympic Games are staged in what is then the world's largest stadium, the Coliseum in Los Angeles.

1933 Construction begins on San Francisco's Golden Gate and Bay Bridges.

1933 An earthquake (measuring 6.3 on the Richter scale) kills 120 people in Los Angeles.

1937 The Golden Gate Bridge is opened to an uproarious reception, six months after the Oakland Bay Bridge.

1939 LA's Union Station, the last of the great railroad terminals, opens.

1945 The United Nations Organizaton is born in San Francisco with 50 countries agreeing to sign its Charter.

1947 The California legislature passes a law against smog.

1951 In the San Francisco Opera House, the Japanese Prime Minister signs the treaty ending World War II.

1953 Lawrence Ferlinghetti opens City Lights bookstore in San Francisco's North Beach which becomes the hang-out for the country's "Beats" or beatniks.

1955 Disneyland opens at Anaheim.

1960s Hippies, leftists and idealists are drawn to San Francisco's Haight-Ashbury district and, in 1967, celebrate the Summer of Love.

1963 California's population exceeds that of every other state.

1965 Rioting in the Watts area of Los Angeles kills 34 people.

1968 Presidential candidate Robert F. Kennedy is shot and killed in Los Angeles.

1971 An earthquake measured at 6.6 on the Richter scale claims the lives of 64 Southern Californians.

1974 Oil tycoon J. Paul Getty donates his Los Angeles home as a museum.

1974 The BART (Bay Area Rapid Transit System) starts a regular transportation service.

1978 San Francisco mayor George Moscone and supervisor Harvey Milk are assassinated by a conservative political opponent.

1980 Former actor and governor of California Ronald Reagan becomes the 39th president.

PRECEDING PAGES: Central Pacific Railroad, 1867.
LEFT: Native tribes settled as early as 500 AD.
RIGHT: California's movie industry, which began *circa* 1910, had an impact around the world.

1980s Phenomenal growth in the computer industry, particularly in the Northern California region, puts Silicon Valley on the map.

1989 An earthquake (7.1 on the Richter scale) collapses a freeway and causes chaos and destruction in the San Francisco Bay area.

1992 The acquittal of LA police officers charged with beating a black motorist starts riots which kill 51 people.

1993 Los Angeles' first subway – the Metro Red Line – is opened, with the first route running between MacArthur Park and Union Station.

1994 An earthquake (6.7 on Richter scale) centered on Northridge in the San Fernando Valley

JUNE 1/-

NICELY SUITED FOR HOLLYWOOD

kills 61 people and causes billions of dollars worth of damage.

1995 The opening of the Museum of Modern Art in San Francisco's SoMa (South of Market Street) district spearheads a downtown building boom.

1995–97 The Los Angeles trials of football star O.J. Simpson accused (and eventually acquitted) of two murders enthrals the nation.

1997 Dramatic mass suicide in a San Diego mansion of 39 members of the Heaven's Gate alternative religion.

2000 Completion of Anaheim Convention Center in Los Angeles, which includes Disney's 55-acre California Adventure. Completion of popular Pac-Bel Park baseball stadium in San Francisco.

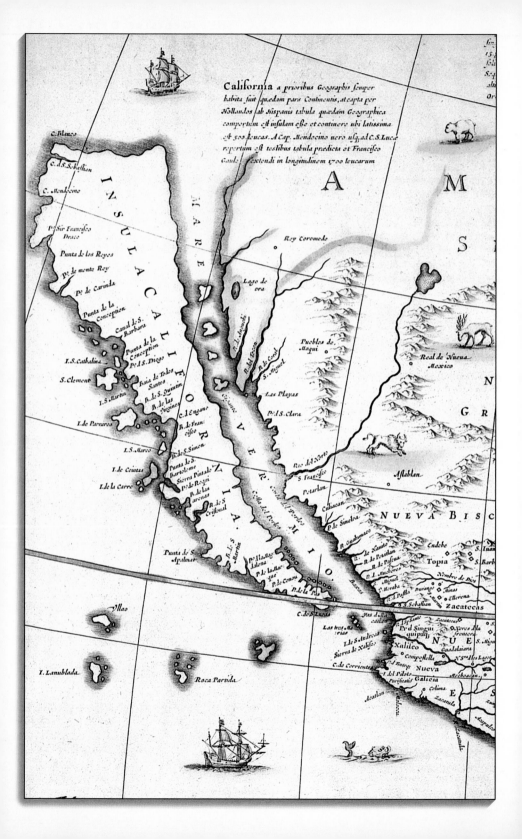

NATIVE TRIBES AND EUROPEANS

California tribes thrived and prospered for 10,000 years.
Then the white man brought disease and religion

The first tenants of the rich land that became California were the tribes that, through the centuries, crossed the land bridge of the Bering Strait and slowly filtered down into the North American continent. So many native people died soon after white people arrived that anthropologists have had to rely on patchy mission records for their estimates – a reasonable guess being that 230,000 Native Americans originally inhabited the northern region.

California tribes led a simple life, their igloo-shaped homes of reed providing breezy shelter in summer, while deerskin roofs afforded protection during the rainy season. When it grew cool, open fires were built in the homes, with holes in the roof allowing the smoke to escape.

In warm weather, the men and children were naked except for ornamental jewelry such as necklaces, earrings, bracelets and anklets. They kept warm when needed with robes of yellow cedar bark or crudely tanned pelts. Some groups practiced tattooing. The women wore two-piece aprons made of deerskins or reeds.

Tribal identities

Customs, talents and preoccupations varied from tribe to tribe, each with separate identities and distinct languages. The Miwoks and Ohlones around San Francisco Bay moved in short nomadic spurts, sometimes trekking from their ancestral shell mound up to the oak groves on what are now the Berkeley Hills. Here they ground acorns into rich and oily meal, and socialized warily. Then they would pack up for the meadowland and its rich harvest of deer and elk, at each stop along the trail being greeted and heartened by ancient landmarks: a venerable oak tree, a mossy boulder, a lively stream, a soft meadow.

The land around the Bay probably supported more humans than any other California locale, but one area not much frequented was that where the city of San Francisco now stands. It

LEFT: map by Dutchman Joannes Jansson, 1638.
RIGHT: early painting of Californian natives.

was a sandy, windy, desolate place compared to the lushness of the Berkeley Hills, the mild slopes of Mount Tamalpais, or the woods of the southern peninsula. San Francisco today, in fact, has more trees and wildlife than at any time in its history.

In the south, the Chumash tribesmen, living

habitants de Californie

in what is now Santa Barbara, were adept fishermen who used seashell hooks, basket traps, nets and vegetable poisons, even catching fish with their bare hands. The tons of shellfish eaten over the course of centuries have left us with mounds of discarded shells which can now reach 20 foot (7 meters) deep.

Canoe-making was usually with easily worked timbers such as red cedar and redwood. The canoes were distinguished by their symmetry, neatness of finish, and frequent decoration. All of this was achieved with limited tools, the principal ones being chisels, curved knives, abrasive stones, wedges and sharkskin. The Chumash in particular were expert boatbuilders. One of their elegant vessels can still be admired today at the Santa Barbara County Courthouse.

The California tribes' lifestyle continued and prospered for 10,000 years with few major changes and, by our standards, few possessions. The arrival of white people bewildered them but their acquisition of manufactured articles such as guns, metal utensils, axes, knives, blankets and cloth led inevitably to a decline of the native arts and crafts. With the coming of the immigrant wagons and the encroachment of white settlements, warfare became a unifying force.

Tribes that had been enemies often united

against the intruders. But even this did not save them and, in the end, they were overwhelmed. The culture of all Native Americans was radically changed and remains so today. They had survived regular earthquakes and droughts, but the white man proved too strong for them.

Hernando Cortés, the Spaniard who conquered Mexico, sailed up the west coast of North America. Stumbling upon a "peninsula" which stretched down between the sea and a gulf, he believed he'd found a long-lost fabled island, and he named it "California." But the discovery of the state of California is officially credited to Juan Rodriguez Cabrillo, Portuguese commander of two Spanish caravels, who is thought to have embarked from the Mexican port of Navidad in June 1542. He explored most of the coast of what is now the state of California, entering San Diego harbor in September 1542 and labeling it "enclosed and very good."

Sir Francis Drake, sailing around the world in 1579 in the *Golden Hind,* passed by the entrance to the bay of San Francisco without noticing an opening. But his log shows that he did anchor just north and sent several landing parties ashore. One of these groups left behind a small brass plate that was discovered only in 1936 near what is now Drake's Bay.

Twenty-three years later, Sebastian Vizcaíno arrived in the south, searching for suitable ports of call for his Manila galleon on its annual return to the Philippines. What Spain most needed was a safe haven from marauding Dutch and British pirates for the treasure ships en route back to Spain with the riches from their empire as far afield as the Philippines. But the canny and ambitious Spanish king, Charles III, was also keenly aware of Russian incursions from the north, where otter-hunting had reached as far south as Bodega Bay.

Vizcaíno gave lasting names to several California sites, such as San Clemente Island, San Diego and Santa Catalina Island. Of more importance was his glowing report on the virtues of the California coast that urged Spain to colonize the state.

Converting the natives

What followed was another 150 years of lassitude until the overland arrival in 1769 of Gaspar de Portola from Baja. Crossing the Santa Ana River and exchanging gifts with friendly tribes, de Portola's band passed by the bubbling tar pits of La Brea, through the mountains at Sepulveda Pass to Lake Encino and headed northwards to open up the route to Monterey.

"The three diarists in the party agree that the practical discovery of most significance was the advantageous site on the Los Angeles River," noted John Caughey in a volume published by the California Historical Society to mark the city's bicentennial. "Equally important were the numerous able-bodied, alert and amiable Indians because Spanish policy looked towards preserving, Christianizing, hispanizing and engrossing the natives as a major element in the Spanish colony now to be established."

Over the centuries, Spain had developed a

standard method for settling new territory, using the sword to cut down any opposition from the natives and pacifying the area with the introduction of Christianity. This was the approach used in California, where between 1769 and early in the following century a chain of 21 Franciscan missions was established between San Diego and Sonoma. These missions played a major role in enslaving hundreds of coastal Indians into an endless round of work and prayer.

As early as 1775 the natives rebelled: in an

DRAKE'S PLATE

Sir Francis Drake's party left behind a brass plate only discovered in 1936.

White diseases, such as measles and chicken pox, killed thousands. Hundreds more fell ill with other diseases and, as a result, the Indians developed a mortal fear of mission life. But benevolent despotism kept thousands in the missions and it was their labor that made the system successful. Not until the Mexican government's secularization decrees of 1834 were the native people freed – only to exchange their status for that of underpaid peons on the vast ranches.

In theory, the Secularization Act of 1834 gave

uprising at the San Diego mission one of the Franciscans was killed. But abolishing age-old tribal customs and introducing a complex religious structure centered around endless work eventually converted the Indians into obedient servants. The object of every mission was to become self-sufficient, to which end its subjects became cooks, blacksmiths, farmers, tanners, vintners or underpaid laborers. Indian men were taught to tend cattle, women to sew.

LEFT: California Indian tribes prospered for nearly 10,000 years – until the white man came.
ABOVE: Sir Francis Drake (left) in his ship the *Golden Hind* (right) sailed past San Francisco Bay in 1579.

lay administrators and Native Americans the right to ownership of the missions and their property; a potential ranchero could ask for as many as 50,000 acres (20,235 hectares). In practice, however, the acts were barely observed: tribes were driven out into the world of poverty and helplessness, ill-equipped to deal with white men's laws.

Some returned to the hills, others indentured themselves as ranch hands or turned to drinking and gambling. Meanwhile, the orange groves and the productive gardens were cleared or ploughed under, and the so-called "string of pearls" which were the missions transformed into a patchwork quilt of ranches. ❑

THE MISSIONS OF OLD CALIFORNIA

The "string of pearls" – the 21 Franciscan missions spread out along California's coast – offer a serene look into California's history

Heading north from their Baja California settlement in 1769, Franciscan missionaries led by Father Junípero Serra established 21 missions during the subsequent 54 years. Most now lovingly restored, the missions form a uniquely serene look at California's past. Each mission lies roughly a day's journey apart in a line (the "string of pearls") that stretches between San Diego and Sonoma, 600 miles (965 km) to the north. Following the Secularization Act of 1834, the missions fell into disuse and were abandoned for almost half a century until interest was sparked with a series of magazine articles by Helen Hunt Jackson in the 1880s which brought attention to the plight of former mission Indians, many of whom had been used as slave labor in the construction of the buildings.

Each of the timber and adobe missions has some architectural or historical distinction, although all feature the thick walls, small windows and elegant bell towers usually associated with Mexican churches. A few had specific functions: the northernmost mission, San Francisco Solano (1823) was there to discourage the Russians – who for the previous decade had garrisoned Fort Ross on the northern coast – from occupying any more of the still-sparsely populated country. Solano, one of the last missions to be built, and to which at one time 1,000 Indians were attached, was to have a short life as a religious center, for barely a decade later secularization led to its abandonment. A highlight of Solano's museum today is a collection of 62 watercolors of the other missions, painted by Chris Jorgensen in 1903.

For more information on missions see the relevant chapter: ie, Santa Barbara p293 or San Diego p331.

△ **MISSION DOLORES GLASS**
In reality called San Francisco de Asi, its name derived from its location at 16th and Dolores streets. The mission was opened in 1776 by Father Serra, whose biography was written here by Father Palou.

▷ **MISSION SAN GABRIEL**
This 1832 work by Ferdinand Deppe is one of the earliest paintings showing a mission. San Gabriel was very prosperous, with over a million acres and 40,000 head of cattle. At its peak, almost 2,000 Indians lived here. Currently being restored.

Santa Clara de Asis, California, 1777

◁ **FATHER JUNÍPERO SERRA**
A tireless zealot and a mere 5ft 2ins (1.5m) in height, Father Serra was responsible for establishing the chain of missions along the coast.

△ **MISSION SANTA CLARA**
Reconstructed in 1929 as a faithful copy of the mission of a century before, it sits on the campus of Santa Clara University, surrounded by gardens as lush and splendid as the original grounds.

THE SWALLOWS OF CAPISTRANO

The fame of Orange County's Mission San Juan Capistrano has spread around the world: each year on March 19 – St Joseph's Day – a flock of swallows returns to roost here. Legend says the influx began back in the mists of time when the original brood took refuge in the mission's eaves after a local innkeeper destroyed their nests.

The birds have been coming here for at least two centuries, building their nests out of mud in the tiled roof *(see above)* and, after a summer in California, heading south again in the fall. The arrival of the swallows, although not always on the exact day, is celebrated with a festival.

Another legend that is associated with the mission – described as "an American Acropolis" – is that of a woman named Magdalena whose penance was to walk up and down the church aisle with a lighted candle to atone for disobeying her father by courting a man of whom he disapproved. On occasions, it is said, her candle can still be seen shining among the ruins of the cruciform Great Stone Church in which she perished during an earthquake.

The Stone Church, one of the oldest sections of the mission still standing, is currently being restored to its former glory.

For more information on Mission San Juan Capistrano, see p309.

◁ **SAN JUAN CAPISTRANO**
Behind Father Serra's statue is a tiny stone chapel, (the only one remaining) in which he celebrated mass. The oldest building in use, it houses a magnificent 350-year-old altar.

△ **MISSION SANTA BARBARA**
Replacing the earlier adobe destroyed by an earthquake, the present "Queen of the Missions" – the most visited in the state – was completed in 1833 based on a design of the Roman architect Vitruvius.

EMIGRATION TO CALIFORNIA !

Do you want to go to California? If so, go and join the Company who intend going out the middle of March, or 1st of April next, under the charge of the California Emigration Society, in a first-rate Clipper Ship. The Society agreeing to find places for all those who wish it upon their arrival in San Francisco. The voyage will probably be made in a few months.— Price of passage will be in the vicinity of

ONE HUNDRED DOLLARS !

CHILDREN IN PROPORTION.

A number of families have already engaged passage. A suitable Female Nurse has been provided, who will take charge of Young Ladies and Children. Good Physicians, both male and female go in the Ship. It is hoped a large number of females will go, as Females are getting almost as good wages as males.

FEMALE NURSES get 25 dollars per week and board. SCHOOL TEACHERS 100 dollars per month. GARDNERS 60 dollars per month and board. LABORERS 4 to 5 dollars per day. BRICKLAYERS 6 dollars per day. HOUSEKEEPERS 40 dollars per month. FARMERS 5 dollars per day. SHOEMAKERS 4 dollars per day. Men and Women COOKS 40 to 60 dollars per month and board. MINERS are making from 3 to 12 dollars per day. FEMALE SERVANTS 30 to 50 dollars per month and board. Washing 3 dollars per dozen. MASONS 6 dollars per day. CARPENTERS 5 dollars per day. ENGINEERS 100 dollars per month, and as the quartz Crushing Mills are getting into operation all through the country, Engineers are very scarce. BLACKSMITHS 90 and 100 dollars per month and board.

The above prices are copied from late papers printed in San Francisco, which can be seen at my office. Having views of some 30 Cities throughout the State of California, I shall be happy to see all who will call at the office of the Society, 28 JOY'S BUILDING, WASHINGTON ST., BOSTON, and examine them. Parties residing out of the City, by enclosing a stamp and sending to the office, will receive a circular giving all the particulars of the voyage.

As Agents are wanted in every town and city of the New England States, Postmasters or Merchants acting as such will be allowed a certain commission on every person they get to join the Company. Good reference required. For further particulars correspond or call at the

SOCIETY'S OFFICE,

28 Joy's Building, Washington St., Boston, Mass.

FROM RANCHOS TO STATEHOOD

*It started as a simple war with Mexico. But it ended by transforming a wild
and savage wilderness into the 31st state of the Union*

After three centuries of Spanish rule, Mexico finally broke away in 1821 and, on September 27, declared itself a republic; coincidentally, secularization of the missions was sought by Spanish-Mexican settlers, known as the Californios. Eight million acres (3.3 million hectares) of mission land were fragmented into 800 privately-owned ranches with some governors handing out land to their cronies for only a few pennies per acre.

Soldiers who had finished their time in the army often stayed on in California rather than return to Spain or Mexico. Under Mexican law, a ranchero could ask for as many as 50,000 acres (20,200 hectares) and Indian slave labor became part of the plunder.

The *vaquero's* values

Orange orchards were cleared for firewood and herds were given to private hands. The predominant lifestyle quickly changed to that of an untamed frontier-style cattle range, although cattle ranching in this part of the world made few demands upon its owners. With no line fences to patrol and repair on the open range, and no need for vigilance because of branded stock, the *vaquero* had little to do but practice feats of horsemanship to improve his masculinity and impress the *señoritas.*

His sports were violent, including calf branding, wild horse roundups, bear hunts, cock- and bullfights; his entertainment included dances, such as the Spanish fandango and the Western waltz, and at his fiestas he was bedecked in gold-braided clothes dripping with silver. Crops and game were plentiful; wildlife included badgers and coyotes; the lordly condor circled overhead and grizzly bear, deer, gray wolves, mountain lions and wildcats roamed the hills.

Author Richard Henry Dana, who visited the state in 1835, called the Californians "an idle thriftless people," an observation lent considerable weight by the lifestyle of so many of the rancheros, who found it a simple matter to maintain and increase their wealth. The sudden influx of prospectors to the north created an immense demand for beef which the southerners were readily able to supply.

In his novel, *Two Years Before the Mast,* Dana

described how cattle hides and tallow in 500-lb (227-kg) bags were thrown from the cliffs to the waiting ships. Accepted as a basic unit of barter, these hides were turned into rugs, blankets, curtains, sandals, chaps and saddles. Rawhides were twisted into *reatas* (used for roping cattle) or used to lash timbers together. Edible meat not eaten immediately was sun-dried as beef jerky or pickled for barter with trading ships. All fat was rendered into tallow, the basis for candles and soap.

Yankee trading ships plied up and down the coast, operating like floating department stores offering mahogany furniture, gleaming copperware, framed mirrors, Irish linen, silver candle-

---

LEFT: enticing New Englanders to join the migration.
RIGHT: an 1842 portrait of Richard Dana, author of the influential *Two Years Before the Mast.*

sticks, and cashmere shawls. For many of the native-born Americans these were their first amenities from the civilized world. Sometimes the trading ships, which had survived the precarious Straits of Magellan, would stay an entire year, working up and down the coast.

A genteel contraband soon developed. To reduce import taxes ships worked in pairs to transfer cargo from one to the other on the open seas. The partially-emptied ship would then make port and submit to customs inspection. With duties paid, it would rejoin its consort and reverse the transfer. Sometimes the Yankee traders used lonely coves to unload their car-

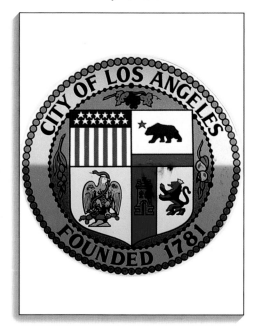

goes which were eventually smuggled ashore. Both sides fared well: the Yankee traders sailed south with full holds and the rancheros displayed their new finery with yet another fiesta.

The weather remained temperate except for the occasional hot, dry, gale-force wind the Native Americans called "wind of the evil spirits." The Spaniards called them *santanas*, a name which today has become corrupted to Santa Ana winds. Now and again an earthquake rumbled down the San Andreas Fault. The rancheros spent their energy rebuilding damaged haciendas, made from red-tile roofing set on white-painted adobe brick walls, while allowing the missions to fall into ruins. Resto-

ration of the missions began only this century after they were declared historical landmarks.

In 1834, Governor Figueroa issued the first of the Secularization Acts, which in theory gave lay administrators and Indian neophytes the right to ownership of the missions and their property. In practice, however, these acts were widely ignored; secularization drove the Native Americans out into the world of poverty and helplessness. Like other slaves, they were psychologically ill-prepared to cope with freedom. Some returned to the hills, others indentured themselves as ranch hands or turned to drinking or gambling in the pueblos.

Official Washington soon became aware of this land of milk and honey on the Pacific coast. President Andrew Jackson sent an emissary to Mexico City in the 1830s to buy California for the sum of $500,000. The plan failed.

The Mexican War

When James K. Polk took office in 1845, he pledged to acquire California by any means. He felt pressured by the English financial interests which plotted to exchange $26 million of defaulted Mexican bonds for the rich land of California. On May 13, 1846, he surprised no one by declaring war on Mexico. News of the war had not yet reached California, however, when a group of settlers stormed General Mariano Vallejo's Sonoma estate. Vallejo soothed the men with brandy and watched as they raised their hastily sewn Bear Flag over Sonoma.

The Bear Flag Revolt is sanctified in California history – the flag now being the official state flag – but, for all its drama, it was immaterial. Within a few weeks Commodore John Sloat arrived to usher California into the Union.

Most of the fighting in the War of American Conquest took place in the south. The war in the north effectively ended on July 9, 1846, when 70 hearty sailors and marines from the ship *Portsmouth* marched ashore in Yerba Buena village and raised the American flag in the village's central plaza.

The bloodiest battle on California soil took place in the Valley of San Pasqual, near Escondido. The Army of the West, commanded by General Stephen W. Kearney, fought a brief battle during which 18 Americans were killed.

Kearney's aide-de-camp was US naval officer Robert F. Stockton. Together they skirmished with Mexican-Californians at Paso de

Bartolo on the San Gabriel River. The Californios, however, soon readily capitulated to the Americans and California's participation in the Mexican War ended at last with the Treaty of Cahuenga.

The treaty, which came into force on July 4 (US Independence Day), 1848, ended the War with Mexico. By the Treaty of Cahuenga, California became a territory of the United States of America. Only through fierce negotiation was San Diego saved from being on the south side of the Mexico-California boundary.

BEAR FLAG

The state flag of California commemorates the Bear Flag Revolt of 1846.

Alta California in 1848 following its war with Mexico, Los Angeles remained a predominantly Mexican city infused with a Latino culture and traditions. But the arrival of the Southern Pacific Railroad triggered a series of land booms with the subsequent influx of Anglo-American, Asian and European immigrants eventually outnumbering Mexicans 10 to 1.

Next to suffer from marginalization and racist attitudes were the Chinese, thousands of whom had poured into Northern California from the gold fields and, later, into Los Angeles after

1822 MEXICAN RULE

From 1850 onwards the Federal government signed treaties (never ratified by the Senate) under which more than 7 million acres (70,000 hectares) of tribal land dwindled to less than 10 percent of that total.

Apart from being denied legality and having their labor exploited and their culture destroyed, the Native Americans themselves had been fatally exposed to not only alcoholism, but to all manner of dreaded foreign diseases.

For three decades after America had acquired

LEFT: the historic seal of the city.
ABOVE: a Southern Californian mural shows the transition of California to Mexican sovereignty.

their (mostly unappreciated) building of the railroads had been completed. In one notorious incident in 1871 during an economic slump that had led to widespread unemployment, a mob of frustrated whites descended on LA's Chinatown and killed a score of its residents.

California was rushed into the Union on September 9, 1850, as the 31st state, only 10 months after convening a formal government. But it had already drafted a constitution which guaranteed the right to "enjoying and defending life and liberty, acquiring, possessing and protecting property, and pursuing and obtaining happiness," with hindsight a typically Californian mix of the sublime and the practical. ❏

THE CALIFORNIA GOLD RUSH

Gold and silver were the stuff of dreams. They made millionaires out of mountain men and, sometimes, paupers out of millionaires

Gold was discovered in Placeritas Canyon, north of Mission San Fernando, in 1842. Francisco Lopez, rounding up stray horses, stopped to rest beneath an oak tree. He opened his knife to uproot some wild onions, and their roots came out attached to something gleaming bright in the sun – a nugget of gold. Six years later, gold was discovered in quantity at Sutter's Mill near Sacramento in Northern California. Word quickly spread east and the stampede began. Soon a torrent of gold-dazzled prospectors was running through the Sierras to California. Entire parties in covered wagons made their way west. When they encountered the sheer cliffs of the Sierra Nevada, they winched up the wagons or took them apart and lowered them down the steep precipices.

Population explosion

Nowhere was the Gold Rush's magic more powerful than in San Francisco. When storekeeper Sam Brannan ambled down Montgomery Street with a recently prospected vial of gold, the town's population was less than 1,000. By early 1850, when the madness was in full swing, the population topped 30,000. Brannan, who had recently settled in San Francisco heading a group of Mormons, saw the potential of this future city (and the success of his own store), and he excitedly spread the word.

Bayard Taylor, a reporter for the *New York Tribune*, described the atmosphere as a "perpetual carnival." What he found when he returned from four months at the diggings was not the town of "tents and canvas houses with a show of frame buildings" that he had left but "an actual metropolis, displaying street after street of well-built edifices… lofty hotels, gaudy with verandahs and balconies… finished with home luxury and aristocratic restaurants presenting daily their long bills of fare, rich with the choicest technicalities of Parisian cuisine."

By the end of May, the word had spread all over California: stores closed, city officials left their offices, soldiers deserted, sailors jumped ship and the exasperated editor of the *Californian* announced the suspension of his daily newspaper because the staff had walked out. "The whole country from San Francisco to Los Angeles and from the sea shore to the base of

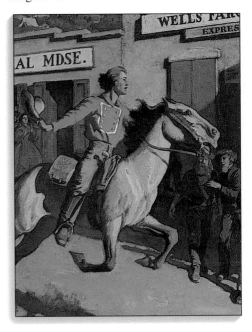

the Sierra Nevada," he wrote, "resounds with the sordid cry of gold! GOLD! GOLD! – while the field is left half-planted, the house half-built and everything neglected but the manufacture of shovels and pickaxes." Before the year was out more prospectors arrived in California from Oregon, Mexico, Peru and Chile.

The first big discovery of gold took place at a sawmill beside the American River in the Sierra Nevada foothills. (Today a recreation of the fabled mill stands at Coloma, 50-odd miles east of Sacramento.)

The mill was the idea of John Augustus Sutter – a man, one contemporary wrote, with a disastrous "mania for undertaking too much." Born

LEFT: gold miners drawn by William McIlvain.
RIGHT: Pony Express rider brings the news.

in Switzerland in 1803, Sutter arrived in San Francisco in 1839. Despite a disorderly career as a Swiss Army officer and dry-goods merchant, he somehow impressed Alta California's authorities enough to offer him the largest possible land grant, nearly 50,000 acres (about 20,000 hectares) of the Central Valley. Naming his land "New Helvetia" and using Native Americans as serf labor, Sutter set out to create his own semi-independent barony.

Sutter's Fort, at what is now Sacramento, was often the first stop for bedraggled overlanders

GOLD FEVER

"Gold! Gold! Gold on the American river!" he shouted.

applying "every test of their ingenuity and the *American Encyclopaedia*," decided that it was indeed gold. They raced back up to the sawmill, poked and panned awhile, and found quite a bit more.

Realizing that New Helvetia would be overrun if word of the discovery leaked out prematurely, Sutter swore his mill hands to secrecy. But nuggets kept popping up in bars and stores all over the region. "As a lumber enterprise, the mill was a failure, but as a gold discovery, it was a grand success," said a later report. And when Sam Brannan strolled

after their harrowing Sierra to the valley crossing. Sutter gloried in providing comfort and goods (at a price) to California's new settlers. He planted wheat and fruit orchards, bought out the Russians at Fort Ross, lent his aid to several of Northern California's jostling factions, and, in 1847, decided to build the sawmill that was his ultimate undoing.

James Marshall, who had been hired to oversee the mill's construction, peered into the mill-race on January 24, 1848, and noticed a bit of shiny material, one of the millions of smithereens of gold that had been tumbling down the streams of the Sierra for millennia.

He took the nugget to Sutter and the pair,

down San Francisco's Montgomery Street shouting "Gold! Gold! Gold on the American river!" the secret was well and truly out. The Western world had been waiting for the myth to come to life for centuries. The Spanish had uprooted and discarded more than one civilization in their search for the country of gold. The myth had eventually grown into a prophecy.

The news spread as rapidly as the times allowed. San Francisco was left nearly deserted, its shops stripped of axes, pans, tents, beans, soda crackers, picks and whatever else might conceivably be of use. Monterey, San Jose, all of Northern California's mission towns and farms joined in the scramble. Gold fever worked its way to the states of Utah and Oregon, where "two-thirds of the able-bodied men were on their way to the diggings."

Ships in the Pacific spread the word to Peru, Chile, Hawaii and Australia. Lieutenant L. Loeser carried a "small chest... containing $3,000 worth of gold in lumps and scales" back to Washington DC, where it was exhibited at the War Office, increasing greed in the capital. On December 2, President Polk told Congress that the "extraordinary accounts" were true. A few days later, the *New York Herald* summed it up: "The El Dorado of the old Spaniards is discovered at last."

Hundreds of thousands of reveries were fixed on the fabled Mother Lode region, which ran for 120 miles (190 km) from north of Sutter's Mill to Mariposa in the south. Forty-niners (as the Gold Rush miners were known) first worked the streams of the Klamath Mountains in the far north: later, the southern deserts had their share of boom towns. But the Mother Lode's wooded hills and deep valleys were the great centers of the raucous, short-lived argonaut civilization.

How claims were staked

Gold Rush mining, especially in the early days before the streams were panned out, was a simple affair. The Mother Lode was owned by the federal government, and claims were limited to the ground a man and his fellows could work. Stockpiling claims was impossible and hiring a work force was unlikely. There was scant reason to make another man rich when one's own wealth-spouting claim was so easily achieved.

There was money to be wrung out of those hills. The problem lay in keeping it. In 1849, $10 million of gold was mined in California; the next year, four times that amount. In 1852, the pinnacle of the Gold Rush, $80 million wound up in prospectors' pockets.

The Sierra streams did much of the miner's work for him. The rushing waters eroded the hillsides and sent placer gold (from dust to nugget size) rushing downstream. A miner crouched by the streambank scooped up a panful of gravel, shifting and turning his pan as the debris washed out and the gold sank to the bottom. Later, sluices were built and holes were dug. Finally hydraulic mining took over,

although this was banned in 1884 after causing dramatic ecological damage to the foothills.

The endless disputes over water rights, which continue to this day, mostly date to the days of the gold prospectors when miners, whose claims were far from stream beds, collaborated to build ditches funnelling water from sources whose "riparian rights" (that is, owning the adjoining land) were in conflict with "appropriation rights." The introduction of hydraulic mining bringing streams of water to bear on hillsides intensified the problem. The extensive network of canals and flumes which eventually brought water a long way from its original

source came to be worth more than the claims it served, but the conflicting arguments over who had a prior right to the water were never entirely solved. (However, as the mines petered out, the agribusinesses of the state's central valleys gained the lions' share.)

As easy as it was to find, the Mother Lode's gold was easier to lose – to rapacious traders, in the gambling halls and bawdy-houses, to the simple unwiseness of young men. But for most prospectors it was a grand adventure. Many returned home sheepishly but full of stories for their grandchildren. *California as It Is and as It May Be, Or, A Guide to the Goldfields* was the title of the first book to be published in San

---

LEFT: a 19th-century illustration of mining life.
RIGHT: pre-Gold Rush Yerba Buena.

Francisco (in 1849). In it, the author F.B. Wierzbicki wrote that the city looked like it had been built to endure for only a day, so fast had been its growth and so flimsy its construction.

"The town has led the van in growth… there is nothing like it on record. From eight to 10 thousand may be afloat on the streets and hundreds arrive daily; many live in shanties, many in tents and many the best way they can… The freaks of fortune are equally as remarkable in this place as everything else connected with it; some men who two years ago had not a cent in their pockets, count by thousands now…"

For most of the '49ers it was rough and

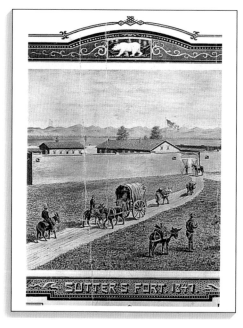

expensive. Eggs from the Farallone Islands sold for $1 apiece. Real-estate speculation was epidemic. Each boatload of '49ers represented another batch of customers. As the city burst from the boundaries of Yerba Buena Cove, "water lots" sold for crazy prices on the expectation they could be made habitable with landfill. Much of today's downtown San Francisco is built on landfill.

Most of California's new tenants had little desire to lay the foundation for the orderly society that would surely follow the Gold Rush. The popular conception was that the foothills were crammed with gold. "Ages will not exhaust the supply," Bayard Taylor wrote. In the end, the

winners in the great money-scramble were those who took the time to sink roots by establishing businesses and buying land, taking advantage of the '49ers' disdain for tomorrow. Each fire was an opportunity for the arising bourgeoisie to build anew.

In 1853, the Gold Rush began to wind down. Real-estate values fell 20 to 30 percent. Immigration slowed to a trickle and merchants were cornered by massive oversupplies ordered during the heady days. The men who started the Gold Rush, John Sutter and James Marshall, were only two of the many losers in the great game. Marshall ended his days in 1885 near the site of his discovery, broken-down, weepy, shaking his fist at fate. Sutter, whose barony was overrun just as he'd feared, kept a brave front for some years. But history had swept him aside, too, and he died in 1880 after years of futile petitions to Congress for restitution.

Robberies and the Silver Rush

None of California's new towns, much less San Francisco, were built with much care or foresight. Pre-Gold Rush street plans, based on tight grids, were expanded out from flat Yerba Buena Cove with a flick of pen on ruler, jauntily ignoring the city's hills – which is why San Francisco's streets barge up and down those hills, rather than gracefully following their contours. Most buildings were hasty wooden edifices and, between 1849 and 1851, six major fires ravaged San Francisco. Sacramento, smaller, marginally quieter, also had its share of blazes.

In San Francisco, hoodlums (a word coined in late-19th-century San Francisco) had organized themselves into gangs like the Sydney Ducks and the Hounds. At least some of the city's fires were set by these gangs, in addition to routine robberies, beatings and generally ugly behavior. In 1851, the forces of social stability asserted their constitutional right to "acquire, possess and defend property" by warring against the criminal elements in the community.

The robbery and beating in early 1851 of a merchant named C.J. Jensen inflamed the righteous, especially Sam Brannan – a man who, according to historian Josiah Royce, was "always in love with shedding the blood of the wicked." Newspapers like the *Alta* brought up the specter of lynch law, and Brannan shouted that the time had come to bypass "the quibbles of the law, the insecurity of the prisons, and the laxity of those who pretend to administer justice." A Committee of Vigilance was formed; soon a Sydney Duck named John Jenkins was hanged for stealing a safe. Within two weeks Sacramento also had its vigilante corps and other California towns followed its lead. California's first bout of vigilantism put a damper on crime only for a while. Whatever chance California had of becoming placid was swept away in 1859 by yet another torrent of riches flowing down the Sierra slope. This time it was silver, not gold, that geared up the rush.

One of the most comfortless outposts of the Gold Rush had been centered around Nevada's Sun Mountain on the dry eastern slope of the Sierra near Lake Tahoe. There was a little gold up in the Virginia Range, but eking a living out of the area's irritating bluish clay was wicked work. In June, 1859, a sample of that "blue stuff" found its way to Melville Atwood, an assayist in Grass Valley. Examining it closely, Atwood found an astounding $3,876 worth of silver in that sample of ore.

At first it appeared that the Silver Rush would mimic the Gold Rush of a decade earlier. "Our towns are near depleted," wrote one spectator. "They look as languid as a consumptive girl. What has become of our sinewy and athletic fellow citizens? They are coursing through ravines and over mountaintops," looking for silver.

Mark Twain as prospector

One of the athletic young men who rushed up to the Virginia Range was Mark Twain. In his marvelous book, *Roughing It*, he describes how he and his fellow almost-millionaires "expected to find masses of silver lying all about the ground." The problem for Twain and the thousands like him was that the silver was in, not on, the steep and rugged mountains. And getting it out was no matter of poking and panning.

The Silver Rush, it turned out, was a game for capitalists, men who possessed the money to dig tunnels, purchase claims, install the expensive machinery and mills that transformed the "blue stuff" into cash. They were men like William Ralston of the Bank of California in San Francisco, and the four legendary "Bonanza Kings" – James Flood and William O'Brien, former

saloon-keepers; and James Fair and John W. Mackay, old miners whose Consolidated Virginia regularly disgorged $6 million a month.

As usual, the treasures of the Comstock Lode (named for an old-timer who ended up broke) flowed from the boomtown of Virginia City to San Francisco. By 1863, $40 million of silver had been wrestled out of the tunnels, and 2,000 mining companies traded shares in San Francisco. Fortunes were made and lost in moments and at one time, more speculative money was wrapped up in Comstock mining shares than actually existed on the whole Pacific Coast.

The Comstock Lode lasted until the 1880s,

plumping up California's economy with the $400 million that the Virginia Range yielded. In San Francisco, Billy Ralston, the Comstock's greatest mine-owner, had taken over from Sam Brannan as the city's top booster. (But Sam was going broke trying to make his resort at Calistoga into "the Saratoga of the West" and died, dollarless, in 1889.) Ralston he built America's largest city hotel; he bought sugar refineries, lumber and water companies; and as the 1860s drew to a close, he happily made confident preparations for what he and his fellow plutocrats thought would be the capstone to the state's greatness – the long-awaited completion of the Transcontinental Railroad. ❑

LEFT: gold was first found on John Sutter's property, but Sutter himself lost a virtual fortune.
RIGHT: panning and posing for the camera.

BOOM AND BUST YEARS

After enjoying immense wealth, the state was hit by massive unemployment.

But California was far too rich to suffer for long

Plans for a railroad linking the coasts had been floating around for many years. When the American Civil War broke out, Congress, intent upon securing California's place in the Union, at last stirred itself. In the winter of 1862, the Pacific Railroad Act granted vast tracts of western land, low-interest financing and outright subsidies to two companies – the Central Pacific, building from Sacramento, and the Union Pacific, building from Omaha, Nebraska, in the Midwest. As it happened, the Civil War largely bypassed California, but it nonetheless prompted the building of a railroad that brought unexpected havoc to the residents of the state.

In his widely-read book, *Progress and Poverty*, Henry George, a journeyman printer and passionate theorist, had warned that the increasing dominance of the railroads would prove to be a mixed blessing. He predicted that California's immature factories would be undersold by the eastern manufacturing colossus and that the Central Pacific's ownership of vast parcels of land along its right of way would drive prices of agricultural land shamefully high. George even foresaw the racial tensions that would result from the railroad's importation of thousands of Chinese laborers. "Crocker's Pets," as they were called, flooded the state's job market in the 1870s.

Railroad woes

George's prophecies began arriving with the first train. In San Francisco, real-estate dealing of $3.5 million a month fell to $1.5 million a month within a year. "California's initial enthusiasm soon gave way to distrust and dislike… an echo of the national conviction that the railroads were responsible for most of the country's economic ills," was the assessment of historian John W. Caughey in his book *California*. "The railroad became a monster, the Octopus. It was

---

LEFT: a vigilante committee membership certificate.
RIGHT: the domination of the railroad by the "Big Four" was a target of indignant press protest.

a target for criticisms by all those made discontented and bitter by the hard times of the Seventies." The genius of the Central Pacific was a young engineer named Theodore Dehone Judah who had built California's first railroad, the 22-mile (35-km) Sacramento Valley line, in 1856. He spent years crafting the crucial route across

the Sierra at Donner Pass. Unfortunately for Judah, the Central Pacific's other partners were uncommonly cunning and grabby men.

Charles Crocker, Mark Hopkins, Collis Huntington and Leland Stanford, who became known as "The Big Four," had been lured west by the Gold Rush. They were Sacramento shopkeepers when they invested in Judah's scheme. Shortly after Congress dumped its largesse in their laps, they forced Judah out of the Central Pacific. He died, aged 37, in 1863, still trying to wrest back control from his former partners.

The Central Pacific made the Big Four almost insanely rich. The government's haste to get the railroad built, and Stanford's political manoeuvering, made the Central Pacific the virtual dictator of California politics for years. Between them, the railroad barons raised private investment, earned government subsidies, acquired bargain-priced land, imported cheap labor from China and by their exploitative and monopolist practices made themselves multi-millionaires.

.JOINING OF THE RAILS

In 1869, the Union Pacific and the Central Pacific met at Promontory Point, Utah.

As the biggest landowners and biggest employers, the immensely rich railroad barons were able to manipulate freight rates, control water supplies, keep hundreds of thousands of productive land acres for them-

a firm and fabulous prosperity to California.

In April, 1868, five years after construction had begun on Sacramento's Front Street, the first Central Pacific train breached the Sierra at Donner Pass. Where, on May 12, 1869, the Golden Spike was driven at Promontory Point, Utah, the coasts were finally and irrevocably linked. "San Francisco Annexes the Union" read one San Francisco headline. But the rush of prosperity failed utterly to materialize. Only a few deep thinkers – none of them ensconced in boardrooms – had

A NEW AND MAGNIFICENT CLIPPER FOR SAN FRANCISCO.
MERCHANTS' EXPRESS LINE OF CLIPPER SHIPS!
Loading none but First-Class Vessels and Regularly Dispatching the greatest number.
THE SPLENDID NEW OUT-AND-OUT CLIPPER SHIP

CALIFORNIA

HENRY BARBER, Commander, AT PIER 13 EAST RIVER.

This elegant Clipper Ship was built expressly for this trade by Samuel Hall, Esq., of East Boston, the builder of the celebrated Clippers "SURPRISE," "GAMECOCK," "JOHN GILPIN," and others. She will fully equal them in speed! Unusually prompt dispatch and a very quick trip may be relied upon. Engagements should be completed at once.

Agents in San Francisco, } Messrs. DE WITT KITTLE & CO. }
RANDOLPH M. COOLEY, 88 Wall Street, Tontine Building.

NESBITT & CO., PRINTERS.

selves and with their wealth subvert politicians and municipalities. It was years before state regulation of the railroads became the norm; when Frank Norris wrote *The Octopus* in 1901, no one had to guess at the reference: the Southern Pacific (as it was renamed in 1884) had its greedy tentacles in every corner of the state.

In the beginning, at least, carping at the Big Four's use of the railroad's treasury as a kind of private money preserve was a game for malcontents and socialists. In the mahogany boardrooms of San Francisco's banks, on the editorial pages of its newspapers, in the overheated stock exchange, up and down Montgomery Street, the verdict was the same. The railroad would bring

understood the financial calamity the railroad would bring. In the winter of 1869–70, a severe drought crippled the state's agriculture. Between 1873 and 1875 more than a quarter of a million immigrants came to California. Many were factory workers and few could find work. The "Terrible '70s" had arrived which certainly for William Chapman Ralston were a calamity. As head of San Francisco's Bank of California, he had presided over the boom mentality that was a legacy of the Gold Rush.

The mid-Seventies saw the depression at its deepest. On "Black Friday," April 26, 1875, a run on the Bank of California forced it to slam shut its huge oaken doors at Sansome and California streets. Driven into debt by Comstock mining losses and by the failure of the railroad to bring prosperity, Bill Ralston drowned while taking his customary swim in the Bay.

Ralston's death signalled the end of California's booming affluence. Those hurt most by the great shrinkage of capital in the 1870s were the state's working people. During the Gold and Silver rushes, California's laborers had enjoyed a rare freedom to move easily from job to job and to dictate working conditions. Now, however, with mas-

BLACK FRIDAY

On April 26, 1875, a run on the Bank of California forced it to slam its doors.

minerals, the state developed its agricultural lands as never before. In the Central Valley, wheat, rice and cotton became major cash crops. The splendid Napa Valley began to produce fine wines in earnest in the late 1870s.

Sometime between 1873 and 1875, two or three orange trees were sent from the Department of Agriculture in Washington to Eliza and Luther Tibbetts in Riverside, not far from San Diego. The young trees had been budded from a seedless orange whose origin was Bahia, Brazil. The Tibbetts planted the trees, lit-

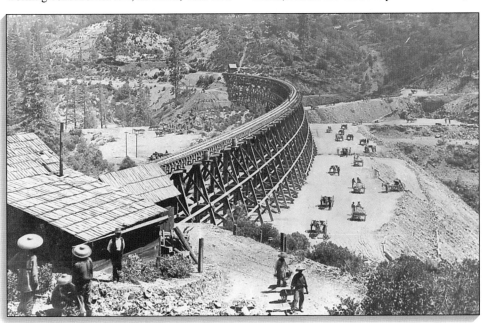

sive unemployment, unionization began to take hold. For the next 60 years California suffered recurrent bouts of labor strife.

The depression was slow to disappear, but California was too rich to suffer permanently. In the next few decades, it slowly built its industrial strength up to the point where it could compete with America's prosperous East Coast. After decades of depending on the land to deliver riches in the form of gold or silver or

---

LEFT: canny 19th-century travel agents encouraged migration to the West by sea.
ABOVE: the railroad was built in large part by imported Chinese laborers, many of whom settled in the state.

tle knowing that a decade later navel oranges would dramatically alter the agricultural, economic and social patterns of the entire region. The Washington navel orange, as the seedless and sweet fruit was officially known, became (in the words of Charles F. Lummis) "not only a fruit but a romance."

Durable enough to survive long-distance shipping, this citrus fruit hit its prime in 1889 when more than 13,000 acres (5,260 hectares) of land in the six southern counties were devoted to its cultivation.

Growers formed a marketing cooperative, the California Fruit Growers Exchange, famed for its ubiquitous trademark, Sunkist. In a mere 18 months, Horace Greeley's "Go West, young man" philosophy became a reality. Many boom-towns took root and soon the population of the south equalled that of the north.

This vast semi-tropical, often desert-like land reached its potential. Thousands of acres of good farmland sold by the railroads at low prices were planted with wheat, oranges, grapes, cotton, tea, tobacco and coffee. Irrigation converted vast tracts of this arid waste to fertile land bearing fruit and field crops. Agriculture, crucially boosted by rail transportation, became the backbone of Southern California's economy.

Well before the new century began, the enter-

prising Edwin Tobias Earl had made a fortune from his invention of the refrigerated railroad car. Meanwhile San Francisco's boomtown mentality may have taken a beating, but as the century wore on, the city's historic predilection for high living remained. Rudyard Kipling, visiting during the Gilded Age at the end of the century, called it "a mad city, inhabited for the most part by perfectly insane people whose women are of a remarkable beauty." San Francisco's society had "a captivating rush and whirl. Recklessness is in the air."

The city by the Bay reached a peak in the 1870s, a now-graceful community whose 1,700 architects were perfecting the characteristical-ly Victorian and "Queen Anne"-style homes which still predominate in at least half a dozen neighborhoods today. Hundreds of others, however, failed to survive the 1906 earthquake.

The rise of the south

Los Angeles, too, was now growing fast: in every decade from 1870 onwards it doubled its population. Before the end of the 19th century, the *Los Angeles Times* with Charles Lummis, a man who had hitchhiked across country from the Midwest on the way to becoming the newspaper's city editor, was proclaiming that it was no place for "dudes, loafers, paupers… cheap politicians, business scrubs, impecunious clerks, lawyers and doctors."

It is hard to imagine what they had against the last-mentioned category, especially in a city growing so sophisticated that by 1897 it boasted the first orchestra to be established west of the Rockies. Eight years later, Abbott Kinney's ambitious reconstruction of Venice on coastal marshland added an international touch, although his initial high-minded attractions soon gave way to motor racing and carnival events.

The pueblo of Los Angeles had become a prosperous community, facing its perennial problem: a shortage of water. To assure a steady water supply, the city fathers made plans for a lengthy trench running from the river and hired a Vermont-born shopkeeper, Ozro W. Childs, to dig this *Zanja Madre* or Mother Ditch, paying him off with land instead of scarce city funds.

The land, a tract bordered by today's 6th & Main streets and Pico Boulevard and Figueroa Street, eventually made Childs so prosperous that, in 1884, he spent $50,000 to build an 1,800-seat opera house. At the ocean, frontage at Santa Monica owned by Southern Pacific Railroad magnate Collis P. Huntington almost became the Port of Los Angeles, but intensive lobbying by rival Santa Fe railroad chiefs won out and San Pedro was chosen instead. Already the region was annually producing almost 5 million barrels of oil, the exporting of which was greatly facilitated by the subsequent opening of the Panama Canal.

The new sales pitch

Southern California's growing reputation as a health resort was responsible for the next big wave of newcomers, enticed by the climate, the abundance of thermal and mineral springs and the boosterism of such communities as Pasadena, Riverside, Ojai and Palm Springs. The state was already first in honey production; vineyards, citrus and walnut groves blossomed over thousands of acres. "Buy Land in Los Angeles and Wear Diamonds" was typical of the slogans that lured newcomers into the area where they were met straight from the train with bands, barbecues and fast-talking salesmen.

The increasing use of the refrigerated railroad car not only escalated freight shipments of oranges throughout the country but spread even more widely the appeal of this fruitful land. In Califiornia's vast deserts and verdant valleys,

Wilcox's death, his widow, Daieda, sold a plot of land on Cahuenga to a French flower painter named Paul DeLongpre and it was his palatial house and floral gardens that became the area's first major tourist attraction.

Hollywood signs up

That same year, ground was broken at Hollywood and Highland for the soon-to-be-famous Hollywood Hotel and also for Whitley Heights, an elegant hillside community that became for early movie stars what Beverly Hills was to become in later years. Planned as a completely separate community, Hollywood was obliged in

figs, rice, vegetables and cotton became profitable. The balmy climate encouraged dairy farming, livestock and poultry raising. And, from the turn of the century, in this already bountiful land oil production became the most profitable of all.

Due to early huckstering by the big railroads, whose salesmen had gone to such lengths as spiking thorny trees with oranges to sell worthless land, real-estate had long been big business. In 1887, Horace H. Wilcox had given the name Hollywood to his new sub-division. After

1903 to join up with the city of Los Angeles, along with so many neighboring communities, to obtain an adequate water supply.

Since 1854, California's capital had been Sacramento, but it was San Francisco that ruled a rapidly coalescing state. Agriculture in the Central Valley had grown in response to the needs of the exploding population; in the decade of the 1850s, California's cattle herds grew from 262,000 to more than 3 million. Towns like Stockton and Monterey were thriving as '49ers set up shops and sank roots. The Gilded Age, with its extravagance and corruption, continued right up to that fateful morning in 1906, after which nothing was the same again. ❑

LEFT: tropical fruit became an early industry in sunny Southern California.
ABOVE: the first map of Hollywood, *circa* 1900.

THE 20TH CENTURY

The Great Earthquake of 1906 had immediate devastating consequences for San Francisco. It also helped Los Angeles inch ahead in popularity

Southern California mushroomed from an agricultural community to an industrial complex spurred on by the discovery of oil in 1892 in what is now the Westlake Park area. It made Los Angeles aware it was sitting on a fat reservoir of wealth. The "Salt Lake Field" in southwestern Los Angeles was developed, followed by fields in Huntington Beach, Santa Fe Springs and Signal Hill. Oil derricks sprouted from the hills to the sea. Even Venice, constructed with canals rather than streets and sporting gondolas like its Italian counterpart, became an oil city. Fresno struck oil in 1899 and began steady oil refining, as well as producing cotton, alfalfa, potatoes and fruit.

Trains and trolley cars

Downtown LA was linked to Pasadena and Santa Fe by an urban railway. But, not to be outdone, the Southern Pacific's Collis P. Huntington had, in 1901, devised a vast inter-urban network of electric trains to blanket the entire area. "I will join the whole region into one big family," he promised, adding that Los Angeles was "destined to become the most important city in the country, if not in the world. It can extend in any direction, as far as you like." Within a decade, his trolley cars on which passengers could ride 20 miles (30 km) for a nickel stretched everywhere from a city whose population had tripled to 300,000.

"The whole area within a radius of 70 miles of the city took on a new life," wrote Huntington's biographer, Isaac Marcosson, in 1914. "Villages became towns; towns blossomed into miniature cities." When the author Henry James came by on a lecture tour in 1905, he said he'd never seen such an efficient transit system in all his worldwide travels.

But within five years, the *Times* noted that "with thousands of motor cars passing and

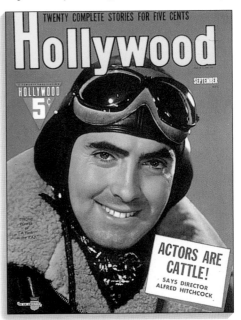

repassing, the traffic question has become a problem." A transportation expert brought from back east to anticipate transit needs for the next decade (during which the population was expected to triple again) urged the creation of a planning commission "to replace the present haphazard system of growth." When Los Angeles held its second annual motor show in 1909, it had more cars on its streets than any other city in the world.

The Big One

An earthquake measuring 8.25 on the Richter scale preceded the fire that first shook Northern Californians from their beds at 5.12am on April 18, 1906. When the deadly San Andreas Fault lurched that morning, it sent terrifying jolts through an area 210 miles (338 km) long and 30 miles (48 km) wide, from San Juan Bautista in the south to Fort Bragg in the north. Other towns, like San Jose and Point Reyes Station near Drake's Bay, suffered more from the ini-

---

LEFT: Los Angeles as a transportation hub: at its second annual motor show in 1909, the city had more cars on its streets than any other place in the world.
RIGHT: Hollywood hunk smolders happily.

tial shock than San Francisco. Church bells jangled chaotically, dishes fell, windows shattered, dogs barked, Enrico Caruso (appearing locally in the opera *Carmen*) was scared voiceless, and San Francisco's new City Hall crumbled. In 48 seconds, it was all over but the city lay in ruins.

The subsequent fire destroyed 28,000 buildings over an area of more than 4 sq. miles (7 sq. km). It killed 315 people; the bodies of 352 more were never found. The city had experienced many earthquakes before, but none on this scale, and in a

EARTHQUAKE AFTERMATH

The 1906 earthquake killed 315 people; a further 352 bodies were never found.

the fire from spreading. Experts were lacking and improvisations by the commandant of the Presidio, Brigadier General Frederick Funston – who had leaped in unauthorized to fill the gap in authority – served only to destroy scores of beautiful Victorian mansions along Van Ness Avenue and to spread the fire still further.

Hundreds were dead or still trapped in smoking ruins, 500 city blocks were leveled and a handful of people had been shot or bayoneted by Funston's inexperienced militia who had poured into the streets to keep order

city that hosted more than 40 percent of the state's population (it is now less than 4 percent) the effect was cataclysmic. Although the awareness of the mighty San Andreas Fault extended back a dozen years, there had been no prior warning of, or preparations for, this major upheaval. Only an unearthly low rumble preceded fissures opening up and spreading wavelike across the city.

With its alarm system destroyed, the Fire Department lacked coordination. When the brigades did arrive, they found mangled mains lacking any water supply. The situation was worst in the area south of Market Street where expert demolition work might have prevented

and prevent looting. Golden Gate Park became the home of as many as 300,000 people for at least the next few weeks. Cooking inside the tents was banned, sanitation was rudimentary, water was in very short supply and rats (and therefore the threat of the bubonic plague) a dark, lingering menace.

But there was a strong will to recover. A Committee of Forty on the Reconstruction of San Francisco was formed to define the tasks to be undertaken and A.P. Giannini's tiny Bank of Italy, making loans to small businesses intent on rebuilding, was at the forefront of those determined to revive the city's fortunes. The bank was later to become the Bank of America, the country's largest. Aid poured in from all over the world, $8 million worth within the first few weeks. Even the much-reviled Southern Pacific Railroad pitched in generously, freighting in supplies without charge, offering free passage out of the city and putting heavy equipment and cranes to work on the enormous task of clearing the debris.

The photographer Arnold Genthe wrote, "While the ruins were still smoking, on top of a heap of collapsed walls, a sign would announce: 'On this site will be erected a six-storey office building to be ready for occupancy in the fall'." San Francisco's renaissance was inevitable. The

Francisco's giddiest times. The 1915 Panama Pacific International Exposition, which occupied 600 acres (244 hectares) of reclaimed land in what is now the marina, is still considered one of the greatest of the world's fairs. Today, only one vestige of the flamboyant celebration remains: the Palace of Fine Arts, intended by its architect, Bernard Maybeck, to impart a certain "sadness modified by the feeling that beauty has a soothing influence." It was saved from gradual decay by civic benefactors in the 1960s.

The initial unparalled growth of Southern California was due in large part to the Owens Valley scandal (see below), and additional water

new, improved, taller buildings of Montgomery Street, the Wall Street of the west, were needed to process all the money churned out by the state's industries, farms and banks. The Port of San Francisco was still one of the world's busiest harbors. San Francisco's historic business of making business was unstoppable.

In 1911, San Francisco elected a new mayor, James "Sunny Jim" Rolph, a purveyor of goodwill whose reign encompassed some of San

LEFT: despite measuring 8.25 on the Richter scale, San Franciscans did not let the 1906 earthquake dampen their appetites or dining habits.
ABOVE: something fishy going on in 1920s Hollywood.

WATER BY STEALTH

An infamous plot hatched in 1904 to steal water from the Owens Valley via a 250-mile pipeline over the Tehachapu Mountains to Los Angeles made fortunes for a private syndicate and allowed LA to grow to unprecedented levels. One of the syndicate's members was General Moses H. Sherman, whose advance knowledge of what land was about to be enriched came from serving on Los Angeles' Board of Water Commissioners. This scandal, which left the Owens Valley dry, formed part of the storyline for Roman Polanski's 1974 film *Chinatown*.

brought in by Los Angeles' Water Bureau Superintendent William Mulholland. Today these aquaducts supply 525 million gallons (nearly 2 billion liters) of water a day, and all firmly believed this would take care of Southern California's thirst forever. But LA has been adding sources ever since: more water from the Parker Dam on the Arizona border arrived in 1941, but it cost the city a staggering $200 million. Electric power now comes mostly from the Hoover Dam on the Colorado river, about 206 miles (330 km) away.

Even as water problems slowed to a trickle, the flood of newcomers to Southern California

continued at an astonishing rate. "California became that legendary land of perpetual summer, of orange groves in sight of snowy peaks, of oil wells spouting wealth, of real-estate promising fortunes, of cinema stars and bathing beauties. It seemed to promise a new start, a kinder providence, a rebirth of soul and body," enthused a writer in the Federal Writers Project guide to the state in the 1930s, by which time the movie industry was one of the country's top 10 industries.

"Have you no slum districts?" an admiring President Taft had asked during a 1909 visit to Los Angeles, to be answered a year or two later by a writer in *Sunset* magazine who rhap-

sodized: "Go north, south, east, west or any point in between on both urban and inter-urban lines and just inside the city limits or outside… you will find climbing the hillsides, slipping along the valleys, stretching across the plain until they join fields still planted in grain, street after street of cozy homes – miles and miles of houses for one man and his family. *These* are the tenements of Los Angeles…"

Six years after the Wright brothers made their pioneering 59-second airflight in North Carolina, Los Angeles hosted America's first international air show, partly financed with a $50,000 contribution from Huntington, the railroad magnate. Among the half a million visitors who thronged the old Dominguez Ranch to watch Glenn Curtis set a speed record of 55 mph (88 kph) was Glenn Martin, who promptly set up a plant that by World War I was turning out a plane a day. One of his employees, Donald Douglas, peeled off to begin his own company. Douglas's DC3, the first commercially successful aircraft, was within a couple of years carrying 95 percent of all US air traffic.

Cecil B. de Mille had an airport at Fairfax and Wilshire across from one operated by Charlie Chaplin's brother, Sydney. Goodyear began a blimp service to Catalina, and Western Air Express was formed to carry mail across the country. In 1920, scheduled flights began from Los Angeles to San Francisco.

Movie madness

It was the film industry that shot Los Angeles to fame and, unwittingly, it was Leland Stanford whose wager about a galloping horse helped launch it (*see page 75*). With its origins in the nickelodeon, the movie industry began to emerge around the turn of the century and headed west partly to escape the stranglehold patents held by the New York-based Edison company and partly because of California's superb climate, which made outdoor filming cheaper and easier.

Within a dozen years, the streets of Horace Wilcox's sedate town of Hollywood were filled with intruders bearing cameras and megaphones, roping off streets, crashing cars and staging pretend shoot-outs. Some prolific directors were turning out one-reel Westerns or comedies almost daily. The locals didn't like it at all. "They thought we were tramps," recalled screenwriter Anita Loos. "They saw themselves as being invaded and supplanted as elegant ladies and gentlemen so they ganged up on us."

For years directors could only shoot outdoors due to a lack of sophisticated photographic equipment. Even indoor scenes were shot outdoors in strong sunlight. From 1926, the Pickford-Fairbanks Studio immortalized such luminaries as actor Charlie Chaplin and directors D.W. Griffith and Cecil B. de Mille. Comedy became king. Mack Sennett's Keystone Kops had the whole nation laughing. Before long, studios sprang up in Culver City,

LA TAKES THE LEAD

By 1920, the population of Los Angeles surpassed that of its rival, San Francisco

started instant fads, and shaped tastes and ideas the world over.

In the summer of 1920, the population of Los Angeles for the first time surpassed that of San Francisco's 508,000, undoubtedly initiating the furious jealousy that still exists between the two cities today. The southern portion of the state was "the world's closest approach to bedlam and babel," sneered George Creel, with columnist Westbrook Pegler urging that the same territory "be declared incompetent and placed in charge of a guardian."

Universal City as well as Hollywood. The latter name, particularly, had by now become more or less synonymous with the word "movies."

Silent movies accompanied by organ music gave way to the "talkies." Hundreds of movie houses sprang up. If a movie wasn't doing good box-office business, dishes were given away. Instant fortunes came to stars, directors and producers. Novelists earned more from film rights than from their original novels. Studios

LEFT: oil wells like these at First and Temple streets, Los Angeles, boosted the southern economy.
ABOVE: the construction of the Golden Gate Bridge in the 1930s gave San Franciscans a morale boost.

During the 1930s, troubles broke out in the great central valleys of the state which, with ample supplies of water for irrigation, combined with skilful techniques developed by the new agribusiness barons, were bidding to feed the world. The workers, long exploited by greedy and brutal bosses, staged spontaneous strikes which were met not with an improvement in their condition but by arrests under the oppressive Criminal Syndicalism Act.

Fortunately, amidst all of this strife, the completion in San Francisco of the Bay Bridge and the Golden Gate Bridge gave the whole state a much-needed shot of enthusiasm and an undisputed cause for celebration. ❑

MODERN TIMES

Beatnik bards and happy hippies flocked to find fulfillment

in the state where experimentation was encouraged

World War II gave a tremendous boost to California's aircraft industry, which increased statewide from fewer than 10,000 employees to more than 300,000. When the war was over, a gradual shift in the industry's workers from mainly blue-collar laborers to scientists and technicians meant, as historian Bruce Henstell wrote, that "aeronautics was replaced by something called aerospace." In 1940, the population of Los Angeles was 1.3 million, of which about 9 percent was Mexican, 3 percent Asian and 3 percent black. By 1950, the City of Angels' 2 million population made it the fourth largest city in the United States.

War rewards

The war had plunged California into a spasm of activity. Twenty-three million tons of war supplies and 1½ million men and women passed through the Golden Gate during the war's 46 months. The ports of San Francisco, Sausalito, Oakland, Vallejo and Alameda were busy around the clock building and repairing ships, and loading supplies for the war machine.

In the Bay area alone, the federal government spent $3 billion on shipbuilding. A dramatic new wave of immigration swept into the region as new factories needed new workers – 100,000 at the Kaiser Yards in Richmond, 90,000 more at Sausalito. Within two years of America's entry into the war, the number of wage-earners in San Francisco almost tripled. The federal government doled out $83 million in contracts to the California Institute of Technology (Cal Tech) alone.

Even though 750,000 Californians left for military service, the state's wage-earners increased by nearly a million in the first half of the decade. After the war, the great suburban sprawl got under way as war workers and their families settled down to post-war prosperity.

LEFT: 1967's Summer of Love in San Francisco's Golden Gate Park made international headlines.
RIGHT: America's favorite tough guy, Humphrey Bogart, reached the heights of Hollywood stardom.

Eventually, the film industry shook down into the seven major studios that dominate the industry today: MGM/United Artists in Culver City, 20th Century Fox in Century City, Paramount in Hollywood, and four studios in the San Fernando Valley: Columbia Pictures, Warner Brothers, Walt Disney Productions in Burbank

and Universal Pictures in nearby Universal City. Also in Burbank is television's NBC. ABC is in the northeastern part of Los Angeles; CBS is at Fairfax and 3rd Street.

The Hollywood area is still host to a few smaller production companies and all kinds of ancillary businesses and services such as recording studios, prop houses, talent agencies, lighting equipment companies and equipment rentals. Also remaining in Hollywood are Eastman Kodak and Consolidated Film Industries, which process millions of feet every day. Technicolor, which in 1931 developed the three-strip color process, was for 40 years located in an Art Deco building on Romaine Street.

The entertainment industry is one of the most highly unionized industries in Southern California, with the Screen Actors Guild (of whom Ronald Reagan was once president), and the American Federation of Radio and Television Artists collectively claiming more than 100,000 members nationwide, with most of them in Los Angeles. The Directors Guild of America and the Writers Guild of America account for most of the rest of the talent, in addition to all the behind-the-camera workers such as grips, gaffers, film editors, car-

CITY OF LOVE

Long-haired youths went to San Francisco to pen odes and wear flowers.

arrivals, have come to the state to escape the burdens of conformity elsewhere. The great majority of Californians have always been settled and to one degree or another, God-fearing. But the anti-conformists – the colorful, sometimes crazy minority – have given California its name for verve and drive.

In the 1950s and 1960s, according to author Mike Davis, Los Angeles became "the capital of youth" but it was in San Francisco that the first stirrings of post-war protest and florid eccentricity were felt. While

penters, plasterers, publicists, costumers, art directors, sound people and cinematographers, who are represented by the International Alliance of Theatrical Stage Employers and the Musicians Union. Studio drivers are in the Teamsters. It is very difficult for a non-union person to get a job in the movies. In the '30s and '40s, the IATSE was headed by a Chicago hood named Willie Bioff, who took payoffs from studio presidents to keep down union demands. He was eventually convicted and ousted.

As a new, almost instant society, California has always felt free to experiment. Many of its newcomers, from the "Anglo hordes" of the 1840s to Gold Rush adventurers to present-day

the American nation was settled into a prosperous torpor, the city's historically Italian North Beach area became the haunt of a loosely defined group of poets, writers, declaimers and pavement philosophers – the beatniks.

In the 1950s, they seemed titillating and somehow significant, a tempting combination for the nation's press who ogled at their rambling poetry readings, sniffed at the light marijuana breezes drifting out of the North Beach coffee houses, and wondered if civilization could stand such a limpid assault. The beatniks, it seems, mostly wanted America to go away. But it wouldn't, and before long "beat" had become a fashion and North Beach a tourist attraction.

The beats, however, had struck a nerve of dissatisfaction and alienation in America. Though it was never a coherent movement, it produced juice-stirring literary works like Allen Ginsberg's *Howl* and Jack Kerouac's *On the Road*. That inspired alienation gave rise to two parallel, dissimilar, but oddly congruent movements: the angry politics of the New Left and the woozy love fest of the hippies.

The first great protest of the great, protest-rich 1960s took place in San Francisco in the decade's first year. In mid-May, the House Un-

CITY OF UNCERTAINTY

"I had already wondered whether God intended for people to live in LA."

Movement kept up a steady assault against racism, materialism and the stifling "multiversity" itself. As the war in Vietnam grew in horror, the New Left spread across America and the world, tilting at governments, bombing, marching, changing the way America looked at itself.

The hippies attacked their target with gentler weapons. While the New Left ranted at the evils of an affluent and smug, hypocritical society, the hippies tried to undermine that society with glimmering love and peace, and wearing far-fetched clothes.

American Activities Committee opened a series of hearings in City Hall. When hundreds of demonstrators met the committee in the rotunda, the police reacted furiously, turning water hoses and billy clubs on the crowds. Dozens of protesters were carted off to jail, but the angry shouts in City Hall were heard around the world.

The locus of dissent was the University of California at Berkeley. There the Free Speech

FAR LEFT: the beat generation's Jack Kerouac.
LEFT: beatnik bard Allen Ginsberg.
ABOVE: 1992's riots over the acquittal of Rodney King's arresting officers left 51 people dead.

The Summer of Love

In the mid-1960s, San Francisco became the center of the hippie revolution. It was a natural refuge for spacey idealists, having been created by youthful myth-chasers. Former beatniks slid easily into the free-and-easy hippie style centered around the Haight-Ashbury neighborhood, with its funky, cheap Victorian houses and Golden Gate Park handily nearby for roaming. By 1967, the Haight was thronged with long-haired young men and women, the movement reaching its apogee in the massive Be-In assemblage and the celebrated Summer of Love.

At first, San Francisco was amused by the hippies. But as altogether too many sons and daughters of wealthy, respected citizens took to marijuana-induced meandering, and as the LSD hysteria took full flight, public sympathy for the nomads gradually began to evaporate.

Tensions and trial by TV

By the mid-1960s, blacks in LA had multiplied tenfold and were fed up with discriminatory employment and "unwritten" housing restrictions. On one hot summer evening in 1965, the palm-shaded ghetto of Watts exploded. For six days the inner city boiled until the National Guard restored order. In April, 1992, with conditions in the black and Chicano areas largely

unchanged, violence erupted again. The acquittal of four police officers recorded on video beating a black man, Rodney King, sparked the worst racial violence in California's history. By the time the dawn-to-dusk curfew was lifted, there were 51 dead, 2,500 injured and 5,200 fires had occurred. South Central LA was devastated. The Rodney King case provided the spark for already existing tension, setting off the intricately-connected time-bomb of race, poverty and the state of the inner city. The recent and seemingly never-ending explosion of gang violence in Los Angeles, for example, has focused national attention on the worryingly intractable problem of urban poverty.

Barely a year goes by without major events making headlines the world over. From 1994 to 1997, TV viewers were glued to their screens by the arrest and trials in Los Angeles of former football hero O.J. Simpson. In late 1997, the mass suicide of 39 members of the Heaven's Gate cult in a San Diego mansion had people, once again, wondering about life in sunny California. These acts of human passion are, of course, conducted alongside the regular earthquakes, floods and brush fires.

Sometimes all this hubris has predictable consequences. "I had already begun to wonder whether God intended for people to live in LA. Certainly he never meant for millions of them to live there," noted writer Richard Reeves, commenting on how often homes built on slopes continually slide back into canyons above earthquake fault lines veined deep into the earth. "LA," he suggested, "is not at peace with nature – that's why we get these periodic punishments. It's a man-made city, a tribute to rapacity and tenacity. There were people who could make money by putting a city here – the last place there should have been one."

Developers still pit their wits and legal expertise against the environmentalists. Yet these "eco-freaks" now have a vocal constituency. The Sierra Club has become caretaker of the wilderness; the Coastal Commission reviews all construction near the coastline; and all plans for major construction must be preceded by a federal environment impact report. Nuclear power plants have strict legal controls. New voices are not only speaking; today, they are being heard.

The growth goes on

In the 1990s, almost a million new residents moved into the state, 10 percent from Asia. Ninety languages are spoken in Los Angeles district schools. In an optimistic forecast of life in 2013, the *Los Angeles Times* concluded that the region will be prospering because of its large, skilled workforce, technical and design expertise, and university-based research and development capabilities. It will also continue to be a center for trends and fashion and a fertile ground for entrepreneurs. ❑

LEFT: the arrest and trials of former football hero O.J. Simpson riveted the nation from 1994 to 1997.
RIGHT: carefree scenes like this one on Santa Monica Pier continue to attract residents to sunny California.

CULTURAL DIVERSITY

Newcomers bring new values. California's changing ethnic mix has
significant political, social and artistic implications

California, the third largest state in the Union, ranks highest in number of inhabitants, but perhaps what is less appreciated is that no other part of America can claim such ethnic diversity. The students of the Unified School District of Los Angeles, for example, speak more than 90 different languages. From the onset of the industrialized era, the state's population has been melded by boom cycles of immigration: Mexicans, Anglos from the Midwest, the Chinese and Japanese, African Americans from the South, Russians, Armenians, Asian Indians, Koreans, Salvadoreans, Iranians, Filipinos, Samoans, Vietnamese. Almost half a century ago, the well-known historian Carey McWilliams was already referring to Southern California as an "archipelago of social and ethnic islands, economically interrelated but culturally disparate."

State of being

When California joined the Union in 1850, it was considered to be the final frontier, a land promising spiritual and social riches. Pioneers armed with little more than faith came in search of sunshine, fertile soil and freedom from oppression. Like the grape vines and citrus trees, the people could bloom under the gentle sun. Boosters furiously sold the fable of the Golden State to the rest of the Union, a dream that more than a century later has yet to lose its tenacious hold on the imagination.

The eruption of civil unrest in Los Angeles in 1992 was a reaction to California's apparent failure to achieve the myth, to become an egalitarian plurality that offered up a better life for migrants' children. California's multi-culturalism was founded on a dream, but also on the backs of minority labor. The uprising in Los Angeles was a wake-up call to the entire US, an indication that the ethnic stew was boiling over.

PRECEDING PAGES: California Koreans taking a stroll; everyone's a star at this Los Angeles diner.
LEFT: flashy sax at Fisherman's Wharf.
RIGHT: love in Lincoln Park, San Francisco.

The miscegenation of cultures had an early start two centuries ago when Spanish Franciscan monks arrived to set up a string of missions throughout the state, spreading a Catholic hand across the souls of the heathen indigenous peoples. In 1834, by now the state having passed from Spanish to Mexican rule, a proclamation

was issued providing for the secularization of all the missions.

Before the end of the century, the American Indian population had been decimated and their offspring, the Mestizos, found themselves pushed southward by an influx of miners flooding the foothills of the Sierra Nevada mountain range. To this day, the preponderance of the Latino population rests in Southern California where people with at least part-African ancestry were also found in large numbers.

When Los Angeles was founded in 1781, more than half of the settlers were Mulattos (those of mixed black, American Indian and Spanish blood). Beverly Hills, once called *Ran-*

cho Rodeo de Las Aguas, was owned by Maria Rita Valdez, the granddaughter of black founding settlers.

The development and growth of California's industries throughout the 19th century brought a tide of immigration. The Chinese initially came as railroad workers on the Central Pacific construction gangs, before branching into agriculture and fishing. African Americans also came as railroad employees, in smaller numbers at first and then, during World War II, to fill manufacturing and service jobs. And towards the turn of the century, Japanese immigrants arrived in search of opportunities in the emerg-

ing produce industry, which they eventually came to dominate, from packing and shipping the fruit to setting up small stands to sell it.

Enter the Okies

Nothing, however, compared to the tidal wave of Anglos who arrived from the Midwest during the 1880s (and then again – fleeing the parched dustbowl farms of the prairies – in the 1920s). Already having established major colonies around the San Francisco and Sacramento areas, they saturated Southern California with visions of manifest destiny.

But destiny's capricious nature has a habit of throwing a dash of irony into the stew. During

the 1980s, hundreds of thousands of Mexicans and Central Americans fleeing civil strife and political persecution immigrated, both legally and illegally, to California. By the year 2020 – some people say even sooner – it is estimated the number of Latinos in California will surpass that of Anglos, becoming once again the majority ethnic group.

The mix has understandably had significant political implications. More than any time in the history of the state, multi-culturalism is beginning to be reflected in the offices of elected and appointed officials: mayors and congressional representatives, city council members and police chiefs. As a consequence of lawsuits brought by such groups as the Mexican American Legal Defense and Education Fund and the American Civil Liberties Union in the past decade, districts have been reshaped to give African Americans and Latinos a chance to elect representatives of their communities. (Asian-American populations in California – as well as most other ethnic communities – tend to be more geographically spread out, making voting blocs more difficult.)

Although Latinos in California are heavily involved in community activism, they are vastly under-represented politically, one reason being that the number of Latinos who are citizens and therefore capable of voting is much smaller than the actual population. For many years the only notable leader was the late Cesar Chavez, the widely-admired president of the United Farm Workers of America, who gained fame during the early 1970s for his battle to gain decent working conditions for the mostly Mexican farm laborers.

American immigrants from Asia and the Pacific Islands, who are the third largest ethnic community in California after Anglos and Latinos, in many ways tread the same path as Latinos. To bolster their power they have formed various cross-cultural alliances and coalitions throughout the state. In Sacramento, for example, after friction between newly-arrived Vietnamese and other minorities – as well as with the police – some ethnic groups have joined members of the Latino community to form an Advisory Coalition on Minority Law Enforcement Issues.

It is African Americans, however, who have probably had the most success with community and political organizations. Groups ranging from the Black Panthers (which originated in Oakland) to Recycling Black Dollars have made great strides in forwarding black causes. But California's African-American population has been declining in the past few years with a consequent stagnation in their political progress. With notable exceptions, most of the influential African-American politicians were elected in the fervor of the civil rights movement of the 1960s and '70s.

Some non-whites have become police chiefs around the state, with a commitment to revamping police departments with long histories of repression of and blatant racism towards

decade that African-Americans who escaped the repression of the Deep South found that they were barred from living in certain neighborhoods by restrictive housing covenants.

As a result, clusters of ethnic communities formed where people could be protected and cultures preserved – San Francisco's famous Chinatown being one such example. Now considered a charming tourist attraction, Chinatown developed out of necessity as a refuge from abuse: until the 1960s when immigration laws changed, the Chinese had been subjected to severe and continual harassment, and discriminatory legislation had deprived them of eligi-

minorities. They are transforming the relationship between law-enforcement departments and the public by installing community-based policing programs – taking cops out of the isolation of police cars and putting them on foot patrol, where they can better interact with the citizens.

How Chinatown was born

Early in World War II, the notorious Executive Order 9066 authorized the internment of all Japanese on the West Coast – most of whom lost everything they owned. It was during that same

LEFT: San Francisco sushi bar.
ABOVE: Juanita's restaurant near Sonoma.

bility for citizenship, ensuring that they had no legal recourse.

In California's sprawling metropolitan areas, many without any recognizable center, it has often been the churches and temples that have served as the nexus of a community – spiritually, socially and politically. First was the African Methodist Episcopal Church in South-Central Los Angeles, which began in the home of a former slave and became the first African-American church in the city. One of its pastors, Dr Cecil L. Murray, considered one of the community's most vocal and visible leaders, established close ties with former mayor Tom Bradley during the latter's 20-year reign. As a result, the media tends to descend upon First AME for statements relating to African-Americans in the city.

It is perhaps the necessity of asserting one's identity in this Babel-like sea of cultures that has made California the state in which more trends and artistic movements take flight. East Coast pundits have long joked about California's lack of culture. To be sure, it is a culture without a face – without *one* face, anyway. It is as much a refined performance of *Swan Lake* at San Francisco's War Memorial Opera House as a barrio mural spray-painted by talented teenaged graffiti artists.

> **2020 VISION**
>
> By the year 2020, it is thought the number of local Latinos will surpass Anglos.

"Tagging" (initialing) property provided inner-city teens – primarily Latino – with a voice that the larger culture refused to hear. Today, rap's impact on the media and advertising has been palpable. And Anglo kids from essentially conservative areas like Orange County, San Diego and Santa Barbara, infatuated with the image of defiance, have been known to don "gangsta wear," the cartoonishly oversized, fall-down clothing favored by gang members, rappers and taggers.

Arching towards the exotic Far East (or West,

Multi-culturalism in California is a fact, not something to be argued by theorists. Ideas, language, art – these are generated by the streets, by the co-mingling of people's needs and desires. Rap music, for example, has been linked to the malaise that occurred after the Watts rebellion in 1965. Assembled from the shards of the uprising, the Watts art renaissance delivered up a number of visionaries. Theirs was the poetry of frustration, self-assertion and, unlike some contemporary rap, hope. Bold, bright graffiti art also arrived hard on the heels of disenfranchisement.

depending on one's point of view), California inevitably adopted the customs of Asian immigrants. Health-conscious Californians submit to strenuous programs of yoga and meditation, while eating brown rice and soy sauce. Beat generation writers, who tumbled around San Francisco in the '50s, derived much of their inspiration from Buddhism, and Japanese and Chinese poetry.

The experience of facing society as "other" in California has produced some of America's finest writers and artists of the past half-century, including playwright William Saroyan, who grew up in an Armenian enclave of grape growers and farmers in Fresno; poet and novelist

Alice Walker, best known for *The Color Purple*; essayist Richard Rodriguez, who writes about gay and Latino assimilation and the politics of multi-culturalism; Filipino-born artist Manuel Ocampo, whose paintings often depict symbols of racism and the brutish imperialism of the colonials; theater artist Anna Deavere Smith, whose performance piece *Twilight: Los Angeles, 1992* concerned the riots that devastated the city, told through the voices of the people who experienced it; and novelist Amy Tan, who found the characters of her widely acclaimed *Joy Luck Club* from the Chinatown (San Francisco) of her childhood.

what being a truly multi-ethnic society can mean. There are some who believe that the obsession with tribalism is a leading factor in causing the sometimes bitter divisiveness throughout the state; viewing others always through the prism of your culture deepens the trenches and hinders society's gains. It's the cult of "other." Critics of this argument say that recognition of California's many ethnic groups is the first step towards peaceful coexistence. Promoting minorities to meaningful positions in public policy – whether it be through affirmative action or some nebulous sense of political correctness – will eventually mitigate the issue.

Mingling of styles

What has become more and more evident, though, is that the people of California have slowly amalgamated each other's habits and styles, tastes and mannerisms. While most California towns and suburbs do tend to stay relatively homogeneous, pockets of cultures border one another, stitched by the colorful religions and customs of their people. California is hip-hop and cha-cha-cha wrapped in a dazzling gold-flecked sari.

California epitomizes the best and worst of

LEFT: California girls getting golden brown.
ABOVE: California boys getting body conscious.

FESTIVALS

There are celebrations up and down the state honoring California's multi-enthnicity. Chinese New Year in San Francisco is one of the biggest in America; Vietnamese New Year has devotees in Santa Clara. Oakland has an African cultural festival in March; Paso Robles a Polish festival in April. Cinco de Mayo, the Mexican holiday, is celebrated in all major cities, while Brazilians, Scots, Irish, Germans and Lithuanians all have their own street parties. For a list of monthly festivities, consult the "Calendar" section of the *LA Times* or check the *San Francisco Chronicle*.

The recession that hit California in the 1990s knocked the smile from its sunny face. As has occurred throughout the history of the state, tensions between ethnic groups amplify when the job market plummets and the window of opportunity slams shut – and illegal immigrants are always the first to feel the blow. During the depression in the 1930s, the county of LA "repatriated" thousands of Mexicans on relief, loading them like cattle onto trains. When the need for cheap labor beckoned, Mexicans once more became a necessary commodity in the burgeoning economy.

Today, politicians and economists have once

again latched onto the issue of immigration. Even in liberal San Francisco, where law enforcement is prohibited from reporting illegal aliens, there's been an uproar about the growing number of Central Americans standing on street corners attempting to get hired out for menial work.

In San Diego, suburban residents have taken action against nearby encampments of immigrants, citing to government officials everything from unsanitary conditions to spousal and child abuse. (Border crossings from Mexico into San Diego County are so prevalent that there are signs cautioning drivers to be watchful of immigrants running across the highway.)

It has been suggested by the media that California is becoming dangerously Balkanized, that the cities especially are starting to resemble such racially- and ethnically-driven areas as the former Yugoslavia. What is evident, however, is not that the hope for multi-culturalism is withering, but that it is being realized.

At the very least from an economical standpoint, many business and political leaders are making a concerted effort to adapt to California's quickly shifting social landscape. Neighborhoods that had previously been abandoned after the flight of the whites are now targeted for revitalization according to the new communities they serve.

Los Angeles' Broadway, once the hub of the white entertainment industry with Sid Grauman's spectacular Million Dollar Theater premiering the films of stars such as Charlie Chaplin and Mary Pickford, is now mostly a Latino commercial district. Broadway is vibrant with the exchanges of everyday life – racks of clothing spilling onto the sidewalk, the smell of espresso wafting over crates of fresh produce, trinkets and gifts, and food and toiletries. Its centerpiece, Grand Central Market, houses Chinese herbalists, black-owned juice bars and tortilla stands operated by inner-city Latino youths.

The future of democracy

California urban theorists like Mike Davis, author of *City of Quartz: Excavating the Future in Los Angeles*, have proposed the idea of neighborhood planning councils in order to give responsibility to the many ethnic populations that are not adequately represented. The basic premise is that a rotating group of representatives elected from each neighborhood would convene on issues concerning their community – including revitalization, law enforcement and public safety, business development, education, health and arts programs.

These representatives would then meet with their city council member or county supervisor. Bringing an additional level of representation to the local citizens might help to render impotent the power-breaking restructuring of districts. Maybe this, at least in California, is the future of democracy. ❑

LEFT: Yurok tribesman at a festival in Klamath.
RIGHT: love conquers even knobbly knees in the amusingly Scandinavian town of Solvang.

CALIFORNIA CUISINE

The menu is as varied as the people. From soya burgers to sushi to sun-dried tomatoes, the state is a food-lover's fantasy

What are you hungry for? It is often said that California is the land of fantasy, and why should food be any exception? Walk just a few blocks in most sizeable cities and you'll have a choice to whet even the most cosmopolitan of appetites: hamburgers and fries, tacos and burritos, pasta and pizza, noo-

dles and sushi, tandoori and curries, Mongolian barbecue, falafel and bagels, piroshki and baklava, and on through the global menu.

To understand what makes this incredible array possible, it helps to consider California's geographic and cultural orientation: the influence of Mexican neighbors to the south and Asian neighbors to the west; the vast tracts of rich soil that make it one of the most fertile and productive places on earth; a climate friendly to growing just about every kind of crop all year round; local waters that yield a bounty of fish and seafood. Mix all this with liberal dashings of sun and easy living, and there's California's recipe for innovation and culinary awareness.

But more than these factors, local food is defined by the many people who call themselves Californians. Most came from other parts of the world (many recently, others a generation or two ago), bringing native regional foodways with them. This has created a food scene that is much more than just a few ethnic restaurants scattered around. Particularly in California's large cities, sizeable ethnic communities support their own specialty food shops and produce markets, as well as an often remarkable number of restaurants (Los Angeles, for example, claims to have around 500 Korean eateries).

This results in a vitality, availability and diversity within a native cuisine that, for the curious diner, can make for a fascinating food experience. Not, however, that every ethnic restaurant is authentic (or, for that matter, very good) and it isn't always easy to find the best ones. Especially in small cities and towns, the highways are lined with the ubiquitous multitude of fast food outlets, coffee shops and diners serving "American food" found everywhere around the country. To locate the individually owned gem, you may have to ask the locals. An excellent place to do this is at a farmers' market where you've stopped to buy food for yourself.

Links with Europe

Traditional European fare, especially Italian and French, has long been available in California, particularly prominent among the more expensive restaurants. Today, these upmarket restaurants have also become highly regionalized, reflecting Californians' passion for European travel and an increased familiarity with specific regional dishes from, for example, Tuscany and Provence. In fact, the chefs at these fine California establishments are likely to have trained at equally good restaurants in Europe. Many European food trends – as in other areas of life – make their US debut in California, where the transference of culinary ideas, techniques and food fashions is picked up, adapted as needed, and passed on eastward across the country.

Perhaps it was inevitable that this state of

agricultural abundance, with its myriad intersecting food traditions, would also have a cuisine named in its honor, a cuisine that has swept the world and produced thousands of imitators. But what exactly is it?

There is no strict definition of California Cuisine, and rightly so. Using classic French cooking techniques and what used to be known as "continental cuisine" as its base, the California phenomenon seeks to combine disparate tastes and textures, with an emphasis on the freshest seasonal ingredients to create

KOREAN COUNTDOWN

Los Angeles claims to have around 500 restaurants serving Korean food.

and Sonoma valleys northeast of San Francisco first achieved world-class status in the 1970s, and along the way have been joined by ever-better wines from other parts of the state. To augment the vast selection of viticultural selections, the micro-brewery, offering patrons beer brewed on the restaurant premises, has recently been introduced in the state.

To round out a good meal, you won't have to look far to find a selection of sidewalk cafés and espresso bars in cities and towns throughout the state. Imported from Europe, and augmented by

imaginative and delicious presentations. In other words, think of tofu loaf made with whole grains and vegetables, covered in sautéed mushrooms and jack cheese. Weird but wonderful.

A thirst for life

No discussion of California eating pleasures would be complete without mentioning its world-famous wines, of which locals are justifiably proud. California vintages from the Napa

---

LEFT: the California emphasis on healthy food using natural ingredients has spawned many imitators.
ABOVE: San Francisco's Chinatown, the biggest in the western world, offers dining opportunities galore.

the wonderful weather, this habit suits perfectly the California "hangin' out" lifestyle.

It would be remiss not to mention California's magnificent supermarkets. Competing keenly for the allegiance of the state's increasingly discriminating household shopper, these 24-hour super-convenience emporia are definitely worth a visit: a trip up and down the aisles, perusing special displays and sampling frequently showcased freebies, can be as enlightening as an outing to the local museum. If time permits, seek out the town's weekly outdoor farmer's market, a recent trend in many communities that allows urbanites to buy direct (and often organically grown) produce from local growers. ❏

THE FINE WINES OF CALIFORNIA

Wine grapes are grown in 45 out of 58 counties, with local wines winning awards and making headlines around the world

In the 18th century when the Franciscan fathers began winemaking, the grapes were dumped into troughs, trampled into pulp and hung in cowskins to ferment before leaking into casks. "In those days the flavor was not described with enthusiasm," wrote the Napa Historical Society's Meredie Porterfield, "but that is what passed for wine in early LA." Today, wine grapes are grown in 45 of California's 58 counties, the state produces 90 percent of total US production and the wines themselves consistently win awards in blind tastings against the world's best.

More than 330,000 Californian acres are planted as vineyards and although Napa and Sonoma get the lion's share of publicity, they produce only about 20 percent of the wine, many more millions of gallons emanating from the San Joaquin Valley, the so-called "jug wines" which are mass-produced and low-priced. Other major wine areas are around Paso Robles, Santa Cruz, the Santa Ynez Valley near Santa Barbara and, in the far south, the emerging vineyards of Temecula.

US wine exports jumped 25 percent in the 1990s, to 48 million gallons a year, with prices rising by 8 percent. Top wine grapes now routinely fetch $2,000 per ton. Chardonnay is still the leader, with 56,000 acres devoted to its grapes, although white Zinfandel and more recently, Merlot, have been coming on strong behind.

Despite increasing sophistication in bottling, manufacturing and marketing, basic winemaking has changed very little over the centuries. Wine is just fermented grape juice, not manufactured but generated by living yeast cells that ferment grape sugars into grape alcohol.

For more about wine and the Wine Country, see the chapter on p.177.

△ **NAPA WINE TRAIN**
Passengers can sample local vintages during a three-hour lunch or dinner on the relaxing 38-mile roundtrip up the valley and back. Tel: 707-253 2111 for information and bookings.

◁ **WINE PRESSING**
The basic function of the press is to separate the juice from the stems and seeds. This basket press is from the Zaca Mesa Winery.

△ TREFETHEN VINEYARDS
More than a century old and restored in the 1970s, Trefethen typifies the tranquil beauty that visitors associate with the Wine Country.

▽ BARREL ROOM OF MERRYVALE WINERY
The perfect setting for dinner or even the sort of "tasting class" that this and many other wineries offer to educate the public palate.

△ AGING WITH ATTITUDE
For aging wine, barrels have a life of five to ten years and come in many sizes, although 225 liter-barrels are the standard.

▽ VALLEY VISITORS
Napa's five million visitors each year bring about $500 million to the valley.

THE CIA AT GREYSTONE

Before the Culinary Institute of America (CIA) was founded half a century ago in Connecticut, many cooks were so secretive about their recipes that it was hard for a beginner to break into the profession. These days, the California branch of the CIA, established at St Helena in what was once the largest stone winery building in the world, Greystone Cellars, works hard to ensure that knowledge is shared, embellished and preserved.

It is appropriate that the CIA is headquartered in the Wine Country because the "pairing" of food and wine is very much a preoccupation of today's culinary industry. At Greystone, students are shown the scientific reasons that food behaves the way it does. In the enormous kitchen, (its windows offering sweeping views of the Napa countryside), they are taught among other things to dice, slice and chop vegetables to $\frac{1}{16}$ of an inch square, more meticulous than restaurants demand. The CIA's restaurant has professional chefs and an open kitchen so diners can watch. Tel: 707-967 1100.

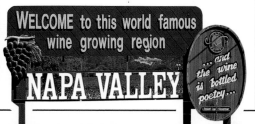

WELCOME to this world famous wine growing region

NAPA VALLEY

...and the wine is bottled poetry...

THE MOVIEMAKERS OF SUNSET BOULEVARD

From such humble beginnings as filming in directors' living rooms,

the movie industry became both star-maker and style-setter

Although its beginnings were elsewhere, Hollywood is what comes to most people's minds when they think of the film industry. Many also think that the first half of the 20th century was both the most interesting and the most important. That's when things were at their peak, when the studio system was in flower and when the major changes were made, from silence to sound and from black and white to color. On or around Sunset Boulevard – the road leading to the "Sunset Sea," as the Pacific Ocean was then called – was where most of the early studios grew up, and *Sunset Boulevard,* the quintessential movie about the industry, came along at the halfway point of the century. The street and the film together neatly encapsulate the story of the movies.

Eccentric pioneers

The ostensible inventor of the moving picture, an English eccentric named Eadweard Muybridge, set out to prove that a trotting horse had all four hooves off the ground simultaneously to enable Leland Stanford, then governor of California, to win a bet. It took five years' work, but in 1877 Muybridge eventually filmed a horse galloping at 20 mph (30 kph), using a series of 12 cameras. Printing the individual shots onto a revolving disk enabled Stanford to win his $25,000 bet. Tripling his battery of cameras, Muybridge devised faster film, mounted his photographs on a wheel combined with light and called his process Zoopraxiscope.

The Paris inventor Étienne-Jules Marey improved on this by developing a photographic gun with a long barrel for the lens and a circular photographic plate that rotated 12 times in the chamber during the single second the shot was being taken – the first movie camera.

PRECEDING PAGES: the Babylon set from *Intolerance*.
LEFT: Gloria Swanson in front of the street sign that immortalized them both.
RIGHT: sound arrives with *The Jazz Singer*.

By 1888, George Eastman had produced celluloid film and Thomas Edison, who at first envisioned film as being merely a pictorial addition to his phonograph, added sprockets to synchronize the sound. It was the director of his

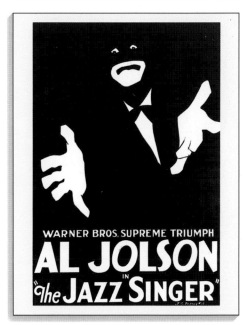

WARNER BROS. SUPREME TRIUMPH
AL JOLSON in "The JAZZ SINGER"

project, William Laurie Dickson, who filmed an assistant sneezing who is on record at the Library of Congress as producer of the earliest movie: *Fred Ott's Sneeze* (1890). Eadweard Muybridge died in 1904, unaware of the industry to which he had given birth, an industry which was about to move west.

The first Hollywood census, in 1907, showed that among its population of 3,500 were 103 immigrants from England, 102 from Germany, 86 from Canada, 20 from France, 28 from Ireland, 24 from Scotland and 158 fom New York. There was also one man from Chicago named Francis Boggs, a film director from that city's Selig Polyscope Studios which had been doing battle with Thomas Edison's movie trust over the important subject of patents.

A year later, when Selig's production of the *Count of Monte Cristo* was enduring a severe winter in Illinois, Boggs recalled the warmth of Hollywood and moved cast and crew to the coast to complete the production near Laguna Beach, thereby earning his place in the reference books as the first director to shoot at least part of a film in California.

In 1911, David Horsley from New Jersey paid $30 a month to lease the dormant Blondeau Ranch. Meanwhile, Cecil B de Mille, Jesse Lasky, Samuel Goldfish and Arthur Friend formed a company under Lasky's name and planned to make *The Squaw Man* starring Dustin Farnum in Arizona, but found the scenery unsuitable. They continued westwards to Hollywood, rented part of a barn one block north of Sunset at Vine and Selma, completing the film there at a total cost of $15,000. It earned $225,000.

The greatest name in early film, David Wark Griffith – "the teacher of us all," said Charlie

WHAT'S IN A NAME?

The movie mogul Samuel Goldwyn changed his name from Samuel Goldfish.

Tavern (Hollywood had gone "dry") at Sunset and Gower, for his Nestor Film Company and made Hollywood's first studio film, *The Law of the Range*. On a budget of just $1,200 a week, the company churned out a dozen movies each month, shipping the roughly-cut negatives back east to be processed, rarely seeing the completed films until they played Hollywood's Idyll Hour theater several months later.

The following year, Carl Laemmle's Universal Film Manufacturing Company began operations at Sunset and Gower, and quickly absorbed Nestor, eventually moving through the Cahuenga Pass to found Universal City on 350 acres (142 hectares) of what had been the Taylor

Chaplin – had begun as an actor and playwright, working in bit parts before being offered a job as a director. With the hundreds of stylish two-reelers he directed for Biograph, he brought respectability to the movies, helping them attract middle-class audiences. Wanting to make longer features, he left to strike out on his own.

Other pioneers on the scene were Lubin, Essanay, the Kalem Company, the New York Motion Picture Company, and the prolific Vitagraph Company, which eventually became Warner Brothers. It was scarcely a decade since the Los Angeles Chamber of Commerce had launched a publicity campaign boasting the attractions of its climate, scenery and sunshine.

Charlie Chaplin, then 21 years old, was not impressed with LA when he paid his first visit in 1910 while touring with one of Fred Karno's variety troupes. It was, he thought, "an ugly city, hot and oppressive, and the people looked sallow and anemic." London-born Chaplin and his fellow Brit, Stan Laurel, both playing on tour in vaudeville, were invited by Sid Grauman, the owner of San Francisco's Emperor's Theater, to create their own vaudeville team.

In May, 1913, Chaplin received a telegram from director Mack Sennett who remembered having seen him in a variety show. Sennett, an actor-turned-director who had appeared in early Griffith two-reelers, was now producing three silent comedy shorts a week through his own company, Keystone. He offered Chaplin $125 a week, which was double the amount he was then being paid. Chaplin held out for $200 and got it. Subsequently, he built his own mock-Tudor-style studio near Sunset on La Brea Boulevard. Today, it houses a record company.

Birth of a notion

In 1915, Griffith joined up with Thomas Ince and Sennett to make films in the old Majestic Reliance Studio (4500 Sunset Boulevard), which was renamed Fine Arts Studio. His first major feature, *The Klansman* (which later became *Birth of a Nation*), was a sensation, introducing new techniques and a grandeur that impresses even today. The controversy over its apparent glorification of the Ku Klux Klan has retained its inflammatory powers.

Griffith followed up with an even more remarkable work, an anti-censorship tract called *Intolerance,* for which he erected an enormous set at the corner of Sunset and Hollywood boulevards which towered over its neighbors for years afterwards. Griffith is credited with many of the basic stylistic devices that define the modern film, and was one of the first to move dramatic action off the stage.

Louis B Mayer, a scrap merchant in New York, discovered the movie business when he dropped into a nickelodeon in Boston and was amazed to discover that there were 3,000 of them throughout the US – double the previous

year. It was a cheap entertainment that even non-English-speaking immigrants could enjoy, and more than 20 million Americans were frequenting the 5¢ theaters regularly every week.

It was "the academy of the working man, his pulpit, his newspaper, his club," commented *The World Today* in October, 1908. Many of the earliest movies were adapted from newspaper stories. Nickelodeon audiences were mostly working-class, prompting a member of the Canadian parliament to express the view, as late as 1920, that pictures were "an invitation to the people of the poorer classes to revolt. They bring disorder into the country."

Spotting a trade paper ad about a vacant 600-seat theater on the East Coast in Massachusetts, Mayer rented and renovated the place and negotiated with the Jesse Lasky company to distribute their films, first *The Squaw Man* and then *Brewster's Millions*. He eagerly acquired the New England franchise to show Griffith's *Birth of a Nation,* later boasting it had made his company a million dollars (although records show it was nearer to $600,000).

Films were still being shot quite casually around Hollywood, using private homes for domestic dramas, banks during weekends for hold-up scenes, and passers-by conscripted on the spot for crowd scenes. But making movies

LEFT: the first moving picture machine, Eadweard Muybridge's 1877 Zoopraxiscope.
RIGHT: 1921 photograph of the studio Charlie Chaplin built near Sunset on La Brea Boulevard.

had become expensive because they were no longer simple. The easy days when sound pioneer Jack Foley was able to simulate galloping horses with coconut shells in a sandbox were giving way to times when the people required to make a film would include visual effects researchers, recording mixers, wranglers, gaffers, caterers, dialect coaches and boom operators, not to mention caterers.

In the early days, Gower Gulch – the corner of Sunset and Gower – had been the rendezvous of dozens of would-be movie cowboys hoping to be called for work in one of the dozens of small companies operating in the adjoining

streets. The formation of Central Casting eliminated this casual approach (although in the 1928–29 season only about 200 of CC's 10,000 extras worked for more than two days per week – earning about $14 when studio bosses were already making $500,000 a year).

A big merger

In 1924, both Metro and Goldwyn – which had moved onto the former lot on which the Pickford-Fairbanks studio had begun in 1922 – were merged. Mayer was hired at $1,500 a week as first vice-president and general manager of Metro-Goldwyn, with Irving Thalberg as second vice-president and production supervisor.

Mayer was quoted in *Motion Picture Weekly* as saying they aimed to produce 52 films per year, which he hoped would fill the 250,000 seats owned by the Loews theater chain.

This era saw the birth of the new system under which directors virtually ceased to be independent agents and became employees of "a massive, assembly-line organization." "So began the great debate about studio versus artist, commercialism versus personal integrity, the desecration of great masterpieces and promising careers through the insensitivity of philistine management," wrote Gary Carey in the Mayer biography *All the Stars in the Heaven*.

By 1927, cinema attendances were slumping. The four Warner Bros – Harry, Albert, Sam and Jack – had added a musical background to their film *Don Juan* (John Barrymore and Mary Astor) which was greeted enthusiastically. They had Al Jolson say a few words in *The Jazz Singer*. Although mostly background music with a few songs, the picture made millions and forced the other studios into sound.

In July, 1928, Warner released *The Lights of New York*, another instant hit. One month later MGM's trademark, Leo the lion, roared from the screen showing a semi-documentary called *White Shadows in the South Seas*. The first MGM sound film was *Broadway Melody*. One scene was reshot and MGM experimented with leaving the music as it was and having the players mime the number for the cameras – the beginning of prerecording. It cost $280,000, grossed $4 million and won an Oscar for the best picture in the Academy's third year of awards.

From the beginning there were reformers who wanted to censor the films and keep the industry under some restraints. In 1921 and '22, such scandals as the Fatty Arbuckle rape case, actor Wallace Reid's drug death and the (unsolved) murder of director William Desmond Taylor lent them ammunition at the same time as movies were appealing to wider and a more middle-class audiences. Lewis Jacobs (author of *The Rise of the American Film*, 1968) wrote that "as the poor became less important as the mainstay of the movies, the ideals and tribulations of the masses lost some of their importance as subject matter."

Hoping to pre-empt the would-be censors, the movie industry invited Will H. Hays, an Indiana crony of President Warren G Harding, to be its moral watchdog. Only months after taking office, Hays banned Arbuckle from the screen, although even when the ban was lifted the actor was never again a major star.

Hays's authority as head of the otherwise toothless National Association of the Motion Picture Industry was only moral – a smoke-screen, charged some critics – although for a while most producers obeyed at least the letter of the law. But late in the decade such daring productions as Raoul Walsh's *Sadie Thompson*, in which actress Gloria Swanson portrayed the sad prostitute of W. Somerset

PICTURE PALACES

By 1934 there were around 100,000 movie houses – a third of them in Russia.

Loew's Inc (the theater chain that owned MGM), Paramount Pictures, Twentieth Century Fox and RKO – while Universal, Columbia and United Artists (which had been set up by Chaplin, Pickford, Fairbanks and Griffith to distribute the work of themselves and other independents) played a minor role.

Accelerated by the Depression of the 1930s was the development of color on celluloid, which by 1934 had progressed enough for Walt Disney to produce his first full-length animated feature, *Snow White and the Seven Dwarfs*, an

Maugham's novel *Rain* and the MGM filming of another banned title, Michael Arlen's *The Green Hat* as a vehicle for Greta Garbo, reduced the Hays Office's credibility.

The big five

By the 1930s the industry – one of America's top 10 – was dominated by the Big Five majors, all with production studios, large theater chains and worldwide distribution – Warner Brothers,

LEFT: Charlie Chaplin hit the big time in Hollywood, despite being unhappy when he first arrived.
ABOVE: the closing scene from *Sunset Boulevard*, the quintessential movie about the film industry.

assemblage of 250,000 separately painted frames. *Ben Hur*, three years in the making, cost around $4 million.

By this date there were almost 100,000 movie houses in the world – a third of them in Russia; only half that number were in the US. Every country's film industry needed foreign sales in order to be viable, which created a touchy situation for the US with the rise of Nazism because Germany was a major market for US films. MGM was cautious and not until Germany had actually declared war on Poland did it start producing anti-Nazi films.

Gone With the Wind was passed up by Mayer and instead was developed with great difficulty by David Selznick, who had to turn to Mayer for help. In return for the loan of Clark Gable, Selznick was obliged to let Loews distribute the movie. He also had to borrow money from Mayer in return for which 50 percent of the film's profits went to MGM. *Gone With the Wind* turned out to be MGM's top-grossing release of 1939 and 1940.

The US Courts, after a decade of hearings, ruled in 1947 that the film studios' method of production and distribution violated anti-trust laws and that the studios must divest themselves of their theater chains. It took Loews 10 years before finalizing this move.

At the end of the 1940s, the studios also underrated television and concentrated too much on films for younger audiences. Attendances began to drop. In 1947, the House Un-American Activities Committee (HUAC) targeted the industry for promoting communist propaganda, and influential columnists urged a boycott of "red" actors.

The Hollywood Ten were cited for contempt and denied work. Most top stars escaped attention, although actress Katharine Hepburn, who had addressed a large gathering of people supporting Henry Wallace (a presidential candidate who had been labeled a communist by far-rightists), came in for a good deal of criticism.

Boulevard beginnings

When director Billy Wilder and producer Charles Brackett (together with co-writer DM Marshman) finished their script for *Sunset Boulevard* in 1949, they were "acutely conscious of the fact that we lived in a town which had been swept by social change so profound as that brought about in the old South by the Civil War. Overnight the coming of sound brushed gods and goddesses into obscurity. At first we saw [the heroine] as a kind of horror woman… an embodiment of vanity and selfishness. But as we went along, our sympathies became deeply involved with the woman who had been given the brush by 30 million fans."

Several former silent stars were approached: Mae West, then 55; Mary Pickford, 57; and Pola Negri, 51. All of them rejected the role as being too close to real life. The final choice, Gloria Swanson, 50, had left Hollywood a decade earlier after a 45-movie career that began in Mack Sennett comedies when she was still a teenager.

Swanson embraced a lifestyle which typified its time – extravagant parties at which hundreds of the movie elite were presented with gold cigarette cases as party favors. "The public wanted us to live like kings and queens," Swanson recalled. "We were making more money than we ever dreamed existed and there was no reason to believe it would ever stop."

The ultimate Hollywood movie

Sunset Boulevard, which portrayed the pathos of a former silent superstar in her declining years in a broken-down Hollywood mansion, struck a chord with critics as the ultimate inside-Hollywood movie. It garnered eight Academy Award nominations and won three Oscars (best writing, score, art direction). But not everybody in the city was pleased by the way the industry was depicted. "You bastard," shouted an outraged Louis B Mayer to Wilder at a preview screening made on the Paramount lot. "You have disgraced the industry that made and fed you. You should be tarred and feathered and run out of Hollywood."

Half a century later, the success of Andrew Lloyd Webber's retelling of the tale in a stage musical demonstrates how timeless the story of Sunset Boulevard and the movies really is.   ❏

LEFT: Valentino vamps – in French.
RIGHT: West was one of many considered for *Sunset*.

THE GREAT OUTDOORS

Like a surfer waiting for a wave, the outdoors enthusiast in
California floats on a sea of possibilities

There are endless ways to enjoy the outdoor landscape of California, but to experience the state as its natives do, you'll do well to elevate your heartbeat by some activity – walk, roller-skate, ride a bike, paddle a kayak, climb a granite face, or "catch a wave." California is rife with outfitters, schools, clubs, rental shops, guides, resorts – and even tour buses – that specialize in outdoor adventure. There is as much choice in things to do as there is in the breathtaking landscape itself.

The far north

The far northern corner of the state, still partly populated by native tribes, is home to the legendary Sasquatch, Bigfoot to modern locals, a huge reclusive ape-like creature whose red fur camouflages him among the towering redwood trees and river canyons. The rivers and streams bear names that join in a confluence of Indian mythology and whims of 19th-century prospectors: Klamath, Ukunom, Trinity, Salmon, Smith. Fishing and floating on these rivers is by no means limited to natives; the streams are big and cool in hot summers, and rafting and fishing guides take visitors down many of the most inviting canyons.

Prospectors of adrenalin seek out the thundering rapids of Burnt Ranch Falls on the Trinity, the cataracts of Hell's Corner Gorge or the Ikes Falls on the Klamath. The breathtaking forest drops of the California salmon are at once beautiful and thrilling. On the other hand, you can float for many days in inflatable kayaks with nary a ripple on the lower Klamath and parts of the Trinity.

Salmon and steelhead trout still spawn in these rivers and the fall run is unparalleled in the state. The Hoopa and Klamath tribes own ancestral fishing rights, and still set their traps and dip their nets at the foot of Ishi Pishi Falls.

PRECEDING PAGES: Yosemite National Park.
LEFT: the Big Sur coast.
RIGHT: Death Valley, the lowest point on the North American continent.

Guides with graceful, swept-ended rowboats, called "MacKenzies," will lead you to the finest holding pools. Stealthy visitors are sometimes rewarded with sightings of eagle, river otter, great blue heron, duck, fox, bobcat, and the occasional great bear.

Here, and especially in the old-growth state

parks of these northern coastal mountains, can be found the redwood trees. Some of these majestic giants, 1,000 years old and reaching 300 feet (90 meters) into the sky, are the largest living things on earth.

Sun filtering through the redwood canopy as if through leaded glass, the cool enveloping shade, and the imposing sense of age, often draw comparisons to the cathedrals of Europe. Rain in the summer and snow in the winter keep forests lush and rivers flowing. Backpackers can explore a vast wilderness, called the Trinity Alps, a region of high, craggy peaks and sparkling lakes.

The northwest coast is somberly beautiful:

long, empty beaches littered with driftwood, rugged sea cliffs, sawmills and fishing towns, and forests that come to the edge of the cliffs. Swimming is none too inviting here – the sky is usually gray and the water is a constant 50°F (10°C) – but you can enter the surf with a wetsuit. Surfing has a loyal following, particularly at the point breaks of river mouths and harbors.

Because of undertows and riptides, the waves here are powerful and dangerous, and no place for the novice. Cold-water diving gear (a 7-mm wetsuit, hood, booties, fins, mask, snorkel, and 20 lbs/9 kg of lead to sink all that neoprene) equips you to hunt for abalone. This giant mol-

Northeast corner

By far California's most remote region, the northeast part of the state was home to its most recent volcanic eruption: Mount Lassen blew its lid in 1914 and, at Lassen National Park, you can view the bubbling mud pots of Bumpass Hell or hike to the rim and peer into the crater. Backpackers will find hot springs and geysers throughout the huge park.

North of Lassen, near the town of Redding, an ancient volcano named Mt Shasta (14,162 feet/4,316 meters), the southern point of the volcanic Cascade Range that extends all the way to Alaska, stands solitary sentinel at the head of

lusk is a delicacy, but prying them off the rocks at depth is not for the casual swimmer. Sometimes, at low tides, the intrepid wader will find a legal-sized "ab" in the tide pools.

Fishing abounds on the coast. You can cast from rocks or piers, or embark on a "party boat" to probe the depths for salmon, ling cod, rockfish and other denizens of the deep. Unusual, chilling sport can be had pursuing surf smelt. The fisherman uses a big triangular net on a frame. Plunging the net into oncoming breaking waves, he tends to get soaked completely. The nets are available for rent; the smelt, sometimes caught by the bucketful, are deep fried for dinner and then eaten whole.

the Sacramento Valley. The glacier-capped peak is a moderately difficult all-day climb in the summer, with climbers offered a sweeping view of the Central Valley to the south, the Trinities to the West and the Sierras to the southeast. In the winter, the mountain is buried in snow, but still open to enthusiastic skiers.

Backpackers and cross-country skiers will revel in the wilderness of Lassen National Park and the surrounding National Forest. Many alpine lakes dot the area and children will spend long days paddling driftwood logs like surfboards and watching the big, wary trout cruise slowly below.

Fishermen, particularly fly fishermen who

enjoy floating tiny nymphs in the surface film of chalk streams, will find abundant game and frequent caddis and mayfly hatches in the McCloud, Pitt and Fall rivers, as well as within the winding banks of Hat Creek, Hot Creek, Battle Creek and the many other notorious streams of the area.

HARD DAY AT THE LAKE

Children will spend long, lazy days paddling drift-wood logs like surfboards.

Eagle Lake, an anomalous, highly alkaline body of water straddling the Eastern Sierras on one side, sage desert on the other, is home to a splendid species of oversize Eagle Lake rainbow trout, found nowhere else in the state. As the name of the

much more solitary than their handsome African cousins), black bear, and North America's only antelope, the Pronghorn. From the foothills to the high Sierra ridges, this region is more wilderness than otherwise. Bicyclists (of both the road and mountain variety) will find abundant trails and out-of-the-way roads to explore on two wheels, as long as the bikes are sturdy. (Be sure to have them checked out before you undertake a trip like this; garages are few and far between.) Backpackers will find endless untrammeled trails.

lake implies, osprey, golden eagle and bald eagle – the national bird – are often seen skimming this lake for hapless, loafing fish.

Nearby Lake Almanor, a massive man-made reservoir, is a resort area with plentiful opportunities for waterskiing, sailing, lake trolling and sunbathing.

All the mountains of this region are notorious for their massive deer herds, stealthy cougar (aptly called "mountain lions," but smaller and

LEFT: gathering seaweed for personal use has become a popular pastime on the Northern California coast.
ABOVE: Southern California's image of sea and endless sunshine is reinforced by residents of Malibu.

The Central Coast

California's Central Coast is a region about 50 miles (80 km) wide beginning roughly 100 miles (160 km) north of San Francisco, and extending all the way to Point Conception, where the coast takes a sharp bend and heads east towards Santa Barbara and then on south to Los Angeles.

Within that span, adventurers will find redwood forests, lakes, rivers, estuaries, San Francisco Bay, which contains many environments unto itself, rolling grass-covered hills and down-sized mountains, hundreds of miles of trails for hiking, horseback riding, biking and mountain biking. Travelers will find massive herds of marine mammals; kelp beds alive with fish, birds and sea otters; cypress gardens; underwater marine sanctuaries; and fishing fleets for salmon, sturgeon and crab.

Just north of the Golden Gate Bridge, opposite San Francisco, the Marin Headlands and Mount Tamalpais are considered the birthplace of mountain biking. Miles of scenic trails are the perfect routes for this bouncy recreation, bikers sharing the trails with hikers and equestrians.

The valleys of Napa and Sonoma, about 30 miles (48 km) north, are the heart of California's

HIGHWAY 1

The coastline is a rough jumble of broken cliffs and long, misty beaches.

popular here, as is hang-gliding and, closer to Santa Cruz, competitive surfing.

On a spring or summer afternoon, you're likely to catch sight of hundreds of windsurfers braving the cracking swells and blowing sands of Gazos Creek, Scott Creek and Waddell Creek, the last considered one of the best windsurfing spots in the country, where experts are often spotted jumping waves and pulling spectacular aerial manoeuvers with names like "killer loop" and "cheese roll."

Año Nuevo State Park, a mile or two upwind,

wine country. Road cyclists take long wine-country tours on the rolling hills that wind through the scores of vineyards. On rainy spring days in the forest slopes above Sonoma, thousands of red-bellied salamanders come literally out of the woodwork, crawling to the stream beds to spawn. Within sight of fertile vineyards and cottage-style wineries, the Russian River and Cache Creek are popular rafting and canoeing streams.

Monterey

Heading south from San Francisco along Highway 1, the coastline is a rough jumble of broken cliffs and long, misty beaches. Surf fishing is

is a carefully protected nursery for the giant, billowing elephant seals, most noted for the male's ability to inflate its prodigious fleshy nose, and the fact that the male is often five times the size of the females in its harem. The seals don't trouble boardsailors and surfers, but this is the one area in California that's truly a lunch counter for the great white shark. One attack per year is the norm, although few turn out to be fatal.

Actually, the sharks are under far more predatorial pressure than the surfers and windsurfers are; many biologists fear that the prehistoric fish are being hunted to extinction out of misplaced fear and misunderstanding.

A popular pastime in Monterey is to rent simple open-topped kayaks, called "scuppers," to paddle out to the local kelp beds. The kelp, long and spindly at the base and stretching up to form thick mats at the surface, ranges all along the coast, forming fantastic underwater forests through which divers swim in search of the Garibaldi, lingcod and many types of rockfish. Scuba diving is extremely popular in Monterey and southwards along this particular coast.

Where the divers and kayakers converge at the surface, both are likely to encounter one of California's most delightful wild animals, the winsome and intelligent sea otter, once hunted for its fur but now a favorite of animal-lovers.

enter a wide, twisting delta that has been formed by the confluence near sea level of the Sacramento and San Joaquin rivers. As has often happened at many other huge river mouths, the Sacramento Delta has been turned into an agricultural bonanza.

The water of the Sacramento River, by far California's largest, is a hotly contested commodity. A major dam, Shasta, at the northern end of the state, is the first plug in the Sacramento's flow and other dams block the progress of most of its tributaries. The huge river is the source of all kinds of wild scenery. People have been known to canoe it, swim it, drive boats up

The creatures are often seen floating on their backs with an infant sleeping on their belly, lolling about in the water, fastidiously cleaning their fur, or just happily crunching on a just-caught shellfish.

The Sacramento Valley

Heading inland from San Francisco on a freighter toward the source of the muddy water that flows into San Francisco Bay, you will soon

LEFT: Southern California's wonderful weather and laid-back lifestyle lends itself to beachside cafés.
ABOVE: Northern California and the Central Coast are full of safe harbors for sailboats.

and down its length, and in summer to spend long hours floating in the tube of a truck tire.

The Sierra Nevada range, 400 miles (645 km) long and up to 100 miles (160 km) wide, peaks at the summit of Mt Whitney, which is 14,495 feet (4,420 meters) high. The range is only 50 miles as the crow flies from the lowest point in the continental US's 48 states, Death Valley (150 feet/45 meters below sea level). This gives some idea of its severity; an imposing wall facing east. To the west, however, are the long, sloping Sierra foothills, ponderosa, alpine meadows and granite domes. The sky here is clear and brilliant, the rivers steep and serious.

A wilderness trail of several hundred miles

bears naturalist John Muir's name, as do a vast wilderness and a University of California college. Any visitor to these mountains will find a deep spiritual connection in Muir's writing *(see next page).*

Yosemite, now a national park, was his chief inspiration, a wondrous collection of granite domes and towers thousands of feet high, as sheer as if they had been lopped off with a knife. In summer, the high season, avoid the crowds and buses of Yosemite Valley, opting instead for a visit to the more remote locations of the park, perhaps not

PEAKS AND LOWS

Towering Mt Whitney is only 50 miles as the crow flies from Death Valley.

enly is just as good; it's a question of choice.

Many smaller areas, with names like Kirkwood, Homewood, Sugar Bowl, North Star and Donner Ridge, are homier, more friendly spots to ski, although the sheer vertical drops are not as great. In summer, adventurers can carry mountain bikes on the lifts of many ski areas to explore the alpine network of trails, some with a bird's-eye view of Lake Tahoe.

On the Sierra's east slope, Mammoth Mountain is Southern California's premier ski area. Here the mountains slope down to the desert

as spectacular but just as scenic – and lacking bumper-to-bumper traffic.

Lying almost due east of San Francisco and Sacramento is the sapphire of the Sierra, Lake Tahoe, the largest and most scenic lake in two states (it is split down the middle by the California-Nevada line). Tahoe offers California's best snow sports – skiing and boarding – plus golfing, riding and waterskiing.

Attracting the most skiers are Squaw Valley on the North Shore, and Heavenly Valley at the South Lake, both huge, full-featured resorts. Squaw has a giant hotel, an Olympic history, an ice-skating rink on top of the mountain, a bungee-jumping tower and a golf course. Heav-

plain of the Owens River Valley, not far north of the precipitous drop into Death Valley. Near this mountain is Devil's Postpile National Monument, the gigantic, geometrically-fractured core of an ancient volcano. The streams and lakes of this region are famous for their trout fishing. Hikers marvel at the ruggedness of the high peaks and the tiny sky-colored lakes.

California went from Indian settlement dotted with Spanish missions to a gold-frenzied boomtown nearly overnight. The rush of 1849, which forever changed the wilderness with hydraulic mining, began at a mill in Coloma, on the South Fork of the American River. Although the gold is mostly gone, Coloma still profits from a summer rush of visitors when throngs float the Chili Bar run and Gorge of the South Fork, California's most popular whitewater.

Close to the masses of Southern California, the Southern Sierra is an anachronism somehow remaining more isolated and remote than most of the mountains to the north. The most spectacular region – due east of the sprawling valley town of Fresno – comprises the adjoining John Muir Wilderness, Kings Canyon National Park and Sequoia National Park, separated only by the ridge lines of spectacular alpine mountains, yet each pristine wilderness area sporting its own distinctive flavor.

lakes which are stocked from the air by the Fish and Game Department. Kern Canyon is the nearest west-slope river to Los Angeles (about six hours away) and is the entry point to a vast wilderness of high sierra landscape, as well as to the Kern River itself.

On the end of Point Conception, the jutting corner of the state where the coast turns east, is a rugged spit of sand called Jalama State Park where the fury of the northern Pacific collides with warm serene waters. Wind that whips across the point propels windsurfers up and over the biggest and ugliest of the waves.

Below Jalama, the road meanders towards

Good backpacking

Kings Canyon, less accessible and more rugged than Yosemite National Park, is, like the latter, alternately chiseled and smooth granite. Here is some of the Sierra's best backpacking country where one can hike for many days without reaching a road. Careful planning and wilderness permits are required.

Smart hikers will carry very light fly or spin fishing gear to try for trout in the hundreds of

LEFT: Cathedral Rocks in Yosemite National Park is a popular site for hikers.
ABOVE: shy and elusive Thule elk can be seen in the San Joaquin Valley.

THE SIERRA FOOTHILLS

"Probably more free sunshine falls on this majestic range than on any other in the world I've ever seen or heard of. It has the brightest weather, brightest glacier-polished rocks, the greatest abundance of irised spray from its glorious waterfalls, the brightest forests of silver firs and silver pines, more starshine, moonshine, and perhaps more crystal shine than any other mountain chain, and its countless mirror lakes, having more light poured into them flow and spangle most" – a poetic description by naturalist John Muir (1838-1914), founder of the Sierra Club.

Morro Bay and San Luis Obispo. The region's long beaches, interspersed with high cliffs, are a haunt of surfers, and diving and fishing is popular among the kelp beds. Just north of Santa Barbara, surfing and ocean sailing predominate at a seaside campus of the University of California, a bonus for any student. Mountaineers will be interested to know that at Ventura the popular suppliers Patagonia and Chouinard both have discount outlets.

The 130-mile (210-km) area between LA and San Diego stands out for the sharp blue line of the ocean. The water is warm here, pushed north by the Japan current, and the swells are man-

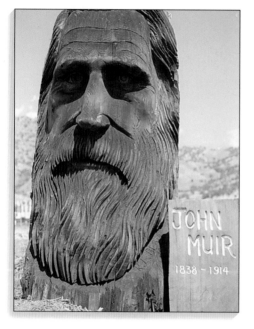

ageable in most places, even for novice surfers. But be aware that surfing has become a sharply territorial pastime and has gained a somewhat unfriendly reputation. However, if you're willing to settle for mushy waves, you can paddle out at almost any non-surfing beach and be assured of a good time.

Southern desert

The desert landscape is alternately twisted and folded, then smoothed over. Wide planes of sage and low desert scrub soon give way to high jagged mountains covered in smooth, house-sized boulders.

Climbing out of the desert toward the eastern

ridges of the Sierras will bring hikers to many trailheads that lead into the vast sierra wilderness areas. Joshua Tree National Monument, widely publicized by the album cover of a popular Irish rock band, is a strangely alien place. Huge sandstone boulders the color of sunsets and rust are interspersed with oddly-shaped and often very old joshua and yucca trees.

Back in the desert, the Mojave – named after a southwestern native tribe, and pronounced *mo-hahv-ee* – covering much of the southeast portion of California, floats like a mirage out of Arizona, ending against the precipice of the Sierras at their southern extreme. Death Valley National Monument is the lowest point on the North American continent. If the sea were to have access here, Death Valley would drown under some 150 feet (45 meters) of water. Death Valley is the result of a geological phenomenon. At least 5 million years ago, the deep gap between the Panamint and Funeral mountains was formed by earthquakes and the folding of the earth's crust. This created, technically speaking, not a valley, but what geologists tend to call a graben rock.

The name comes from the stupefying summer heat which sometimes exceeds 130°F (54°C). Shade trees are rare. In the springtime, however, Death Valley suddenly comes to life. Spring rains bring brilliant blooms of cactus and desert wild flowers. Their color is glorious against the spare desert backdrop.

Opening your senses to the nuances of desert life, you may be lucky enough to spot California's horned lizard, a chuckwalla, or diamondback rattlesnake, a desert tortoise, a gila monster (North America's only poisonous lizard, which is high on the endangered species list). Pack rats and kangaroo rats, bats, hawks and low-swooping falcons make their home here, too. At night you'll very probably fall fast asleep to the melancholy yipping and howling of coyotes.

California could be a dozen states, each with its own outdoors personality, its own climate, its own natural wonders, its own rules for being and behaving. For many Californians – and visitors, too – the outdoors is synonymous with activity. It's a big state, the theory goes, and you'll have to keep moving to see it. ❑

LEFT: monument to John Muir
RIGHT: Mono Lake, one of the oldest in the US.

EARTHQUAKES AND OTHER DISASTERS

"Living in paradise" has its downside, although Californians usually regard its crop of natural disasters as a worthwhile price to pay

Living in anticipation of "the Big One" is a fact of life in the state, rarely discussed but an ongoing subtheme for all who live here. It has given rise to a series of myths, the main one focused on "beachfront property in Arizona," (a jocular reference to the state being washed away). "The idea of California falling into the ocean has had an enduring appeal to those envious of life in the Golden State," wryly observes a brochure issued by the Southern California Earthquake Center (SCEC). "Of course, the ocean is not a great big hole into which California can fall but is itself land at a somewhat lower elevation with water above it."

California is big-time earthquake country. According to official records, the southern part of the state alone has experienced more than 200,000 earthquakes in the past decade even though most of them were too mild to be felt. The cause of earthquakes is fairly well understood as the constant shifting of huge blocks of the earth's crust. The southern portion of the state straddles the boundary between the Pacific plate (extending as far west as Japan) and the North American plate (eastwards to Iceland) with the former moving northwest at a rate of 1¾ inches (45 mm) per year, (about as fast as fingernails grow).

Unfortunately, this shift is not steady but one that stores up the energy, releasing it with the enormous burst which we know as an earthquake along one or another of the scores of fault lines. Although there have been recorded earthquakes since 1765, it was not until 1935 that Charles F. Richter devised the scale by which seismographs plot today's tremblors. Still, according to SCEC, awe-inpiring holes exist only in movies. "If the fault could open there would be no friction, and without friction there would be no earthquake," they explain.

△ **LOS ANGELES 1994**
The 6.7 quake resulted in 57 deaths, almost 9,000 injuries as well as 12,000 buildings damaged or destroyed.

▽ **FLOOD ALERT**
Brush fires destroy trees and hillsides, leaving the country-side vulnerable to flooding.

▽ **BRUSH FIRES**
Multi-million dollar homes like this one are not spared when brush-filled hillsides catch fire and flames, fanned by erratic Santa Ana winds, sweep across parched crests and canyons.

▷ **SAN ANDREAS FAULT**
An 835-mile (1,609 km) troublemaker stretching from the Mexican border to Cape Mendocino has averaged a major earthquake every 130 years with the last major upheaval, ominously, in 1857

SAN FRANCISCO 1906
...udden right slip movement
...p to 16 feet (4.9 meters)
...the San Andreas Fault
...used an 8.2 tremblor which
...eled the city, killing 315
...ople, and causing a fire
...ich took days to extinguish.

SAN FRANCISCO 1989
...en the Bay Bridge
...lapsed, over 250 people
...re killed and 1,700 injured.

COPING WITH CALAMITIES

After a series of natural disasters in the 1980s and 1990s that included fires, earthquakes and floods, Californians began to joke that maybe its telephone area code should be changed to 411 (the number for emergencies), and more than one writer has suggested that the southern portion of the state, at least, should never have been developed.

Maybe a stoic but light-hearted approach is the best way to handle the hazards of living in a state with the potential for so many natural calamities. It seems that way: the photo above, of a globe with a bandage around its head, dates from very early this century. More recently, Universal Studios' simulated earthquake was popular from its inception (even though it featured what looked suspiciously like a New York subway train), and Chinatown's souvenir of an earthquake in a can (*see lower left-hand corner*) became an instant hit. "Make the earth move for you" chortled the blurb, as the battery-operated can rocked dizzily out of control.

After spring floods have repeatedly poured down Malibu hillsides and inundated coastal homes, residents are invariably seen on TV sweeping up the mess. "Leave? Why should we leave paradise?" they always say to the camera.

CALIFORNIA'S CAR CULTURE

There's a revered rite of passage in California. You truly regard yourself
as an adult when you can legally get behind the wheel of a car

The coming of age in California is marked by the ability to obtain a car or at least a driver's license, without which one is likely to feel like a second-class citizen. It is not only mobility that is conferred on the driver, but a kind of nobility, too, an exalted state from which he or she can survey the world with bemused tolerance.

Increasingly, though, automobile ownership – or at any rate its side-effects – is becoming one of the state's most insoluble problems. In Los Angeles County alone, there are more than 5 million cars registered – some representing two- or even three-car families. And as the average Californian drives more than 100 miles (160 km) a week, traffic pumps 18,000 *tons* of carbon monoxide into the air each year.

Car crazy

A poll by the *Los Angeles Times* reported that although 40 percent of the respondents believed cars had ruined that city, 80 percent of those hadn't ridden a bus in the past year, a not unfamiliar pattern throughout the state. And so, as it's unlikely that drivers are going to abandon their cars to any great extent, the major current campaign is to persuade more of them to share daily rides.

In addition to the sharing of passengers, however, there are other plans under way to thin out the traffic. Six counties in Southern California are currently spending $2.3 billion in state and federal funds on rail projects – including LA's subway system – compared with $1.5 billion on highways. In the Bay area, similar plans are on the books.

Such ideas are long overdue. In 1911, Bion J. Arnold, consulting engineer on the development of New York City's subway and the planner responsible for Chicago's transport system, was brought to LA to anticipate the city's transport

needs for the next 10–15 years, during which the 350,000 population was expected to triple.

He recommended a "one city, one fare" railroad to add 80 miles (130 km) to LA railways' 320 miles (515 km) of single track, and urged the creation of a Planning Commission "to replace the present haphazard system of growth".

But instead of taking this advice and extending or even maintaining its extensive network of light rail services, Southern California scrapped it in favor of more highways.

Ecology and the economy caused a sea-change in attitudes in the 1990s." I think we're talking about strategies and forces that will lead people to use their autos more wisely," says transportation analyst Steve Heminger of the Bay Area Councils.

An old idea, in fact, is getting a new lease of life. At the turn of the century, more electric cars than gasoline models were being built in the US, with about 6,000 electric cars and trucks being produced annually by 1913. Registered for road

PRECEDING PAGES: fins to the fore in downtown LA; classic cars are seen everywhere in California.
LEFT: valley girl with her vehicle of choice.
RIGHT: uptown babe with classy convertible.

The Feeway

For more than half a century, one of California's proudest boasts was that its highway system was extensive but not expensive – roads, in fact, that are literally freeways. But now a new wrinkle has been added: feeways. In different parts of the state toll roads have appeared. Cal Trans has signed a franchise agreement with the California Private Transportation Corps (CPTC) in Irvine, Ca., allowing the latter to collect tolls for 35 years, after financing construction costs of $88.3 million.

CPTC expects to turn a healthy profit on the first

STAR-5B

private road – a 10-mile (16-km) stretch in Orange County between the Riverside County line and the Costa Mesa Freeway (Route 91) – from electronically-collected tolls. Other fee-paying roads include an 85-mile (137-km) highway between Vacaville and Freemont; a short 1-mile link from Anaheim Stadium to Interstate 405 in Orange County, and a stretch in southern San Diego County that extends to the Riverside County line. Several new toll roads are being constructed annually.

The toll roads are one of the ways in which the state's transit officials are trying to solve the problem of increasing congestion, whose undesirable byproducts include pollution, human stress and expense, plus too many fatal accidents.

The top four of America's 10 busiest freeway interchanges, all in LA County, carry an average of 500,000 vehicles each a day. The busiest interchange is the one in East LA connecting Interstates 5 and 10, State Route 60 and US 101. The second busiest is where the Santa Monica and Harbor freeways meet near downtown.

In the Los Angeles area alone, there are an average of 75 freeway accidents every day – 27,000 a year – of which about one-third cause injuries, and 1 percent are fatal. The main reasons for accidents are driver fatigue, alcohol and cars following each other too closely. Highway officers also notice men shaving, reading, or using car phones, women putting on make-up, drivers doing crossword puzzles or even engaging in heavy sexual activity.

Attempting to reduce freeway congestion, authorities have been experimenting with co-ordinating helicopter traffic surveillance with tow-truck routes to get stalled cars out of the way as soon as possible, well aware that every minute a static car is on the freeway causes at least four minutes of stalled congestion.

"There simply (isn't) enough room for more freeways to be built," says Catherine Wasikowski, transport director of the clumsily-titled Air Quality Management Department, "so we must maximize our resources." The department heavily promotes a program called Regulation xv, which requires employers to reduce the number of single-occupant drivers commuting to work.

Potential ride-share commuters can call a special number posted along the area's freeways to find willing matchmates. This can cut commuting costs by half which, say the organizers, can amount to well over $1,000 per year for a commuter traveling 20 round-trip miles a day. For some drivers this arrangement brings a bonus in other ways. Some people are so nervous about driving the freeways that they develop what USC Professor L Jerome Ozil describes as "an avoidant lifestyle," always making excuses to vacationing visitors as to why it's taking so much longer to get to their destination. In fact, they're taking different, often less direct routes that eliminate the freeways entirely.

At least 1 million drivers in the state have paid for personal license plates which the issuing department vets with a full-time staff to avoid offensive or illegal suggestions. The most requested plate is for one which says peace. ❏

LEFT: the top four out of America's 10 busiest freeways are all located in LA County; "feeways" are an attempt to reduce congestion.

use were 34,000 buses, cars, trucks. But cheap gasoline, the invention of the electric starter, mass production of the Model T and the extended range of the internal combustion engine all combined to virtually eliminate electric car production by 1930.

Now, with state legislation demanding reduced pollution, coupled with the demands of the federal government's Clear Air Act, electric cars are seen as the only likely solution. California originally ordered 10 percent of cars – 200,000 vehicles – to be pollution free by the year 2003 but because of stalling by the industry this goal is unlikely to be achieved.

Even though recent statistics suggest that the automobile accounts for less pollution in California than previously thought (industry is now seen as the main contributor), electric cars cause 97 percent less pollution than gas-powered automobiles. Highly relevant to the new controls is the fact that America's oil is expected to run out in the year 2020, and the world's supply, together with natural gas reserves, only a couple of decades later.

Gas-guzzlers preferred?

The new requirements are not being universally welcomed by the automobile and oil companies. "It's a mandate to sell, not a mandate to buy," says Ric Geyer, a marketing executive for Ford's electric vehicles, referring to the California legislation. At what price, he asks, can several thousand people be enticed to buy cars that cost more than existing models and need constantly recharging?

Even so, General Motors has invested hundreds of thousands, if not millions, in "a bunch of mavericks in the San Fernando Valley who had never made a real car before," vowing to become first in the marketplace. Amy Rader, designer of GM's electric car advertising strategy, says, "GM sees a profit opportunity here and sees that it is probably the only one with all the resources to pull something like this off. For us, it's a moonshot."

Meanwhile, other ideas are constantly emerging: Los Angeles-based Luz International, the world's major supplier of solar energy, has devised a silvery liquid zinc slurry which can be charged and recharged and thus used to refuel batteries instantly when they run down.

Tops for design

It is not, of course, surprising that America's auto-crazy state should be in the forefront of such developments. Southern California in particular has been the automotive world's key design center since Toyota first established its design studio here in 1973. Today, it is home to 11 foreign and domestic automakers.

Gerald P Hirshberg, former chief designer for the Buick division of General Motors, who was

PETERSEN AUTOMOTIVE MUSEUM

Los Angeles' Petersen Museum is one of the world's largest devoted exclusively to the history and cultural impact of the car. With a board of advisors comprising high-profile enthusiasts like actor Paul Newman and racing ace Parnelli Jones, the four floors of this $40 million building detail everything you ever wanted to know about four wheels. The second floor is the best, housing racing cars, classic cars, hot rods, movie-star cars and vintage motorcycles. Open Tues–Sun, 10am–6pm, tel: (213) 930-CARS or website www.petersen.org. Admission charge.

RIGHT: the Petersen Automotive Museum is a division of the Natural History Museum of Los Angeles County. It is located at the corner of Wilshire Boulevard and Fairfax Avenue, on LA's "Miracle Mile".

hired to run Nissan's design company more than a decade ago, is himself car crazy and exclaims: "It's a car-loving culture. It's very exciting. We're working in a place where people enjoy driving, enjoy cars, and don't give a damn where they come from. California has long accepted foreign cars. It's had more than 50 percent foreign cars for 20 years. Living out here is like living in a permanent international automobile show."

Selling cars is big business, of course, with salesmen making anything up to a $500 com-

AUTOMANIA

Some drivers commute 100 miles or more each way in order to go to work.

designer at GM's center in California's Thousand Oaks, says, "This is the place where trends start, and we're here to pick up on them before somebody else does."

Of course, much of this is in the future. Both residents and visitors who try driving here are troubled by a much more mundane problem: the difficulty of finding a parking space. The city of Los Angeles has 40,000-plus parking meters, almost half the total for the whole county, as well as 150,000 NO PARKING signs, 41,000 NO STOPPING signs, and 40,000 signs noting a time

mission per car, and some salesmen earning as much as $200,000 a year. Mercedes is the car that most people say they would like to own, but Hondas sell the best. The automobile industry has its own prototype of "the Calif Car", currently the Mazda Miata convertible.

When the Miata was launched, some customers were willing to pay more than double the $14,000 sticker price to avoid joining the waiting list. Nissan's $38,000 Inifiti was the result of years of study which included a Japanese researcher's lengthy stay in a California household, noting the family's views and habits before concluding that what they sought most was "an antidote to stress." John Schinella, head

limit. Sometimes there is a confusing mix of up to four signs posted on a single pole.

LA has about 600 meter maids (parking enforcement officers), who in the past decade have more than tripled their parking ticket issuance to 4 million each year. This means revenue of $100 million a year from meters and fines, a quintuple increase in less than a decade.

Some avoidance methods: passengers jump out of cars to save spots until the motorist can get to them; motorists feign poverty after they are parked in a pay lot; they place old tickets under their wipers or spray paint curbs a different color. Officers chalk tires, motorists rub it off. Drivers keep refeeding meters past the posted limit, or pull out of one space when time has run out and park in a new space a few feet away, both illegal practices. If a valet parks your car and it then gets ticketed, you are responsible, because tickets follow the car, not the driver.

Los Angeles locates offenders with the aid of 13 two-man teams from its Habitual Parking Violators division. Its avid members drive randomly around feeding license numbers into mobile computers. A huge, 40-lb (15-kg) orange metal boot is placed on 60 or 70 vehicles a day that have accumulated

STOP-START

Los Angeles has 150,000 "No Parking" signs and 41,000 "No Stopping" signs.

of cases are won by the motorist. If the description of the vehicle on the ticket differs from the actual car, the judge usually dismisses the ticket, as he does if the driver shows up in court and the parking cop doesn't bother.

Photographs are helpful evidence, especially if they show an unreadable sign. Some people even take in video tapes, a receipt from a repair shop, or a note from a doctor giving legitimate reasons for being illegally parked. With the difficulty of parking, valet parking is big business, with women tending to

more than five current parking tickets.

Needless to say, the Boot Officers are even more unpopular than the meter maids, which is partly why they travel in pairs, one distracting the motorist while the other takes less than a minute to install the device. Having it removed costs money, on top of the ticket's cost. If the matter isn't resolved within 72 hours, the car is towed away, with additional penalties. Half the cars that are towed away never get reclaimed.

Of the 50,000 or so parking tickets that are disputed in the average year, about 20 percent

take better care of cars, according to a (somewhat biased) representative of the parking service Valet Girls.

In 1954, Los Angeles mayor Norris Poulson, trying to deal with the growing traffic problems, argued for a ban on curbside parking during rush hours, more one-way streets, and the provision of parking lots at bus and street car terminals. Four decades later, the parking problem is universal throughout the state, with LA, the biggest city, having the biggest problem.

"The practice of making love on the highways is becoming alarmingly prevalent," the LA's Board of Supervisors was told by a captain in the LA Motorcycle Squad in the year

LEFT: just another car in Bolinas, California.
ABOVE: just another day on Sunset Boulevard.

1921. The state's once-envied network of free-ways has become so congested that traffic has slowed to a crawl at almost any time of the day.

Because of escalating housing costs, some drivers commute 100 miles (160 km) or more each way daily, which employers note is caus-ing increasing stress. Around 1,150 bright yel-low call boxes placed along Orange County freeways for stranded motorists can sometimes cause unexpected problems. An enterprising hacker made 11,733 calls, charging them all to a single box on Route 57, after apparently match-ing the individual electronic serial number for the call box to its telephone number.

Along a stretch of freeway in Oakland, a pair of sea lions emerged from the chilly waters of San Francisco Bay, wandering into traffic and causing three accidents. Scientists explained that, because uncommonly warm ocean currents had reduced the population of fish the sea lions eat, they were beginning to seek food on land.

Extra attractions

One design quirk that appears to be more impor-tant in California than elsewhere is the need for car accessories to aid those who guzzle as they drive. Local drivers who invest $40,000 or so on a European car are united in their complaints about the lack of cup-holders. Eating at the wheel is such a common preoccupation of free-way drivers who are always "in a McHurry" that Jerry Hirsrchberg, vice-president of Nissan Design International, speculates that future in-novations might include ashtrays replaced by larger cup-holders, a built-in trash container and an arm-rest made of double-walled plastic to act as a Thermos.

Peter O'Rourke, director of the California Office of Traffic Safety, says he has already encountered such munching-while-motoring aids as refrigerators plugged into cigarette lighters, dashboard hotplates and mini micro-wave ovens that fit under the seat. Ted Sturges, a California Highway Patrol officer, says that citations written for "unsafe speed at existing conditions" have included not only eating while driving, but also using laptop computers, talk-ing on cellular phones, retying pony tails, grop-ing a passenger, and passing around sushi. ❏

RIGHT: pretty as a painting: the mural, by T Bernard, is called Miss Liberty; the decorative car is the owner's pride and joy.

NORTHERN CALIFORNIA

The following chapters provide a detailed guide to the region,
with main sites cross-referenced by number to the maps

Almost a century ago, a perceptive author declared: "California, more than any other state in the Union, is a country by itself, and San Francisco a capital". The statement is still absolutely true, although boosters of Los Angeles doubtless crow that it, too, has become a capital since that time. (As it happens, neither of them is the state capital – an honor that goes to Sacramento.)

Southern Californians, it's said, spend much of their time exploiting the attractions of Northern California – its water, its crops, its lumber. Then, as if to add insult to injury, they want to come and visit it as well.

But it's certainly understandable, because so do millions of tourists worldwide. To begin with, San Francisco is most Americans' favorite city. The Golden Gate Bridge and Fisherman's Wharf are the stars of a thousand postcards. But consider, too, the austere glacial cirques around Desolation Valley... the small peaceful tidepools on the Monterey Peninsula... the windswept meadows on the Mendocino coast.

Northern California isn't Paris or the Pyramids, compact and easy to explore. It helps to make a little time, to take a few chances. The upper half of the state of California harbors more places of interest than the Gallo family has grapes.

There is rich bottomland and high desert plains, raging whitewater rivers and sweeping freeways, roller coasters and ski runs, and lava caves and granite cliffs. And, as if that wasn't enough, Northern California is also home to Yosemite, arguably the most beautiful valley to be found anywhere worldwide.

Imagine a line drawn north of San Luis Obispo and south of Paso Robles, over the mountains and through the central valley just south of Fresno, with a dip down to the southern tip of the Sierra then up to the Nevada state line. Within this arbitrary border which we have assigned to Northern California lies more natural and social variety than in any similar-sized territory in the world.

Visitors can follow the crowds, or be utterly alone. They can drink America's best wines, eat the West Coast's best seafood, slither around in the best mud baths. They can try the top golf courses, climb the highest mountain, see the oldest tree, surf the biggest waves. Or, better yet, they can just take a map – and a walk – and discover a few other natural wonders the authors of this book don't even know about.

Certainly, this is a place worth exploring, a place with secrets worth discovering by foot, bicycle, bus, car, train or plane. Where else can you find a state that takes as its official motto the confident name of one of its remotest northern towns? The town is Eureka. And its meaning? "I have found it!" ❏

PRECEDING PAGES: homesteaders at home near Orleans in Northern California; San Francisco's Nob Hill.
LEFT: Fisherman's Wharf, a fisherman, and its attractions.

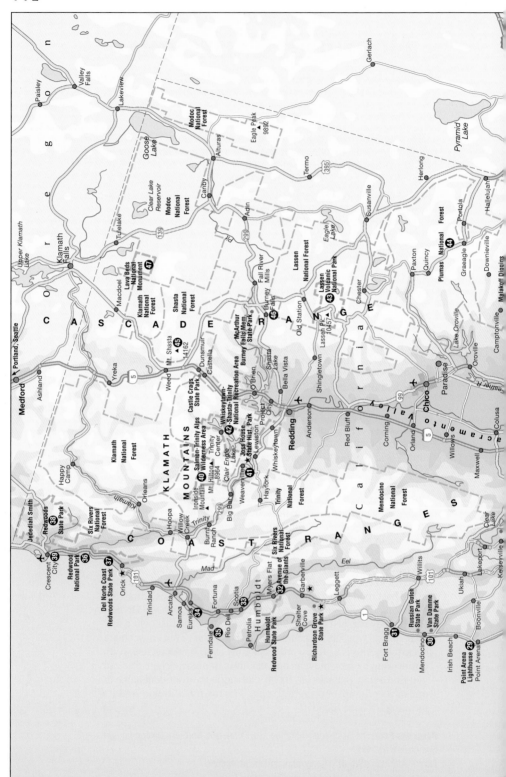

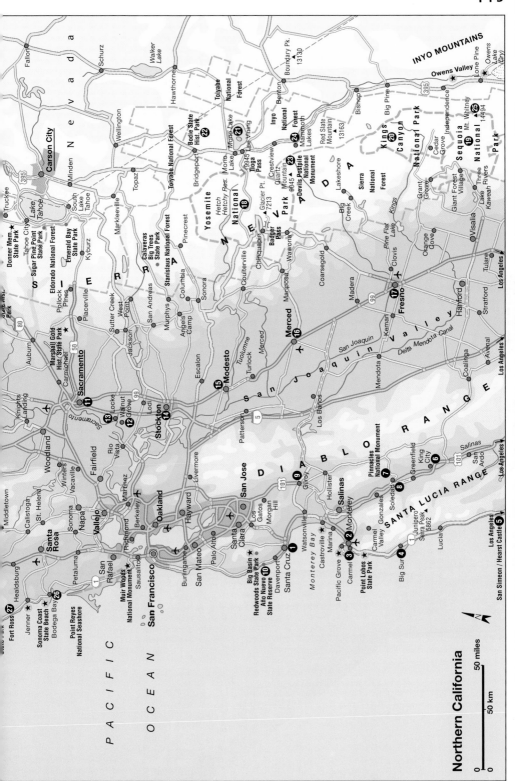

Northern California

INYO MOUNTAINS

SAN FRANCISCO

Map, page 116

Tony Bennett sang it like it is. The City by the Bay, long celebrated in lyrics and postcards, wins visitors' hearts straight away and effortlessly

San Francisco is a pastel city for lovers and pleasure-seekers, soft and feminine and Mediterranean in mood. Foghorns and bridges, cable cars and hills, Alcatraz and Fisherman's Wharf, Chinatown and North Beach – all invite feelings of fascination or enchantment.

The city sits like a thumb at the end of a 32-mile (50-km) peninsular finger, surrounded by water on three sides and blessed by one of the world's great natural harbors. It is joined to the mainland by two of the acknowledged masterpieces of bridge design and construction, which blaze at night like strings of glittering jewels. In the daylight, San Francisco's profile of towers and hills looks promisingly like a foreign land of exotic dimensions. In many ways, it is – elegant and cosmopolitan, San Francisco is a sleek courtesan among the cities of the world, beautiful, narcissistic and proud of it.

Poll after poll acclaims San Francisco as the city Americans most like to visit, while nine out of 10 people who come to the United States on foreign-exchange programs ask to be taken here. As a result, more than three million visitors a year come to the city and leave behind more than $1 billion annually, making tourism San Francisco's most profitable industry.

LEFT: view from Pier 39. **BELOW:** cable car shopping.

San Francisco is a city of at least a dozen neighborhoods, as distinct and original as the people who live in them. Traveling from one to another is like watching a tightly-edited color movie. The character of each area comes clearly into focus – different, and yet connected to the others by a common history. Only a resident like Dickens could do justice to the vast incongruities of the city. But, unlike so many other places, social and economic diversity is embraced here. The boundaries between social classes are less clearly drawn than elsewhere. The promise of social mobility at least seems more tangible.

Stake in the city

Of course, the vast majority of San Franciscans are middle-class. The people who fall within this broad category range from the ambitious young professionals who have invaded the city's fashionable districts to the immigrant families who run neighborhood businesses. More than other people, all San Franciscans – from the richest to the poorest, from the hushed precincts of Presidio Terrace to the run-down projects of Hunters Point – have a stake in their city. They are all an integral part of San Francisco's heritage.

The residents of this charmed city, the nation's 13th largest, form a demographic bouillabaisse not found elsewhere on the North American continent. Although the descendants of early Italian, German and Irish families are still found in snug neighborhood enclaves, their numbers have been greatly diminished over the past

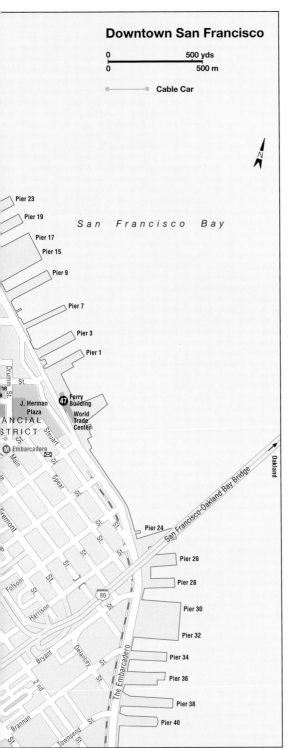

Downtown San Francisco

| 0 | 500 yds |
| 0 | 500 m |

●━━━━━━━● Cable Car

Pier 23
Pier 19
Pier 17
Pier 15
Pier 9
Pier 7
Pier 3
Pier 1

San Francisco Bay

Drumm St.
J. Herman Plaza
FINANCIAL DISTRICT
Steuart St.
Ⓜ Embarcadero
Main
Spear St.
Fremont
2nd
Folsom St.
Harrison St.
Bryant
Brannan St.
Townsend St.
Delancey St.
The Embarcadero

❹⓻ Ferry Building
World Trade Center

80

Pier 24
San Francisco-Oakland Bay Bridge
Oakland
Pier 26
Pier 28
Pier 30
Pier 32
Pier 34
Pier 36
Pier 38
Pier 40

couple of decades by the lure of suburbia, with its cheaper and bigger houses. Their place has been filled by an influx of Asian and Latino people.

The city in recent years has become a mecca for Filipinos, the fastest-growing minority; refugees from Southeast Asia; and both wealth and people from jittery Hong Kong. One consequence has been that the small 23 square blocks of Chinatown haven't been able to absorb the new arrivals. So they have spread their cultures west into the formerly all-white Richmond and Sunset districts.

San Francisco is to an extraordinary degree a city for young singles. In just one 10-year period, the number of singles aged 25 to 34 jumped an astonishing 40 percent – to more than 150,000 people. The traditional family was, meanwhile, decamping. During the same decade, the number of children below 18 in San Francisco dropped by a startling 27 percent.

Many of the new singles who arrived were homosexuals fleeing hometown disapproval for San Francisco's famed easygoing tolerance. During the past 20 years, San Francisco's gays have emerged from a guilt-ridden existence to play a major role in the city's political, cultural and economic life. They have even been elected to the 11-member board of supervisors, which governs the city along with the mayor. The police department recruits both gay men and women.

Waiting for "the big one"

No one can predict when the next earthquake will come and lay waste to the great beauty of San Francisco as it did in 1906 and, more recently, in October, 1989. This last quake caused billions of dollars of damage to the city (although most of the downtown remained intact) and cost many people their lives. Although the 1989 quake was a major one, and there have been smaller "shivers" since, none have proven to be "the big one" Californians talk of someday facing.

Perhaps this underlying tension is what gives the city of San Francisco its special zest. It may also help explain why it abandons itself so freely to self-indulgence. ❑

UNION SQUARE TO NOB HILL

Map, page 116

Some of the most famous attractions in America are contained within these few square miles, from Chinatown and Fisherman's Wharf to the notorious offshore prison of Alcatraz

Every visitor takes a different memory away from San Francisco. There is the street that drops off steeply toward the whitecapped bay, where sailboats heel before the wind. There is the fog drifting through the Golden Gate, blurring the bridge's sparkling lights. There are the savory dishes that expertly blend to make the perfect meal. There is the simple fun of a cable-car ride. San Francisco – the city that may be gone tomorrow – has mastered the art of today.

Union Square ❶ is within easy walk of most of the city's hotels. It was regarded during pioneer days as San Francisco's geographical center, and was deeded to public use in 1850. The square received its name a decade later from meetings held to demonstrate solidarity for the union of American states, then threatened by southern secession in the impending Civil War.

Apart from the shaft supporting the winged statue commemorating Admiral George Dewey's naval victory over the Spanish in 1898, there is not a great deal to be said about Union Square, which tends to be on the way to interesting places rather than being of interest itself. Its main denizens are multitudes of pigeons and indigents seeking small contributions toward the purchase of potable fluids.

Just west of the square is the **Westin St Francis ❷**. The city's second-oldest hotel, it's a majestic reminder of the past and has one of the best afternoon teas in town. On the south of the square, facing Geary Street, are two department stores – one, **Neiman-Marcus ❸**, featuring a glorious rotunda saved from its predecessor on the same site. To the north, on Post Street, are the **Grand Hyatt** hotel, with a detailed fountain by sculptress Ruth Osawa; and a couple of other, rather posh, department stores.

LEFT: street classics.
BELOW: east meets west.

The theater district

A couple of blocks west from Union Square along Geary Street, shopping ends and San Francisco's theater district begins. The **Curran Theatre** and the **Geary Theater** stand side by side. The Geary is the home of the **American Conservatory Theater**, one of the nation's best repertory companies and winner of several Tony awards. The Curran offers some of the biggest hits and stars from New York.

As well as the **Jewel Theatre** on Geary, there are no fewer than four theaters on Sutter Street – the **Lorraine Hansberry Theater**; the nearby **Marine's Memorial**, which specializes in Broadway musicals; the **Plush Room**; and the **Actors' Theater**, which performs classics by luminaries like Tennessee Williams.

Buddhist temples occupy the upper floors of buildings on Waverly Place.

Follow **Maiden Lane ❹** from Stockton Street on the east side of Union Square for cafés serving good coffee. It's easy to see how this little pedestrianized street got its name; during the tough Gold Rush era men came here to look for female company. At the junction of Maiden Lane and Grant Avenue, the attractive green roofs of the **Chinatown Gate ❺** appear.

Chinatown

This is the entrance to exotic **Chinatown ❻**, a cramped neighborhood where no sane resident attempts to enter with a car. If Chinatown were the only attraction San Francisco had to offer visitors, it would still be worth it. While this is no secret to tourists, the clacking of mahjong tiles from overly-populated apartments and crowds of Chinese residents vying for space on the sidewalk ensure that the area still caters to the local populace.

Extending for eight blocks, it's the biggest Chinatown outside of Asia, and the steady influx of immigrants keeps it growing. Its streets are narrow, crowded, and alive with color and movement. You feel after a while that you might almost be in Hong Kong or Shanghai. Mysterious alleys abound. Tiny cluttered herb shops offer powders and poultices promising everything from rheumatism relief to the restoration of sexual powers.

In Chinatown's dozens of hole-in-the-wall shops, one can buy anything from cheap trinkets to exquisite screens and massive hand-carved furniture costing thousands of dollars. Silken clothing, hand-painted vases, paper lanterns, rattan furniture, and many other Asian articles are for sale.

BELOW: the city's Chinatown is the biggest to be found outside Asia.

Dozens of Chinese restaurants can be found in this quarter, from the fancy and the famous to any number of obscure eateries and tiny cafés where diners can sit down with the Chinese locals and eat well and very cheaply. Veteran foodies have been known to cry out in ecstasy after a meal of *dim sum*. These delicious pastries, filled with meat, chicken, shrimp or vegetables, are a favorite Chinatown lunch. Waitresses push them from table to table on carts like peddlers. Diners select the dishes they want; the number of empty dishes on the table at the end of a meal determines the charge.

Intriguing though it is, **Grant Avenue** should not be the sole focus of Chinatown exploration. Grant is the face Chinatown wears for tourists. One block west of here, between Washington and Sacramento streets, is **Waverly Place ❼**, an alley renowned for its colorful Asian architecture. Northeast of Grant on Washington is the **Bank of Canton ❽**. Its bright, three-tiered edifice is the oldest of its kind in Chinatown. West is **Stockton Street,** where the real business of life is carried on. Tiny Chinese women, ancient enough to have had their feet bound many decades ago, totter along on shopping errands. Old men smoke cigarettes and read Chinese-language newspapers.

South of Grant, between Washington and Clay streets stands **Portsmouth Square ❾**, an urban park where children play and men gather to bet over mahjong and Chinese cards. Across the street inside the Holiday Inn on Kearny Street is the **Chinese Cultural Center ❿**. Well worth a visit, the center offers art shows, entertainment and guided tours.

North Beach

East to the busy thoroughfare of Columbus Avenue, Chinatown ends where North Beach ⑪ begins. The once tawdry **Broadway** strip has been gentrified quite a bit in the past few years. While a few seedy clubs still beckon with promises of lap dances and naked girls, critically acclaimed restaurants, posh nightclubs and jazzy swing bars entice a different crowd altogether. You will also find a variety of wonderful coffee shops where midnight snackers can sip espresso or *caffe latte*, fork down pastry, and eavesdrop on some first-rate conversation at neighboring tables.

This area has always been congenial to writers, artists and deep thinkers. At the same time, it has retained the flavor of an old-fashioned Italian neighborhood, full of little working-men's bars where elderly Italians sip red wine and muse about life. The outside tables at **Enrico's** on Broadway are a good place from which to study the passing scene. Many interesting local characters and homegrown celebrities drop by at night, including entertainers from up and down the street who are taking their breaks between shows.

Woody Allen and Bill Cosby had their taste of the limelight at the Hungry I; Barbra Streisand, Johnny Mathis and Lenny Bruce also plied their trades in the area's nightspots. A favorite venue from the old days is the **Condor**, a historical site that became famous when a waitress named Carol Doda peeled to the waist one night in 1964 and ushered in the topless boom. The venerable Doda used to descend nightly from the ceiling atop a piano. She was clad only in a G-string, showing her debt to silicone technology. The scene is a lot tamer since it became a sports bar frequented by neighborhood Yuppies (a term that was coined in this very city).

Map, page 116

TIP

Parking in North Beach at night is virtually impossible, and police are very strict on illegally parked vehicles. It's best to walk or take a taxi.

BELOW: North Beach street artists.

Founded in 1953 by Beat poet Lawrence Ferlinghetti, City Lights bookstore is still a favorite haunt of wordsmiths.

BELOW: the ever-popular sea lions of Fisherman's Wharf.

The **Washington Square Bar and Grill** is a hangout for lawyers, politicians, writers and others who make their livings from words. Rugby experience is helpful in getting a drink from the small crowded bar. Another favorite North Beach haunt of the wordsmiths is the **City Lights** ❷ bookstore on Columbus Street (open late) which has been operated since 1953 by poet Lawrence Ferlinghetti, one of the literary luminaries of the 1950s Beat era. Across the alley is **Vesuvio's**, a wonderfully atmospheric bar where intellectuals in rimless glasses sip aperitifs and think long thoughts. And nearby, on Columbus, is the **Tosca Cafe**, where off-duty cops and society swells listen to opera records that play on the jukebox. The little street which crosses Columbus Avenue was renamed **Jack Kerouac Street** in honor of the area's Beat status.

Above North Beach, at the end of Lombard Street, is **Telegraph Hill** ❸. As well as being one the city's most famous sites, it also offers spectacular views across San Francisco Bay. The *moderne* tiara crowning the hill is **Coit Tower** ❹ (415-362 0808), built in 1934 by Mrs Lillie Coit in memory of San Francisco's heroic corps of firefighters. Its momentous views and WPA frescoes entice thousands to wait bumper-to-bumper for a coveted parking space.

At the intersection of Columbus and Union is **Washington Square** ❺, a grassy expanse, favored morning tai chi location and perfect picnic spot.

Fisherman's Wharf

Straight up Columbus Avenue is another of the city's premier attractions. Tourism surveys claim **Fisherman's Wharf** ❻ – and, perhaps, its unruly but entertaining gang of resident sea lions – is what 84 percent of all San Francisco visitors have come to see. Although the fishing boats look like parts of a quaint

set designed in the Disney studios, they are actual working vessels that put out before dawn to fish the abundant waters outside the Golden Gate. The catch they bring back often determines the "special of the day" at the numerous restaurants clustered around the wharf. Italians historically skippered and manned the boats and also ran the restaurants. A glance at the names of the restaurants indicates that not all that much has changed, with Italian dishes a not-always-second choice to some of the freshest food around.

Chances are Fisherman's Wharf will be where visitors have their first encounter with one of the city's proudest legends, its crusty sourdough bread. It is quite unlike anything found elsewhere. Natives swear the secret ingredients roll in with the fog, working a mysterious influence on the bacteria in the sourdough starter. The best way to enjoy this bread is with sweet butter, Dungeness crab and a crisp Chablis.

The wharf has catered to generations of tourists and knows how to do it with skill. At sidewalk concessions, strollers can watch crabs being steamed and can buy shrimp or crab cocktails as takeaway treats. A recent attraction is **Forbes Island**, based on a self propelled motor vessel – with palm trees, a sandy beach, waterfall and 40ft (12 meter) high lighthouse with observation deck.

Ripley's Believe It or Not! Museum assembles under one roof a collection of some 2,000 peculiar things once belonging to the late cartoonist Robert Ripley. **The Guinness Museum of World Records** offers a gallery of biggest, smallest, fastest, slowest and other such pacesetters from the pages of the Irish brewer's bestsellers. It is only a short, hop, step and jump from here to the other attractions on nearby **Piers 39** and **41**, which also serve as the departure points for boat trips around the harbor and the extremely moving tour of Alcatraz island.

**Map,
page 116**

BELOW: peering at the attractions on Pier 39.

Chicago mobster Al Capone (1898–1947) was one of Alcatraz island's better-known residents.

BELOW: Alcatraz prison lies a mile offshore.

Alcatraz Island

Due to age and vacancy, **Alcatraz** ⑰ (last ferry from Pier 41 around 2pm tel: 415-773 1188) is slowly falling apart. Its steel bars are being eaten away by salt air and its pastel buildings are giving way to the ravages of time. In the case of Alcatraz, part of its appeal lies in its location and its notorious past. Just over a mile offshore from San Francisco, it is windswept and scoured by swift tides. When it was first sighted in 1775 by Spanish Lieutenant Juan Manuel de Ayala, the only occupants were pelicans, so Ayala named it Isla de los Alcatraces – the Island of Pelicans. Its strategic location in the bay suited it to military purposes and it was garrisoned with soldiers in the 1850s. Because escape from the island was a remote possibility, renegade servicemen were incarcerated on Alcatraz, to be followed by Apaches, taken prisoner in Arizona during the 1870s Indian wars, and then prisoners from the Spanish-American War.

Alcatraz evolved into a federal prison that housed such case-hardened criminals as Mafia leader Al Capone and the notorious Machine Gun Kelley. Those few desperate inmates who managed to escape their cells in bids for freedom perished in the frigid waters surrounding the island. The prison was finally closed in 1963 when the costs of repairing the constant ravages of wind and weather grew too great.

So the prison buildings crumble away bit by bit as people increasingly think the best thing to do with Alcatraz is just to leave it as it is, a symbol of "man's inhumanity to man." It is now part of the Golden Gate National Recreational Area: park rangers give guided tours of safe parts of the island, including a peek at some of the cell blocks, while the evocative, award-winning taped cassette tour features voices of some of the original prisoners.

(Less visited than Alcatraz is the larger **Angel Island**, accessible by Bay ferries, which has picnic sites, hiking trails, historic buildings and an educational tram tour. Call 415-897 0175 for information.)

Pier 39 is another popular section of Fisherman's Wharf, perhaps due to those previously mentioned sea lions. This 45-acre (18-hectare) collection of shops, arcades, fast-food restaurants and other diversions lure tourists by the thousands to places like the big-screen **Cinemax Theatre**, the **Cyberstation Arcade** and the **UnderWater World** aquarium. The oldest thing at Pier 39 is the **Eagle Cafe**, a fixture favored for decades by fishermen and longshoremen before it was moved intact from its original site a couple of blocks away.

TIP

When boarding your ferry from Pier 41, be sure to bring a jacket, as warm protection against the wind is essential.

Ghirardelli Square

Heading west along the water's edge and back near the main section of Fisherman's Wharf, you'll soon come to the popular **Cannery** ⑲. Built in 1909 to serve as Del Monte's canning plant, it capitalized on the success of nearby tourist sites and now houses dozens of shops and restaurants. A couple of blocks west is the popular and fanciful **Ghirardelli Square** ⑳ (tel: 415-775 5500, open 10am–8 or 9pm during summer, 10am–6 or 7pm during winter), another superb example of putting the past to work in the present. Ghirardelli Square was built as a wool mill during the Civil War era and later became a chocolate factory. When the chocolate business moved elsewhere, it could easily have been torn down to make way for something modern. But William Matson Roth, a financier with a keen aesthetic sense, saw the possibilities for a rebirth of the building. Over a five-year period, starting in 1962, it was transformed into a brilliant showcase for retail shops, restaurants, bookstores and bars.

BELOW:
Lombard Street, star of movies and car chases.

Map, page 116

There's usually free entertainment going on somewhere in the square, likely including tomfoolery by theater troupes or mime artistes, who are nearly as common as seagulls.

Only a few steps west of Ghirardelli Square is **Aquatic Park ㉑**, a terraced greensward that leads out to a small beach and curving municipal pier usually crowded with fishermen. The park houses the **National Maritime Museum ㉒**, which has all kinds of natural displays and photographs, and is adjacent to the Hyde Street Pier, where the museum's floating displays are docked. These include a sidewheel ferry and three schooners that carried heavy freight in the days of sailing ships.

The tall masts and rigging at the water's edge belong to the graceful Scottish-built clipper *Balclutha*, a 265-feet (81-meter) beauty open to the public. It put to sea in 1886 and made many voyages around Cape Horn. Two piers away is the *Pampanito*, a World War II submarine whose narrow passageways may awaken claustrophobia. Yellow helicopters take off at regular intervals near the *Balclutha*. The price for a ride around the bay is steep, but circling around Alcatraz in a pulsating chopper is an unforgettable experience.

Two blocks inland from the Hyde Street Pier is the **cable-car turnaround**, where the Powell-Hyde car begins its ascent into the wealthy neighborhood of **Russian Hill ㉓**. A ride on this route is one of the best ways to see the hill, whose high-rise apartments and mansions have cashed in on the vistas and charming neighborhood appeal; several celebrities live here. The cable car passes near to that curvy section of **Lombard Street ㉔** made famous in countless movies and TV shows for its twisting, winding lanes and rarely fatal celluloid car chases.

BELOW: Grace Cathedral.
RIGHT: Coit Tower and Telegraph Hill.

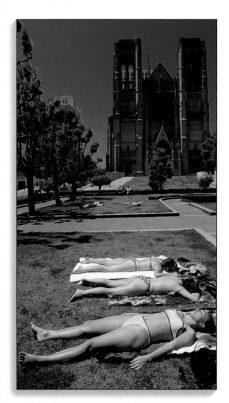

The mansions of Nob Hill

The cable-car ride continues up to one of the best-known of the city's hills – just to the west above Chinatown – **Nob Hill ㉕**. An epicenter for the city's elite, the hill is celebrated mostly for the size and elegance of the mansions built there a century ago. Writer Robert Louis Stevenson called Nob Hill the "hill of palaces."

Here, the **Mark Hopkins Hotel ㉖** occupies the site of the former Mark Hopkins mansion where a cocktail at the **Top of the Mark** bar on the 19th floor is on most visitors' must-do lists (tel: 415-392 3434). The lovely **Stanford Court** and **Huntington hotels** were also built on the ashes of mansions, and the **Fairmont Hotel ㉗** retains an aura of (rebuilt) splendor, having been open only two days before being burned down in the fires that raged after the 1906 earthquake. It reopened for business just one year later.

All these lavish structures encircle and provide the perfect setting for the neo-Gothic **Grace Cathedral ㉘**, where acoustics are unparalleled for the house organ and boys' choir. The cathedral is said to have been a copy of Notre Dame in Paris, and is the seat of the bishop of the Episcopal Church.

Northeast, at the corner of Washington and Mason streets, stands the **Cable Car Barn Museum ㉙**, which exhibits the city's transit history as well as the actively operating machinery and cables that pull the glamorous transportation throughout town. ❑

SAN FRANCISCO'S CABLE CARS

They're much more than a means of transport.
They've been designated a National Landmark,
and in 1962 even featured on a postage stamp

Operating on three routes – the Mason-Taylor, Powell-Hyde and California lines – San Francisco's cable cars are almost the only remaining ones in the United States, at least 100 cities having abandoned this type of transit in favor of buses. Underestimating the universal fame of its famous tourist attraction, San Francisco tried to abandon them back in 1947, but after a vigorous local campaign they were saved by a City Charter perpetuating the system.

Today, the cars service 12 million passengers a year, more than half of them local residents. It is the visitors, of course, who buy the vast numbers of engraved knives, belt buckles, coins, posters and T-shirts, all emblazoned with pictures of the beloved cars. Real aficionados can also find for sale genuine cable car bells and walnut music boxes that play crooner Tony Bennett's sentimental hit song *I Left My Heart in San Francisco*.

On June 3 1981, after a $65 million refurbishment which had deprived San Franciscans of the cable cars for 21 months, a city-wide party celebrated their return. During their absence, the number of visitors to Fisherman's Wharf dropped by 15 percent. "They're Back" read the inscription on thousands of colored balloons, and employees of MUNI, the city-owned transit system that operates above-ground transportation, served free coffee, brownies, donuts and wontons to lines of customers who had waited since dawn to be among the first passengers. Three weeks later, Tony Bennett himself turned up for the official party.

Even from their earliest days, visitors have been impressed. "They turn corners almost at right angles, cross over other lines and for aught I know run up the sides of houses," wrote Rudyard Kipling, who visited in 1889 on his way to India.

▷ **POSTCARD ON POWELL**
This 1848 image of a cable car on the turntable at Powell and Market streets shows how little things have changed.

△ **JEALOUSY ON WHEELS**
San Francisco has a bus and trolley system too, but some of the tour buses envy – and on occasion emulate – their more famous stablemates.

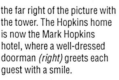

◁ CABLE CAR TURNAROUND

The car is pulled by a wire rope running beneath the track's route, passing through the machinery in the Cable Car Barn at Mason and Washington streets, also a working museum, tel: 415-474 1887. The turnaround must be done manually.

▽ MAKING TRACKS

At the beginning of the century, 600 cars rolled over 115 miles (185 km) of track. But a fleet of electric trolleys powered by overhead wires hastened their demise. Today, the system has only 30 cable cars and a mere 17 miles (25 km) of track.

GOING FOR A SONG

ring the tourist season, es to board a car can be so ng buskers have taken to tertaining the crowds.

▷ CALIFORNIA STREET

is old photograph *(below)* m 1890 shows the lifornia Street cable car ssing railroad magnate ark Hopkins' mansion, on

the far right of the picture with the tower. The Hopkins home is now the Mark Hopkins hotel, where a well-dressed doorman *(right)* greets each guest with a smile.

ANDREW SMITH HALLIDIE

Andrew Hallidie, a British-born inventor, is usually credited with creating the cable car system in 1876. Seven years before, it's said, he saw a horse slip, causing the chain to break on an overloaded streetcar it was pulling uphill. Hallidie rushed to devise a system to eliminate such accidents.

Although Hallidie and his friends put up the $20,000 to get the cable cars operating, he was anticipated in 1870 by Benjamin Brooks, son of a local lawyer, who had been awarded a franchise to operate a similar system, but had failed to raise the necessary financing. When the Hallidie plan finally came to fruition, scepticism was the order of the day. "I'd like to see it happen," said realtor L. C. Carlson, "but I don't know who is going to want to ride the dang thing."

Criticism of the system is still around today. Some say that the cars, which are of course on a fixed track and thus have no ability to duck potential collisions, are inherently unsafe. Columnist Dick Nolan called the braking system "unimprovable" or "blacksmith shop crudity at its worst." And one family living at Hyde and Chestnut streets initiated an (unsuccessful) law suit against the loud noise, which measures 85 decibels at street level.

MARKET STREET TO THE FINANCIAL DISTRICT

Art meets high finance in three distinct neighborhoods: the high culture of the Civic Center, the trendy culture of SoMa, and the money culture of the Financial District

Map, page 116

While Union Square acts as the hub of downtown's shopping, entertainment and tourism, a few blocks in either direction lead to more locally utilized sections of the city. To the west, the Civic Center area, though downtrodden with homeless and litter, still harbors grand civic buildings, such as City Hall and the Opera House. To the northeast, high-rises pronounce the banking capital of the west, the Financial District. Everywhere just south of Market in the downtown area is known as SoMa (South of Market), a vast area crammed with museums, restaurants and nightclubs.

Market Street ❸, the southern border of Union Square, leads to all these areas and is a thoroughfare of variety. Along the Financial District, it's comfortably interesting. But it turns seedy down toward 5th Street, and stays that way for four blocks before beginning to revive. The street finally ends at the multi-intersection that includes 24th and Castro streets, one of the busy hubs of gay action. Broad, tree-lined and well-lit at night, it has all the elements needed to become one of the world's great avenues. The city even spent millions of dollars building a tunnel beneath Market Street to eliminate the clutter of streetcars. Yet the street has never achieved its potential.

LEFT AND BELOW: contrasting views of Embarcadero: the soaring center and the farmers' market.

The Civic Center

Equally infiltrated with depressed urban living is the **Civic Center** ❸, both a neighborhood and a huge grassy area where protests and celebrations are often held. Off Market a few blocks north on Polk Street, its grand buildings surround the square.

The stately main branch of the **Public Library** ❸, built in 1916, is closed and now moved to a neighboring building; it's thought that the Asian Museum will move into these handsome, unoccupied premises. The south end of the plaza is occupied by the **Bill Graham Civic Auditorium** ❸ built in 1913 and now renamed in honor of the city's late, great rock entrepreneur.

The north side has the **State Office Building** ❸, constructed in 1926. Together, they present an appearance of order and harmony. The brutal federal building standing behind the state building on Golden Gate Avenue is a reminder of how badly the Civic Center could have turned out had it been planned less carefully.

West of the square is **City Hall** ❸, one of the most beautiful public buildings in the United States. It was designed by Arthur Brown, an architect so young and so unknown that he figured he might as well shoot for the moon in the early 20th-century competition to select the building design. To his surprise, Brown and his partner, John Bakewell, won with a design that called for

the lavish use of costly marble, and a dome that was patterned after St Peter's Cathedral in Rome. Built in 1914, City Hall is honeycombed with municipal offices, and both civil and criminal courts. The full effect is best felt from its Polk Street entrance, which faces a plaza. The magnificent stairway inside leads to the second-floor Board of Supervisors' chambers.

This is the building in which Supervisor Dan White shot Mayor George Moscone in 1978 for refusing to reappoint him to the seat White had resigned. White then shot gay Supervisor Harvey Milk for smirking at him. After White was convicted of manslaughter and given a remarkably lenient sentence, mobs descended on City Hall. The episode made headlines around the country, and the world. In the the past few years, the old building has undergone lavish retro-fitting and restoration to ensure its livelihood through the next millennium.

Opposite City Hall on Van Ness Avenue is a series of distinguished buildings. The **Veterans Auditorium Building** ❸ at the corner of Van Ness and McAllister streets was built in 1932 and houses the **Herbst Auditorium**. Next to it is the **Opera House** ❸, one of the country's greatest, and built the same year as the Veterans Auditorium. It has a summer opera festival and a regular season running from September to December. The opera company, which draws the foremost artists of the day to its stage, shares quarters with the highly-regarded San Francisco Ballet. Across the street from the Opera House is the lavish **Louise M. Davies Symphony Hall** ❸, which was completed in 1980.

Davies Hall has triggered quite a boom in the Civic Center area. Expensive condominium buildings are rising to the north, hotels are being smartened up, and excellent restaurants have opened. The **Opera Plaza** complex, where apartments go for astronomical sums of money, is a good example of the quality.

BELOW: interior of City Hall.

SoMa's attractions

In the past decade "**South of Market**," or **SoMa**, has become one of the hottest locations in the city, and keeps right on booming. Centered around **Yerba Buena Gardens** ③⑨, the area has become a focal point for art galleries, cafés, and general places to see and be seen in. Encapsulating it all is the **Metreon Center**, a Sony entertainment, food and shopping complex with 15 cinemas and an IMAX theater. The Discovery Channel store, on Metreon's ground level running along Mission Street, is a well-planned space where talks and events are often held; the Metreon Marketplace is good for original souvenirs of the city.

Nearby is the bold **San Francisco Museum of Modern Art** ④⓪ (151 Third Street, tel: 415-357 4000, Friday–Tuesday 11am– 6pm, Thursday 11am–9pm, closed Wednesday; admission charge). Some locals think the building is better than the art contained inside, but of course it's all a matter of taste. Across the street from the museum is Yerba Buena Gardens. What started out as a lovely public park with a waterfall monument honoring Martin Luther King, Jr has now become a mecca for art and entertainment. Buildings around it house, for instance, the **Center for the Arts** ④①, where plays, modern art exhibitions and experimental multi-media performances are staged.

Across the street from the square are the **Cartoon Art Museum** ④②, dedicated to pop cartoon art (and where children will particularly enjoy the comic playroom); the as-yet-uncompleted Mexican Museum; the **Museum of the California Historical Society**, and the most interesting of all, the **Ansel Adams Center for Photography** ④③ (250 4th Street, tel: 415-495 7000, Tuesday–Sunday 11am–5pm, the first Thursday of each month 11am–8pm).

The Ansel Adams Center contains some wonderful examples of the famous

Map, page 116

Matisse's "Femme au Chapeau" at the SFMoMA.

BELOW: Yerba Buena Gardens with the Museum of Modern Art behind.

MUSEUM OF MODERN ART

San Francisco's answer to New York's Museum of Modern Art was completed in 1995, and was, among other things, an attempt to regain cultural supremacy over Los Angeles. The Southern California city had in recent years swiped the cultural mantle, due mainly to the astonishing collection and wealth left to his LA-based trustees by J Paul Getty. SF MoMa was designed by the Swiss architect Mario Botta and cost over $60 million to build.

It is worth stepping inside if only to admire the sunlight effects in the entrance hall beneath the five-story glass-roofed staircase. But many also come here to admire its collection. Works by American and European expressionists, such as Max Ernst, Picasso, Paul Klee and the Californian painter Richard Diebenkorn, are exhibited on the first floor. The second floor consists of the architecture and design sections and also stages special touring exhibitions.

Very interesting displays of experimental 1920s and 1930s photography can be found on the third floor, while the fourth floor is devoted mainly to contemporary works of art. Even if you're seduced by the art and the interior, be sure to leave enough time to visit the museum shop, which sells some of the best souvenirs in the city, and have a cup of coffee in the steel and chrome café.

**Map,
page 116**

photographer's works, along with traveling exhibitions by other photographers. Adams was a master of Absolute Realism who, during the 1930s, produced some of the finest black and white landscape photographs of the US, particularly the Southwest and Yosemite National Park. Just across 4th Street is the **Moscone Convention Center** ❹, which accommodates 30,000 people and is constantly busy due to the conventioneers who pour into the city most weeks.

A couple of blocks away on 5th Street is another fine old building (*circa* 1875), San Francisco's **Old US Mint** ❺. Dating from the days when the city was still a Wild West town, it was in this massive building that silver from Nevada was first converted into dollars and then stored in huge safes in the cellar.

Walking around SoMa is a treat, as it is the area where things are changing the fastest. As well as the locale for some of the city's trendiest nightclubs and local theaters, it is also emerging as the high-tech district with many innovative design and programming firms moving in.

To the east bordering Market Street and New Montgomery Street is the venerable **Palace Hotel** ❻, which hails from the ranks of the city's premier hotels. The Palace, opened in 1875, is San Francisco's oldest luxury hotel. Its 150-foot Palm Garden, with its leaded-glass dome roof bathing diners in light, remains as striking as ever. The Pied Piper bar with its beautiful Maxfield Parrish mural is a fine place to have a drink. Seven American presidents have stayed here, from Ulysses S Grant to Franklin Roosevelt. One of those presidents, Warren G Harding, died at the Palace in 1923 while still in office.

Where Market Street ends, the bay begins with the **Ferry Building** ❼, whose design was influenced by the Cathedral Tower in Seville, Spain. Built in 1894, it's still the gateway for ferry riders from all over the bay. It's especially convenient for commuters who need only to cross the Embarcadero intersection to reach the **Financial District**.

BELOW: the highly visible Transamerica Pyramid.
RIGHT: the soaring Garden Court of the Sheraton Palace.

The Financial District

Roughly bounded by Kearny Street on the west; Washington Street, a quaint neighborhood of tasteful antique shops and interior decorator showrooms, on the north; and Market Street on the southeast, the most immediate attraction in the Financial District is the sprawling $300 million **Embarcadero Center** ❽. In its four-square-block structures connected by bridges this city-within-a-city has numerous shops, restaurants and high-rise apartments, as well as the **Hyatt Regency Hotel**, which boasts a spectacular 20-story atrium lobby. Noticeable from any part of town is the **Bank of America** ❾ building, which is so tall its roof sometimes disappears in the fog.

Equally distinctive is the **Transamerica Pyramid** ❺⓿ on Montgomery Street, its 48 floors making it the tallest building in the city. When it was completed in 1972, a lot of people were appalled by its pointy, unorthodox appearance, but now almost everyone has come to appreciate its architectural eccentricity. South on Montgomery is the **Wells Fargo History Museum** ❺❶ (420 Montgomery Street, tel: 415-396 2619, Monday–Friday 9am–5pm), which displays Gold Rush relics alongside the history of the Wells Fargo company. Exhibits include a 19th-century stagecoach. ❑

AROUND SAN FRANCISCO

Map, page 140

*Latino culture meets gay culture in this trip around the city,
which also takes in Haight-Ashbury, Golden Gate Park
and the most famous bridge in the world*

While it's easy to get caught up in the excitement of downtown, the neighborhoods that make up the rest of the city are equally intriguing and wonderfully diverse. Exploring these areas may seem daunting at first, but they're easily navigated and full of what makes San Francisco one of the most beloved towns on the planet. Mission Street heads due south into the heart of the **Mission district**, San Francisco's great melting pot of Latin American cultures. **Mission Dolores ❶** (Dolores Avenue near 16th Street) was founded less than a week before the American Declaration of Independence was signed in 1776, and its thick adobe walls still form what is the oldest building in San Francisco. The graves of many early pioneers, and thousands of native Costonoan Indians can be found in the mission cemetery.

The Mission district oozes Hispanic culture. Nowadays, while Mission still caters to the Latino community, many newcomers are settling in the area because it's more affordable than most. But the expanding community hasn't yet affected the district's night-time reputation: it's still not the safest place to stroll after dark. In a town as condensed as this one, you need only head a few blocks to find yourself in an entirely different community. To the west of Mission, near Dolores, the sunny districts of **Noe Valley** and the Castro are comprised of many well-kept Victorian homes and shopping streets.

LEFT: local twins pose.
BELOW: ever body-conscious Castro.

Gay abandon

More a neighborhood than a district, the **Castro** is the world's most celebrated gay community. The streets are filled with same-sex couples, rainbow flags, hopping bars, and such poignant landmarks as the **Names Project Aids Memorial Quilt Visitors Center ❷** (2362a Market Street, tel: 415-863 1966, staffed by volunteers, so call first). It is here that the Names Project began in 1987 to commemorate Aids victims. Each square of each quilt has been made by the victims' friends, lovers, and/or family. Today, if the quilts were combined, they'd cover 14 football fields, although sections are usually on tour throughout the world. Another testament to the gay community is **Harvey Milk Plaza ❸**, a MUNI bus stop that's been dedicated to celebrated gay resident Supervisor Harvey Milk who was shot and killed in 1978, along with Mayor Moscone, by anti-homosexual Supervisor Dan White.

The western most section of the Castro leads into the **Twin Peaks ❹** area, full of elegant homes. The neighborhood is named after the two 900-plus-foot-tall hills that provide stunning views of the entire city, and are well worth the short ascent to the top. Heading north, ie, back towards downtown via Stanyan Street leads to lively Haight-Ashbury and tranquil Golden Gate Park. Stanyan Street borders the eastern edge of the park and

intersects with **Haight Street,** a world-famous thoroughfares in the 1960s, when long hair, tie-dyed fabrics, hallucinogens and a belief in the power of love and peace persuaded a generation that they could create an alternative lifestyle.

They were called "hippies." They openly smoked marijuana, took up forms of Eastern mysticism, declined to fight in foreign wars, and otherwise were a thorn in the sides of their elders, who sometimes sent police in riot gear to the middle of the **Haight-Ashbury** ❺ district to clean it up. Haight Street was once so gaudy and bizarre that tour buses full of goggle-eyed tourists ran up and down it. Like most such radical departures from the social norm, the hippie experiment fell victim to time and fashion. The neighborhood still retains its anti-establishment roots, but today flower power has been replaced by piercing shops and tattoo parlors. It's still a lively, colorful stretch, however, with great shopping and a wide range of good, inexpensive restaurants and cafes.

Golden Gate Park

The squatters keep mostly to themselves, in fact, and pose no threat to the hordes of tourists and locals who pass through their makeshift bedrooms into one of the greatest – and most famous – urban parks in the world. **Golden Gate Park** (tel: 415-831 2700) is 3 miles long and half a mile wide (5 by 0.8 km), and consists of groves of redwoods, eucalyptus, pine and countless varieties of other trees from all over the world. It is dotted with lakes, grassy meadows and sunlit dells. There can be thousands of people within its borders, but Golden Gate Park is so large that one can easily find solitary tranquillity in a misty forest grove or by a peaceful pond. More than a century ago, the park was painstakingly reclaimed from sand dunes through the Herculean efforts of a Scottish land-

ABOVE AND BELOW:
The world-famous hippie haven. Wear flowers in your hair.

Map, page 140

cape architect named John McLaren. Park superintendent for 55 years, McLaren so disliked statuary that he shrouded all human likeness in dense vegetation. Most statues remain "lost" today.

Along John F Kennedy Drive about seven blocks into the park, it's impossible to miss the **Conservatory of Flowers** ❻. The incredible glass structure was built in 1878, modeled after the Palm House at London's Kew Gardens. But the park has feasts for the mind as well as the eyes. Further along JFK Drive, a road branches off to the left for the **Music Concourse** ❼, an esplanade built in 1894 offering Sunday concerts. The nearby **California Academy of Sciences** ❽ (tel: 415-750 7145, daily 10am–5pm with extended hours during summer; admission charge) comprises three museums in one. The natural history section incorporates displays of anthropology and ethnology with dioramas of North American and African animals. The **Steinhart Aquarium** has nearly 16,000 specimens of marine and shore life on display in its 190 tanks. The Steinhart's attractions include a look at the intricate pattern of sea life around a living coral reef, and the fierce anatomy of a frozen great white shark. The entertaining **Morrison Planetarium** has a whiz-bang laser light show about our tiny, undistinguished corner of the universe under its 65-feet (20-meter) dome.

Across the enormous plaza complete with an old-fashioned band shell where locals often practice tai chi is the **M.H. De Young Memorial Museum** ❾ (tel: 415-750 3600, Wednesday through Sunday 9.30am–5pm; admission charge). Blockbuster traveling exhibits are presented here, but even without these shows, the De Young – which opened in 1921 – is the one of the city's best museums. Its collection includes Renaissance and medieval paintings and tapestries, sculpture and suits of armor, and African and Polynesian galleries.

BELOW: the 1878 Conservatory of Flowers was based on the Palm House built in London's Kew Gardens.

An adjunct of the De Young is the **Asian Art Museum** (tel: 415-379 8800, Wednesday–Sunday 9.30am–5pm; admission charge), donated to the city by the late Avery Brundage, the iron-willed millionaire who dominated the international Olympic movement. The Brundage collection, the largest of its kind outside Asia, has 10,000 items. It includes precious jades, ceramics, sculptures, bronzes, vases and figurines, some dating back 3,500 years. Next door is the beautiful **Japanese Tea Garden ⑩**. Built in 1894, it's a harmonious blend of architecture, landscaping and pools. It is said that fortune cookies were invented here. The custom spread to Chinatown, then traveled throughout the Chinese food industry in the western world. The garden was disassembled during World War II, then restored when the threat of wartime vandalism had passed.

The stretch of neighborhood north of the park is the **Richmond district**, fogbound much of the summer and renowned for its orderly streets which blend well into the **Sunset district,** equally conservative and flanking the south side of Golden Gate Park. The simple grid of numbered streets is as mundane as the quiet neighborhood itself, so the best thing drivers can do is to follow the signs that guide them along the more fascinating **49-Mile Scenic Drive**.

The drive can be picked up as it snakes past the **Cliff House ⑪**, which overlooks the Pacific Ocean and peers down upon barking seals clinging wetly to the rocks below. The present Cliff House is the fifth to have been built here since 1863; its predecessors have all burned down or suffered some other disaster. The food's not great, but down the steps from the cliff-hanging restaurant there's still a fanciful blast to the past at the **Musée Mechanique**, a penny arcade featuring bygone entertainment combined with today's latest arcade games.

North of the Cliff House is verdant **Lincoln Park**, whose 270 acres (109

This drive takes about a day.

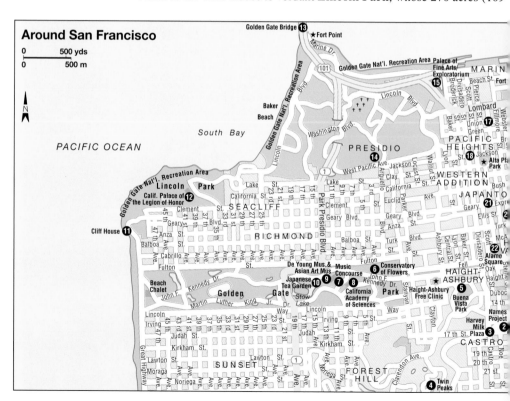

Around San Francisco

0   500 yds
0   500 m

N

ectares) include an 18-hole municipal golf course and the stunning neoclassi-
al French-style **California Palace of the Legion of Honor** ⑫ (tel: 415-863
330, Tuesday–Sunday 9.30am–5pm; admission charge). Smack dab in some
f the hottest real estate in town, the $35 million renovated museum is spectac-
lar: at the entrance is one of five existing bronze casts of Rodin's *The Thinker*.
he cliffs wind east along a protected area known as the **Golden Gate National
Recreation Area**, under the Golden Gate Bridge, past **Fort Point** to **Golden
Gate Promenade**. Further down the promenade is the **Marina Green**, beloved
y kite flyers and joggers. The big yachts in the harbor belong to the members of
he **San Francisco Yacht Club**, whose Spanish-style clubhouse looks out on
he bay, which is often alive with windsurfers.

Map,
page 140

Golden Gate Bridge and the Presidio

Whether sailing under the **Golden Gate Bridge** ⑬ or taking in its enormity
rom the Marina's shore, it is interesting to consider that at one time many rep-
itable engineers argued that it would be impossible to build a span at this point
ecause of the depth of the water and the powerful tidal rush in and out. The
ity authorized the first studies in 1918, but it was 1937 before the bridge was
inished at a cost of $35 million and the lives of 11 construction workers.

Part of the promenade goes through **Crissy Field**, an airfield-turned-picnic
rea belonging to the 1,480-acre (599-hectare) **Presidio** ⑭. Established by the
Spanish in 1776 and once owned by the US Army, the Presidio is a very unwar-
ike military installation. Decommissioned in 1992, this green and attractive
pot is perceived as some of the most valuable real estate in the country and
here have been plenty of debates about how best to use the land: so far preser-

*The Art Deco towers
of the Golden Gate
Bridge (see below)
reach a height of 746
feet. When first built,
they were the highest
structures in the West.
With a span consist-
ing of 3,950 feet, the
Golden Gate, when
completed, was also
celebrated as the
longest suspension
bridge in the world.*

Map, page 140

vationists and film director George Lucas (who has his eye on offices here) seem to be winning. The National Parks Service currently oversees the manicured grounds, which include stands of pine and eucalyptus, and even a lake. It also offers tours (tel: 415-556 4323, daily).

One of the most beautiful man-made sites stands a few blocks inland from the promenade. **The Plaster Palace**, across Marina Boulevard to the south, is the classic rococo rotunda of the **Palace of Fine Arts ⓯**. It stands before a reflecting pond where ducks and swans glide. Designed by Bernard Maybeck, the palace was originally built of plaster of Paris for the Panama Pacific Exhibition of 1915. It wasn't meant to last, but somehow it did. Not until 1967 was it strengthened and made permanent. The palace houses the **Exploratorium** (3601 Lyon Street, tel: 415-561 0360, Tuesday and Thursday–Sunday 10am–5pm, Wednesday 10am–9.30pm; admission charge), an interactive children's museum with more than 500 exhibits to awaken even the most dormant interest in science. Further east along Marina is **Fort Mason ⓰**, a decommissioned military base whose long huts house art galleries, ethnic museums, workshops and a good restaurant, called Green's.

Union Street

Turn inland to **Chestnut** and then on to **Union Street ⓱**. By day, Chestnut acts as one big outdoor café where the next generation of yuppies congregate in sportswear, when they're not shopping in the trendy boutiques. After dark, the same crowd meets in the plethora of tasty and inexpensive restaurants, then heads to the post-collegiate-type bars. Union Street is a chic stretch of boutiques, antique stores, gourmet shops, delicatessens and classy restaurants. At night, the singles bars are the main attraction where the beautiful go in search of each other's images.

When not out shopping, residents of this area, such as writer Danielle Steele and the Gettys, head to the hills just south of Union Street, into the city's wealthiest area, **Pacific Heights ⓲**. Stunning mansions line every steep-and-wide street whose integrity is maintained by the upkeep of underground telephone lines. A stellar example of Queen Anne Victorian architecture that can be visited is the **Haas-Lilienthal House ⓳**, (Franklin and Washington streets, tel: 415-441 3004).

Further south, the hill crests at Jackson Street to demark the beginning of **Fillmore Street ⓴**. Further south of Fillmore at Post Street is the heart of **Japantown ㉑**. The **Japan Center,** the neighborhood's focal point, is an Asian-oriented shopping center, which stretches three blocks and is filled with affordable Japanese restaurants and little stores featuring everything from kimonos to bonsai trees. The handsome, distinctive five-tiered peace pagoda stands as a monument of ever-lasting goodwill between the Japanese and the United States.

Nine blocks south, at the corner of Fulton and Steiner streets, a very different history is preserved. The rows of perfectly maintained Victorian houses surrounding a grassy square with skyscrapers peeping over the top is called **Alamo Square ㉒** and the subject of thousands of photographs of the streets of San Francisco. ❑

BELOW: the rococo Palace of Fine Arts. **RIGHT:** Alamo Square, star of a thousand photos.

OAKLAND, BERKELEY AND THE PENINSULA

Jack London's Oakland and the people's Berkeley lead the way to Stanford University and the high-tech communities of Silicon Valley

Maps, pages 148 & 152

Despite all the hard knocks – especially Gertrude Stein's infamous quip that "there is no *there* there" – Oakland **❶** is doing all it can to emerge from the long shadow cast by its older sister to the west. Oakland and the rest of the East Bay – which existed, said the late *San Francisco Chronicle* columnist Herb Caen, only because "the Bay Bridge had to end somewhere" – seems to thrive on such adversity. And diversity. Cheaper rents and a slightly slower urban pace have attracted would-be San Franciscans, much like Brooklyn can draw frustrated Manhattanites in New York City.

At second glance, Oakland seems to offer much of what San Francisco has – even a Chinatown and thriving waterfront – without the fog, the crowds, and stop-and-go traffic. More than half a century after Stein passed through town, visitors might reconsider: there is a there here. It's just a little harder to find.

Jack London's legacy

Oakland's version of Fisherman's Wharf is the restaurant and shopping pedestrian walk **Jack London Square** and **Village ❶**. The author of *The Sea Wolf* and *The Call of the Wild*, who died in 1916, might not be impressed to see the overpriced restaurants and T-shirt shops, but he'd be able to munch crab, listen to live music and watch the sailboats pass by without having to elbow his way through crowds to the pier.

The **First and Last Chance Saloon**, that London himself (an Oakland native) used to frequent, is here, as is London's sod-roofed Yukon cabin, which was moved from Alaska to the waterfront as part of a tribute to the city's native son. On Sundays, there's a farmers' market, open until early afternoon.

Oakland's most obvious landmarks are the handsome **Tribune Building ❸**, with its distinctive tower; the post-1989-earthquake renovated **Oakland City Hall ❹**, with its wedding-cake cupola; and, in the hills above, the five-towered, white granite **Mormon Temple ❹**, which is the only Mormon temple in the state. From its lofty heights are wonderful views of the bay.

Visible from the Nimitz Freeway, if you're driving toward the airport, is the **Oakland-Alameda County Coliseum Complex**, which is the home of the Oakland A's baseball team, the National Basketball Association's Golden State Warriors and the Oakland Raiders AFC football team.

On the eastern edge of town is a natural landmark, **Lake Merritt ❺**. This large salt-water lake and wildlife refuge, rimmed by Victorian houses and a necklace of lights, is home to **Children's Fairyland** (tel: 510-452

PRECEDING PAGES: Pigeon Point lighthouse on Highway 1 west of San Jose. **LEFT:** ferry tale. **BELOW:** Oakland's well-known harbor.

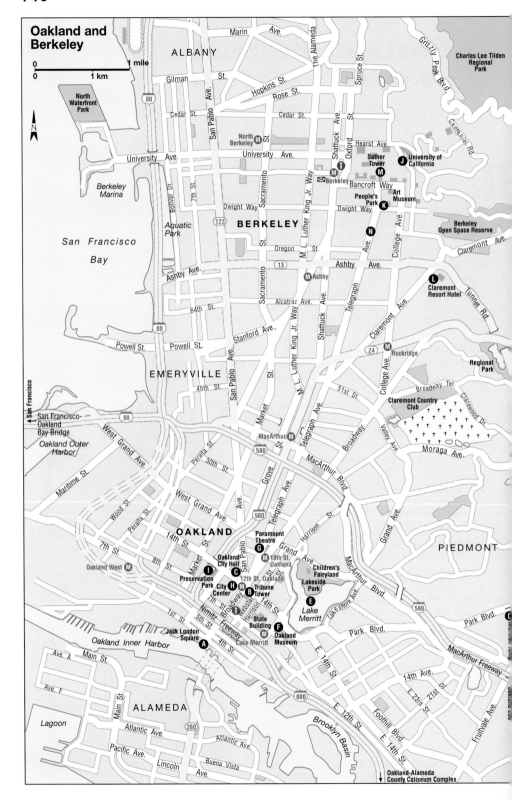

Oakland and Berkeley

0 _____ 1 mile
0 _____ 1 km

N

ALBANY

BERKELEY

EMERYVILLE

OAKLAND

PIEDMONT

ALAMEDA

San Francisco Bay

San Francisco

North Waterfront Park

Berkeley Marina

Aquatic Park

Charles Lee Tilden Regional Park

University of California

Sather Tower

Art Museum

People's Park

Berkeley Open Space Reserve

Claremont Resort Hotel

Regional Park

Rockridge

Claremont Country Club

Moraga Ave.

San Francisco-Oakland Bay Bridge

Oakland Outer Harbor

Paramount Theatre

Oakland City Hall

Preservation Park

City Center

Tribune Tower

State Building

Oakland Museum

Jack London Square

Oakland Inner Harbor

Children's Fairyland

Lakeside Park

Lake Merritt

Lagoon

Oakland-Alameda County Coliseum Complex

2259), touted as the country's first "3-D" theme park. Visitors can board a pirate ship reminiscent of Peter Pan, or step into the mouth of the whale that "swallowed Pinocchio." The lake is also good for sailing or picnicking all the year round. At the modern **Oakland Zoo** (tel: 510-632 9525), visitors can ride in the sky in gondolas overlooking some of the zoo's 330 animals.

Within walking distance of the lake are two wonderfully contrasting architectural delights – the **Oakland Museum ❻** (1000 Oak Street, tel: 510-238 2200, Wednesday–Saturday 10am–5pm, Sunday noon–7pm; admission charge, except free on Sunday 4–7pm) and the Art Deco-style **Paramount Theatre ❼** at 2025 Broadway. The Oakland Museum, wonderfully landscaped with terraces and gardens, occupies three levels, and is considered the finest museum in the state for information on California's art, history and natural science. The Cowell Hall of California History has a huge collection of artifacts, while the Gallery of California Art is known for its oil paintings of Northern California sites. (Tip: before you leave, be sure to take the museum's fun, simulated walk across the state.)

The Paramount is the home of the Oakland Ballet and the Paramount Organ Pops, and shows old movies, complete with newsreels. Among Oakland's newer attractions are the **City Center ❽**, a pedestrian mall with quaint restaurants, jazz concerts and changing art exhibits, **Preservation Park ❾**, a restored Victorian village complete with 19th-century street lamps and lush gardens, and the **African American Museum** at 659 14th Street. For many black Americans, Oakland has a special significance; it was here in the 1960s that the Black Panther Movement was founded. The politics espoused by the Panthers spread from here to the East Coast and then to college campuses around the country.

Map, page 148

In the books Martin Eden *(1909) and* John Barleycorn *(1913), Jack London wrote about the waterfront home in Oakland in which he grew up.*

BELOW: Jack London Square.

Berkeley

Just north of Oakland is Berkeley ❷, another East Bay rival of San Francisco. A city famous for social experimentation and the birth of the Free Speech movement, Berkeley has, in recent times, become slightly less flamboyant, slightly more commercial and the home of Chez Panisse (one of the country's most coveted restaurants, tel: 510-548 5049).

The city grew up around the **University of California** ❿ (tel: 510-642 5215), considered one of the country's finest public universities, and outranking all other American universities in the number of Nobel laureates it has educated. Berkeley began as a humble prep school operating out of a former fandango house in Oakland, and eventually grew into the nine-campus University of California system. But it was the Free Speech movement of 1964 that put Berkeley on the map. At issue was a UC Berkeley administration order limiting political activities on campus. This touched off massive student protests and, in turn, similar protests on campuses nationwide. For several years the campus remained a smoldering center of protest and politics.

In 1969, students once more took to the streets to stop the university's expansion in an area they wanted to preserve as **People's Park** ⓚ. They prevailed ultimately, despite the intervention of 2,000 National Guard troops and violence that led to the death of an onlooker. Years later, People's Park began to draw more drug dealers and drifters from the city's homeless than it did students. Today, the student unrest here has turned to rest and recreation: the city has added basketball and volleyball courts to People's Park.

On the approach to Berkeley from Oakland, two buildings catch the eye. On a hillside toward the south is a fairy-tale white palace, otherwise known as the

ABOVE: power to the people.
BELOW: Claremont Resort Hotel.

Claremont Resort Hotel ⬤ (tel: 510-543 3000), which, like San Francisco's Palace of Fine Arts, was finished just before the Panama Pacific Exposition of 1915. The other landmark is a tall,pointed structure, the university's bell tower. Its official name is **Sather Tower** ⬤, but it's known to everyone simply as the "Campanile" because it's modeled after St Mark's Campanile in Venice, Italy.

To get the feel of Berkeley at its liveliest, visitors should take a walk down **Telegraph Avenue** ⬤ from Dwight Way to the university. Here students, towns-people and "street people" pick their way between rows of shops and street vendors offering jewelry, pottery, plants and tie-dyed everything.

Like Oakland, Berkeley offers respite for those who run screaming from the headaches of San Francisco traffic and weather – it can be freezing and fog-bound in the city, but sunny here – but who still yearn for a lively, cosmopolitan community that represents urban life, albeit on a slighter, smaller scale.

The Peninsula

Back to the west side of the Bay Bridge, orchards once graced the fertile land-scape south of San Francisco where today industrial parks and seemingly end-less commercial and condominium strips now spread inland from the edge of the bay. But this is also the land of high-technology and suburban dreams, a place that sprang up with its own, virtually-created industry as quickly as the original *Sputnik* satellite came down.

The San Francisco **Peninsula**, roughly a 55-mile (89-km) swath of high hills, tall trees and beautiful estates, is wedged between the Pacific Ocean and San Francisco Bay. To its north is San Francisco. At its southern end lies the sprawl of the **Silicon Valley** – or what used to be known as Santa Clara Valley when

Maps, pages 148 & 152

BELOW: Berkeley was a hotbed of student unrest in the 1960s.

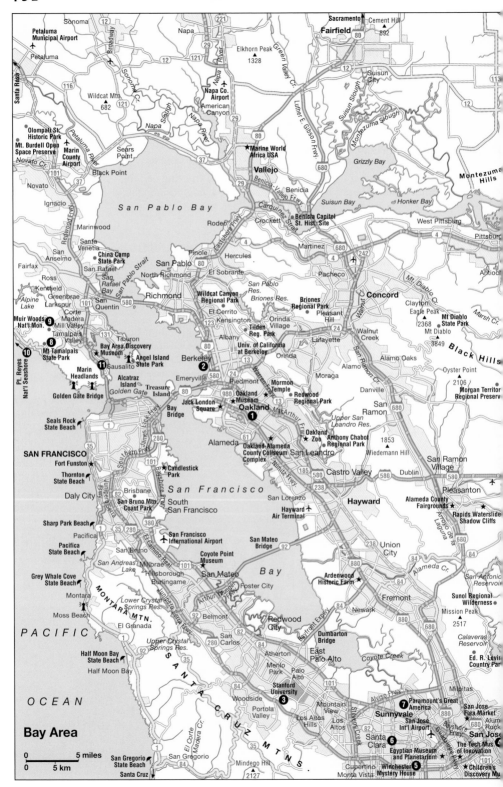

Bay Area

| 0 | 5 miles |
| 0 | 5 km |

pples and pears, not computers and silicon chips, were harvested here. In the valley, the peninsula's highlands segue into the affluent, high-tech communities of Palo Alto, Los Altos, Sunnyvale, Santa Clara and San Jose. As the drive south on **El Camino Real** – the main thoroughfare that runs through all these cities down to San Jose – will prove, the only true borders between peninsula cities seem to be stoplights. Where the commercial and spartan-finish industrial strips end, the wealthy suburban homes begin, spread like a heat rash across the ample flatlands. In fact, housing in Silicon Valley is now so scarce, its impact can be felt in commuter-distance San Francisco, where rents in the Bay City soared during the latter half of the 1990s, and continue to rise.

The style of the peninsula is sophisticated, shamelessly commercial, and contemporary. Six thousand residents have doctorate degrees, and Stanford University is the hub of academic and cultural activity. Mixed with the high-mindedness, however, is lots of new money (millionaires from scratch as common as tennis courts) and old money (San Mateo is one of the four wealthiest counties in California). Both types shop at the impressive **Stanford Mall**.

Map, page 152

Stanford University

A farm – blue-blooded horse ranch – is exactly what the campus of renowned **Stanford University** ❸ (tel: 650-723 4177) was a little over a century ago when Leland Stanford and photographer Muybridge began their experiments with moving images (which were to lead to the creation of motion pictures). Today, it is the academic lifeblood of the peninsula, located in the northwestern corner of **Palo Alto**, a city known for its strict environmental policies and praised as one of the best "model little cities of the world." Architecturally, Stanford's

ABOVE: the republic of California.
BELOW: Memorial Church, Stanford University.

Map,
page 152

handsome, rough-hewn sandstone buildings are Romanesque in style, though the red-tiled roofs, the burnt adobe color of the stone, and the wide arches give the university a Spanish mission look. The exception to the overall prosaic qualities is beautiful **Memorial Church**, which dominates the **Inner Quad** (the quad is also known as the central courtyard). The church is resplendent in stained glass and with a domed ceiling.

South peninsula

San Jose ❹ was the first pueblo to be founded in Northern California by the Spanish, in 1777. Until 1956, the San Jose area was providing America with half its supply of prunes. But the orchards of three decades ago have now sprouted condominiums and industrial parks. Today, San Jose is the third largest city in California with a population that is booming due to the influx from around the world of high-tech personnel and like-minded groupies.

It is a busy, fast-paced community, with several major hotels, nightclubs and no fewer than 100 shopping centers that cater to all the techies with money to burn. Sightseeing is pretty minimal in metropolitan San Jose, although three major wineries are located within the city limits and all offer free tours and tastings – the **Almaden, Mirassou** and **Turgeon and Lohr**.

For entertainment of a more eccentric bent there is the red-roofed, sprawling touristy but nonetheless fascinating **Winchester Mystery House ❺** (tel: 408-247 2101, near I-280, -880 and Highway 17, daily 9am–5pm; admission charge), in downtown San Jose. It was built in convoluted stages by local eccentric Sarah L Winchester, who inherited the fortune of her father-in-law, the famed gun manufacturer. Sarah was a spiritualist who believed that she would live as long as she kept adding to her house. Sixteen carpenters worked on the mansion for 36 years, adding stairways that lead to nowhere and doors without any rooms.

BELOW: oarswoman in Oakland.
RIGHT: bending with the wind.

The spiritual realm is also the basis and reason for the **Rosicrucian Egyptian Museum** and planetarium (tel: 408-947 3636, closed holidays) in San Jose on the way to **Santa Clara ❻**. A recreated walk-in tomb of 2000 BC and the West Coast's largest collection of Egyptian, Babylonian and Assyrian artifacts are contained within the building, which draws a half-million visitors annually. The Ancient, Mystical Order Rosae Crucis is an international philosophical order said to have been established nearly 3,500 years ago.

Lighthouse and laser show

Anyone longing for the sea should nip over to Highway 1 west of San Jose near the little town of **Pescadero** to see a particularly atmospheric site – **Pigeon Point Lighthouse**, the second tallest lighthouse in the US.

Youngsters are more likely to wail for **Paramount's Great America ❼** (tel: 408-988 1776, hours vary, closed during winter; admission charge) located off the Bayshore Freeway near **Sunnyvale**. A theme park drawing on five venues of old America, it has stage shows, arcades and shops. There's also a Lost In Cyberspace laser show, and a vomit-inducing bungee jump-like ride, Extreme Sky Flyer. The IMAX theater has film produced for its stunning 90-ft (27-meter) screen.

MONTEREY BAY TO BIG SUR

Highway 1, the first scenic highway in the state,
hugs the coast from Santa Cruz to Monterey to Carmel,
before meandering past Big Sur towards San Simeon

Map, page 112

San Francisco
California
Los Angeles

The stretch of Northern California coast from Santa Cruz to San Simeon is one region that does not exist in a state of implicit apology for not being San Francisco. The pace might be slower, but the highly differentiated and individualistic communities which occupy this shore are so busy leading their own lives, the thought of doing otherwise does not occur to them.

At the northern end of Monterey Bay is **Santa Cruz ❶**, a cool, green, redwood-shingled beach town hoisted for the moment on the leftward swing of its own political pendulum. The **University of California** opened its Santa Cruz campus in 1965 and within a few years this influx of academic activity transformed what had previously been a quiet backwater town into an activist community. Santa Cruz was rejuvenated with excellent restaurants, cafés, pastry shops, bookstores and a multitude of shops selling everything from 10-speed bicycles to Japanese kites. Old buildings were refurbished, cement block and aluminum replaced with natural redwood and hanging ferns. Santa Cruz has sparkling clean air in the summer; its only drawback is the torrential winter rain that turns canyons into rivers.

PRECEDING PAGES: Big Sur coastline. **LEFT:** rural living. **BELOW:** chipmunk on Bird Rock, 17-Mile Drive.

Amusing attractions

The Santa Cruz **municipal pier** features restaurants, fish markets and fishing facilities. Next to it is a wide white sandy beach. On the other side is the **Boardwalk Amusement Park**, with its carousel, Ferris wheel, thrilling roller coaster and old-fashioned arcade containing shooting galleries. Note: Santa Cruz is one of the sunniest spots on this stretch of the coast, usually unaffected by the chilly winds and blinding fog that can blanket Big Sur further south in minutes. Sun-lovers should linger here, and, to enjoy the atmosphere to its fullest, keep your swimming suit handy: not for nothing does the town have one of the few – if not the only – monument to a surfer on the promenade looking out over the water.

Highway 1, probably the most beautiful road in the state, hugs the coast here in a beautiful arc around Monterey Bay. During the spring, the high sand dunes are covered in a colorful carpet of marigolds. The road is fairly built up around the beach town of **Capitola**, but then chills out dramatically towards Big Sur. Peanut stands and agricultural produce stands make brief stops pleasant; they're also good for picking up snacks.

Cannery Row

The busy city of **Monterey ❷**, located at the northern end of the Monterey Peninsula, comes as a surprise after this peaceful journey. Thanks to John Steinbeck, the most famous attraction in town is the former Ocean

View Avenue, now known as **Cannery Row**. During World War II, Monterey was the sardine capital of the Western hemisphere, processing some 200,000 tons a year. As Steinbeck described it then, the street was "a poem, a stink, a grating noise, a quality of light, a tone, a habit, a nostalgia, a dream".

When the fishing boats came in, heavy with their catch, the canneries blew their whistles and the residents of Monterey came streaming down the hill to take their places amid the rumbling, rattling, squealing machinery of the canning plants. When finally the last sardine was cleaned, cut, cooked and canned, the whistle blew again, and the workers trudged back up the hill, dripping wet and smelly. After the war, for reasons variously blamed on overfishing, changing tidal currents and divine retribution, the sardines suddenly disappeared from Monterey Bay and all the canneries went broke.

But, as Steinbeck pointed out, it was not a total loss. In those heady early years of the industry, the beaches were so deeply covered with fish guts, scales and flies that a sickening stench covered the whole town. Today, the beaches are bright and clean, and the air is sparkling fresh. Cannery Row, located along the waterfront on the northwest side of town just beyond the Presidio, has become an impressive tourist attraction, its old buildings are filled with lusty bars, gaudy restaurants, a wax museum, dozens of shops, a carousel and food vendors.

California-born John Steinbeck (1902–68) is best known for his 1939 novel "The Grapes of Wrath." He won the Nobel Prize in 1962.

A spectacular aquarium

A trip to Cannery Row these days invariably includes visiting one of the world's premier aquariums: the **Monterey Bay Aquarium** (886 Cannery Row, tel: 831-648 4888, open daily but different hours, call for details; admission charge). The enormous building, with its outdoor pools overlooking the sea, stands on

BELOW: Cannery Row, Monterey.

Map,
page 112

the site of what was Cannery Row's largest cannery, the Hovden Cannery. More than 100 galleries and exhibits include over 350,000 specimens, from sea otters, leopard sharks, bat rays and giant octopuses, to towering underwater kelp forests. Feeding time is particularly fascinating, when keepers in glass tanks talk to spectators through underwater microphones. Although always crowded, this spectacular sanctuary – the biggest in the US – is worth any amount of waiting time, but be warned: it may spoil visits to lesser aquariums.

In downtown Monterey, the main visitor attraction is **Fisherman's Wharf**. (The real working wharf is two blocks east.) Fisherman's Wharf is lined with restaurants, shops, an organ grinder with a monkey, fish markets and noisy sea lions which swim among the pilings. To see the rest of Monterey, a 3-mile (5-km) walking tour, called **The Path of History**, leads past the more important historical buildings and sites. These include the Customs House, the oldest public building in California, now a museum; Pacific House, a two-story adobe with a Monterey balcony around the second floor; and impressive historical exhibits from the Spanish, Mexican and early American periods.

Other attractions include **Colton Hall**, a two-story building with a classical portico which was the site of the state's first (1849) constitutional convention; Stevenson House, a smaller former hotel where the romantic (and sickly) Robert Louis Stevenson lived for a few months while courting his wife; and the **Royal Presidio Chapel**, in constant use since 1794. (US President Herbert Hoover was married in a courtyard here.)

The **Presidio**, founded in 1770 by Gaspar de Portolá, now serves as the **US Army Language School**. Other points of interest in Monterey are the **Monterey Peninsula Museum** of regional art, and the **Allen Knight Maritime**

The aquarium in Monterey keeps expanding: in 2001 there will be a floor devoted to life-forms of Monterey Canyon, some of which glow in the dark.

BELOW: Monterey squid festival.

The Lone Pine Cypress is at the southwestern corner of the 17-Mile Drive.

BELOW: the mission in Carmel was once the administrative center of Northern California.

Museum, featuring relics of the era of sailing ships and whaling. In mid-September each year, the hugely popular **Monterey Jazz Festival** (tel: 800-307 3378) attracts many of the biggest names in music to the Monterey Fairgrounds. It was here that Jimi Hendrix was brought to the attention of the world.

Kayaking on Monterey Bay is growing in popularity, too, offering a delightful opportunity to get out among the otters and sea lions. A local company operates tours out to see the gray whales on their migration past here between Alaska and Baja, California, down Mexico way.

17-Mile Drive

Just north of the foot of Ocean Avenue is the Carmel Gate entrance to the 3-hour-long **17-Mile Drive,** which meanders around the Monterey Peninsula, via the **Del Monte Forest,** to Pacific Grove. Because all the roads in the Del Monte Forest are privately owned, travelers on the 17-Mile Drive must pay a fee to the Pebble Beach Company (note: no motorcycles allowed). Close to the **Ghost Tree** cypress, a big stone mansion looks like something seen in a lightning flash which cleaves the midnight darkness of the Scottish moors. The peninsula has several other houses of note.

The attitude of the Pebble Beach Company toward tourists seems more than a little condescending, however. Along its exclusive golf courses are many signs warning visitors that trespassing on the course is a misdemeanor punishable by a fine and imprisonment. At the famous **Lone Pine Cypress,** a single gnarled and windswept tree near the top of a huge wave-battered rock, the sign on the protective fence reads: "No Trespassing Beyond This Point," as if merely being in the forest were a trespass in itself.

Charming Carmel

The southern gateway to the Monterey Peninsula is the town of **Carmel ❸**. A couple of chance factors made Carmel (population: 4,239) what it is today: starving writers and unwanted painters in flight from the devastation of the 1906 San Francisco earthquake; and canny property developers who, to reduce their taxes, covered the treeless acres with a thick, lush carpet of Monterey pines.

The result is one of the most endearing seaside towns on the West Coast. When the evening fog rolls in from the bay, the lights inside the cozy houses, combined with the faint whiff of wood smoke from roaring fires, give Carmel the peaceful feeling of an 18th-century European village. Although some 3 or 4 million people visit each year – popularity boosted when actor Clint Eastwood became mayor for a couple of terms – Carmel has resisted any temptation to yield to fast-food franchises and neon signs. The street, plazas and upscale little shopping malls attract pedestrians to wine shops and antique stores, art galleries and numerous boutiques. The local market offers good produce, fresh artichokes and racks of wines.

At night, on the side streets, a dozen couples might be dining quietly by candlelight behind dark restaurant windows. In the residential parts of town, the streets meander casually through the forest, sometimes even splitting in two to accommodate an especially praiseworthy specimen of pine. Having said all this, the town is not to everyone's taste. Its sweetness can be cloying, and its plethora of gift shoppes just a little too removed from real life to digest without a healthy touch of irony. Nevertheless, **Carmel mission** (1770) is definitely worth a visit, and the beach at the bottom of the hill is stunning.

South of Carmel is **Point Lobos State Reserve**, a rocky park overlooking the

Map,
page 112

BELOW: Carmel is full of antique shops and quaint bed-and-breakfast inns like this one.

Map, page 112

sea. Nature trails crisscross the reserve, and big natural rock pools are home to lolling sea lions. Be sure to take water and a picnic: there are no food facilities.

Highway 1 south of Point Lobos begins to swoop and curve in dramatic fashion. The San Lucia Mountains rise steeply to the left; the foamy sea to the right changes shape and color constantly. Only the two-lane road separates the two, which means the curling ribbon of road has its own distinct weather pattern. For this read: fog. Although the sun may be shining brightly on the other side of the mountains, and can often be seen through the trees, Highway 1 can be distinctly chilly (travelers in convertibles or on motorcyles take note), and the fog comes on very quickly, obliterating the world for unexpected moments.

Big Sur

This is a suitably theatrical entrance to **Big Sur ❹** arguably California's most beautiful stretch of coastline. Its most photogenic site is **Bixby Bridge**, north of Big Sur Village, spanning the steep walls of Bixby Canyon. Until 1945, Big Sur was mainly populated by ranchers, lodgers and miners. But soon literary people began turning up, attracted by the idea of living cheaply, growing marijuana in remote canyons and communing with what long-time resident Henry Miller called "the face of the earth as the creator intended it to look." The **Henry Miller Memorial Library**, (tel: 831-667 2574), near **Nepenthe** restaurant where everyone goes for sunset, has works by and about this local hero.

Big Sur Village is really little more than a huddle of shops and a post office. Places to stay in Big Sur are few and far between, and if planning a weekend visit, book well in advance for any of them. There's a couple of camp sites, a couple of motels and inns, and a couple of beautiful but pricy hot-tub-and-fireplace country inns, usually described in glossy travel brochures as "hedonistic hideaways" and "sensuous, sumptuous and serene." Notable among them are the **Ventana Inn** (tel: 831-667 2419) and the **Post Ranch Inn** (tel: 831-667 2200), designed by local architect Mickey Muenning. South of Big Sur Village, Highway 1 winds past several state parks, including stunning **Julia Pfeiffer Burns State Park**, with its twisting nature trails and silvery waterfall, and the entrance to 1960s alternative haven the **Esalen Institute**, before ending 16 miles (25 km) north of **Hearst Castle ❺** *(see page 166)*.

Beyond Hearst Castle, Highway 1 branches off to hug the coast passing close to **Morro Bay**, dominated by a 576-feet (176-meter) rock just offshore. To take the fast track back to San Francisco, turn at Morro Bay onto State 41, which eventually joins US 101.

Heading north, US 101 passes through the town of **King City ❻**; to **Pinnacles National Monument ❼** with its ruined mission on the fringes not far from **Soledad ❽** and on to **Gilroy ❾**, best known for its Garlic Festival. If Big Sur has made you long for the coast, head for **Año Nuevo State Reserve ❿**, off Highway 1, 20 miles (32 km) north of Santa Cruz near the San Mateo-Santa Cruz county line. Here, whiskered and roly-poly elephant seal pups are born in January, when entire seal families are visible from lookout points along the beachfront. It's a popular sight, however, so book a place in October. ❑

BELOW: rustic retreat.
RIGHT: Bixby Bridge, Big Sur, was called an engineering marvel in 1932.

HEARST CASTLE AT SAN SIMEON

Tycoon William Randolph Hearst was larger than life and so is his mansion. Indeed, it is so lavish that it is often referred to simply as "Hearst Castle"

After Disneyland, California's most visited site is the baroque home that newspaper and movie tycoon William Randolph Hearst *(left)* had built for himself by his favorite architect, Julia Morgan. Craftsmen labored for 28 years to create *La Cuesta Encantada*, "the Enchanted Hill" with its acres of gardens, terraces, pools and walkways.

It was Hearst's father George, a multimillionaire from his gold, silver and copper mines, who first acquired the 275,000-acre (111,300-hectare) ranch. On his parents' death, the younger Hearst hired Morgan to design the highly ornate twin-towered main house which ended up with 38 bedrooms (some high up in the elegant belltowers), a Gothic dining room, two swimming pools and three sumptuous guest houses.

Next, he stocked the grounds with animals from all over the world, and filled the buildings with carvings, furnishings and works of art from European castles and cathedrals. To hide from view a water tank on the adjoining hill, Hearst had 6,000 pine trees planted.

Hearst, who at his death in 1951 owned the country's largest newspaper chain, and was the subject of Orson Welles's 1941 movie *Citizen Kane*, lived in his 130-room hilltop mansion at San Simeon for 20 years until 1947, when ill health caused him to move to Beverly Hills. Ten years later the Hearst Corporation deeded the San Simeon property to the state of California, where it is an historical monument.

Hearst Castle, 750 Hearst Castle Road, San Simeon, tel: 805-927 6811. There are three to four tours most days.

△ UNDERWATER ROMANCE
The indoor Roman swimming pool took over three years to build. Replete with decorative tiles in Venetian glass and hammered gold, the pool room is big enough to house twin tennis courts on its roof.

◁ WORKS OF ART
In addition to statues, paintings and tapestries, Hearst's collection included oriental rugs, Navaho blankets, furniture, silver and stained glass.

△ NEPTUNE POOL
This enormous outdoor poo was the favorite among the castle's guests. Marble colonnades and white marb statues front an impressive Greco-Roman temple facad

◁ **CASTLE IN THE CLOUDS**
Perched up so high, San Simeon is often wreathed in fog. All supplies were brought up the coast by steamer, then had to be hauled up the hill.

▽ **THE ASSEMBLY ROOM**
This lavish room is 85 feet (26 meters) long and constructed around a 400-year-old carved wooden ceiling from Italy.

Virtually every weekend San Simeon welcomed moviedom's elite. A special train with a jazz band and open bar from Glendale station brought the party guests 210 miles (338 km) from Hollywood to San Luis Obispo, where limousines transported them through the estate's grounds filled with lions, bears, ostriches, elephants, pumas and leopards. On arrival at the floodlit mansion, each was allocated a personal maid or valet and was free to wander – except for a mandatory attendance at the late-night dinner. There were also special occasions: among the hundred guests who attended a covered wagon party were the Warner Brothers, the Gary Coopers and William Powell.

"The society people always wanted to meet the movie stars so I mixed them together," wrote actress Marion Davies *(above)*, Hearst's longtime mistress. "Jean Harlow came up quite frequently. She was very nice and I liked her. She didn't have an awful lot to say... all the men used to flock around her. She was very attractive in an evening dress because she never wore anything under it." Clark Gable was another regular guest. "Women were always running after him but he'd just give them a look as if to say 'how crazy these people are' and he stayed pretty much to himself."

▷ **THE REFECTORY**
Most nights the publisher would preside over dinner at the 16th-century monastery table *(right)* where catsup from bottles and the absence of tablecloths preserved the illusion of "camping out." Liquor was strictly banned (so guests drank in their rooms). After dinner Hearst often showed an as yet unreleased movie; *Gone With the Wind*, for example, was screened six months before its December 1939 premiere.

MARIN COUNTY

One reason why San Francisco is so popular lies just across the Golden Gate Bridge. Here are pristine forests, pretty beaches and old-fashioned towns that lend themselves to strolling

Map, page 152

San Francisco
California

Los Angeles

For decades San Franciscans have been quietly passing lazy Saturday and Sunday afternoons in the windswept, mist-soaked towns of Marin County, where the trappings of city life seem to fall away as soon as you cross the Golden Gate Bridge. Small wonder: life here seems to fall into a cycle of great repose. In this sparsely populated landscape, you find your way around on two-lane roads, braking sometimes for deer. Dine in old-fashioned, uncrowded restaurants, and sleep in empty bed and breakfasts. Sift for sand dollars on lonely beaches and hike on mossy wilderness paths. Lean into the salt spray and watch the waves pound the rocks. Venture inland into the hillside neighborhoods, and you come across more than a few redwood cottages with stained-glass windows. Is this place for real?

Hot-tub heaven

Encircling San Francisco Bay from the north, and lying at the tip of a metropolitan area of some 5 million inhabitants, Marin County is home to tens of thousands of acres of pristine coastline, unspoiled redwood groves and mountain meadows, untrammeled by development. This luxurious, green belt offers seemingly limitless options for hikers and nature-lovers, as well as those following the self-gratifying regimen of hot tubs, relaxing massage and good food that the stereotypically upscale Marin lifestyle affords.

We don't know for sure what the hot-tub-per-capita ratio is as enter the 21st century, but what will remain constant is that the county offers some of the finest scenic and outdoor experiences anywhere around.

In recent years, **Mount Tamalpais ❽** has become a weekend traffic jam of hikers, mountain bikers, and runners. Still, there seems to be enough beauty to go around. Over 30 miles (48 km) of trails wind their way through 6,000 acres (2,430 hectares), as well as many more miles of hiking in the contiguous watershed lands. (Biker-hiker relations have soured in the last few years. If you're walking, watch your step. If you're riding, beware: bike cops now issue speeding tickets even on the mountain.)

On Mount Tam's lower elevations, often shrouded in fog, are stands of virgin redwood. Above, the mountain's chaparral-covered high slopes jut proudly into the sunshine, overlooking San Francisco Bay and the Pacific. It's a fantastic sight.

At the very base of Mount Tamalpais is wonderful, woodsy **Muir Woods National Monument ❾**. At the turn of the 20th century, the Marin water district planned to condemn a property called Redwood Canyon, cut the timber on it, and with the profits build a dam and reservoir. The scheme so appalled one wealthy

PRECEDING PAGES: a California dreamlife. **LEFT:** sailing past Sausalito. **BELOW:** Muir Woods.

MUIR WOODS
NATIONAL MONUMENT
NATIONAL PARK SERVICE DEPARTMENT OF INTERIOR

*Elephant statue in
Vina De Mar Park,
Sausalito.*

BELOW: view of
San Francisco
and the bay from
Mount Tamalpais.

Marinite, named William Kent, that he bought the land outright, then cleverly deeded the redwood stand to the government, who turned it into a national monument. Kent modestly declined to have the monument named after him, out of deference to his old friend, naturalist John Muir.

About 1 million visitors a year visit the giant sequoia trees here, which grow to 200 feet (61 meters) in height, 16 feet (5 meters) in diameter, live up to 1,000 years, and are spread out through Muir Woods' 300-plus acres (120 hectares). Energetic walkers might be advised to leave parked cars behind and head up the steep slope of Mount Tam on the **Ben Johnson Trail** through deeply shaded glens rife with ferns and mushrooms, past ever-changing groves of bay, tan oaks, madrona and nutmeg.

Marin Headlands

Beyond Mount Tam, Marin County's green belt extends some 50 miles (80 km) to the distant tip of Point Reyes National Seashore. The coastal country, known as the **Marin Headlands** (easily accessible off Highway 1 just north of the Golden Gate Bridge), has miles of coastal and beach-bound trails. Stellar views can be had by driving up the Fort Baker Road.

Muir and Stinson beaches, at the foot of Mount Tamalpais, are popular among anglers hoping to hook surf perch and rockfish, and among bird watchers who want to spy such out-of-the-way creatures as the sooty shearwater, brown pelican, Western grebe, killdeer and millet. When the fog pulls back, the beaches also attract sunbathers. They get crowded only on fine weekends, or when sweltering inland weather drives inland home-dwellers as near to the sea as possible.

Map, page 152

Point Reyes

A triangular peninsula, **Point Reyes ⑩** is separated from the rest of the world by the main fissure line of the San Andreas Fault, which is nudging Point Reyes northeast at an average rate of 2 inches (5 cm) a year. This 65,000-sq.-mile (105 sq.-km) seashore park, which draws over 2 million visitors a year, is one of the most frequented of the country's national parks.

Add quaint inns and diners in the little towns of **Inverness** and **Point Reyes Station**, and it seems as close to untouched paradise as you can get. (Word to the wise: avoid the weekend crowds.) The epicenter of the 1906 San Francisco earthquake was a half-mile from where the main park headquarters now stands on Bear Valley Road. On **Earthquake Trail**, visitors can see where the quake moved one old stone fence a distance of at least 15 feet (5 meters).

To get to the park headquarters and most of the trailheads in the National Seashore, drivers must travel up State Highway 1 past the town of **Olema** to Bear Valley Road. The park is open only to those who are willing to walk or ride a horse. The terrain is varied; much of it very steep. Gloomy forests suddenly open on lush, sweeping meadows. The coast is rockbound with occasional pocket beaches. Hikers may see owls, foxes, raccoons, bobcats, deer and almost every kind of bird imaginable, especially herons, egrets and ducks.

A hike up wind-whipped, 1,400-foot (427-meter) **Mount Wittenburg** rewards out-of-breath hikers with a truly breathless view of the California coast: green-black forests and golden meadows that roll down to a coastline the eye tracks for miles without seeing a soul. Below is **Drake's Beach**, where the famous Elizabethan sea captain Sir Francis Drake is said to have set ashore in 1579 for ship repairs.

At the tip of the Point Reyes promontory perches a **lighthouse** which warns ships away from the treacherous coast. One of the foggiest places in Marin County, it usually has no view at all. When the fog lifts and at the right season, however, it is a good place from which to spot migrating whales.

On the northern edge of the seashore, Pierce Point Road meanders around to several beaches – **Abbott's, Kehoe**, and the most ruggedly dramatic, **McClure's**. These beaches are not recommended for swimming because of the danger of sharks, undertow and rip tides. Better to head for Drake's Beach on the southern side, which is somewhat protected from winds.

Sausalito

With the lighter regimen in mind, the first – or last – stop for most Marin visitors is **Sausalito ⑪**, tucked inside the bay to the east behind the Golden Gate. There is a ferry service to the Sausalito dock from San Francisco. The waterside shops, the warrens of pricey but perfect boutiques, and the houses perched behind them on a steep slope draw inevitable comparisons to Mediterranean *villes* of the Riviera. The Spanish word *saucelito* (meaning "little willow") is said to have been the name's origin. There is, in fact, very little to do in Sausalito except stroll around, have lunch or dinner in one of the restaurants – California Cuisine a speciality – and admire all the boats and pretty people. ❑

BELOW: the streets of Sausalito.

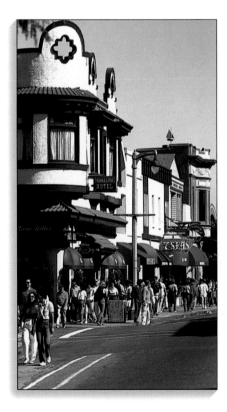

WINE COUNTRY

Map, page 178

Although wine is grown all over the state, it is the Napa and Sonoma Valleys that personify California Wine Country for most visitors

Standing on the summit of Mount St Helena, you can see the vast expanse of emerald vineyards of Napa, Sonoma, Mendocino and Lake counties stretching for miles below your feet. From the redwood groves surrounding the Russian River to the burgundy-hued Mendocino ridges, the Northern California vineyards are renowned for producing some of the finest wines in the world. The area owes its premier grapes to the excellent growing conditions found here: temperate climate and rich, drainable soil. In fact, there is no one California wine county. Wine grapes are grown in 45 of California's 58 counties, and the northern wineries produce just a fraction of the state's total output. Most of the remaining grapes come from the hot, arid San Joaquin Valley, several hundred miles south, and are often used to make modestly-priced "jug" wines.

Some vintners have even discovered pockets of land throughout the rest of California which can match the growing conditions of the great north, among them Monterey's Gavilan Mountain foothills, the south central coast in San Luis Obispo and Santa Barbara counties, and the Temecula Valley outside San Diego. But when most people think of California Wine Country, they think of the areas discussed here: the Napa and Sonoma Valleys.

First vintage

The first wine-makers in California were 18th-century Spanish missionaries who used wine in religious ceremonies. Father Junípero Serra, who founded the state's earliest mission in San Diego in 1769, had no taste for California's indigenous wild grapes and instead imported quality vines from his native Spain. Large-scale vineyards were established around the Los Angeles area in the 1830s by Jean-Louis Vignes, a French vintner. Vignes's wine operation lasted until 1862; after that, California's first commercial vineyards closed and were swallowed by Los Angeles' expanding suburbs.

In the north, it was two men – Father Jose Altimira, founder of the Mission San Francisco de Solano at Sonoma, and General Vallejo, who colonized Sonoma and Napa counties with land grants to his relatives and friends – who first dabbled in California wine-making. But it was Count Agoston Haraszthy who pushed the Sonoma region into wine stardom.

Haraszthy, a flamboyant Hungarian political refugee, began Buena Vista, Northern California's oldest winery, in 1857. He trekked across Europe to cull wine-grape cuttings for California's growers. Ever restless, Haraszthy migrated to Nicaragua, but his career there was unfortunately short-lived; he was killed and eaten by alligators.

He wasn't forgotten, however. One of Haraszthy's protégés, Charles Krug, a German political exile,

PRECEDING PAGES: winery wedding. **LEFT:** grapepickers. **BELOW:** stained glass in Sonoma.

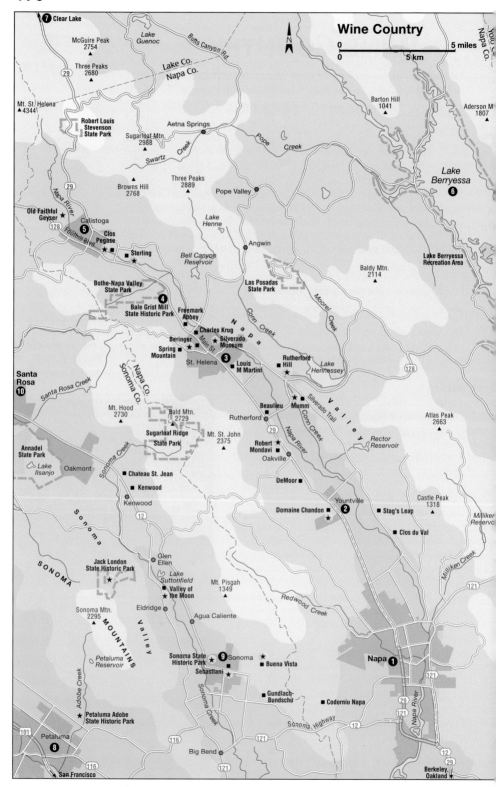

Wine Country

0   5 miles
0   5 km

⑦ Clear Lake

McGuire Peak
2754 ▲

Lake
Guenoc

Butts Canyon Rd.

Lake Co.
Napa Co.

Three Peaks
2680 ▲

29

Mt. St. Helena
▲4344

Robert Louis
Stevenson
State Park

Aetna Springs

Sugarloaf Mtn.
2988 ▲

Swartz   Creek

Pope

Creek

Barton Hill
1041 ▲

Aderson M
1807 ▲

Lake
Berryessa
⑥

Browns Hill
2768 ▲

29

Three Peaks
2889 ▲

Pope Valley

Napa River

Old Faithful
Geyser ★

Calistoga

128   Foothill Blvd.

⑤ Clos
Pegase
★ ■ Sterling

Lake
Henne

Angwin

Bell Canyon
Reservoir

Baldy Mtn.
2114 ▲

Lake Berryessa
Recreation Area

Bothe-Napa Valley
State Park

④ Bale Grist Mill
State Historic Park

Freemark
Abbey ■

Las Posadas
State Park

Moorel Creek

Charles Krug ■

Beringer ■   ★ Silverado
Museum

Spring
Mountain ■ ★

St. Helena

③ ■ Louis
M Martini ■

Main St.

Corn Creek

N a p a

Rutherford
Hill ★

Lake
Hennessey

128

Santa
Rosa
⑩

Santa Rosa Creek

Napa Co.
Sonoma Co.

Mt. Hood
2730 ▲

Bald Mtn.
2729 ▲

Rutherford ●

Beaulieu ■   ★ Mumm

Silverado Trail

V a l l e y

Atlas Peak
2663 ▲

Sugarloaf Ridge
State Park

Mt. St. John
2375 ▲

Robert ★
Mondavi ■

29

Oakville

Corn Creek

Napa River

Rector
Reservoir

Annadel
State Park

Lake
Ilsanjo

Oakmont

■ Chateau St. Jean

■ Kenwood

Kenwood ●

12

DeMoor ■

Domaine Chandon ■

Yountville ●
②

Stag's Leap ■

Castle Peak
1318 ▲

Milliker
Reservo

■ Clos du Val

S o n o m a

SONOMA

Jack London
State Historic Park
★

Glen
Ellen ●

Lake
Suttonfield

Valley of
★ the Moon

Mt. Pisgah
1349 ▲

Redwood Creek

Milliken Creek

121

Sonoma Mtn.
2295 ▲

MOUNTAINS

Eldridge ●

Agua Caliente

V a l l e y

Adobe Creek

Petaluma
Reservoir

Sonoma State ★
Historic Park   ⑨ ● Sonoma   ★
Sebastiani ■   ★
★

■ Buena Vista

Napa ①

121

★ Petaluma Adobe
State Historic Park

■ Gundlach-
Bundschu

■ Codorniu Napa

29

121

Napa River

101

Petaluma

⑧

116

Sonoma Creek

121

Sonoma Highway

12

121

Big Bend ●

San Francisco

116

121

12

Berkeley,
Oakland ▼

29

opened Napa Valley's first commercial winery in 1861. And by the 1880s, valley wines were winning medals in Europe. The advent of Prohibition nearly decimated this blossoming industry. Following repeal of Prohibition in 1933, Beaulieu Vineyard's Georges de Latour, the Mondavi family and others began resurrecting the wine industry.

In the 1960s, a wine boom began as large corporations marketed vintage-dated varietal wines at reasonable prices, and small, privately-owned wineries produced more expensive, estate-bottled wines at higher costs. Old-time wine-making families were joined by oil barons, engineers, doctors and actors who revitalized old wineries and opened new ones. Many vintners began exploring the regions beyond the Napa-Sonoma Valleys and they established premier wineries elsewhere. By 1976, California wines were beating French vintages in European tastings.

Map, page 178

Napa County

Wineries, delicatessens, restaurants and country inns lie close together in compact **Napa Valley** (*napa* meaning "plenty" in the local Indian dialect) and the little town of **Napa ❶**. Although rural, the area's mix of San Francisco socialites, titled Europeans, semi-retired Hollywood directors and producers gives Napa County a genteel, wealthy, if sometimes slick, aura. A 30-mile (48-km) thrust of flatland between the pine-forested Mayacamas Mountains and the buff-colored Howell Mountains, the Napa Valley is pinched off in the north by **Mount St Helena**. The valley's expanses of vineyards are broken up by farmhouses, stone wineries and a series of towns stretched along State Highway 29, "The Great Wine Way." Strict land-control measures have kept valley development

ABOVE AND BELOW: grapes: after and before.

A WINE PRIMER

Wines begin at the crusher, where the juice is freed from the grapes. Red wines are created when the grape skin and pulp are put into the fermenting tank, where yeast is added to convert sugar to alcohol and carbon dioxide. Grape skins are pressed to extract more juice, then the reds are aged in stainless steel or wooden tanks. The wine is clarifed, then aged further before bottling.

White wines are made from the fermentation of the juice alone, drawn off from the grapes immediately after crushing. Yeast is added, and fermentation occurs in stainless steel tanks. Leaving the yeast in creates very dry wines; stopping yeast action makes sweeter wines. Champagne, or sparkling wine, begins the same way, then undergoes a second fermentation. The carbon dioxide is trapped within the bottle, hence the heady bubbles.

Most wineries are open 10am–4pm daily; some are by appointment only. It's a good idea to try a tour (usually 1–2 hours) and a tasting at one of the larger wineries, then follow that up with tasting-room stops at a few of the smaller wineries. For more information and a list of local wineries, contact Napa Valley Tourist Information at 1310 Napa Town Center, tel: 707-226 7459 and Sonoma Valley Tourist Information, 453 1st Street E., tel: 707-996 1090.

confined to the towns and the freeway south of Yountville, but these have also escalated land prices.

The town of Napa is mainly an administrative center, so wine country itself begins in earnest at **Yountville ❷**, where the vineyards abut the village's historic, renovated brick and stone buildings. Yountville's city-park picnic stop is across from George Yount's grave at the pioneer cemetery. One of General Vallejo's beneficiaries, Yount received his 11,000-acre (4,450-hectare) land grant for roofing Vallejo's Petaluma adobe – surely one of history's most lucrative contracting deals. **Domaine Chandon Winery** (tel: 707-944 2280) just west of town is French throughout; in deference to Gallic law, the champagne is called sparkling wine. The winery, owned by Chandon of Moët and Chandon fame, makes sparkling wine in the *méthode champenoise*; that is, it is fermented in the same bottle from which it is poured. The outdoor restaurant is good, too. Just north of Oakville is the **Robert Mondavi Winery** (tel: 707-259 9463), a huge, sleek operation, as befits such a famous local name. Guided tours only.

St Helena

The undisputed capital of the wine country is **St Helena ❸**, noted for its 40 (or thereabouts) wineries, historic stone buildings, picnic parks, chic shops, pricey restaurants and country inns. The **Silverado Museum** is stuffed with Robert Louis Stevenson memorabilia – collectables like first editions of his work and souvenirs of his global jaunts. South of town, the **Louis M Martini Winery** (tel: 707-963 2736), run by one of the valley's oldest wine-making clans, offers reasonably-priced wines in an unpretentious setting. Two historic wineries lie just north of St Helena. Jacob and Frederick started the **Beringer Vineyards**

BELOW: the Rhine House at Beringer Vineyards.

tel: 707-963 7115) in 1876, modeling the Rhine House (1883) after their ancestral estate in Mainz, Germany. They dug limestone caves for ageing wine. Today's winery, owned by Nestlé (yes, the chocolate people), features Fumé Blanc and Cabernet Sauvignon in the mansion tasting room. Outside, spacious lawns and a regal row of elms fronts the winery. The building of the other founding father, **Charles Krug Winery** (tel: 707- 963 5057), dates from 1874. The lavish Greystone building nearby was the world's largest stone winery when it was erected in 1889 by mining magnate William Bourn; today, the mansion is run by the California headquarters of the **Culinary Institute of America**, a brilliant cooking school with a restaurant that is open to visitors (professional chefs). To clear your head and take a break from wine tasting, the **Bale Grist Mill State Historic Park ❹** is three miles north of St Helena.

Between Bale Grist and the town of Calistoga are two excellent places to stop: **Sterling Vineyards** (tel: 707-942 3344) – part-Spanish mission, part-fantasy – reigns over the upper valley atop a knoll. A tram whisks visitors 300 ft (91 meters) up for a self-guided tour. The tram fee is applicable toward the purchase of Sauvignon Blanc and other wines. Close by is **Clos Pegase** (tel: 707-942 4981), designed in 1986 by architect Michael Graves in sleek, modern style. Clos Pegase is known almost as much for its art collection as for its wines.

The one-street town of **Calistoga ❺** is a gem, wooden hangings shading the shopfronts give it a Wild West feel. In fact, Calistoga is a spa town, rich in mineral springs and hot, therapeutic mud. A variety of low-key treatment centers are scattered around town, busy making beautiful Californians even more beautiful. Two miles north of town, **Old Faithful Geyser** (tel: 707-942 6463) spouts jets of boiling water high into the sky every so often. Although the tickets are somewhat expensive for what takes place, there are tables inside the little waiting area, so you can have a pleasant picnic while waiting for the water to take off. Just west is the disappointing **Petrified Forest**, where redwoods were turned to stone millions of years ago.

Calistoga is surrounded by wineries, far too many to mention. Of note for its historic (1882) lakeside setting with a Chinese feel, however, is **Chateau Montelena** (tel: 707-942 5105), which produces classic Chardonnay and Cabernet Sauvignon. A limited number of reservations are accepted for the picnic sites on Jade Lake in view of the pagoda; if you're an organized kind of wine drinker, booking one of these in advance of a visit would be well worthwhile.

The Silverado Trail

Running alongside State 29 between the towns of Napa and Calistoga, the **Silverado Trail** joins with the highway as the route into Lake County's resort and wine region. Built as the road from Mount St Helena's cinnabar mines to Napa's river docks, it is an elevated, two-lane road above the valley floor offering panoramic views, uncrowded wineries (most with picnic areas) and hidden valleys deep in the Howell Mountains. **Stag's Leap**, a rocky promontory near Yountville where a 16-point Roosevelt elk once plunged to its death, overlooks the award-winning **Stag's Leap Wine Cellars** (tel: 707-944 2020) and **Clos du Val** (tel: 707-259 2200).

Map, page 178

Domaine Chandon has landscaped grounds and a museum devoted to champagne.

BELOW: lake walk at Chateau Montelena near Calistoga.

Wine-making has attracted a wide variety of people from all over the US.

Towards St Helena, a popular stop is the **Rutherford Hill Winery** (tel: 707-963-7194), an ark-like structure with picnic grounds and Chardonnay, Cabernet Sauvignon and Zinfandel wines.

St Helena is also the turn-off to a warm-water paradise. The tragedy-ridden Berryessa family lost sons and soil in the Mexican War; today, their Napa land grant is better known as **Lake Berryessa ❻**, reached via State 128 from St Helena or State 121 from Napa. Fishermen pull in trout, bass and catfish, while sailors, waterskiers, campers and swimmers have their choice of several resorts around this lake, which has more shoreline than Lake Tahoe.

Back on State 29 and past **Robert Louis Stevenson State Park,** the road heads towards **Lake County** and its bold, friendly, visitor-seeking wineries scattered around **Clear Lake ❼**, California's largest natural lake. (Lake Tahoe lies partly in Nevada.) Besides producing Cabernet Sauvignon, Zinfandel and Sauvignon Blanc grapes, Lake County is famous for Bartlett pears and walnuts. Resorts and campgrounds ring the lake, and there's good walking in **Clear Lake State Park** at the foot of conical **Mount Konocti**, an extinct volcano.

Sonoma County

BELOW: olive oil is now the region's second produce.

A patchwork of country roads, towns, orchards, ridges and hills is an apt description of Sonoma, west of Napa and only about one hour's (jam-free) drive from San Francisco. US 101, the wine country's only freeway, traverses the north-south length of **Sonoma County**, entering it near **Petaluma ❽**. The freeway continues on through Santa Rosa, Healdsburg (gateway to the Alexander, Dry Creek and Russian River valleys) and Cloverdale, which is located on the Mendocino County border.

The **Sonoma Valley** is steeped in wine, wineries (about 35), literary and political history. *Sonoma* is a Patwin Indian word meaning "Land of Chief Nose," after an Indian leader with a prominent proboscis. Vallejo romanticized it as the "Valley of the Moon," and author Jack London took up the call with a book about frazzled urbanites rejuvenated by clean country living. State 12 runs the length of the valley, passing through the towns of Sonoma and Kenwood.

Father Altimira founded California's last mission, **San Francisco de Solano**, in 1823. Vallejo set up the town in 1835, making **Sonoma** ❾ the northernmost outpost of a Catholic, Spanish-speaking realm that, at its peak, extended all the way to the tip of South America. It briefly became a republic after the Bear Flag Revolt in 1846, when Americans stormed Vallejo's home. Haraszthy's wine-making innovations at Buena Vista Winery a decade later forced residents to recognize the region's vinicultural potential. The **Sonoma Plaza**, the largest in California, today dominates this attractive town. Several restored adobes ring the plaza and nearby streets, including the mission, Vallejo's old house **Lachryma Montis** and the **Sonoma Barracks**, all known as the **Sonoma State Historic Park**. The town is a pleasant place, relaxed and well-heeled.

Two blocks from the plaza stand **Sebastiani Vineyards** (tel: 707-938 5532), some of the land dating from mission days. This winery is one of the largest and most popular in Sonoma and is still in the hands of the Sebastiani family. East of Sonoma, **Buena Vista Winery** (tel: 707-938 1266) has old-style connections with Count Haraszthy. South of town, the Gundlach and Bundschu families were involved in wine-making for more than 125 years; **Gundlach-Bundschu** (tel: 707-938 5277) produces wines that are exported around the globe. Nearby, the pricey, beautifully decorated **Sonoma Mission Inn and Spa** (tel: 707-938 9000) offers health and fitness facilities, and tasty meals.

The **Valley of the Moon Winery** (tel: 707-996 6941), north on State 121, occupies part of George Hearst's 19th-century vineyards (George was the father of William). Today, these vineyards produce a fine Zinfandel. North on State 1 are two fine wineries in Kenwood. **Kenwood Winery** (tel: 707-833 5891) features Zinfandel, Cabernet Sauvignon and Chenin Blanc. Chardonnay lovers head for **Château St Jean** (tel: 707-833 4134), with its medieval-style tower and fine Johannisberg Riesling.

Famed botanist Luther Burbank picked the area around **Santa Rosa** ❿ on State 12 as "the chosen spot of all the earth" to conduct his plant experiments. He developed more than 800 new plants, including many fruits, vegetables and flowers, yet relished few of them except asparagus. Visitors can tour the **Luther Burbank home and gardens** (home open only certain days April to October, but the gardens are open all year round). Children will want to head for Santa Rosa's **Snoopy's Gallery**, selling the widest range of Snoopy products in the world, thanks to the fame of Santa Rosaite and dog creator Charles Schultz.

The town's trinity of adjoining parks form a 5,000-acre (12,000-hectare) urban oasis with a children's amusement park and lake in **Howarth Park**; camping, picnicking and boating in **Spring Lake Park**, and hiking and equestrian trails in **Annadel State Park**. ❑

Map, page 178

BELOW: Sonoma; the word means Land of Chief Nose.

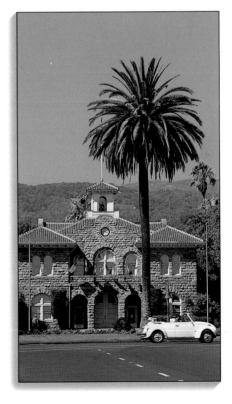

SACRAMENTO

*California's state capital was an important cutural center
even before the discovery of gold made it a mecca
for miners hell-bent on making fortunes*

Map, page 112

E ven as the state's capital city, Sacramento has always lived in the long shadows of prominence and popularity cast by San Francisco and Los Angeles. Located about two hours north of San Francisco, nestled in the middle of California's 500-mile (805-km) long Central Valley, this once hot and dusty cow town has endured the same dubious distinction that author Gertrude Stein once bestowed on the city of Oakland: there is no *there*, there. At one time, there was at least *gold* to be found here, which was what first put Sacramento on the map. A town called John Sutter's New Helvetia Colony did exist here earlier, but it wasn't until 1848, when James Marshall discovered gold deposits in the nearby Sierra foothills, that it became a substantial draw for goldrush settlers.

The town grew up where the American and Sacramento rivers join, where steamers from San Francisco let off passengers headed for the gold fields. From the ensuing Gold Rush emerged Sacramento, which had been named the state capital in 1845. Sacramento was also the western terminus of the Pony Express, then later of the Transcontinental Railroad.

Today, the area surrounding **Sacramento** ⑪ is home to more than a million people, countless industrial parks, spacious, tree-lined parks, expansive shopping malls, suburban tracts and a tangle of multi-lane highways that joins it all together. But even when the locals speak about going to "the city," they often mean San Francisco. Until comparatively recently, in fact, Sacramento was the ultimate cow town, a nice, big, prosperous, comfortable, tree-shaded cow town.

High temperatures

In contrast to its glamorous coastal neighbor, Sacramento is a blazing furnace in midsummer, with temperatures often passing 100°F (38°C) for days at a time. But the weather can still be pleasant, as humidity is low, it seldom rains for long, and the prevailing wind is a marine breeze from San Francisco Bay that cools the nights. In the winter, the city, which lays low in the 150-mile (240-km) long Sacramento Valley, is a resting bed for thick tule fog, which, like the summer sun, can last for many weeks.

In recent years, Sacramento has joined the ranks of progressive, major-league US cities, becoming a serious player in Pacific Rim trade, as well as the smallest American city to build a light-rail commuter transit line. Sacramento also added a National Basketball Association franchise, the Kings, to its entertainment line-up, and, in 1989, became the first American city to close a nuclear power plant by a vote of the people.

Beneath the imposing facade of Sacramento's mirrored-glass office buildings and slightly away from all the traffic lies a distinct image of the old West. Tucked

PRECEDING PAGES: exhibit from the Railroad Museum. **LEFT:** California State Capitol. **BELOW:** Governor's Mansion.

*Old Sacramento:
both the Pony
Express and the
Transcontinental
Railroad stopped
here on the way to
San Francisco.*

BELOW: reliving
the Wild West.

just below the fork of the Sacramento and Americans rivers is **Old Sacramento**, where the old Pony Express and Transcontinental Railroad stations have been fully restored. Stop off at the **Visitor's Center** (1100 Front Street, tel: 916-442 7644) for a list of the sites, which include the **California State Railroad Museum**, with over 50 restored engines; the **Sacramento History Center**, a reproduction of the 1854 City Hall and Water Works building; and the **Crocker Art Museum**, the oldest art museum west of the Mississippi River, with its constantly changing exhibits and its pleasant, relaxed ambience.

Elsewhere in downtown Sacramento you'll find the interesting and nicely restored **California State Capitol**, which is surrounded by the 40-acre (16-hectare) **Capitol Park**. This manicured arboretum has a vast collection of California flora and examples of plants from many different climates and continents. A 400-seat IMAX **theater** has recently opened next to the **Convention Center**. Daily tours of the Capitol building are offered on the hour. Also, while downtown, don't miss the handsome, old **Governor's Mansion**, an 1877 Victorian building where 13 California governors lived between 1903 and 1967.

Now almost overtaken by suburbs, **Sutter's Fort** (2701 L Street, tel: 916-324 0539; admission charge) was once one of the most important in the West. It was an employee of John Sutter's who discovered gold in 1848, but 11 years earlier Sutter had already established the fort as a rest stop and refueling station for immigrants crossing the frontier from the east. The present site, which includes a prison and a bakery, has been reconstructed to give one of the most authentic pictures of pioneer life in the state.

Seasonal events in Sacramento have also lent it big-city prominence. The **Dixieland Jazz Jubilee**, held each May in Old Sacramento, is the world's larg-

Map,
page 112

est celebration of dixieland jazz, featuring more than 120 bands from around the world. The highlight of the summer is the **California State Fair**, a colorful occasion which attracts thousands of people from all over the county. It runs for around 18 days before Labor Day at California State Exposition, the city's outdoor exposition facility.

During the fall months, the excellent and well-attended **Sacramento Blues Festival** draws the biggest names in the business, while a drive up Highway 50 to the east brings you to the **Apple Hill Growers Festival** held in the town of Camino, where scores of apple ranches offer their finest fruits and pies for public consumption.

River recreations

When the temperature gets too hot to handle, take the cue of thousands of houseboaters, waterskiiers, anglers and sailors, and head south on Highway 5 or 99 toward the **Sacramento River Delta**, where hundreds of miles of interconnected river channels percolate slowly toward San Francisco Bay and the Pacific Ocean. The *Delta King* is a moored paddle-steamer operating as a hotel and restaurant. This river country contains hundreds of islands, as much of the area is accessible only by water. Still, even land-locked car passengers can choose from a variety of charming olde-worlde towns such as **Walnut Grove** ⓬ and the 80-year-old Locke.

Locke ⓭, created by Chinese laborers then building the railroads, has a porticoed street with wooden sidewalks that is right out of the Old West. The deepwater port of **Stockton** ⓮, the "Gateway to the Delta," has 1860s homes, the **Haggin Museum**, which is full of local history, and several wineries. ❑

BELOW: Sutter's Fort was an important cultural center prior to the Gold Rush.

SAN JOAQUIN VALLEY

*The Valley is the lifeline of California, while Fresno is the
only community in the United States to be
within an hour's drive of three national parks*

Map,
page 112

Stuck between the brash, self-indulgent coast and the awe-inspiring
Sierras, the San Joaquin Valley suffers the kind of image problem more
associated with the Midwest than the Golden State.

That's because, in many ways, it *is* the Midwest. Perhaps as many as 500,000
so-called "Okies" – the Dust Bowl victims of the Great Depression that gave
life to John Steinbeck's *The Grapes of Wrath* – migrated here. Like ants on a
honey trail, they piled into overloaded flivvers and streamed west on old Route
66, through the chalk-dry Mojave Desert, past "bum barricades," and the abuse
heaped on them by native Californians.

What became of them? One-eighth of the current California population – or
nearly 3.75 million residents – claim Okie ancestry, and the core of that gritty,
family-based community is still here in the heart of the San Joaquin. Stop by
any town in San Joaquin Valley and, as one Dust Bowl survivor said himself,
"You might as well be in Tulsa or Little Rock or Amarillo… Same music, same
values, same churches, same politics."

The valley

Though its name is often mistakenly applied to California's entire Central Valley, the San Joaquin comprises just the southern two-
thirds of that 450-mile (720-km) long, 50-mile (80-km)
wide basin. It follows the course of the **San Joaquin
River**, flowing south to north, to the Sacramento-San
Joaquin Delta, where both rivers empty into San Francisco Bay.

Mostly treeless, the valley doesn't at first appear to
offer much to an outsider. Interstate 5, running the
length of it, is the main link between Los Angeles and
the Bay Area, and the east-west routes to Lake Tahoe
and the Sierras all cross the valley. So it can only sell
itself by virtue of being in the middle of it all. Fresno,
for instance, boasts of being the only community in the
United States within little more than an hour's drive of
three national parks.

The San Joaquin *is* known for some unpleasant natural phenomena. Valley fever – a little-known respira-
tory illness – is spread when strong winds stir up the
spores of a fungus indigenous to the arid soil in parts of
the valley. And in December and January, dense "tule"
fog blankets the area for days at a time, making driving
around hazardous.

But its second-class status bothers San Joaquin Valley
residents very little. The business of the valley is farming, and it succeeds at that like few other spots on earth.
Agriculture, after all, is California's biggest industry,
and more than half of its $14 billion a year in farm
goods is produced in the San Joaquin. Fresno County

LEFT:
working ranch.
BELOW: time
for lunch at the
Fresno County Fair.

alone accounts for some $2 billion of that, making it the number one farming county in America. The valley's soil, covering more than a million irrigated acres, supports some of the most productive farming in the world.

Recently, with substantial growth in population, the area's cities have experienced a boom as commercial and manufacturing centers. But employment in the valley is most closely tied to farming and rainfall, and it is the abundance of that most precious of the state's resources – water – that makes the San Joaquin Valley a recreational as well as an agricultural heartland. Aside from the Sacramento River Delta and the mammoth irrigation projects it supports, several great rivers flow through the area – the San Joaquin, the **Stanislaus**, the **Tuolumne**, the **Merced**, the **Kings** and, farther south, the **Kern**. Most are renowned for outstanding – and occasionally terrifying – stretches of whitewater rafting. This sport is for serious enthusiasts only, but there are gentler stretches of water where the faint-hearted will also feel at home.

It doesn't take long to see that the valley is the lifeline of California. An hour out of San Francisco going eastward, I-580 crosses **Altamont Pass**, one of the windiest spots on the coast. It is marked by an exquisitely rural sight – a windmill farm, overhead power lines and dairy cows peacefully coexisting. The wind may be only 16 mph but the turbines are driven at ten times that speed, effortlessly creating electricity. As the descent begins, the highway crosses a branch of the **California Aqueduct**. Almost immediately the freeway is full of trucks hauling bottled tomato catsup, ripe golden melons or crates of canned peaches.

Like much of California, **Modesto** ⑮ is the creation of Leland Stanford's Central Pacific Railroad. The Tuolumne River runs almost unnoticed through the southern fringes of town. A turn-of-the-century steel arch along the main

ABOVE:
aviation sticker.
BELOW:
harvesting corn.

thoroughfare promotes the town's virtues: "Water, Wealth, Contentment, Health." As in most of the valley, food is king – not food eating but food producing. A "Gourmet Taste Tour" includes stops at an almond exchange, a mushroom farm, a cheese processor, a Hershey chocolate plant and local wineries.

Map, page 112

Halfway between Modesto and Fresno, **Merced** ⓰ is a major access point to Yosemite. The biggest attraction Merced can call its own may be **Castle Air Force Base**, where lumbering B-52s provide a somewhat chilling background to the **Castle Air Museum's** collection of vintage fighters.

Fresno

The sleeping giant of central California is **Fresno** ⓱. From a train station by the edge of a wheatfield, it has become a city with 11 freeway exits and rows of high-rises. The financial and cultural, as well as the service and commercial center of the San Joaquin Valley, it is also as ethnically diverse as any city, with large Mexican, Asian, Armenian and Basque communities. Cultural institutions include the **Metropolitan Museum of Art, Science and History**, the **Community Theater** and the **Fresno Philharmonic Orchestra**.

For people with children **Roeding Park**, right off State 99 in west Fresno, features a number of family amusements – a zoo, a Playland with rides, and Storyland, a quaint walk-through village where plaster fairytale figures tell their story. **Woodward Park** in central Fresno has a Japanese Garden and a bird sanctuary. But the most bizarre attraction is **Forestiere Underground Gardens**, 5021 Shaw Avenue. The gardens were once the beloved domicile of sculptor-horticulturist Baldasare Forestiere, who single-handedly carved out the maze of 100 rooms, passageways and courtyards over a period of 40 years.   ❑

BELOW: melon farmer displays his produce.

YOSEMITE AND THE HIGH SIERRA

Map, page 112

It's one of America's most visited national parks, which means massive congestion in summer. But, out of season, Yosemite is magnificent and magical

The idea of getting away from it all can seem like a cruel joke as you stand in yet another line in the crowded valley, the heart of Yosemite. Is this any way to celebrate the park's beauty, jostled and jammed together in a supposed wilderness setting?

Unfortunately, if you're one of the 3½ million annual visitors to its 760,917 acres (308,000 hectares) of parkland – most of whom end up in the 7-sq.-mile (11-sq.-km) Yosemite Valley – **Yosemite National Park** ❶ can certainly feel like any other urban vacation, complete with overflowing parking lots, elbow-to-elbow shuttle buses and packed grocery stores. But 94 percent of its area is designated wilderness and, to experience it properly, you have to get out on a trail, preferably one that isn't paved. Alternatively, visit one of the following parks in those overheated summer months, and come back to Yosemite earlier or later in the year.

PRECEDING PAGES: sunset over Half Dome, Yosemite. **LEFT:** backpacker in Kings Canyon. **BELOW:** General Sherman Tree, Kings Canyon.

Sequoia and Kings Canyon

It is tempting to dismiss **Sequoia National Park** ❶ and **Kings Canyon National Park** ❷ as Yosemite but without Yosemite Valley. Judging from the statistics, many California travelers do just that. In any given year, over 3 million visitors converge on Yosemite; the comparable figure for Sequoia/Kings Canyon is barely 400,000. (Although Sequoia and Kings Canyon parks were established separately, their adjoining areas are administered as one unit, and thought of together.)

Even though 7,000-feet (2,130-meter) deep Kings Canyon exceeds Yosemite Valley in sheer vertical relief, and the sequoia forests of the southern park are larger and more numerous than Yosemite's groves, the absence of waterfalls and striking rock formations make them pale alongside their more celebrated northern cousin. The result is a national park bereft of the most common national park headaches and reason enough for those seeking solitude to beat a hasty path to the entry station.

Much more so than Yosemite, Sequoia/Kings Canyon is a wilderness park, with only two developed areas near its western boundaries. The back-country extends east across the west slopes of the Sierras as far as the crest of the range, encompassing the headwaters of the Kern and San Joaquin rivers and the highest Sierra summits, including Mount Whitney.

Ironically, a majority of the park's mountain trails are most easily reached from trailheads out of Lone Pine, Big Pine and Bishop on the Sierra's east side, a 250-

In 1864, pressure on the legislature resulted in the Yosemite Grant, the first attempt in the nation's history to preserve an area of scenic beauty from exploitation.

mile (400-km) drive from park headquarters near **Three Rivers**. As in Yosemite park, permits are required for overnight back-country camping. The most scenic approach to the Kings Canyon section of the park, State 180, begins in the sprawling agricultural city of **Fresno**. A 52-mile (84-km) drive from there through the Sierra foothills leads to the **General Grant Grove**, a stand of massive 3,000-year-old sequoia trees notable for the wide-open parkland that surrounds their bases.

Thirty-eight miles (61 km) past the Grant Grove (where campground sites are available by advance reservation), State 180 drops into Kings Canyon at **Cedar Grove**. In contrast to Yosemite Valley, this gaping chasm is V- rather than U-shaped; the smaller flow of the **Kings River** has yet to deposit enough alluvium to level out the canyon's floor. Cedar Grove offers idyllic camping and fishing; rustic lodging is also available. Two trailheads lead north and east toward the High Sierra, but the 6,500-foot (1,980-meter) climbs on south-facing (and sun-broiled) slopes are only for the fit and experienced.

After backtracking to Grant Grove, visitors can proceed into the Sequoia section by following State 198 south for 28 miles (45 km) to **Giant Forest**. A short nature trail leads to the **General Sherman Tree**, a redwood much loved by photographers, who like to pose very small persons next to the very tall tree for contrast. The tree is believed to be the earth's largest living thing.

Hotel rooms, restaurants, a grocery store and a visitor center make Giant Forest the closest thing to an urban center in the area. Three campgrounds lie a few miles farther south on State 198. The road continues southward past good camping and boating at **Lake Kaweah**, and drops back into the San Joaquin Valley at **Visalia**, 50 miles (80 km) from the park boundary.

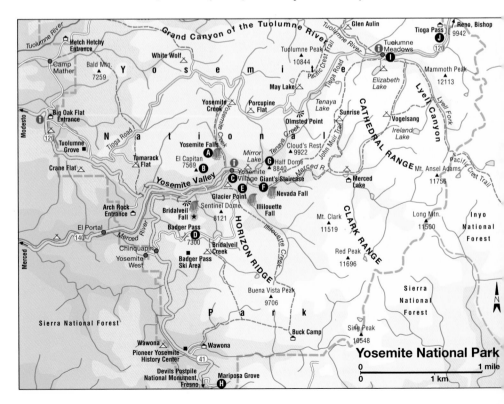

Yosemite National Park

Yosemite: a holy place

A holy place is exactly what Yosemite (*yo-SEH-mih-tee*) Valley was to its original inhabitants, the Ahwahneechee Indians. Because of its isolation, the tribe managed to keep its mountain paradise a secret from whites until 1851, a full year after California attained statehood, when the US Cavalry arrived and herded the natives across the Sierras to a barren reservation near Mono Lake. As with much of the American West, subjugation of the Indians paved the way for settlement. During the decade following its "discovery", Yosemite Valley was fenced, farmed and logged by homesteaders.

Map, page 198

Visitors, drawn by newspaper and magazine accounts of Yosemite's marvels, were appalled to find cow pastures instead of mountain meadows. With thousands of hotel rooms and nearly 2,000 campground sites, restaurants, supermarkets, liquor stores, gift shops and even a jail, Yosemite Valley has become a textbook example of overdeveloped parkland.

But there is a reason the crowds come in such numbers. Nowhere else in the world are there so many big waterfalls in such a small area, including 2,425-foot (739-meter) **Yosemite Falls ⓐ**, the highest in North America. When Ice Age glaciers scoured out 8-mile (13-km) long, mile-wide Yosemite Valley, they left behind several smaller hanging valleys on either side of the main feature, high but not dry, conduits for free-leaping torrents whose very names suggest their infinite variety: **Ribbon, Bridalveil, Silver Strand, Staircase, Sentinel, Lehamite, Vernal, Nevada, Illilouette**.

In early June, one of the rarest of Yosemite sights – the "moonbow" at the foot of lower Yosemite falls – sometimes appears. It shows up only in the spring, when the falls are running full, and only in the days around the full moon, when

BELOW: Yosemite Falls; view of Yosemite when first entering the park.

the moonlight shines on the spray from the falls, producing a ghostly rainbow. Visitors should note, however, that the falls is often dry out of season.

"Great is granite," wrote New England clergyman Thomas Starr King in 1878, "and Yosemite is its prophet." As the prehistoric ice floes melted and retreated, they exposed the colossal building blocks of the Sierra Nevada, shaped and polished into scenery on a grand scale – **El Capitan ❸, Cathedral Rock, Three Brothers, Royal Arches, Clouds Rest**. In the daredevil world of technical rock climbing, this is the one true mecca.

Getting around

Many feel cars ought to be banned altogether, but in the meantime roads in the east end of the valley near **Mirror Lake** have been restricted to shuttle buses, bicycles and pedestrians. A convoluted one-way traffic pattern almost everywhere else makes driving a masochistic experience, especially in summer. If you can resist the shuttle buses for getting around, arrange to take a guided horseback trip through the valley stables, near **Yosemite Village ❸** (the first large developed area on the Yosemite loop road). Bicycles may be rented at the village and at **Yosemite Lodge** (tel: 559-252 4848), and several bikeway trails make two-wheeled travel the most efficient choice of locomotion. Lodging runs the gamut from inexpensive cabins at the village to the palatial suite atop the **Ahwahnee Hotel** (telephone number as above), with Yosemite Lodge somewhere in the middle.

In summer, Yosemite Valley's singular concentration of natural beauty has its far less felicitous human analogue, complete with overcrowded campgrounds, traffic jams and hour-long waits in cafeteria lines. Although the valley com-

BELOW: rafting in the park, Yosemite.

rises only 8 sq. miles (21 sq. km) of the park's 1,189-sq.-mile (3,080-sq.-km) area, it plays host to more than 90 percent of all Yosemite's overnight visitors. The surest way of seeing Half Dome without an enveloping wreath of smog is during the off-season, September to May. Autumn brings a rich gold to the leaves of the oak trees, and the sun's lowering angle etches the granite domes and spires into sharper relief. Nights are cool, mornings are apple-crisp. Autumn also brings herds of wild deer, migrating to winter forage in the Sierra foothills.

Yosemite Valley is emptiest in winter, when the action shifts to the ski resort of **Badger Pass D**, 21 miles (34 km) away and 3,000 feet (900 meters) higher. Badger's gentle, pine-fringed slopes offer few challenges for accomplished skiers, but prove ideal for family groups and novice-to-intermediate skiers who don't mind the 45-minute commute by car or bus from the valley. But spring is the favorite season of many. Wild flowers carpet the meadows, and the roar of wild water resounds throughout the valley.

Map, page 198

TIP

Wilderness permits, available free of charge at park ranger stations and visitor centers, are required for *all* overnight trips in the Yosemite back-country.

Glacier Point

To the south, State Highway 41 climbs 9 miles (15 km) to **Chinquapin** junction, where a 15-mile (25-km) paved road departs for **Glacier Point E**. From this famed viewpoint, 3,200 feet (975 meters) above the floor of Yosemite Valley, the entire park comes into unforgettable, stomach-clutching focus. No less compelling is the 80-mile (129-km) vista to the east and south, a panorama of lakes, canyons, waterfalls and the rugged peaks of Yosemite's High Sierra. Close at hand are the granite steps of the **Giant's Staircase F**, where Vernal and Nevada falls drop the raging waters of the **Merced River** 320 and 594 feet (98 and 181 meters) respectively.

From Glacier Point, **Half Dome G** is the most prominent landmark, a great solitary stone thumb thrusting skyward. What became of Half Dome's other half? In fact, the dome never had another half of solid rock, only slabs of granite on the sheer north face that were peeled away like onion skin by advancing Ice Age glaciers.

At the height of glaciation, 250,000 years ago, Glacier Point itself lay under 700 feet (213 meters) of ice, and interpretive markers explain how the 2,000-foot (610-meter) thick Merced and Tenaya glaciers ground down from the high country to merge near Half Dome and hollow out vast Yosemite Valley. The mighty glacier filled the valley to its brim, and extended all the way down the Merced canyon to **El Portal**, 15 miles (24 km) to the west.

Five miles (8 km) south of **Wawona**, just inside the park's southern boundary, a short side road leads to the **Mariposa Grove H** of giant sequoias, a preserve containing more than 500 mammoth redwood trees. It was here that John Muir slept under the stars alongside President Theodore Roosevelt, and persuaded the chief executive that the forest should be added to the infant Yosemite National Park. The grove's largest tree, the **Grizzly Giant**, is at least 3,800 years old, 200 feet (60 meters) high and with a girth of 94 feet (29 meters). The best way to experience the trees is on foot, wandering among living things that were already giants when Christ walked the Holy Land.

BELOW: horseriding is often the best way to get around.

Unlike the camp-grounds on the west side of the Sierra, many on the east do not accept advance reservations. All ask that you respect Smokey the Bear, however, and put out your campfires.

BELOW: Lambert Dome and the Tuolumne River, Tioga Road.

If Wawona and the Mariposa Grove are Yosemite's Black Forest, **Tuolumne Meadows ❶** is its Switzerland. Reached by an hour's drive north from Yosemite Valley on the scenic **Tioga Pass ❷**, and situated at 8,600 feet (2,620 meters) above sea level, Tuolumne is the gateway to an alpine wilderness. The only way to see the more remote areas of the back-country is to pick up your feet and hike, with the minimum of creature comforts carried in a backpack that may tip the scales at 50 lbs (23 kg) or more. A less arduous alternative – at least on some of the smoother trails – is to arrange a horsepacking trip, details of which can be discovered locally or by calling Yosemite Park information services.

Tuolumne is also the site of **Tuolumne Meadows Lodge**, central star in the summer constellation of high Sierra camps. Arranged roughly in a circle, about 9 miles (14 km) apart, these six permanent tent camps provide lodging, meals and hot showers to hikers and horsepackers on the popular High Sierra Loop trail. Elevations of the camps vary from 7,150 feet (2,180 meters) to 10,300 feet (3,140 meters), and a night of acclimatization in Tuolumne is recommended before departure. In a typical year, camps are open from June 14 through September 1, with advance booking essential.

The Eastern Sierra

Approached from the west, through the foothills of the Gold Country and on into Yosemite or Sequoia and Kings Canyon, the Sierra Nevada begins gently. Low, rolling hills studded with oak trees give way to pine-blanketed higher hills, which in turn give way to an accelerating crescendo of granite domes, spires and ridges. These culminate in the 13,000- and 14,000-foot (4,000-meter) peaks of the crest. But there is nothing gradual about the Sierra when approached from

e east, up US 395 from Southern California. On the east side, the mountains of
e crest drop precipitously nearly 10,000 vertical feet (3,000 meters) in the
ace of a few miles, a single great front nearly 200 miles (320 km) long. From
'alker Pass at the southern end of the range to Tioga Pass on the eastern
osemite boundary, not a single highway cleaves the scarp, the longest con-
guous roadless area in the United States outside Alaska.

kiers and devils

t **Deadman Summit**, north of June Mountain, US 395 begins a long descent
to Mono Basin, once the site of an inland sea. **Mono Lake ㉑**, the last rem-
ant of that sea, is the oldest continuously existing body of water in North Amer-
a, and islands near the lake's northern shore are breeding grounds for 90
ercent of the world's California seagulls. Eerie calcified rock formations on
e shoreline are called *tufa* and some of the best examples are strikingly pre-
erved at **Mono Lake State Tufa Reserve**.

From May until November, or until the first winter snow falls, the town of
ee Vining on Mono Lake's western shore is the east entry to Yosemite Nation-
Park, via 9,990-foot (3,045-meter) Tioga Pass. From Lee Vining, Tuolumne
Ieadows is a 45-minute drive away; it takes at least two hours to reach Yosemite
alley. Campgrounds are spaced every 15 miles (24 km) or so, and, unlike the
est of the park's sites, are *not* reservable in advance; just show up and see if
ace is available.

North of Mono Lake, the Sierra crest begins to lower, although "lower" in
is case still means snowy summits 11,000 feet (3,350 meters) high. Just un-
er 12 miles (18 km) north of Lee Vining, a graded side road leads 13 miles (21

Maps,
page 198
& 112

BELOW: calcified
rocks rise from
Mono Lake, the
oldest body of
water in North
America.

Map,
page 112

km) to **Bodie State Historic Park ㉒**, which offers both an excellent panoram
of the northern Sierras and a reasonably authentic glimpse into the life of a '49e
boomtown. Once the wildest camp in the West, Bodie was home to a ragtag co
lection of miners and confidence men who made silver fortunes by day an
squandered them by night in opium dens, saloons and bawdy-houses. Both pr
fessional and amateur photographers love Bodie Park, whose eerie, abandone
buildings perfectly evoke an era long past.

Heading south past Tioga Pass is **Devils Postpile National Monument ㉓**
just west of Mammoth Lakes. Its abrupt geometric pickets (80 ft/24 meters hig
350 yards/320 meters long) testify to the power of the twin forces that shaped th
Sierras – fire and ice. There's some camping in summer at **Agnew Meadow**
(just before the monument boundary on State 203) and **Red's Meadows** (ju
after the boundary).

Winter sun fanatics head for **Mammoth Lakes ㉔**, the largest downhill s
resort in America. In the snowy season, Mammoth is where Los Angeles goe
skiing, and it is not uncommon to share lift lines with 20,000 other powd
hounds. On the plus side, Mammoth offers gourmet dining at several eatin
establishments, plus wine and cheese shops.

Owens Valley

Heading south further still, dramatic scenery begins on the shores of **Owe
Dry Lake**, near the hamlet of **Olancha**. To the left, the tawny, unforested pea
of the southern Sierras rise abruptly, cresting in granite pinnacles 12,000
(3,650 meters) high. To the right, across the wide, shimmering lake bed, th
softer, more rounded contours of the somewhat lower **Inyo Range** dissolve in

black and purple foothills. These are the portals
Owens Valley, deepest in America, and "The Land
Little Rain". The vegetation here is hardy desert flo
– scrub oak, mesquite and sagebrush. Owens Valley a
the Inyos receive less than 10 inches (25cm) of ra
every year.

Just past the northern end of the lake bed, 21 mil
(34 km) north of Olancha, State 136 departs east f
Death Valley. Located at this junction is the **Visit**
Center which dispenses maps, information and wilde
ness permits for the extensive public lands under fe
eral jurisdiction. In winter, the center is a mandato
stop for the latest word on campground closures an
road conditions. In the busy summer season, range
will steer travelers to campgrounds where spaces a
still available.

On a patio outside the Visitor Center, telescopes a
trained on the summit of **Mount Whitney ㉕** *(also s
page 347)*, at 14,495 ft (4,418 meters) the highest mou
tain in the United States outside Alaska. A trail leads
the very top of Whitney where portable latrines ha
been set up to cope with the tide of visitors. It's a stre
uous three-day hike (two up, one down), but no techni
cal skills are required, and thousands make the tr
every summer. The hardest part can prove to be acqui
ing a reservation: many Mount Whitney trail permi
are reserved up to a year in advance. For details or mo
information, telephone 415-556 0560.

GOLD COUNTRY

*Many of the towns that straddle the Mother Lode,
California's richest mineral vein, have been expensively
restored to their pioneer glory*

Map,
page 210

San Francisco
California
● Los
Angeles

The Gold Rush may have ended, but it wasn't because they ran out of gold. They just ran out of the gold lying near the top of the ground. As the holes got deeper and more dangerous, the work got harder, slower and more expensive, until finally it was no longer cost-efficient to dig.

Geologists say there is at least as much gold in the Mother Lode today as was taken out in the past 100-odd years. Latter-day gold miners say the 7 million pounds extracted by the old-timers was only 10 percent of the wealth that nature had deposited there. Either way, there is a good deal left – and quite a few people are looking for it. Modern mining operations dig deeper and deeper into the Sierra with automated machinery, but there are still the rough-hewn old-timers who crouch by mountain streams, squinting for the glimmer of gold flakes in shallow tin pans.

There's another 20th-century rush going in the gold country foothills from Mariposa to Nevada City, but it's real estate, not just valuable minerals, that is at stake. Travelers on State Highway 49, Gold Country's main highway, are likely to see more real-estate signs than ghost towns. The modern miner now competes with housing developers – not claim jumpers – for land.

PRECEDING PAGES:
Fiddletown, in the
Mother Lode.
LEFT AND BELOW: the
sparkle in his eye
says "Gold!"

Them thar hills

The placid Gold Country landscape hides its treasures well. In the lowest of the Gold Country foothills, spring begins as early as March. The roadsides from the Central Valley towns of Sacramento, Stockton and Fresno are crowded with wild mustard, an edible plant that adds tang to a salad and covers the beef-cattle grazing land with yellow blossoms. In spring, a succession of wild flowers moves up the hills and turns entire mountain-sides blue and purple with lupine and brodiaea. There are larkspur and popcorn flowers, purple vetch and baby blue eyes, and the maroon of the red bud, a local flowering bush.

Sonora ❶, named for the Mexican state from which many of its first '49ers came, is a city again, one that may be losing a struggle with the real-estate hustlers. But the houses and shopping centers have sprung up because Sonora is as beautiful as it was during the Gold Rush – and its quaint downtown has remained true to the miners' spirit.

In the 1870s, there was a pocket mine at the north end of Sonora where the operators found a vein of nearly pure gold and recovered, they say, $160,000 worth of gold in one day. It was part of *La Veta Madre*, otherwise known as **"the Mother Lode,"** from which the legends sprang. It is the kind of story that still keeps miners at work today, toiling in the dark tunnels.

But, for the most part, it is tourism, not treasure, that

This early satirical portrait of a laden-down, roaming gold-seeker says: A Gold Hunter on his way to California, via St Louis.

plays a key role in the area's resources. A real gem of Tuolumne County these days is the town of **Columbia ②**. Just a few minutes north of Sonora and just off State 49, this old town has been restored as the Columbia State Historic Park (information from 22708 Broadway, tel: 209-532 0150). For those who have traveled in the eastern United States, Columbia can be compared to Williams-burg, Virginia, another restored historical town. Columbia once had a population of 15,000, 50 saloons, competing daily newspapers and at least one church. Nearly $90 million in gold was mined there over a 20-year period. Much of restored Columbia is closed to cars, but the easy layout of the town makes it well worthwhile parking and walking around. The best sites are the Wells Fargo Express Office; the old schoolhouse, used until 1937; and the old city hotel.

Around Columbia, as in many of the Gold Country towns, there are several rock or gold shops whose proprietors may be willing to show visitors where to look for gold and perhaps even teach them how to mine. There are even tour companies that will set up trips to local mines.

Mark Twain lived here

Back on State 49, still headed north, a sign indicates the way to the summit of **Jackass Hill**. It is named for the animals so central to gold prospecting, and it is the place where Mark Twain lived in 1864. The Twain cabin has been recon-structed around the original hearth. During the time Twain lived in the cabin, he wrote one of his most famous yarns, *The Celebrated Jumping Frog of Cala-veras County*. The actual jumping frogs were supposed to have been a bit north in **Angels Camp ③** – and that's where they can still be found.

Angels Camp still harbors the **Angels Hotel**, where Twain is said to have

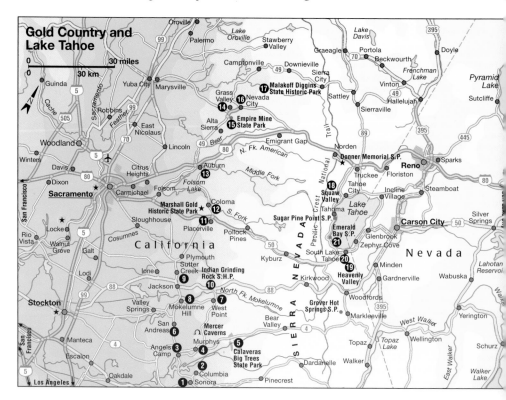

eard the frog story. Better yet, each May the community holds a frog-jumping ontest that attracts thousands of people to the area – so many, in fact, that the only way actually to see a jumping frog is to enter your own in the contest. Any rog more than 4 inches (10 cm) in length is eligible. The wiser course may be to avoid Angels Camp during the week of the frogs. Mark Twain would certainly ave done so. From the Angels Camp area, a detour leads up into the mountains o the town of **Murphys ❹**, a Gold Rush period settlement far enough off the rack to be a natural museum. The excellent **Mercer Caverns**, well worth a visit, re in this area. Farther up State 4 is **Calaveras Big Trees State Park ❺**, with magnificent sequoia trees.

San Andreas ❻ is another town whose present is a triumph of development interests, but whose past is alive with romantic echoes. Black Bart, a real stage-coach bandit, was tried here in 1883 for some of the 28 robberies he allegedly committed. Bart, a San Franciscan with expensive tastes and little income, embarked on a series of polite, bloodless robberies of the gold-laden stages. His hotgun was always unloaded and no one was ever hurt, but he served six years in San Quentin's rough prison. Then he disappeared.

In good weather, the drive from San Andreas to **West Point ❼** on the Mountain Ranch and Railroad Flat roads is beautiful. There have been recent attempts o reopen some of the 500 local mine shafts. A few shafts now crush ore and even welcome visitors. If you stand in the mouth of a mine shaft, even in mid-ummer, you can see your breath condensing in the cold air seeping up from thousands of feet beneath the ground. Modern techniques of deep-rock mining differ little from those used by the '49ers. The gold pan and sluice boxes used by weekend miners are essentially the same tools that were used 100 years ago.

Map, page 210

BELOW: Columbia once had a population of 15,000, plus 50 saloons.

TIP

For those who don't want to spend all their time meditating on history, Coloma is a pleasant place for a raft trip. A number of companies offer one-day and longer trips rafting down the American River.

BELOW: the City Hotel in Columbia.

From West Point, travelers can loop back west to **Mokelumne Hill ❽**, a town once so rich in gold that its claims were limited to 16 sq. ft (about 1.5 sq. meters) According to legend, the lust for wealth ran so high that there was a murder a week here for more than four months. On a more benign note, Mokelumne Hill is the site of the founding of the **E Clampus Vitus Society**, a group devoted to good deeds and good times. The society is still around and active, and generally has an entry in any local parade or fair.

From **Sutter Creek ❾** to Grass Valley, about 75 miles (120 km), the countryside surrounding State 49 is mostly a commuter suburb of Sacramento. For a more authentic look at the old west, drive east to **Chaw'se Indian Grinding Rock State Historic Park ❿** near the town of Jackson, one of the largest Native American sites in the United States. The park and its museum are a celebration of the contributions made by the Miwok tribe.

Placerville gold

At the junction of highways 49 and 50 is **Placerville ⓫**, once called Hangtown because of its chosen method of execution. Placerville was the nexus of wagon, mail, Pony Express and telegraph routes, and consequently a busy and exciting place. Now it may be the only town in America with its own gold mine. The **Gold Bug Mine**, north of town, is located in a public park and is open to visitors for inspection.

North of Placerville on State 49 is **Coloma ⓬**, the birthplace of the Gold Rush. There is a state historic park now at the spot where, in 1848, James Marshall was building a waterway for John Sutter's lumber mill and was distracted by something glittering in the water. The state has reconstructed the mill though not exactly at the same place, since the American River has changed its course in the past century.

Auburn ⓭, at the junction of State 49 and busy Interstate 80, is very much a part of the Sacramento economy. The **Placer County Museum** in Auburn is counted as one of the best in the mountains, with its collections of native Indian materials as well as gold mining paraphernalia. Nearby is the colorful and unusual **Firehouse**.

Auburn is a good place to jump off for a visit to Lake Tahoe (up Interstate 80) with a return via State 20 near **Emigrant Gap**. State 20, the old Tahoe-Pacific Highway, is one of California's great drives. It rejoins State 49 in the Nevada City-Grass Valley area.

Grass Valley ⓮ was the center of the deep mines and there are several splendid places to get a sense of what they were like. Some of them, including the **North Star**, have shafts that go hundreds of feet below sea level. These shafts are now closed and flooded. The **Nevada County Museum** in the town of Grass Valley is good for local history. **Empire Mine State Park ⓯** east of town, is the site of a mine that once produced no less than $100 million worth of gold before it was closed down in the mid-20th century.

Grass Valley is now the center of high-technology industry, most notably the manufacture of equipment for television broadcasting, and is once again a name recognized around the world.

Antique city

Nevada City 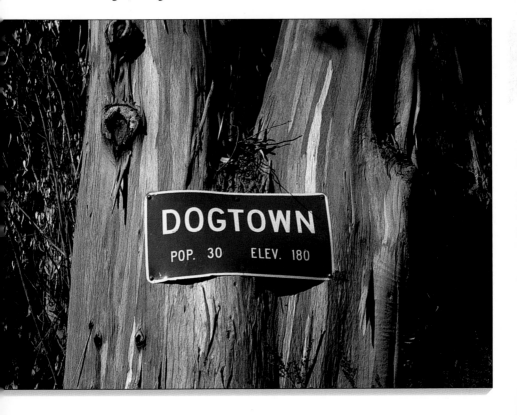 is as old-fashioned as Grass Valley is up-to-date. It is the kind of place that attracted city people early. They busily converted the old factories and miners' stores into restaurants, museums, antique stores and theaters, many of which have been restored. There are a couple of pleasant bars and the **National Hotel** (tel: 530-265 4551) still puts up overnight visitors in rooms tastefully furnished with antiques.

Ten miles (16 km) north of Nevada City is a large state park at the old **Malakoff Diggins** ⑰, a place that generated one of the very earliest pieces of environmental legislation. Visitors to the Malakoff mine can see the effects of hydraulic mining, a method of gold extraction in which high-powered streams of water were directed from cannons at the side of the mountain. This method was highly effective, but it devastated the mountain, and waterways were clogged with mud as far away as San Francisco Bay. The technique was banned in 1884 but the scars, which have been only slightly healed by time, are still grimly awesome.

It's an hour's drive from Nevada City to **Downieville**, a fitting end to a tour of the Gold Country. The country here is higher, cooler and much less crowded than further south. From **Camptonville**, midway along the route from Nevada City, the pretty **Henness Pass Road** veers off into the mountains. In good weather, it is a lovely side trip. There are a number of campgrounds a few miles toward the pass. Downieville itself is almost as perfect as a picture. It is a remote place hemmed in by steep hillsides, with a population of under a thousand people. Despite its seclusion, however, there are a few places for visitors to have a meal or relax for the night, taking in the sweet mountain air. ❑

Map, page 210

BELOW: the isolation of the Wild West can still be found.

DOGTOWN

POP. 30   ELEV. 180

LAKE TAHOE

It's the gambling that makes the headlines, but there's also a wide variety of top skiing in the Lake Tahoe area in winter, and great hiking and biking in summer

Map, page 210

O f Lake Tahoe, the Sierra explorer and America's most famed naturalist John Muir wrote: "A fine place this to forget weariness and wrongs and bad business." Mark Twain was no less impressed. "The lake burst upon us," he wrote in *Roughing It*, describing the moment he reached the summit overlooking Tahoe, a "noble sheet of blue water lifted 6,300 feet (1,920 meters) above the level of the sea, and walled in by a rim of snow-clad mountain peaks… I thought it must surely be the fairest picture the whole earth affords."

Twain might eat his words today. Several communities – and countless casinos, fast-food joints, strip malls, and water- and snow-sports outfitters – now dot the 71-mile (114-km) shoreline of this crystal-blue lake, which straddles Nevada and California, and stands at 6,229 feet (1,898 meters) in the Sierra Nevada, about 50 miles (80 km) southwest of Reno. But in many ways, especially during winter, Tahoe does still possess a unique allure.

When Twain and Muir discovered Tahoe, the lake was as pure and sparkling as the silver being dug out of the nearby Comstock Lode. These days, its blue waters are sometimes green with algae, and its blue skies dimmed somewhat by smog. The indoor attractions (roulette wheels and craps tables) rival the outdoor ones (sun, water and winter snow) for the attention of the travelers, while a seemingly endless array of fast-food outlets, motels, condominiums, video arcades – and, at last count, two miniature golf courses and three McDonald's – cater to their every need.

PRECEDING PAGES, LEFT AND BELOW: winter, summer and night-time activities in Lake Tahoe.

Outdoor attractions

But only a few miles from the furious bustle of the Nevada casinos are wilderness, hiking trails, hidden lakeshore caves, snow-covered backroads ideal for cross-country skiing and quiet beaches that look much the same as when Twain dug a toe into them. Recreation is the lake's lifeblood, and in winter that means downhill and cross-country skiing, and snowboarding. On Friday nights, the weekend exodus from the Bay Area begins. Tens of thousands of cars, skis strapped on their roofs like sections of picket fences, stream up Interstate 80 or US 50 toward the lake.

The largest ski areas are **Squaw Valley** ⑱ (tel: 530-583 0985) at the northwest side of the lake, and popular **Heavenly Valley** ⑲ (tel: 702-586 7000) on the south side. Each has more than two dozen ski lifts and terrain to satisfy skiers of every ability, including novices. (Heavenly now features a "Sky Express" high-speed detachable quad, and two triple chairs, plus expanded snow-making.) Another local favorite, the family-run Sierra Ski Ranch, 12 miles (19 km) west of South Lake Tahoe on Highway 50, has added its third high-speed detachable quad, and snowboarding.

Another way to see the area is from above. Cal-Vada Aircraft Tours (tel: 916-525-7143) take off from Homewood Marina, south of Tahoe City. The Heavenly Tram (tel: 702-586 7000) goes 2000 feet up the mountain from the top of the Ski Run Boulevard in South Lake Tahoe. The Squaw Valley Cable Car (tel: 916-583 6985) also offers great panoramas.

BELOW: sloping off.

Heavenly Valley is the favorite ski area for those who like to duck into the casinos at night, as it is located at **South Lake Tahoe ㉟**, the busiest part of the lake and just a stone's throw from Nevada. For all their commotion, the casinos can actually come in handy for skiers in the evening – most offer inexpensive all-you-can-eat buffet dinners to lure customers to the gambling tables. The preferred buffet is at **Harrah's**, followed by those at **Caesar's Tahoe**, the **High Sierra** and **Harvey's** hotels. There's no law, however, that says a person can't just visit the dining-room, eat his fill after a tough day of skiing, and depart with his fortune still snugly in his pocket.

Most skiers, however, prefer the northern half of the lakeshore on the California side, particularly the area around **Tahoe City**. It's quieter, cleaner and the selection of ski areas is better. In addition to Squaw Valley, skiers can choose **Alpine Meadows, Sugar Bowl, Boreal Ridge** and **Northstar**. The latter caters particularly for families – its gentler slopes keep most of the show-offs away. Boreal, perched on the edge of four-lane Interstate 80, is the easiest to reach. Sugar Bowl is the oldest. Alpine Meadows is preferred by experienced skiers, as runs rated "expert" make up 40 percent of the terrain.

Even if you don't care for skiing, the outdoors is the central focus. To get off the beaten track, **Lake Tahoe Winter Sports Center**, 3071 Highway 50 in Meyers, leads snowmobile tours through a series of meadows, lakes and mountain forest. Wilderness dinners, weddings and overnights in igloos can be arranged. At **Northstar Stables**, off Highway 267 between the towns of Kings Beach and Truckee, visitors can explore the snowy terrain by horse – and sleigh. To take the wintry chill off, try a hot soak at **Walley's Hot Springs Resort**, located 12 miles (19 km) east of South Lake Tahoe on Foothill Road in Genoa.

Cross-country skiing, which is more like a hike in the woods than a flight down a mountainside, is attracting more people each year. The skis are longer and narrower, the uphill stretches can make the legs ache, but the silence and solitude are blessed.

Summertime exploits

Even if there's still snow on the mountaintops, it will likely be hard to choose between outdoor sporting options when the summer sun comes out. Rent in-line skates or a bicycle to explore the local roads, or a mountainbike to blaze down the bare ski runs at Squaw Valley. Several parks and reserves have well-marked hiking trails. The lake offers great fishing, as well as jet-skiing and waterskiing and kayaking. There is usually good river rafting on the nearby **Truckee River**. The local tourist office has information on tour operators and rental shops to help you get going on these activities.

A great way to see Lake Tahoe is to take a ride on one of the large vessels that cruise around the lake all year round. The *Tahoe Queen* (tel: 800-238 2463 or 530-541 3364) is an authentic steam-paddleboat which departs from the Ski Run Marina on the south shore; another paddlewheeler is the *Tahoe Gal* (tel: 800-218 2464), which departs from the North Shore Marina. The *MS Dixie* (tel: 702-588 3508) leaves from Zephyr Cove Marina on the Nevada side of the lake. All offer lunch, dinner and dancing cruises, as well as sightseeing trips along the shoreline and through spectacular Emerald Bay, an isolated, tree-lined wilderness tucked into the southwest corner of the lake.

Hikers and backpackers usually head for **Desolation Wilderness**, a lake-studded area located west of Emerald Bay. Not far away is the well stocked **El Dorado National Forest Visitor Center**, offering orientation programs and guided walks. A wilderness permit must be obtained for backpacking in Desolation Wilderness – it's a popular place that often fills to capacity in summer. The **Granite Peak** area is also good for backpacking, and the extremely pretty **Emerald Bay State Park** ㉑, as well as **DL Bliss** and **Sugar Pine Point** state parks, are excellent for short walks and picnics.

On any summer weekend, joggers and bicyclists take to the roads ringing the lake. The 75-mile (121-km) circle makes a strenuous one-day bike ride or a leisurely two-day trip.

Getting there

Getting to Lake Tahoe is easy and, thanks to the many casinos seeking to lure fresh blood from the Bay Area or even Los Angeles, inexpensive. Package tours (which include accommodation, food and cocktail vouchers, and, sometimes, even some time at the tables) are easy to purchase in the large cities. The drive from San Francisco, where most out-of-towners seem to come from, takes four to five hours in good weather and light traffic. Getting there in the wintertime is a different story: chains should always be carried in case of ice and snow, and drivers should be prepared either to lie on their backs in roadside slush to put them on, or to pay one of the "chain monkeys," young people who cluster on the side of the road hoping to earn money by carrying out the task.   ❑

Map, page 210

BELOW: boating on Emerald Bay.

THE NORTH COAST

*California's huge stands of protected redwood trees
mean that urban civilization has been kept
at bay on this wild coastline*

Map,
page 112

F ew places in America are as wild as California's North Coast. Developers may have tried to replicate Southern California's coastline, but in the upper reaches of the north the elements still rule and the eye can scan miles of majestic coastline and inland hills without spotting a living soul – except perhaps the legendary Sasquatch, the ape-like beast who supposedly roams the redwood forests. Although most towns along Highway 1 are small, visitors are welcome and accommodations plentiful.

The absence of development is partly due to the California Coastal Commission, formed in the 1970s when the state seemed fated to become a 400-mile (644-km) ribbon of private marinas and ocean-view condominiums. The only unchecked development is the Sea Ranch, a chic subdivision north of Marin County designed to blend into the environment. Residents are not allowed to paint their homes or go beyond minimal landscaping.

A comfortable coast

North of **Bodega Bay ㉖**, most of the Sonoma County coast is a state beach, with comfortable access, plenty of parking, thrilling views, no camping, and appropriate beach names like **Mussel Point, Salmon Creek, Hog Back, Shell Beach** and **Goat Rock**. As you travel north on Highway 1 from Bodega Bay, the prevailing scenery is fog, cypress trees, pines, old barns and grazing sheep and cows. As real estate, this grazing land is so valuable that local ranchers are termed "boutique farmers," because they don't really have to farm. They could sell the land for easily more money than they'd make in a lifetime of farming.

"I'd rather look at my cows than count money in a bank," says one North Coast dairyman. "If my cows are happy, I'm happy." The cows, at least, have a million-dollar view. This same man once owned a chunk of Marin County pastureland that was sold a few years back for unknown millions of dollars to film-maker George Lucas for his Skywalker Ranch.

Tourism – as with most of California – is now the growth industry, having overtaken logging and fishing. Although demand for trees and fish is on the increase, the supply is diminishing, as are the people prepared to do the work.

The boats in the Bodega Bay salmon fishery, declared an "economic disaster" in the early 1980s, remain berthed during the salmon season because it is too expensive to cruise for a product that may not be there. As a result, salmon fishermen sell extremely tasty, freshly caught albacore directly from their boats in order to recoup any losses.

The winner in this market may be the camping trav-

PRECEDING PAGES:
flying north by
northwest.
LEFT: Crescent City
fishing fleet.
BELOW: one type of
coastal cuisine.

eler. Fresh barbecued albacore is far better than the deep-fried frozen fish served with professional indifference in tourist cafés along State 1.

North of **Jenner**, State 1 weaves through daily fog, rolling pastures and sudden canyons that drop 1,000 feet (over 300 meters) into the blue and foamy Pacific. The road passes historic **Fort Ross** ㉗, a careful reconstruction of the original fort built by Russian traders in the early 19th century. There are tours, but the best way to see the fort is to stroll through and around on your own. The small Russian Orthodox chapel is worth a special stop.

One compelling way to pass an afternoon in north Sonoma County is to visit the coastal tidepools. At **Stewart's Point State Park** ㉘, a popular place for abalone divers, the pools are accessible at most tides, and there's little risk (present at some North Coast beaches) that the explorer will be swept away by what the California state's warning signs call "sleeper" waves.

Travelers enter Mendocino County just north of Sea Ranch at **Gualala**, notable for its fine old hotel in the center of town. Fifteen miles (24 km) north, a coastal access path leads to **Point Arena**, a tiny bayside beach that comprises several dozen weathered mobile homes, two disintegrating and dangerous piers, and a few shops selling bait and fishing tackle. However, bed and breakfast inns are springing up all along the coast as city dwellers buy up Victorian homes, preserve them, fill them with antiques and surrender with relief to a lifestyle change in the countryside.

The Coast Guard's **Point Arena Lighthouse** ㉙ occupies the point of the US mainland closest to Hawaii. Many ships have crashed near Point Arena. Lots of free literature is available to tell visitors which ships, and where, and what was lost as a result.

B&Bs (bed and breakfast inns) have proliferated so fast in Mendocino, 32 miles north of Point Arena, that the city has passed laws prohibiting any new ones from opening.

BELOW: barbershop in Mendocino.

Preserving its heritage

In a sense, **Mendocino** ㉚ is a victim of its own beauty: it's just too lovely to be ignored. A century-old former logging village, it's set on a long bluff above a small bay and is full of picturesque Victorian structures. The town is now treading the narrow line between "quaint" and "cute."

For a small town with a population under 1,000, Mendocino is hectic. Once visitors find (with difficulty) a place to park, they are confronted with restaurants bearing names like **Whale Watch**, and menus listing such delicacies as "Sempervirens Steak" – a "highly seasoned tofu loaf made with whole grains and vegetables and covered with sautéed mushrooms, onions and jack cheese." Nevertheless, if comfort and good cuisine in the countryside is something you've always wanted to aspire to, Mendocino is difficult to beat. Travelers who want to escape from all this leisure chic can go to two nearby state parks, **Van Damme** and **Russian Gulch**, which offer camping, hiking, bird-watching, fishing, beach-combing and other quiet pleasures.

To the north, the city of **Fort Bragg** ㉛ is the frumpy flipside of Mendocino. It is an unpretentious, working-class, beer-bellied hick town that greets the wayfarer, not with an historical bed and breakfast inn, but with roadside cafés with names like Jerko's Koffee Kup. Fort Bragg's love affair with the architectural present (Safeway supermarkets, Woolworths and Payless drugstores) can be a shock, like a breath of unexpected air freshener. Some of the best of its unpretentiousness can be found in **Noyo Harbor**, a sunny inlet lined by docks, charcterful boats and seafood restaurants. These are likely to be simple cafés with plastic tablecloths, paper-napkin dispensers and bottles of McIlhenny's tabasco sauce on the tables. The fish will be fresh, but be warned: as tourism creeps closer even this atmosphere won't last forever.

The cloud of steam over Fort Bragg is produced by the Georgia-Pacific Corporation's lumber mill. The largest coastal settlement between San Francisco and Eureka, Fort Bragg is still an active logging town.

Redwoods and marijuana

Much of the North Coast's mystique is in the tall redwood trees, which have survived attempts to transform them into everything from lumber and ashtrays to mulch for suburban rose gardens. Most of California's remaining old-growth redwoods are now protected in parks, where tourists are invited to admire them, to drive through holes burnt or cut through the larger ones, and to buy objects made of their wood.

Notices tacked to buildings and utility poles offer "Sinsemilla Tips." Says another bulletin: "Don't get caught with your plants down." The plant in question is marijuana, a multimillion-dollar black market commodity. Until 1981, it was listed in Mendocino County's agricultural report as the largest local cash crop; since then, officials have chosen not to include the estimated marijuana gross. An attraction in **Garberville**, in southern Humboldt County, is the weekly newspaper's "Bust Barometer," a map with the week's pot raids charted from information provided by the sheriff.

North of Garberville a 33-mile (53-km) scenic drive called the **Avenue of the Giants** ㉜ follows the South

Map, page 112

BELOW: Yurok Indian, a fisherman on the Klamath River.

Fork of the Eel River through **Humboldt Redwood State Park**. The giants – redwood trees, otherwise known as *Sequoia sempervirens* – are tall and sometimes surprisingly wide. Their size can be marketed: "Drive through a living tree" is the come-on from the **Drive-Thru Tree** in the town of **Myers Flat**.

Those seeking to avoid this kind of commercialism can take the difficult road west from Garberville over the **King Mountains** to **Shelter Cove**. North of this isolated outpost is **Petrolia**, site of California's first oil well.

An honest glimpse into the spirit of the early Anglo life along the North Coast is aptly afforded by **Scotia ❸**, a crisp little company town built entirely of redwood – the wooden visitors' center is in the style of a classic Greek temple – and dominated by the **Pacific Lumber Company mill**, the world's largest redwood mill. The company owns the town and keeps it tidy.

Eureka's attractions

From the moment you arrive, it is obvious that **Eureka ❸** is a good place to buy such commodities as sewer pipe, lumber, a slab of redwood burl, a life-sized statue of a lumberjack carved from a redwood log, or a fresh fish dinner. Often shrouded in fog, it's the largest Pacific Coast enclave in North America north of San Francisco. It is a sprawling, busy, industrial place, still with a large fishing industry.

Eureka's ubiquitous and impressive Victorian architecture in **Old Town** is highlighted by the **Carson House** at the end of 2nd Street. Visitors can't go inside the house because it is now a private men's club – which makes it seem all the more Victorian. (The little town of **Ferndale ❸**, lying 10 miles (16 km) southwest of Eureka, has a remarkable collection of well-maintained Victorian

BELOW: Eureka's Carson House.

buildings to excite the architectural connoisseur.) Eureka is also the location of the North Coast's only institution of higher learning, called, appropriately enough, **Humboldt State University**.

Orick is the entrance to **Redwood National Park ㊱**, established in 1968 to consolidate 40 miles (64 km) of majestic forested coastline under federal jurisdiction. A visitors' center in Orick gives out directions and shuttle-bus information for excursions up **Redwood Creek** where, southeast of Orick, three of the six tallest trees ever identified, including the record holder – 368 feet (112 meters) in height – are located. They are clustered in the unimaginatively named **Tall Trees Grove**. It is difficult to recommend much of the scenery north of the **Klamath River** bridge, however, because you probably won't see much of it. The stands of redwood in **Del Norte Coast Redwoods State Park ㊲** and **Jedediah Smith Redwoods State Park ㊳**, both extensions of Redwood National Park, are noteworthy. But the foremost fact is fog, which can come in thick and fast and without warning. Be sure to take a sweater, just in case.

Crescent City ㊳ – a grim, gray gathering of plain houses and vacant lots around a semi-circular harbor – has never fully recovered from a 1962 typhoon which devastated the town and the traveler's best bet is to head inland to higher and hotter ground. Fifteen minutes east of Crescent City, on US Highway 199 toward Grants Pass, Oregon, the last undammed river in California flows gin-clear through the 90°F (32°C) summer twilight. Although the **Smith River** is wild, its accommodations are civilized. There's a lodge on **Patrick Creek** with a restaurant and bar. There are clean campgrounds, public and private, under the peeling red madronas. The attractions here are simple: boulder-lined banks, clear pools, good fishing – and no redwood souvenirs. ❑

Map, page 112

Paul Bunyan statue and the Trees of Mystery near the town of Klamath.

BELOW: a home-steader at home.

THE HIGH NORTH

The key to unlocking the secrets of the north is State Highway 299. This two-lane blacktop cuts across some of the state's least populated wilderness

Map,
page 112

San Francisco

California

Los
Angeles

Mountainous State 299 should be savored like a fine wine; at least five days should be allowed. On its winding trek, it cuts across a remote domain of mountains, valleys, volcanoes, rivers, canyons, basins and, at the end, barren desert. The time to visit is mid-April to mid-November, but even under the best of weather conditions, rock slides and heart-stopping curves make driving no experience for the timid, the inebriated or the impatient.

Coming from the Pacific Coast, State 299 branches off US Highway 101 at Arcata, north of Eureka, and crosses the low **Coast Range** to the wilderness realm of the **Klamath** and **Trinity** rivers. These two principal rivers drain the Coast Range and **Klamath Mountains**. The Klamaths comprise a series of smaller ranges – the **Siskiyou**, the **Trinity**, the **Trinity Alps**, the **Marble**, the **Scott Bar**, the **South Fork** and the **Salmon** mountains. They cover about 12,000 sq. miles (about 31,000 sq. km) of Northern California and southern Oregon. **Mount Hilton** is the highest peak in the region.

Bigfoot

The Klamaths are famous as the home of **Bigfoot**, also known as Sasquatch, the giant humanoid who – according to legend – stalks these mountains. There *is* something wild about the Klamaths: with more than 70 inches (1,780 mm) of annual rainfall in some parts, they sustain a lush forest of ferns, hemlocks, pines and spruce. And some native tribes still inhabit the area. Except for the highest of the Trinity Alps, glaciers are rare, so most peaks retain a raw, jagged quality. River canyons lack the graceful horseshoe shape of their glaciated Sierra Nevada counterparts.

Three national forests contain most of California's Klamaths – Klamath, Shasta and Trinity. Within these forests are more strictly-protected wilderness areas. The best-known and most popular is the **Salmon-Trinity Alps Wilderness Area ④**, laced with hundreds of miles of trails for hiking and camping. Ranger stations along State 299 at **Burnt Ranch, Big Bar** and Weaverville, and on State 3 at **Trinity Center**, will issue free permits, answer flora and fauna questions, and provide up-to-date information on weather and trail conditions.

About 10 miles (16 km) east of the Trinity River bridge marking the Humboldt-Trinity county line, near the community of Burnt Ranch, State 299 passes just south of **Ironside Mountain** (5,255 feet/1,602 meters). Ironside's sheer, scenic face is the eroded, exposed tip of a much larger piece of granite – the Ironside Mountain Batholith. About 165 million years old, this batholith is typical of other such intrusions in the Sierra Nevada and Klamaths. Batholiths distinguish the Klamaths from the neighboring Coast Range. Under a recent federal law,

PRECEDING PAGES: redwoods are synonymous with Northern California. **LEFT:** Mount Shasta and a Shasta City farm in its shadow. **BELOW:** cow-persons posing.

PONY ROOM

local power companies must purchase any electricity generated by small entrepreneurs. With this in mind, some mountain residents have developed small hydroelectric plants – like the one run by Mom & Pop Power Company in Trinity's **Minersville**. Only a few such plants now operate, but others are planned.

For residents of Trinity County a "night on the town" usually means a trip to **Weaverville ⓫**, the county seat with a population of around 3,500. It saw its glory days during the mid-19th century, when it was a supply post for Klamath region gold prospectors. Gold hunters still haunt the creeks of Trinity County, but lumbering sustains the economy.

High priestess of the High North.

Old-timers and newcomers

Although lumber ranks first, marijuana ranks second in Trinity County's cash crops. This juxtaposition of enterprises – one traditional, one contraband – is typical of Trinity, and personified in the names given to bars on Main Street – The New York Hotel, or The Diggin's. Trinity County's population breaks into two groups – true locals, and those who have come here since the end of the 1960s. Generally, locals tend to be conservative, the newcomers less so – but both groups share an individualism and a jealous regard for the natural environment. While Trinity often votes conservative, it also displays an abiding sensitivity to ecological issues. This is less ideology than simple self-interest.

BELOW: Chinese joss house in the town of Weaverville.

Many residents hunt their own food and draw water directly from springs, rivers and creeks. (The bedrock of granite and serpentine is too impermeable for aquifers.) So when the county recently tried to stop the federal government from spraying Trinity's woodlands with an herbicide many feared would end up in water supplies, no politicians – Democrat or Republican – openly opposed

the grass-roots effort. This closeness to one another and to the land breeds a native suspicion of outsiders.

Map, page 112

Visiting motorists should know that Trinity County, like most of California's north, has "open range." Cattle have never been a major part of the economy here, and open range is mostly a symbolic vestige of the region's frontier heritage. Open range means that cattle wander beyond their owner's unfenced rangelands. It also means that any driver whose vehicle strikes a cow has just purchased damaged livestock. Hikers must be careful to stay away from creek bottoms on which gold prospectors have staked claims. Likewise, those who come across a patch of marijuana should leave quickly before either (a) they are shot at by its grower, or (b) they are arrested on suspicion of being its growers.

Weaverville is the site of the **Joss House State Historic Park**, a tribute to Chinese history in California, particularly of the Gold Rush days. The oldest Chinese temple still in use in the state is open daily; guided tours are available. Nearby is the eclectic **JJ "Jake" Jackson Museum**.

Weaverville is also the gateway to **Clair Engle** and **Lewiston Lakes,** part of the expansive **Whiskeytown-Shasta-Trinity National Recreation Area ⓬**. A short drive north of town, these lakes were created in the 1960s with the damning of the upper Trinity River. They offer outdoor recreation opportunities in the form of fishing, hiking, boating and camping.

The **Cascades** run almost due north from California to Canada's British Columbia. In California, the range runs 40 to 50 miles (70 to 80 km) across. Farther north, glaciers dominate the range. Here in California, only the highest peaks bear these Ice Age relics. The dominant snow-capped Cascade peaks are young volcanoes. Some, like Washington's Mount St Helens, are still active.

BELOW: logging operation, Trinity National Forest.

Map,
page 112

Unlike the Klamaths, the higher Cascade peaks present a sharply vertical profile of high conical peaks surrounded by lower mountains of the 4,500 to 5,000-foot (1,370 to 1,520-meter) range.

There are few better places to study volcanology than **Lassen Volcanic National Park** . The park is reached via State Highway 36 stretching east from **Red Bluff**, State 44 east from Redding, or from State 89 south from State 299 beyond Burney. Lassen Peak (elevation 10,457 feet/3,187 meters) marks the southern terminus of the Cascade Range, and is one of only two Cascade volcanoes to have erupted in the 20th century.

Much of 108,000-acre (43,700-hectare) Lassen Park lies within a caldera, the giant crater left by the collapse of an ancient volcano. Out of this caldera, Lassen Peak later rose to dominate this expanse of wilderness, but there are small volcanoes in the park as well. There is also **Bumpass Hell**, a steaming valley of active geothermal pools and vents. And there are lakes, rivers, meadows, pine forests and fine trails for hiking and camping.

Most of the California Cascades fall within two national forests, **Lassen** and **Shasta**. At Shasta's southern boundary lies another prime wilderness, **Plumas National Forest**. These upland woods cover the northern end of the Sierra Nevada and cradle the **Feather River**, one of the state's best-known wild streams.

Between Redding and Burney, a distance of 53 miles (85 km), State 299 climbs into a gently undulating country of ranches and volcanic debris. The red rocks that litter the landscape and pastures to the south of the road were deposited by hot mud flows from the eruption of Mount Maidu 7 million years ago. This posthumously-named volcano collapsed to form the caldera within Lassen Park. Just beyond the lumber and livestock marketing center of **Burney** (population 3,200) is the State 89 intersection. South is Lassen Park; north is **Mount Shasta**, 14,162 feet (4,000 meter) high and usually covered with snow. Mount Shasta is the second highest elevation in the Cascades; the other is Mount Rainier in Washington state.

BELOW: whitewater rafts on the mighty Trinity River.
RIGHT: Helen Lake, Lassen Volcanic National Park.

Falls and forests

About 6 miles (10 km) north of Burney is pretty, moss-covered 129-foot (39-meter) **Burney Falls**. East of Burney is **Fall River Mills**, and from here to the Nevada border, State Highway 299 runs across the basins and fault-block mountains of the **Modoc Plateau**, a lava plain similar to the Columbia Plateau to the north. For a large section of its route, the highway follows the deep canyon of the Pitt River, the plateau's main drainage. The plateau extends over some 13,000 sq. miles (33,500 sq. km), taking in the whole of Modoc County and parts of Lassen, Shasta and Siskiyou counties. Vestiges of volcanism make up much of the **Modoc National Forest**, a wonderful green expanse covering 1.97 million acres (800,000 hectares). A pristine example of this volcanic past is **Glass Mountain**, a huge flow of obsidian lava on the forest's western edge.

But the main focus of any geological tour of this region has to be **Lava Beds National Monument**. A more impressive example of basalt flows cannot be found than this moonlike landscape of lava flows, columns and deep, dark caves.

SOUTHERN CALIFORNIA

The following chapters provide a detailed guide to the region,
with main sites cross-referenced by number to the maps

California is the only state in America that describes itself as having two distinct regions. There's a good reason for that description – Northern and Southern California *are* different. Viewed simplistically, one has water and the other has weather, if we take the latter to mean a supply of almost constant sunshine. (It does rain in Southern California, although seldom in the months between April and November.)

But obviously both sections have very much more to offer. In the south's case, these attractions include three of the country's biggest theme parks (Disneyland, Knotts Berry Farm, Magic Mountain), more year-round beaches, zany architecture, easy access to Mexico and – who could forget? – Hollywood. It seems almost superfluous to mention that it also has sprawling, smoggy Los Angeles, which in the past decade has become one of America's most varied and interesting places. And San Diego, which to many people's surprise is the state's second-largest city.

There's a tendency for almost anybody in the southern part of the state to claim they're "from LA," even when they actually live somewhere down (or up) the coast as much as 100 miles away. The Big Orange does tend to sprawl over a great region and certainly gets the lion's share of attention.

But Californians in general, whether from LA or not, all like to think of themselves in trendy terms as taste-makers, arbiters of the future. "All the domestic automobile companies and almost all the Japanese feel they need to keep tabs on the pulse of what is happening in Southern California," says auto market analyst John Rettie. Designer Mark Jordan adds: "People here demand to make individual statements." The Mazda Miata, designed by Pasadena's Bob Hall, was an auto toy created especially for Southern Californians. "You can put the top down year-around and there are a lot of windy roads to drive it on."

Los Angeles novelist Carolyn See says visitors often don't understand the local style because "California culture doesn't pop up on a computer screen. It's like the wind. So outsiders say there's nothing here." Her literary agent, Mort Janklow, says California is "like a teenager growing up." Very nicely, too, most people would say. ❏

PRECEDING PAGES: lounging in LA; up against the wall.
LEFT: triplets on the bed they all shared in Los Angeles.

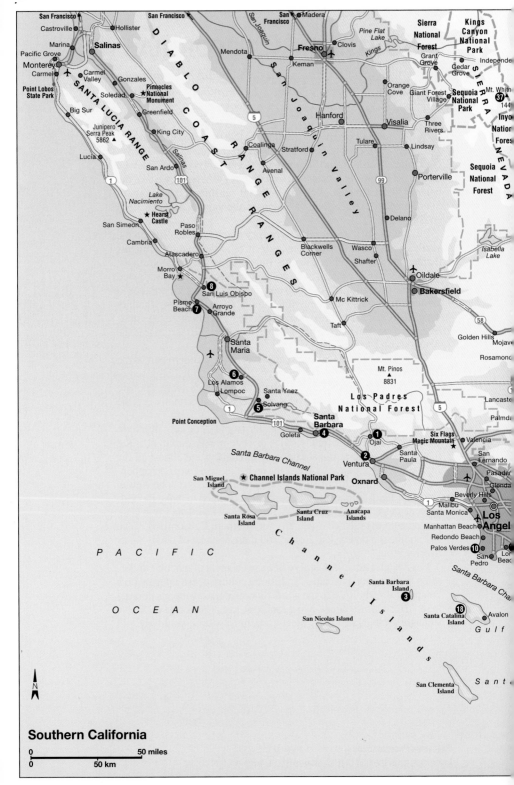

Southern California

```
0                    50 miles
0          50 km
```

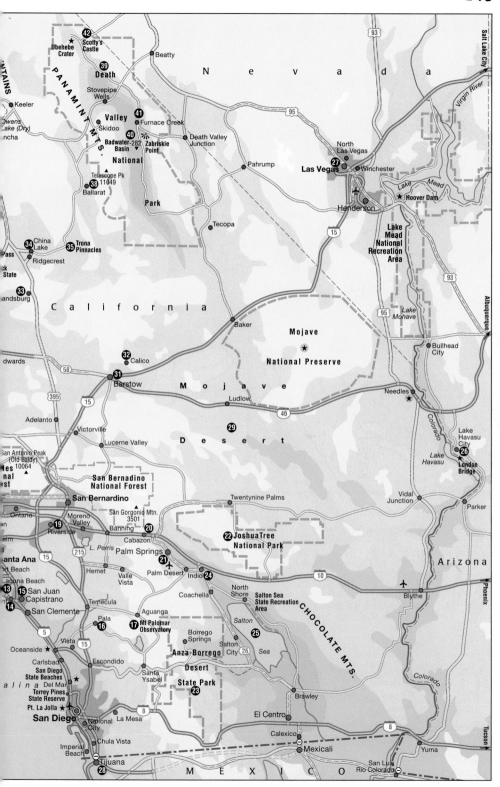

TAINS

Ubehebe
Crater
⁂ Scotty's
Castle
42

● Beatty

N e v a d a

93

Salt Lake City

Virgin River

● Keeler

Owens
Lake (Dry)
ncha

P A N A M I N T
M T S.

39
Death

Stovepipe
Wells

41
● Furnace Creek

● Skidoo
Valley

40
Badwater-282
Basin
⁂ Zabriskie
Point

National

Death Valley
● Junction

Telescope Pk
11049
38 ▲
Ballarat

● Pahrump

95

North
Las Vegas

Las Vegas 27
● Winchester

Lake   Mead

✈ ★ Hoover Dam

Park

● Tecopa

Henderson ●

Lake
Mead
National
Recreation
Area

15

93

China
34 Lake
● Ridgecrest

35 Trona
Pinnacles

C a l i f o r n i a

● Baker

Mojave
★
National Preserve

95
Lake
Mohave

Albuquerque

ass
k
State

33
andsburg

● Bullhead
City

dwards

58

32
● Calico
31
Barstow

M o j a v e

● Ludlow

40

Needles
★

Colorado

Adelanto

395
15

● Victorville

● Lucerne Valley

D e s e r t

29

Lake
Havasu

Lake
Havasu
City
26
★
London
Bridge

San Antonio Peak
(Old Baldy)
▲ 10064
es
nal
st

**San Bernadino
National Forest**

San Bernardino

San Gorgonio Mtn.
▲ 3501

● Twentynine Palms

Vidal
Junction

● Parker

● Ontario
n

Moreno
Valley

19
● Riverside

Banning
● 20

22
**JoshuaTree
National Park**

A r i z o n a

eim

L. Perris
215

Cabazon
Palm Springs

Phoenix

anta Ana
rt Beach
aguna Beach

15

● Hemet

21

Valle
Vista

Palm Desert ●

24
Indio ●

10

✈

● Blythe

13 15 **San Juan
Capistrano**

14
● San Clemente

● Temecula

● Coachella

North
Shore
Salton Sea
State Recreation
Area

C H O C O L A T E   M T S.

Pala ●
16

17 ● Mt Palomar
Observatory

Salton

Borrego ●
Springs

Salton
25 City

Colorado

● Aguanga

Sea
26

5
● Vista
● Oceanside ★

15

Carlsbad ●
San Diego
State Beaches
alina Del Mar
Torrey Pines
State Reserve
Pt. La Jolla ★

San Diego

● Escondido

● Santa
Ysabel

Anza-Borrego

Desert

State Park
23

● Brawley

Colorado

8

● El Centro

8

Tucson

National
City ● La Mesa
● Chula Vista

Imperial
Beach
28 Tijuana

● Calexico

● Mexicali

Yuma

San Luis
Rio Colorado

M E X I C O

LOS ANGELES

*It attracts myths like a magnet. But then, right from its
beginnings, Los Angeles was an unlikely place,
emerging "out of nowhere without much of a past"*

Map,
page 248

Because Los Angeles is such a huge, sprawling city, few of its residents know it well, or even choose to explore many neighborhoods beyond their own, most of which are composed of different ethnic populations. The greater metropolitan area is one of the most crowded in America (8.9 million versus New York City's 8.5 million), although in size its city boundary is second to Houston.

When Los Angelenos leave the self-sufficiency of their homes, they step into their cars and travel long distances (or at least to the supermarket around the corner); walking is rarely an option they would choose. And when they do go from one place to another, they seldom explore communities along the way, infinitely preferring to zoom past on the freeway. It is the destination that matters, not the journey. Los Angeles is one of North America's most Hispanic and most Asian cities. It is sixth in the divorce table, but on average has the largest families. Although it has only one-third as many visible homeless as New York City, it still ranks second in that sad list.

And, although it has the most Rolls-Royce dealers, it also has the most congested traffic (and comes second in the number of cars stolen). It has the least wind, the most sun, the most smog and – according to a recent Gallup Poll – has "the most attractive" men and women (as well as the largest number of cosmetic surgeons).

LEFT: city of angels and mice.
BELOW: waiting for the big break.

Where dreams come true

Where else could you rent a superstar clone such as John Wayne, Dolly Parton or Elizabeth Taylor – all of whom are on hire from a dating service called Celebrity Dream Date – to accompany you to dinner? Or have your apartment, or hotel room, tidied up by the topless girls from Bust Dusters, a cleaning service that charges over a dollar a minute (watch, but don't touch) for providing high-heeled maids wearing fishnet stockings, G-strings and tiny aprons?

Right from its beginning, LA was an unlikely place, emerging "out of nowhere without much of a past," in the words of writer Carey McWilliams who loathed it when he first arrived in the 1920s. "It lacked form and identity; there was no center… never-ending spread and sprawl… a city of strangers, of milling marauders all staring at one another without a glint of recognition." Some of those marauders, he felt, were a little *strange*. In his book, *Southern California: an island on the land*, he quoted the words of contemporary writer Hoffman Birney: "Every religion, freakish or orthodox, that the world ever knew is flourishing today in LA."

In the first 40 years of the last century, the city's population increased 15-fold, making virtually everybody an alien, as well as the notion of a community itself.

And the fact that this spectacular growth "exactly coincided with the automotive age," wrote Dominick Dunne, weakened even further the idea of community. It was, he pointed out, "the first city on wheels… the first city in the country to be entirely lit by electricity… scarcely older than a century (with) a bumptiousness that was as appealing to some as it was aggravating to others."

Since at least the 1950s, Los Angeles has been a mecca for the young – "the capital of youth," according to author Mike Davis (*City of Quartz,* a history of LA) – and it is still a magnet for the adventurous, for those seeking to begin a new life. In the 1990s, more than 750,000 new residents moved into the state, 10 percent from Asia. In the years between 1850 and 1950, almost a score of major utopian colonies were set up in California compared with no more than three in any other state, and this search for the bizarre hardly seems to have abated.

The listings in a 100-page *Spiritually LA* directory published by a local weekly paper include six pages of specialist bookstores, hundreds of religious denominations ranging from Ukrainian Orthodox to Eckankar and ads from practitioners of Pragmatic Buddhism, body harmony, extra-terrestrial communications, and karma-clearing – to name but a few.

The lure of Hollywood

From all accounts, though, it is not spirituality that most of LA's visitors come to seek. Sunshine and sea, shopping and sex symbols – all have their attractions, but in their secret hearts what most people hope to see is a star. Or a place where stars spend their time. Or even a place where stars are buried. (The crypts of Rudolph Valentino and Marilyn Monroe – respectively in Hollywood and Brentwood – still draw sightseers in numbers that smalltown hucksters would die for.)

BELOW AND RIGHT:
Venice Beach.

This, remember, is a company town, or at least a town where it sometimes seems that everybody's major preoccupation is with "the industry" and where the appearance of even a minor celebrity can cause outbreaks of hysteria. Not that this is anything to be ashamed of, after all. Unlike super-cool New York, everyone is star-struck here; it goes with the territory.

Maybe some of this devotion to the here and now derives from the very transience of the place. It's easy to imagine that if everybody left tomorrow, within a year or two most of Los Angeles would be reclaimed by the desert that nibbles at its borders. Water must be pumped in from hundreds of miles away to keep it alive. Windswept fires race across arid hillside devouring entire estates in a matter of hours. Spring rainfalls slipslide celebrity-owned, million-dollar mansions down precarious slopes. Storm tides topple beach homes and century-old piers.

Every year there are earthquakes – on a minor scale in recent years, but everybody knows the Big One is long overdue. Los Angeles, says Richard Reeves, is "not at peace with nature – that's why we get these periodic punishments. It's a man-made city, a tribute to rapacity and tenacity." But with all the hazards, Los Angelenos remain fairly sunny and optimistic in their outlook. Perhaps local publisher Jeremy Tarcher sums it up the best. "We are still the city of the future," he says, "even if nobody knows what the future is." ◻

Los Angeles: West Side

0 ——————— 2 miles

0 ——————— 2 km

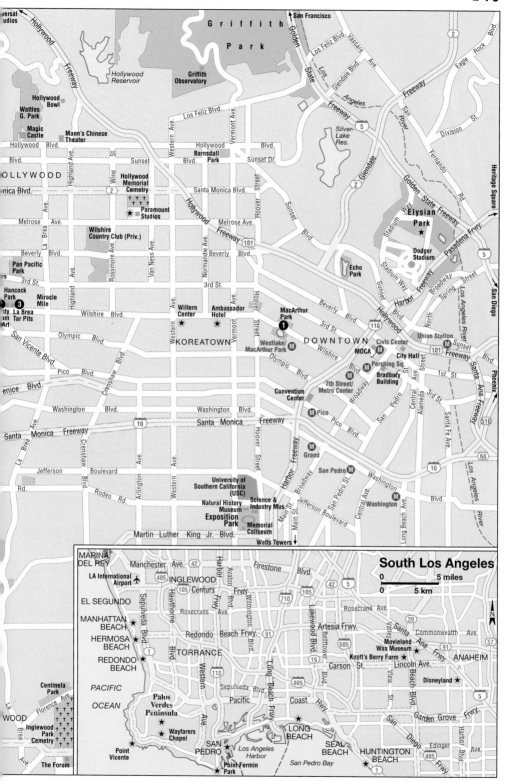

Universal Studios • Hollywood Freeway • Griffith Park • San Francisco • Golden State Freeway • Eagle Rock Blvd. • Los Feliz Blvd. • Vassare Ave. • Glendale Blvd. • Freeway • Los Angeles River • Division St.

Hollywood Reservoir • Griffith Observatory • Silver-Lake Res. • Glendale • State • Fernando Rd. • Heritage Square

Hollywood Bowl • Wattles G. Park • Magic Castle • Mann's Chinese Theater • Hollywood Blvd. • Barnsdall Park • Sunset Dr. • Golden State Freeway • Pasadena Frwy. • San Diego

HOLLYWOOD • Monica Blvd. • Sunset • Wine St. • Hollywood Memorial Cemetery • Santa Monica Blvd. • Hoover Street • Elysian Park • Stadium Way • Dodger Stadium • Broadway • Spring St.

Melrose Ave. • Paramount Studios • Melrose Ave. • Sunset Blvd. • Echo Park • Stadium Way • North Broadway

Beverly Blvd. • Wilshire Country Club (Priv.) • Beverly Blvd. • Hollywood Blvd. • Harbor Freeway • Los Angeles River • San Diego

Pan Pacific Park • 3rd St. • 3rd St. • Beverly Blvd. • Union Station • Santa Ana Freeway • Phoenix

Hancock Park • Miracle Mile • La Brea Tar Pits • Wilshire Blvd. • Wiltern Center • Ambassador Hotel • MacArthur Park • 3rd St. • DOWNTOWN • MOCA • Civic Center • City Hall • 101 Freeway • 1st. St. • 3rd St.

San Vicente Blvd. • Olympic Blvd. • KOREATOWN • Westlake/MacArthur Park • Wilshire • Pershing Sq. • Bradbury Building • Central Ave. • Alameda • 510

Venice Blvd. • Pico Blvd. • Olympic Blvd. • Convention Center • 7th Street/Metro Center • Broadway • San Pedro • 60

Santa Monica Freeway • Washington • Washington Blvd. • Santa Monica Freeway • Pico • Pico Blvd. • 10

Jefferson Boulevard • Crenshaw Ave. • Western Ave. • Grand • University of Southern California (USC) • San Pedro St. • Washington • Los Angeles River

Rd. • Rodeo Rd. • Arlington Ave. • Natural History Museum • Science & Industry Mus. • Jefferson Boulevard • Central Ave. • Washington • Blvd. • Long Beach Ave.

Exposition Park • Memorial Coliseum • Martin Luther King Jr. Blvd. • Watts Towers

South Los Angeles

MARINA DEL REY • Manchester Ave. 42 • Harbor Frwy. • Firestone Blvd. • Aviator Blvd. • 42 • 5

LA International Airport • 405 • Century Blvd. • 105 • Wilmington Ave. • 710 • 105 • Rosecrans Ave. • 39 • Commonwealth Ave. • 57

EL SEGUNDO • Sepulveda Blvd. • Hawthorne Blvd. • Century Frwy. • Rosecrans Ave. • Santa Ana Frwy. • 91

MANHATTAN BEACH • HERMOSA BEACH • Redondo Beach Frwy. • 91 • Artesia Frwy. • Lakewood Blvd. • Bellflower Blvd. • Movieland Wax Museum • Knott's Berry Farm • ANAHEIM

REDONDO BEACH • 1 • TORRANCE • Western Ave. • 110 • 19 • Carson St. • Lincoln Ave. • Disneyland • 5

Centinela Park • PACIFIC OCEAN • Sepulveda Blvd. • Pacific Coast Hwy. • 405 • Long Beach Frwy. • San Diego Frwy. • Garden Grove Frwy. • 5

Florence Ave. • INGLEWOOD • Inglewood Park Cemetery • Palos Verdes Peninsula • Wayfarers Chapel • SAN PEDRO • Los Angeles Harbor • LONG BEACH • SEAL BEACH • HUNTINGTON BEACH • 405 Frwy. • Harbor Blvd. • Edinger Ave.

WOOD • The Forum • Point Vicente • Point Fermin Park • San Pedro Bay • 1

0 — 5 miles
0 — 5 km
N

DOWNTOWN LA

The downtown district of Los Angles, with its skyscrapers and ornate movie palaces, represents both the old and the new faces of the city

Map, page 252

It's fashionable among those living in Hollywood or Beverly Hills to pretend that downtown Los Angeles barely exists – just as many Manhattanites claim they never go south of 34th Street (or north of 14th Street). But downtown LA, in fact, represents both the oldest and newest faces of this multi-faceted city. Millions of dollars have been spent in recent years to transform it into a business and cultural showcase second to none, and, if the results are debatable, they are certainly interesting to see.

Forget about driving; parking downtown is difficult and expensive unless you choose to leave your car on the edge of the area, in a lot opposite The Original Pantry (it never closes), for example, at 9th and Figueroa streets. Only a few blocks east of here is the busy **Flower Market** (7th and Wall) where the main event is over by 8am.

Take the bus

For those on foot, the bus along 7th operates every few minutes in the downtown area from 6.30am on weekdays and Saturday, from 10am on Sunday. Pick up a schedule before leaving the bus.

Further down Figueroa are several interesting sites: the **Convention Center**, the **University of Southern California** (USC) and **Exposition Park**. But before those, first head up past the **Seventh Market Plaza** ◍, a stylish mall whose sunken plaza with its open-air restaurant sits among three-story palm trees shading stores. Scattered around are several art works, including a stooping bronze businessman on the north side of Citicorp Center.

Cross the street and walk half a block to the **Fine Arts Building** at 811 West 7th, its artists' studios long ago converted to offices. A medieval-style lobby, with 15 chandeliers and a tiled fountain, hosts color drawings of some of the ambitious artwork planned for the stations of the city's new Metro system.

Admire the gilded facade of the **Home Savings** building as you head back to Figueroa. The stepped, white tower of the **777 Building** ("subtle profiles and strong silhouettes," says one critic) was created by Argentine-born Cesar Pelli, also responsible for the distinctive Pacific Design Center (known locally as "the Blue Whale") in West Hollywood. A subtle fountain by Eric Orr sits outside the **Sanwa Bank** building in the 80-feet (24-meter) high Art Deco lobby in which, among acres of brown marble, sit two of the largest plants ever seen in captivity. A recent addition to LA's soaring skyline is the **First Interstate World Center** ◓, one of the tallest buildings in the West.

From **Arco Plaza** across the street, an escalator leads into the glitzy **Westin Bonaventure Hotel** ◉ with its

LEFT: in at the deep end in the corporate swim. **BELOW:** interior of the Westin Bonaventure Hotel.

multi-level lounges and engaging perspectives, and from which a bridge heads from the second floor into the other Arco Plaza, which is dotted with pleasing, enormous sculptures.

Between Grand, Hill, 3rd and 4th streets, the **Angels Flight ❹** (tel: 213-626 1901) funicular again makes its 70-second ride up **Bunker Hill** after a 27-year absence. A right turn from Hope up Grand leads to the **Wells Fargo Center ❺** (closed weekends), whose exhibits recall Gold Rush days and the stagecoaches that tamed the West. The Bonaventura's gleaming cylinders look terrific from the bridge over 3rd Street across from which is the **Museum of Contemporary Art** (MOCA) **❻**, (250 South Grand Avenue, tel: 213-626 6222, open Tuesday, Wednesday, Friday and Sunday 11am–5pm; Thursday 11am–8pm; admission charge), an architectural gem harboring notable art created exclusively since the 1930s, in a building outside which is another eye-catching fountain. Even more spectacular is the recently completed waterfall in **California Plaza**. There are numerous tables and chairs in the plaza, which has take-away food counters. This is one of the best spots for a quick lunch.

The Angels Flight funicular, billed as the "shortest railway in the world," was built in 1901. It was dismantled in 1969, but resumed operations in 1996. City Hall is in the background of the picture.

Asian aura

One of the bus stops is right beside MOCA: the B route that goes up past "touristy" Olvera Street to the far edge of **Chinatown ❼** at Bernard. Just around the corner on **Broadway**, the gaudy Asian stereotypes of Gin Ling Way surround a stage-sized plaza. Three long blocks south (on bus route) is **Olvera Street ❽** with its working craftsmen, Mexican stalls and strolling mariachi who serenade diners as they sip frozen margaritas and eat lunch under the sidewalk awning of **La Golondrina**, the city's first brick building (1850). This was home to the Pel-

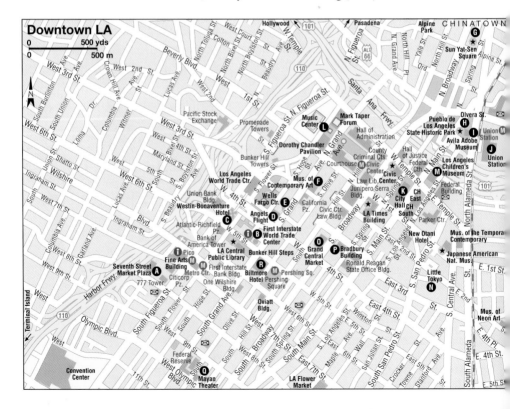

Downtown LA

enconi family whose piano, a neighborly gift, sits across the street in the older Avila Adobe ❶. Deserted for years, the adobe was finally condemned by the city as unsafe, but was saved from demolition by a civic-minded group. Since it was acquired by the state in 1953, it has been restored with some of the original furnishings.

Here on what began as Wine Street is where El Pueblo de Nuestra Senora a la Reina de Los Angeles began in 1780 when Felipe de Neve, California's first governor, laid out what was to become California's biggest city. Apart from being reinforced after a 1922 earthquake, the Avila Adobe, the home of a prosperous rancher who died in 1832, has been restored pretty much as it was left by his widow when she died 23 years later.

Notable in the area are the **Pico House**, the city's first three-story building and once its finest hotel with 82 bedrooms, 21 parlors, two interior courtyards and a French restaurant; the **Garnier House** (1890); and the adjoining **Helman Quon** building (tel: 213- 628 1274), which was originally a Chinese store, but is now managed by the Parks Department who offer morning tours of this neighborhood. In the firehouse is a picture of Blackie, the city's last firehorse.

Between the **Plaza Church** (1818) – also known as Mission Church – scene of an annual Easter ceremony when children bring their pets to be blessed, and Union Station is a statue of Father Junípero Serra (*see Missions on page 26*).

Majestic **Union Station** ❼, opened in 1939, with its leather seats and stratospheric ceiling, has been seen in scores of old newsreels. It is nicely maintained by Amtrak which operates about 20 trains a day up the coast, down to the Mexican border and into the desert. LA's subway system, the **Metro Red Line**, begins at Union Square and the imaginative murals and artwork in this subter-

Map, page 252

BELOW: mainly Mexican Olvera Street.

ranean station and the four others to MacArthur Park are worth going underground to see. Behind the station sits the glass-roofed **Gateway Transit Center**, the mural-and fountain-filled transportation hub of the region.

The bus runs from Olvera Street to **City Hall** ⓚ which has "starred" in many a movie and TV show. On a hill a few blocks northwest is the popular **Music Center** ⓛ which includes the **Dorothy Chandler Pavilion** (where the Oscars are presented); the headquarters of the LA Music Center Opera, the LA Master Chorale and, in fall and winter, the LA Philharmonic. There are two theaters, the **Ahmanson Theatre**, staging plays transfered from New York, and the **Mark Taper Forum**, winner of many awards. Plans to add a Frank Gehry-designed annex, called the **Walt Disney Concert Hall**, have been bogged down in financial difficulties for years. Immediately below City Hall is the excellent **Children's Museum** ⓜ (open erratic hours, so call first on 213-687 8800).

Little Tokyo

Several blocks southeast is the attractive **New Otani Hotel** with its lovely Japanese garden by famous landscape artist Sentaru Iwaki off the fourth floor. The hotel sits at the edge of **Little Tokyo** ⓝ whose interesting stores include a fully-stocked branch of Japanese department store, Yaohan Plaza.

Downtown street life is at its most active on Broadway, where silent screen comic Harold Lloyd once swung from a long-gone clockface in the film *Safety Last*. Broadway's attractions include the lively **Grand Central Market** ⓞ which adjoins one of the city's earliest movie palaces, the **Million Dollar Movie Theater** at 307 South Broadway. Founded by showman Sid Grauman, it had a gala opening on February 1, 1918, with Charlie Chaplin, Mary Pickford and

Lillian Gish in attendance to see the Mack Sennett comedy *The Silent Man.*
Top Mexican stars played the theater in the 1950s, but the decline of Mexican cinema in the 1970s, coupled with the predominance of Central Americans in the area, forced the theater to rent its premises to an evangelist preacher.

The last of the grand movie palaces, S. Charles Lee's **Los Angeles Theater**, which opened with the premiere of Charlie Chaplin's *City Lights* (in 1931), is still operating down the street. Opposite the market is the ornate, 1893-built **Bradbury Building** ❷, whose winding iron staircases, open elevators and rich woodwork has long endeared it to movie-makers.

The Bradbury Building featured in Ridley Scott's cult movie *Blade Runner* and also passed for hard-boiled private eye Philip Marlowe's down-at-the-heels office in the 1969 adaptation of Raymond Chandler's *The Little Sister.* Chandler, the revered documenter of Los Angeles of the 1940s, felt it was a city "rich and vigorous and full of pride... a city lost and beaten and full of emptiness."

Three other distinctive downtown buildings worth seeing are the fanciful **Mayan Theater** ❷ (Hill and 11th streets), now a nightspot, where Norma Jean Baker is said to have appeared as a stripper long before she became Marilyn Monroe; the 1928 **Oviatt Building** (South Olive and 6th streets) whose lobby is still decorated with more than a ton of rare Lalique glass; and the classy, historic **Biltmore Hotel** ❷ with its awe-inspiring lobby and enormous photograph of attendees at the 1937 Academy Awards.

It was here where MGM's art director, Cedric Gibbons, is said to have used a napkin to sketch a design for a still-unnamed Oscar statue. At 5th and Grand streets is the city's **Central Library**. Incidentally, there have been some incidents of violence at downtown nightspots, so be warned.   ❑

**Map,
page 252**

BELOW: Simon Rodia's astonishing Watts Towers.

WATTS TOWERS

In the downtown suburb of Watts, in Los Angeles' South Central area, is one the city's most astonishing sculptures: the Watts Towers. Created between 1921 and 1954 by Simon Rodia, a penniless Italian tilesetter, the trio of lacy columns were intended as an affectionate tribute to his adopted land. Composed of broken bottles, pottery shards, tiles, pebbles and steel rods all stuccoed together and covered with 70,000 seashells, the towers are a set of sculptures so far ahead of their time that they were unappreciated for years: vandals tried to destroy them and the city planned to pull them down.

The towers, the highest of which reaches 100 feet (30 meters), were reprieved after attempts to dismantle them using steel cables pulled by a tractor in full view of TV cameras were unsuccessful. In time, the towers started to accumulate the adulation they had long deserved, but Rodia died in poverty in 1965 at the age of 86, having left town and deeded the site to a friend. The towers can be seen behind the fence even when the adjoining Watts Towers Arts Center, which displays works by African Americans, is closed.

Watts hit the headlines in 1965 when 34 people died in widespread rioting. Take extra care when viewing.
Watts Towers, 1727 E. 107th Street, tel: 213-847 4646.

HOLLYWOOD AND THE WEST SIDE

From Paramount Studios to Mann's Chinese Theatre, from Beverly Hills to Rodeo Drive – when most people talk about Los Angeles, this is what they mean

Almost everything west of downtown is the West Side, or so its inhabitants like to think. In reality, the bottom end of Sunset Boulevard, the section around **Echo Park Lake**, where evangelist Aimee Semple McPherson ("joy! vitality! love!") used to preach at the (still-active) Four Square Gospel Tabernacle, and the stylish Victorian houses of **Carroll Avenue** don't have too much in common with the mansions of "industry" millionaires at Sunset's coastal end. Norma Desmond's mansion in *Sunset Boulevard* was actually on Wilshire Boulevard. In fact, it is Wilshire, running more or less parallel with Sunset Boulevard, 3 miles (5 km) to the south, that became the major road out to the coast when Sunset was little more than a dusty track leading out of the original Mexican plaza. And the automobile made it so.

Wilshire Boulevard

Nowadays, Wilshire is showing its age, although the new Metro Line subway has brought new life to otherwise seedy **MacArthur Park** ❶ and the long-shuttered Bullock's department store now houses a law library which has refurbished this Art Deco landmark. Still closed and fenced off, however, is the Ambassador Hotel, once fabled for the showbiz types who attended (and performed in) its Coconut Grove and later in the 1960s infamous as the site of Robert Kennedy's assassination. It is often used today as a site for movie-making.

Miracle Mile's **Museum row**, on Wilshire near Fairfax, where the Old Masters in the **County Museum of Art** ❷ (5905 Wilshire, tel: 323-857 6000, open Monday, Tuesday and Thursday noon–8pm, also Friday noon–9pm, Saturday–Sunday 11am–8pm; admission charge) are but striplings compared with the old mastodons fished out of the park's **La Brea Tar Pits** ❸ at the George C Page Museum, (tel: 323-934 7243, Tuesday–Sunday 10am–5pm; admission charge), a major tourist attraction. In the 1860s, Rancho La Brea had been bought for $2.50 an acre by Major Henry Hancock, who quarried asphalt and shipped tar to San Francisco to pave streets. The oil company geologists who in 1989 started uncovering fossils here identified some of the bones as belonging to extinct sabre-toothed tigers, dire wolves and giant sloth.

After a decade of oil drilling, Henry's son, George, allowed LA County to examine the site, deeding the 23-acre (9-hectare) ranch to the county in 1913. The skeleton of a woman from 9,000 years ago was found, but no other humans among what were literally millions of bones. The museum opened in 1972; excavations for

LEFT: Hollywood hype captured on cotton T-shirts.
BELOW: LA's MacArthur Park.

Map, page 248

the building uncovered skeletons of complete animals which had been trapped in the tar as they came to drink.

There's *al fresco* eating just a few blocks north at the **Farmers' Market ❹**, where from 1934 farmers parked their trucks and sold produce from the back. The renovated 1852 adobe, in which owner Earl Gilmore was born, and which is the market's business office, sits in an attractive garden on the site.

Paramount Studios

Two-hour tours of Paramount Studios give the low-down on both old and new Hollywood. Call 213-956 5575 for more information.

Most of the movie studios which earned Hollywood its reputation have long gone, but the famous gate seen in *Sunset Boulevard* still guards the entrance to **Paramount Studios ❹**, 5555 Melrose at Van Ness Avenue (tel: 323-956 5000), where *The Ten Commandments* and all the *Godfather* movies were also made. Fans who were not even born when silent star Rudolph Valentino died in 1926 seek out his grave (and those of Douglas Fairbanks, Cecil B de Mille, Eleanor Powell and Marion Davies) in the adjoining **Hollywood Memorial Cemetery**.

Memories of all the low-budget Westerns churned out in moviedom's early days are evoked by **Gower Gulch ❸**, a frontier-style shopping center opposite CBS on the corner at Sunset and Gower. This is where Hollywood's first film studio, the Nestor Film Company, paid $40 to rent a defunct tavern in 1911.

The TV station across the street replaced the old Warner Brothers studios, where in 1927 Al Jolson emoted in *The Jazz Singer*. Just north of Sunset on nearby Vine Street, Cecil B. de Mille and Jesse Lasky in 1913 filmed *The Squaw Man*, Hollywood's first full-length feature. Paying appropriate homage to its location, the McDonald's fast-food joint here on Vine Street is decked out in the style of the movie *Casablanca*. A bust of Rudolph Valentino stands in the minus-

BELOW:
Marilyn Monroe's
hairdresser.

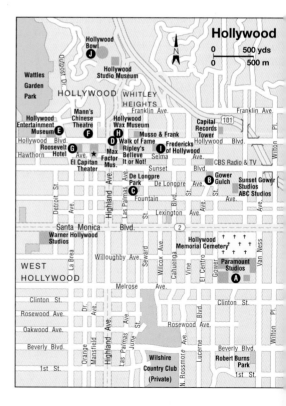

cule **De Longpre Park**  (below Sunset at Cherokee), named after the turn-of-the-century flower painter whose gorgeous house and gardens near Wilcox Street and Hollywood Boulevard was Hollywood's first tourist attraction. Kansas-born Herbert Wilcox and his wife, Daieda, were the founders late in the 19th century of a temperance community they called "Hollywood" that encircled their extensive orchards.

It is this area today that most visitors think of as the heart of Hollywood: the celebrated stars along the **Walk of Fame** ● run along Hollywood Boulevard westwards from Vine Street, with Marilyn Monroe's star positioned outside the McDonald's restaurant. The walk was part of a major restoration of the street back in 1956 when the first batch of stars to be cemented into the sidewalk included Burt Lancaster, Ronald Colman and Joanne Woodward. Only one star, it's said – Barbra Streisand – failed to make the obligatory appearance at a dedication ceremony, although it's presumed that she or her agent paid the usual fee of around $4,000 to be listed. The old Max Factor building on Highland just south of Hollywood is now the **Hollywood History Museum** with hundreds of costumes, film posters and artifacts.

Although it has grown increasingly seedy in recent years, Hollywood Boulevard is still rich in such landmarks as the **Egyptian Theater** in the 6900 block. The theater is a 1,700-seat replica of a palace in Thebes which in its heyday had a man on the roof in white robes announcing times of the movies. When the American Cinematheque has finished restoring some of the theater's original grandeur, it plans daily screenings of a movie about Hollywood history as well as showing other classics, including silent movies with an organ accompaniment.

Nearby, the **Hollywood Entertainment Museum** ●, (6767 Hollywood

Maps, page 248 & 258

Another old movie palace is El Capitan at 6838 Hollywood Boulevard. Built in 1926, movies can still be seen here.

BELOW: Sir Elton's star on Hollywood's Walk of Fame.

Boulevard, tel: 323-465 7900, open Tuesday–Sunday 10am–6pm; admission charge) has incorporated sets from *Star Trek* (you can sit in Captain Picard's chair on the bridge and view clips from old shows) and the bar from the TV show *Cheers* which can be rented for parties. A host of interactive attractions allows visitors to hear short commentaries from stars like Tina Turner, Orson Wells and Walt Disney, and in the Foley Room you are given props and invited to accompany a short film that is screened for you and then played back with your sound effects. There is a fashion display of clothes from the Debbie Reynolds and Cecil B de Mille collections and a dizzying six-minute retrospective film of clips from scores of movies shown twice every hour.

Like the Egyptian two blocks east, **Mann's Chinese Theatre ❺** is a famous landmark most notable for its forecourt of famous footprints, from Mary Pickford to the hoofprints of Roy Rogers's horse etched in cement; the neo-Gothic **Security Pacific Building** (created by the same architects, Meyer & Holler), at the corner of Highland Avenue; and west of La Brea, the extremely glamorous **Hollywood Roosevelt Hotel ❻**, site of the first public Oscars ceremony in 1929. The hotel contains a treasure trove of memorabilia, which includes the first Technicolor camera, used in Disney's *Silly Symphonies* cartoons.

Other notable landmarks close to Vine include **Musso & Frank**, the favorite rendezvous of writers Nathanael West, William Faulkner and Raymond Chandler; **Pantages**, America's first Art Deco theater which was built in 1929; the **Hollywood Wax Museum ❼** (on the site of the old Montmartre Café where Joan Crawford flirted and danced); and **Larry Edmond's Bookshop**, a peerless source of Hollywoodiana, the best place for movie souvenirs in town.

Across from **Fredericks of Hollywood ❽** (tel: 323-466 5151), with its

ABOVE: star stamps.
BELOW: Fredericks bra museum.

BELINDA CARLISLE

AVA GARDNER

AMANDA BLAKE

Map,
page 258

nuseum of famous bras and the lingerie of the famous, steep Whitley Terrace eads up to **Whitley Heights**, a community of elegant mansions much favored by movie stars of the Gloria Swanson era, preceding the rise of Beverly Hills. Access is easier, however, off Highland Avenue, just before the big yellow barn (moved here long ago) which served as the original de Mille and Lasky studio, now the **Hollywood Studio Museum** (tel: 323-874 2276). Across the street is the approach to the **Hollywood Bowl ❶**, a 17,000-seat amphitheater staging "Symphonies Under the Stars" concerts all summer.

chwabs' legendary counter

A movieplex and mall stands on the site of the former **Schwabs Drugstore** at 3024 Sunset, once a prime hangout for unemployed stars, directors and other movie types until it closed in 1983. Charlie Chaplin had been known to scamper behind the counter and make his own milkshakes. F. Scott Fitzgerald once suffered a heart attack in the store while buying cigarettes and composer Harold Arlen said the light coming from the windows as he walked past one day inspired him to write *Over the Rainbow*.

Guitar Heaven and half a dozen similar shops are located at Sunset and Gardner. In the cluster is the Sunset Grill, made famous in an Eagles song by Don Henley; nearby is the Gardner Street School where Michael Jackson studied, and the garage where Les Paul built the first two-track recording machine 50 years ago. Guitars range from $89 to $25,000. The oldest music store is the busy **Guitar Center** (1965), part of a chain, and located in an old movie theater.

Hollywood Boulevard peters out into hillside suburbia beyond La Brea, but if you're driving, it's worth going a few blocks along Franklin to take a look at

BELOW: stars in the sky and on the stage at the outdoor Hollywood Bowl.

the **Yamashiro** restaurant, a recreated Japanese palace, and its Victorian neighbor, the **Magic Castle**. Some delightful Spanish-style architecture can be found in the blocks lying between Sunset Boulevard and Fountain Avenue, west of Crescent Heights. The **Villa Primavera** (1300 North Harper), as well as the **Patio del Moro** (8229 Fountain) and the **Villa Andalusia** (1473 North Havenhurst) were the work of the husband-and-wife architectural team of Arthur and Nina Zwebell; others, including **Villa D'Este** (1355 North Laurel) were done by the Davis brothers, Pierpont and Walter. All date to the 1920s, as does the apartment house located at 1305 N. Harper where Marlene Dietrich is said to have stayed when she first arrived in 1930.

Mi Casa (1406 North Havenhurst) is the genuine foreign article: an irresistible row of balconied apartments around twin patios brought bodily from Ronda, Spain, in 1926, and since designated as a national historic place. The city's denizens have always had an ambivalent attitude about the local architecture and what survives seems to be largely a matter of chance.

The castle-like hotel **Chateau Marmont** ❺, on Sunset near Laurel Canyon (tel: 323-656 1010) where Paul Newman met Joanne Woodward, has become almost an historic monument, largely because of guests such as Greta Garbo and Howard Hughes, and its notoriety as the death site of John Belushi.

Favorite movie location

Dominating the hill above Sunset at 905 Loma Vista Drive is the delightful **Greystone Mansion** ❻. The 18-acre (7-hectare) garden is a popular spot for visitors, although the house itself usually remains closed. It is, however, often rented out to movie companies for location filming. Built at a cost of $6 million

BELOW: seeking out the stars.

in 1926 by the city's first oil millionaire, Charles Doheny, the 50-room mansion is now owned by the city of Beverly Hills.

Down La Cienega at Beverly Boulevard is the **Beverly Center**. For 30 years, until 1974, an amusement park and oil wells stood on the site of what is now an eight-level mall with 160 shops and restaurants and 14 movie theaters. Drilling for oil on what was once the Rancho Rodeo de las Aguas is what led to the birth of **Beverly Hills**, the unsuccessful oil prospectors subsequently deciding to develop the land. One-acre lots were offered for under $1,000 along the length of Sunset Boulevard. In 1912, Burton Green built the **Beverly Hills Hotel** ❼ to be the focal point of the new community *(see page 264)*. One of Beverly Hills' earliest homes is the **Virginia Robinson house and gardens** ❽ (tel: 310-276 5367), built in 1911 for the son and daughter-in-law of the owner of the Robinson department store chain. Lushly landscaped gardens include a mini-forest of palm trees and flower-filled terraces. Only the gardens are open to the public.

Filmdom's elite built ever-bigger homes in this elegant area, fanning out into the hills and canyons, and around Mulholland Drive, the spectacular highway that runs for 50 miles along the crest of the Santa Monica Mountains all the way down to the coast just north of Malibu.

Greta Garbo and John Gilbert shared idyllic poolside afternoons together in a mansion at Seabright and Tower Grove Drive; Rudolph Valentino luxuriated in Falcon's Lair at 1436 Bella Drive; not too far away, the home of Roman Polanski and Sharon Tate at 10050 Cicelo Drive was the scene of 1969 murders by members of the infamous Charles Manson family.

At the canyon's lower end, along immaculate North Roxbury Drive, lived Marlene Dietrich (No. 822), Jimmy Stewart (918), Lucille Ball (1000) and Jack

Map,
page 248

BELOW: a typical night out.

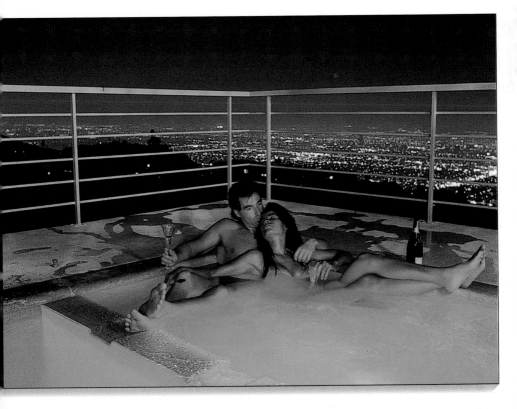

Beverly Hills Hotel

When the Beverly Hills Hotel closed for two years for a $100 million facelift, the doomsayers forecast that it would never regain its old cachet. But now it's back in business and people are ready and willing to pay $150 per day to rent a poolside cabana (on top of the $300 per night for a room).

For the truth is that the famous pink palace is much more than a hotel, it's a legend – the place where Elizabeth Taylor honeymooned in a bungalow that now costs $2,750 a day and where reclusive resident Howard Hughes ordered pineapple upside-down cake from room service almost every night. Hughes also rented four bungalows at the hotel: one for himself, another for his wife Jean Peters, a third for the blueprints of the *Spruce Goose*, the others for bodyguards and guests. One of his eccentricities was to order roast beef sandwiches delivered to a certain tree.

For a long time Katharine Hepburn took

lessons from the hotel's tennis pro and one day after six sets dived in the pool fully clothed. She was also known to curl up outside Spencer Tracy's locked door, waiting for him to let her in after a drinking bout. Greta Garbo chose the hotel as a hideaway in 1932 and Clark Gable checked in to dodge the press after separating from his wife, Rita.

When the world's richest man, Hassanal Bolkish, Sultan of Brunei, bought the hotel for $185 million in 1987, it was rumored he would turn it into a private residence for himself, but instead he ordered extensive renovations. Every room in the hotel has three phone lines, a fax machine, computer, safe and butler-service button. The number of rooms was cut from 253 to 194; gilded ceilings added to the lobby along with crystal chandeliers and rosebud lights. New additions included a kosher kitchen. Finally, 1,600 gallons of Beverly Hills Pink were computer-matched to old paint samples, so the new extensions matched the old.

Some things, of course, stayed the same, especially the Fountain Coffee Shop with its original iron stools still bolted to the floor and the familiar old banana leaf patterned wallpaper. It was in the coffee shop in 1959 that Marilyn Monroe and Yves Montand romanced over afternoon tea. The menu of the Polo Lounge, where big movie deals are still cut, features as previously Neil McCarthy salad, named for the polo-playing millionaire who died in 1972. At first, the bar was called the El Jardin but was rechristened when socialite and polo player Charles Wrightsman turned up with his team's silver trophy bowl. After that, drinkers W.C. Fields and John Barrymore were joined by Will Rogers and Darryl Zanuck who dropped in after their matches.

In a town notorious for its casual attire, decorum still prevails at the Beverly Hills. Mia Farrow was once turned away from the Polo Lounge for wearing pants, and rock manager Arnold Stiefel, who chose the place to sign up Guns N' Roses, recalls that the waitresses "were in shock at all those people with things in their nose. I think it took the coffee shop at least six months to recover." ❏

LEFT: "No one is allowed to fail within a 2-mile radius of the Beverly Hills Hotel," observed writer Gore Vidal after visiting the Pink Palace.

Benny (1002). Greta Garbo's home was nearby at 1027 Chevy Chase Drive and William Randolph Hearst's mistress, Marion Davies, had a home at 1700 Lexington Road. At the time of his death in 1951, Hearst was living with Ms Davies in a house on Beverly Drive, noted for the huge palms that line the street. With a population of 30,000 trees, Beverly Hills has almost one per resident.

Rodeo Drive

Land was cheaper down around Santa Monica Boulevard when the community first began, but these days you'd hardly know it considering the prices along **Rodeo Drive**, especially between Santa Monica and Wilshire where stores with foreign names like Gucci, Hermès, Chanel, Fendi and Cartier have branches – "the most staggering display of luxury in the western world," says novelist Judith Krantz. **Two Rodeo Drive ❾**, with its cobbled street and bow-windows, is a replica of what only Hollywood could believe to be an olde-worlde European backwater; across the street Fred Hayman's red and yellow showplace has a working fireplace surrounded by photos of celebrity customers who can belly up to the bar while waiting for their partners to drop a few thou.

Even **City Hall**, with its handsome tiled dome, is a splendid sight, part of the Spanish Renaissance-style **Beverly Hills Civic Center ❿**. More interesting architecturally, however, is the intriguingly bizarre **Witches Cottage ⓫**, at 516 Walden Drive, which began life as a 1921 movie set designed to look like the home of the fairytale witch in Hansel and Gretel. It was later moved to this site. Conscious of its worldwide fame, Beverly Hills maintains an informed, active **Visitors Bureau** at 239 S. Beverly Drive (tel: 310-248 1015, Monday–Friday 8.30am–5pm). A recent addition to Beverly Hills' exciting list of sites is the

Map, page 248

ABOVE AND BELOW: Fred Hayman's shop on the road that has "the most staggering display of luxury in the western world."

**Map,
page 248**

Museum of Television and Radio ⓬, (465 N. Beverly Drive, tel: 310-786 1000, Wednesday–Sunday noon–5pm; admission charge), where visitors can listen to news and watch old TV shows. A short detour away is a very different experience. The **Museum of Tolerance** ⓭ (9786 W. Pico Boulevard, tel: 310-553 8403, 10am–1pm, longer in summer; admission charge) is a sobering look at the history of racism in the US and the Holocaust experience in Germany.

Santa Monica and Wilshire boulevards intersect at the far side of Beverly Hills, beside the **Electric Fountain** that caused sightseeing traffic jams when it was first built in the 1930s. Santa Monica boulevard heads west past the skyscrapers (filled mostly with corporate law offices and the like) of **Century City**, centered around the luxurious Century Plaza Hotel and another upscale shopping center, before terminating at Santa Monica. Century City's 180-acre (73-hectare) site was once part of the studio back lot of 20th Century Fox which now occupies only the adjoining southern portion.

Westwood Village, home of UCLA

Wilshire Boulevard swerves slightly to the northwest out of Beverly Hills along the southern flank of the shopping complex **Westwood Village**, once the headquarters of William Fox's newsreel operations and now home to the interesting **Armand Hammer Museum** (10899 Wilshire Boulevard, Westwood; tel: 310-443 7000; admission charge), which exhibits European paintings, da Vinci drawings, and traveling art shows.

BELOW: girls having
fun with Chanel.
RIGHT: LA's famous
Chinese Theatre.

It is now better known as a college town because it adjoins the tree-shaded **University of California** (UCLA) ⓮ campus. UCLA's 130 buildings include Schoenberg Hall (named after the composer who taught here), Bunche Hall

Library and the Frederick S Wight Art Gallery, all open to the public. The college's main entrance is on Hilgard Avenue, south of Sunset. A first stop should include the **Visitor Center** (tel: 310-206 0616) in Murphy Hall for maps and information about tours and free movies.

The gated community of ultra-chic Bel Air is north of Sunset, the road up through Stone Canyon passing what some think of as LA's nicest hideaway hotel, the **Hotel Bel-Air** ⓯. Its peaceful grounds are intersected by a stream along which glide graceful swans. Grace Kelly lived here for much of her movie career.

Back on Sunset, the boulevard begins a series of dizzying loops and curves passing through **Brentwood**, site of the impressive **Getty Center** ⓰ *(see page 268)*. One of Raymond Chandler's many homes was at 12216 Shetland Place and Marilyn Monroe died in a bungalow at 12305 Fifth Helena Drive. Sunset continues through **Pacific Palisades** before sweeping down to the Pacific Coast Highway.

Just before the coast, on the left, is a sharp turnoff to the lakeside shrine of the **Self Realization Fellowship**, but a mile or two before that it's worth turning off to the right for the challenging, uphill drive to the **Will Rogers State Historic Park** ⓱. The cowboy philosopher, who had been America's top box-office star, died in a plane crash in 1935. The ranch was turned over to the state which has maintained it as a museum pretty much as it was when Rogers lived.

J. PAUL GETTY MUSEUM AND THE GETTY CENTER

More than a dozen years in the making, the billion-dollar Getty Center has been likened to a Tuscan hilltown by its architect Richard Meier

The white city on the hill high above the intersection of the Santa Monica and San Diego freeways has – like most examples of modern architecture – provoked both praise and criticism. Detractors have claimed it resembles an oversize refrigerator or a strip mall while one admirer claims it is "too good for Los Angeles." Richard Meier, winner of architecture's highest honor, the Pritsker Prize, was chosen for the commission after a worldwide search. He described the site as the most beautiful he had ever been invited to build upon, one whose light, landscape and topography provided the cues for his design. The center, he says, "is both in the city and removed from it… evok[ing] a sense of both urbanity and contemplation."

The collections are displayed in a series of five interconnecting buildings – the J. Paul Getty Museum – but the Getty Center site also houses six other buildings, including a research institute, a library, an auditorium and a restaurant, most offering breathtaking views of the city, the sea and the mountains. Between the museum and the research institute is a central garden, designed by artist Robert Irwin, that changes with the seasons.

The Getty Center, 1200 Getty Center Drive, tel: 310-440 7300. Closed Mondays.

▷ **LANSDOWN HERAKLES**
This statue discovered in 1790 at emperor Hadrian's villa near Tivoli is the inspiration behind Getty's decision to build his own Malibu villa and museum.

△ **THE CRUCIFIXION**
This exhibit is from the *Stammheim Missal*, a German manuscript created in Hildesheim *circa* 1160.

▷ **BUILDING BOOM**
In addition to the five buildings housing the works of art there are six others on-site.

△ **THE HOLY FAMILY**
Buonarotti's drawing, *circa* 1530, was reworked many times in different mediums.

▽ **BERLIN FREE ZONE**
This architectural drawing by Lebbeus Woods of a building facade was one of the inaugural installations.

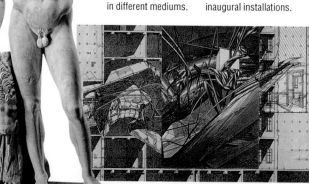

Minneapolis-born oil billionaire J. Paul Getty, who always refused to fly and chose to live his last years as a virtual recluse in England, never saw the Malibu museum which bears his name. From the oilfields of Kuwait in May 1954, he telegraphed regrets that he could not attend the opening: "I hope this museum, modest and unpretentious as it is, will give pleasure..."

Originally the site had been occupied by a ranch house which Getty had opened up to the public to display his collection of art and antiquities, but after he left California, the hillside tract was transformed in 1974 into the elaborate reproduction of a Pompeian villa we see today.

On Getty's death two years later, aged 83, at his mock-Tudor home in England, Getty oil stock was left to the museum – a $700 million endowment which has now grown into billions. Planning for the ambitious Getty Center began almost immediately, but family lawsuits (eventually running up $26.4 million in legal fees) held up events until 1982, after which the hilltop site was acquired.

Despite his five stormy marriages and innumerable mistresses, only one of his 26 heirs – his third son, Gordon – is connected with either of the museums today.

DAVID HOCKNEY MOSAIC

The British-born artist created *Pearlblossom Hwy 11–18th April 1986 # 2* over nine days in the Antelope Valley outside Los Angeles. Ten feet in width by 6 feet high, it is a mounted mosaic of 700 photographs (depicting the vast desert landscape), and is the first major work by Hockney to enter the museum's contemporary collection.

◁ **THE MALIBU MUSEUM**
When the recreated Pompeian villa is reopened in 2001, its focus will be on comparative archaeology and cultures and its exhibits devoted to the vast trove of Greek and Roman antiquities which, from the villa's opening in 1954, was obliged to share space with the rest of the Getty Trust's vast collection, most of which now reside at the Getty Center.

THE LA SEASHORE

From the exclusive Malibu Colony to the roller-blading boardwalk of Venice, Los Angeles wouldn't be Los Angeles without its photogenic beach

Map, page 248

Once upon a time, it took a full day's stagecoach ride to get to Santa Monica from downtown, but when the Santa Monica Freeway opened in 1966, the trip was cut to half an hour: Los Angelenos had discovered the beach. Whereas previously the city's seashores had been the preserve of fishermen and those wealthy enough to build bungalows by the sea, suddenly everyone was sporting a tan and hanging ten.

Where Sunset hits the Pacific Coast Highway (PCH) is one mile south of the fabulous **Getty Villa** ⑱, former home of many treasures from the J. Paul Getty collection now rehoused in the Getty Center. The villa, arguably America's most beautiful museum, will reopen as an evocative, highly suitable permanent home to the Greek and Roman exhibits. Up the highway is **Topanga County beach** with a full range of public facilities, but somewhat territorially-minded surfers.

Malibu

A couple of miles farther north on PCH is the community of **Malibu** ⑲ and its free state beach, and pier. Just north of the pier is the historic **Adamson House** (tel: 310-456 8432, Wednesday–Saturday 11am–3pm). There is a small admission fee for guided tours and parking. The Adamson House was built in 1929 by May Rindge, widow of Malibu's founder and major landholder. It is as attractive outside as inside, and even when the house is closed you can drive or walk up the lane (or even off the beach) and admire the tiled terrace, the lovely fountains, bottle-glass windows and well-kept gardens. Frederick Rindge bought hundreds of acres of surrounding land for $10 an acre back in 1887.

A display in the museum, which features old photographs, explains that the real Malibu Gold is real estate: Bing Crosby's house cost him $8,700 in 1931 and was bought for almost $2 million by Robert Redford half a century later. Harold Lloyd's 1928 house cost him $6,400, but singer Linda Ronstadt paid $1.3 million in 1985. Just south of the lagoon (a preserved wetland in which you can sometimes spot ducks, herons and pelicans) is **Malibu Pier**, built by Rindge just before he died in 1905. The pier closed in 1995 due to storm damage and is undergoing a $4 million restoration.

Dozens of stars live hidden away here, some of them along the well-guarded beachfront **Malibu Colony** at the junction of PCH and Webb Way, but the only place they're likely to be seen in public is the Colony shopping center about a mile to the north of the pier. More interesting is the Malibu Country Mart between the shopping center and the pier. Blockbuster Video at 23705 W. Malibu Road is the local store whose customers include Nick Nolte, Bruce Willis, Demi Moore, Steven Spielberg, Cher and Candice Bergen.

LEFT: sand volleyball, always big in California, is now an Olympic sport. **BELOW:** would-be sailors in the sand.

Broad Beach, like so much of the Malibu coastline, is private but only down to the mean high-tide line. Which means that as long as you stay on wet sand you have every right to be there. Maybe you'll spot a superstar jogging. Easily-missed access to the beach is in the 3100 and 3200 block of Broad Beach Road. Zuma beach and Pt Dume state beach are public, and therefore understandably become pretty crowded. Up in Malibu's Ramirez Canyon, the environmentally friendly Streisand Center for Conservancy Studies (tel: 310-589 2850) occupies the 22.5-acre site of what was formerly one of Barbra Streisand's estates, donated by the singer in 1993. Walking paths shaded by sycamore, walnut and pine trees wind along Ramirez Creek. The center, used mainly for conferences, conducts public tours twice monthly for which reservations must be made.

Santa Monica

At the northern end of Santa Monica, the enormous mansions along the beach were mostly built by moviedom's elite. The grandest, at 415 Pacific Coast Highway, was the 118-room compound designed by William Randolph Hearst's favorite architect, Julia Morgan, for the newspaper tycoon and his paramour, Marion Davies. In 1945, the house was sold for $600,000 to Joseph Drown, owner of the Hotel Bel-Air who turned it into a beach hotel and club. Today, it is not in use, but serves as a good reminder of Hollywood's golden years.

In those days, before the breakwater extended the beach, the sea came to within 50 feet (15 meters) of most of these homes. It was another famous architect, Richard Neutra, who created Mae West's home at number 514, while Wallace Neff, who designed Pickfair, was responsible for the home of Louis B Mayer's son-in-law, producer William Goetz at number 522.

BELOW: the Place for shopping: Santa Monica Place.

The "Bay City" setting of so many of Raymond Chandler's detective novels
s where Wilshire and Sunset boulevards meet the ocean, albeit a couple of miles
part. **Santa Monica ㉟** is something of an anomaly, being an upper-middle
lass town with rent control that's slowly being phased out, a recently discov-
red, affordable office space for Hollywood production companies, and a seaside
esort in which the sea often seems barely relevant. This is apart from the cen-
ury-old **Santa Monica Pier** (which recently underwent a 10-year, $45-million
enovation) with a famous carousel that appeared in *The Sting*.

Discussing the locale of Chandler's novels, his biographer Frank MacShane
aid he felt the detective story was an entirely appropriate form for LA because
uch stories "could involve an extraordinary range of humanity from the very
ich to the very poor and can encompass a great many different places." And as
o involving an extraordinary range of humanity, Santa Monica certainly qual-
ïes, if only for being the largest coastal town in the 100-mile (160-km) stretch
etween Oxnard and Long Beach.

Affluent "industry" types drop in from Malibu or their offices nearby to shop
r use the fine library, and people from all over the area frequent the spacious
edestrian mall, the **Third Street Promenade**, which leads to sparkling **Santa
Monica Place**. This is an attractive and upscale mall designed by the interna-
onally acclaimed local architect Frank Gehry, with major department stores,
cores of eating places and nearby cinemas. A few blocks to the west and south
s the aforementioned pier, with its numerous amusement arcades, eating places
nd fishing stands, where the visitor can gaze at miles of beaches curving gen-
y around the bay, but all too often the ocean is too polluted for safe swimming.

Eucalyptus-fringed **Palisades Park ㉑**, overlooking the pier, was given to

Map,
page 248

*Raymond Chandler
(1888–1959) set
many of his books
in Santa Monica.*

BELOW: Getty Villa.

the city in 1892 for use "forever" by Santa Monica's founders, Col. Robert Baker and his partner, silver tycoon John P Jones. Jones's house at the corner of Wilshire was where the **Miramar Sheraton Hotel** now sits; the enormous fig tree outside the lobby was planted by a member of the family more than a century ago. Greta Garbo spent her first three years living at the Miramar when she first came to the US in 1924. The pool was seen in the "Bermuda" sequence of *That Touch of Mink* with Cary Grant and Doris Day.

Just to the south on Ocean Avenue is **Champagne Towers**, an office and apartment complex set up by bandleader Lawrence Welk, whose national TV program for years was broadcast from the now-defunct Aragon ballroom in Venice, a mile away. The adjoining General Telephone Building, part of **Lawrence Welk Plaza**, was the site of a long-running television series, *Marcus Welby MD*. Adjoining the Towers, the eye-catching Wilshire Palisades Building won an award for its architects in 1960. The Queen Anne house at 1333 Ocean Avenue was once owned by Gussie Moran, a tennis star who was almost as well known for her frilly undergarments. Almost opposite is a handy resource center, the **Visitor Information** kiosk and to the south a **Camera Obscura** ㉒ for which the (free) admission is via the Senior Recreation Center.

South of the pier, a walkway and bicycle path adjoins the beach all the way down to Venice. (Buses run up and down Ocean Avenue, close to **Main Street** with its shops, cafés and **Heritage Square Museum** as well as a small Museum of Modern Art.) Heart of the artistic community is the attractive **Rose Cafe** on Rose Avenue at Main Street, where locally created artworks are sold in a small shop that's part of this lively set-up. Sip espresso and nibble sinfully rich pastries while sitting on stools at high tables or on the outside patio.

BELOW: mood over Malibu.

Some of the city's most interesting murals can be seen around Venice – Christina Schlesinger's *Marc Chagall Comes to Venice Beach* at 801 Ocean Front Walk and Emily Winters' *Endangered Species* six blocks down are notable – which happens to be the headquarters of SPARC, an organization which sponsors such public art. Its greatest triumph is the *Great Wall of Los Angeles*, covering half a mile beside the Los Angeles River in Van Nuys.

Map, page 248

Venice

The closer you get to **Venice ㉓**, the odder the ambience. An early favorite of such silent movie-makers as Charlie Chaplin and Carole Lombard, **Venice Boardwalk** is today jammed almost around the clock with characters who appear to be auditioning for some unannounced contemporary epic. Sights and sounds are likely to include guitar-bearing rollerbladers in robes and turbans, bikini-clad beach bunnies, rainbow-haired punks, lunatic dreamers, outrageous ironmen, barely-dressed cyclists, psychics, chain-saw jugglers and the bicep-bound boasters of **Muscle Beach**. Occasionally fights break out, so be warned. There are sidewalk cafés at which it's a relief to rest and watch all this activity.

But there is another less-explored Venice a few blocks to the east. After you have noted St Mark's, the bar/restaurant/dancehall on **Windward Avenue**, whose colonnaded arches are meant to evoke visions of San Marco Square in Venice's Italian namesake, walk east to the post office which earlier in the century was where most of the canals met. Many are now paved over, but a walk of a few blocks to the south will bring you to what remains of the watery network, a charmingly tranquil area of shallowly-filled canals lined with houses in a myriad styles, mostly with gardens full of flowers that only grow in the hot

ABOVE AND BELOW: just a couple of the outdoor activities to be observed in Venice.

Map, page 248

sunshine. Ducks and geese line the walkways. If you are driving, the route is down Dell Avenue across the humpback bridges. When tobacco magnate Abbott Kinney invested millions in creating his Venice from what was 160 acres (65 hectares) of worthless marshland in the early 1900s, he lined the canals with Japanese lanterns, imported gondolas, encircled the project with a miniature railroad and sold scores of housing lots. Visitors who paid 25¢ to take the new railroad from downtown ended a busy day on the (now-abandoned) pier watching an armored trumpeter serenade the sunset from a replica of Juan Cabrillo's medieval flagship before retiring for the night in the St Mark's Hotel, modeled after the Doge's Palace in you-know-where.

Despite Kinney's ambitious plans, which included hiring Sarah Bernhard and the Chicago Symphony Orchestra for his 3,500-seat auditorium before scaling down the attractions for more plebeian audiences, the project gradually deteriorated. And its collapse was speeded by the discovery of oil (there were 163 wells in the area by 1931) and by the shortage of fresh water. Like so many neighboring communities, Venice was obliged to come under the aegis of Los Angeles if it wanted to ensure a regular water supply. With incorporation came less tolerance for canals when paved roads could occupy the space.

The circulation system for what was originally 16 miles of canals envisaged seawater pulsing through 30-inch (76-cm) pipes from every fresh tide, but it proved unworkable and the canals themselves became sand-clogged and stagnant. In 1993, an extensive renovation began with plans to dredge the canals, refill them with water, repair the paths alongside and rebuild some of the bridges. Kinney's name has been memorialized in **Abbott Kinney Boulevard** – connecting Main Street with **Marina del Rey ㉔** – along which can be found interesting little cafés, restaurants and lots of shops.

BELOW: watery Marina del Rey. **RIGHT:** a smooch by the seaside.

Marina del Rey

On busy weekends Marina del Rey's Villa Marina Marketplace may be the nearest place to park but you can take the bus back to Venice. The marina's tourist attraction is the charming but phony **Fisherman's Village** (the "lighthouse" is a fast-food stand) with a multitude of restaurants for lunch.

These range from reasonably-priced Mexican fare to Shanghai Red's, which has all the appealing ambience of a century-old inn but has actually been there for only 35 years or so, since the marina began. At the end of Basin D is a shallow-water family beach known as "**Mother's Beach**." All the restaurants overlook the harbor – the world's largest artificial harbor for small craft – with its berths for 6,000 boats. From Beverly Hills the bus runs down Robertson Boulevard all the way to Marina del Rey which is also accessible by Santa Monica's Big Blue Bus.

Back on Ocean Avenue, take the Big Blue Bus up a few blocks to Ocean Park and transfer to the bus which runs along the north side of **Santa Monica airport**. From Clover Park, walk a couple of blocks down to the **Museum of Flying ㉕**. It was here, in 1977 at the McDonnell Douglas plant, that the DC3 was born and built, and it is here in this unusual setting that you can have dinner in a restaurant of the same name.

CANYONS AND VALLEYS

*The best-known spots are the San Fernando Valley
and the town of Pasadena, but the fringes of Los Angeles
offer historic houses and gardens galore*

Map,
page 282

Far from the typical glitzy tourist attraction, the San Fernando Valley has a low profile. Tinseltown and the beaches get plenty of television exposure, but aside from Northridge's 15 minutes of fame after the 1994 earthquake the rest of Los Angeles isn't seen too much. In fact, even many of LA's long-time residents know almost nothing of the valley – save that it's the area north-west that floods when it rains and bakes in a dry, desert heat layered in smog in the summer. It's that place they drive through on their way north to ski.

All of the vague and amorphous references to the valleys and canyons of Los Angeles merit some clarification. Of the three main valleys, the smallest is the **Santa Clarita**, known for its abundance of produce stands and the looming presence of the Six Flags Magic Mountain amusement park; next is the **San Gabriel**, which stretches through Pasadena and Monterey Park toward Riverside and San Bernardino. But the star of the three is the sprawling **San Fernando Valley**, and it is this one to which local people are usually referring when they simply say "the valley."

Various passes and canyons are byways to and from the valley: **Sepulveda Pass** connects it to West LA via the San Diego Freeway; the **Cahuenga Pass** takes it to Hollywood. **Laurel Canyon** connects Studio City and West Hollywood, and **Coldwater Canyon** connects Sherman Oaks to Beverly Hills. The last of the large canyons, **Topanga** and **Malibu**, offer dramatic routes from the landlocked valley to the ocean.

Flatlands of LA

In contrast to neighboring areas, the valley is a staggeringly flat expanse of land bounded by the Ventura county line on the West, the San Gabriel mountains to the north, the Verdugo range on the east and the Santa Monica Mountains and Hollywood Hills on the south. San Fernando Valley is about 24 miles (38 km) wide and 12 miles (19 km) north to south. The west and south sides are the more affluent – cities like **Encino**, **Tarzana**, **Woodland Hills** and **West Hills** display few signs of opulence, but a quiet wealth predominates. Heavy industry is almost all concentrated in the northern area, around Pacoima, Sylmar and San Fernando.

Were it a city unto itself, the valley would be the fifth largest in the country, topped only by New York, Chicago, Houston and, of course, Los Angeles. Despite sporadic efforts to secede, the valley is not its own city, however – with the exception of holdouts Burbank and Glendale. All the differently designated areas are merely neighborhoods in the City of Los Angeles, and compose nearly one-third of LA's population.

The valley more or less begins with **Griffith Park ❶** (tel: 323-665 5188), the immense preserve that begins at

PRECEDING PAGES:
Malibu Mountains
rancher.
LEFT: someone to
watch over you.
BELOW: welcome
to the valley.

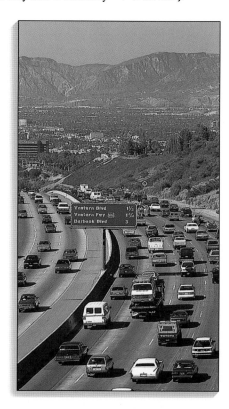

Los Feliz Avenue and extends all the way to the Ventura freeway. It has a **zoo**, a wonderful **observatory,** an **open-air theater**, numerous recreation areas and the excellent **Gene Autry Western Heritage Museum**, but is otherwise more for motorists than for strollers. Not too far away is one of the country's best collections of Native American art, on display at the **Southwest Museum ❷**, 234 Museum Drive, tel: 323-221 2164.

Universal Studios

West of the park, in the Cahuenga Pass which joins Hollywood to the valley, is **Universal Studios ❸** (tel: 818-508 9600 at Hollywood 101, daily 9am–7pm; admission charge), whose daily tours offer glimpses of the studio in what is in effect an amusement park. A 45-minute tram ride visits King Kong and the giant shark from *Jaws,* and negotiates the perils of a collapsing bridge, an avalanche, an earthquake and the parting of the Red Sea. Other additions include *Jurassic Park – The Ride*, the fiery *Backdraft* and a chance to beam aboard *Star Trek*'s Enterprise. You can see numerous outdoor sets, including the Bates mansion from *Psycho* and the facades from *Back to the Future*.

Universal Studios is the world's largest working entertainment studio. It can also be a fun day out.

    Universal CityWalk (tel: 818-622 3801), is a glittery mall with one-of-a-kind shops, a neon art museum and an 18-screen cinema. Admission is free but there is a parking fee; budget-conscious visitors can take a bus to Universal City and a studio tram from there.

    Other tours can be enjoyed back downtown at **CBS Studio Center ❹** (tel: 323-852 2624) where many sit-coms have been made, including *Seinfeld* and *Roseanne*; plus two in "beautiful downtown Burbank" (as the longtime host of *The Tonight Show,* Johnny Carson, dubbed it): the **NBC Television Studios ❺** (tel: 818-840 3537) and **Warner Brothers Studios ❻** (tel: 818-954 6000) which offers a serious VIP tour of its grounds – watch them make whatever program is on the day's shooting agenda. Also in Burbank, but not open to the public, is the unbelievably successful **Walt Disney Studios**.

    Forest Lawn Memorial Park ❼ has two locations flanking Griffith Park (at 4,000 acres/1,618 hectares, the nation's largest): **Glendale**, and the **Hollywood Hills** (tel: 800-204 3131). The Glendale location, the inspiration for Evelyn Waugh's *The Loved One*, is a must-see. All the park literature studiously

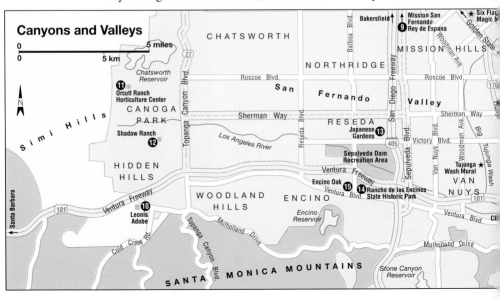

Canyons and Valleys

0   5 miles
0   5 km

N

CHATSWORTH

NORTHRIDGE

MISSION HILLS

Bakersfield
Mission San Fernando
❾ Rey de Espana
Six Flags Magic M
Golden State

Chatsworth Reservoir
❶❶ Orcutt Ranch Horticulture Center
CANOGA PARK
Shadow Ranch ❶❷

Roscoe Blvd.
San Fernando Valley
Roscoe Blvd.
Sherman Way
Sherman Way
RESEDA
Japanese Gardens ❶❸

Simi Hills

HIDDEN HILLS

WOODLAND HILLS

ENCINO

Los Angeles River

Sepulveda Dam Recreation Area
Ventura Freeway
Encino Oak
❶❺ Ventura Blvd. ❶❹ Rancho de los Encinos State Historic Park

Tujunga ★ Wash Mural
VAN NUYS

Ventura Freeway
❶⓪ Leonis Adobe

Encino Reservoir

Mulholland Drive

Cold Creek Rd.
Topanga Canyon Blvd.
SANTA MONICA MOUNTAINS
Stone Canyon Reservoir

Santa Barbara

Ventura Blvd.

Mulholland Drive

avoids the word "cemetery," instead describing founder Huber Eaton's vision of "the greenest, most enchanting park that you ever saw…"

Ultimately a final resting place (for many Hollywood stars, including Clark Gable, Carole Lombard, Nat King Cole and Jean Harlow), Forest Lawn also has reproductions of famous churches from around the world, a stained-glass interpretation of da Vinci's *The Last Supper* and the world's largest religious painting, *The Crucifixion* by Jan Stykam, measuring 195 by 45 feet (59 by 14 meters). The Hollywood Hills branch is dedicated to early American history, and features bronze and marble statuary, including a replica of the Liberty Bell in Philadelphia. Residents include Buster Keaton, Stan Laurel and Liberace.

Northeast a few miles, in the town of **Glendale ❽**, the **Brand Library and Art Center** (1601 W. Mountain Street at Grandview Avenue, tel: 818-548 2051, Tuesday 1–9pm, Wednesday 1–6pm, Thursday 1–9pm and Friday–Saturday 1–5pm) houses the art and music section of the city's public library in a Moorish-style mansion. Inspired by the East Indian Pavilion at the 1893 Chicago World's Fair, it was built in 1904 by Leslie C. Brand, and the peaceful, landscaped grounds are perfect for picnicking.

The *Tujunga Wash* **mural** (west wall of the concrete flood control channel at Coldwater Canyon Boulevard between Burbank Boulevard and Oxnard Street, North Hollywood) claims to be the world's longest mural. It recounts the history of California from dinosaurs to the present, and doesn't leave out the nasty bits. So it's quite a learning experience for participants and visitors alike.

Fascinating missions

Near the junction of US 5 and US 405 in Mission Hills is the historic and interesting **Mission San Fernando Rey de Espana ❾** (tel: 818-361 0186, daily 9am–4.30pm; admission fee), California's 17th mission, founded in 1797. Its history has been marked by destruction in two earthquakes (1806 and 1971) and reconstruction. The tour of the working, sleeping and recreation areas, and an extensive collection of artifacts recreate a sense of daily early mission life.

Nearby, the **Andres Pico Adobe**, the oldest home in San Fernando and second oldest in the Greater LA area, was built by Mission San Fernando Indians in 1834. After years of disuse, it was purchased and restored in 1930 by the cura-

Map, page 282

Universal Studios' scary, theme-based action ride: you'll wish it was just a movie, they say.

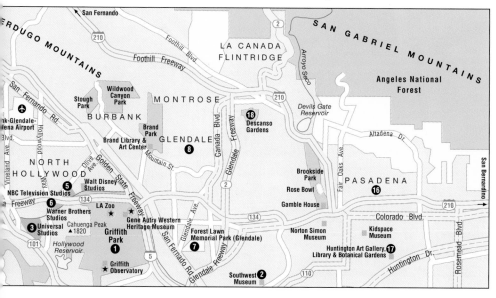

TIP

A stunning scenic
route is Mulholland
Drive, which goes
across the local Santa
Monica Mountains
from the Hollywood
Hills and almost to the
ocean. The drive offers
– among other plea-
sures – a 360-degree
view of Los Angeles.

tor of the Southwest Museum, housing the **San Fernando Historical Society**. Just to the northeast is the very different **San Sylmar Tower of Beauty Museum** (15180 Bledsoe Street, Sylmar, tel: 818-367 2251), a private museum owned and operated by the Merle Norman Cosmetic Co. It offers the visitor a world-class collection of antiques, vintage automobiles, rare musical instruments and music boxes. Tours require reservations, so call ahead, and don't forget that there is a dress code; children under 12 are not allowed.

US 5 continues northwest to **Valencia**, site of the popular **Six Flags Magic Mountain** amusement park that has 2,100-plus rides and other attractions.

At the valley's western end, near Mulholland Drive, is the **Leonis Adobe** ⑩ (23537 Calabasas Road at Mulholland Drive), a two-story 1844 Monterey-style ranch house transformed by "King of Calabasas" ("pumpkin" in Spanish) Miguel Leonis into this charming home, fully restored and furnished. Located on the same property is the **Plummer House** (serving as the **park visitor center**), a pretty Victorian cottage which was transported from a site in Hollywood to avoid demolition.

Orcutt Ranch Horticulture Center ⑪ (23600 Roscoe Boulevard, West Hills) perfectly recalls a vanished moment in California history – citrus groves bounded by majestic and stately oaks, ancient on their native soil. When the Orcutts purchased the 200-acre (80-hectare) estate in 1917, they named it Rancho Sombra del Roble, ranch in the shadow of the oak, which is quite literally the case. There is one magnificent valley oak 33 feet (10 meters) in circumference that is estimated to be at least 700 years old.

The gardens enclose other areas, decorated by statuary and sundials, that are now variously favored for picnics and weddings. The orange groves are open

BELOW:
Universal CityWalk.

o the public on one weekend announced in July, and the proceeds augment the garden's city-allotted budget. **Shadow Ranch** ⓬ (22633 Vanowen Street, Canoga Park) is a restored 1870 ranch house built by LA pioneer Albert Workman and located on the remaining 9 acres (4 hectares) of a 60,000-acre (24,280-hectare) wheat ranch. After being damaged in the 1994 earthquake, it is being repaired and will reopen soon. The stands of eucalyptus are purported to be parents of the towering trees that now blanket the state, and the ranch is currently used as a community center.

The **Japanese Gardens** ⓭ (6100 Woodley Avenue, Van Nuys), a 6-acre (2-hectare) botanical delight, is little-known despite having been created almost a decade ago on the Donald C. Tillman Water Reclamation Plant. Morning tours visit three gardens in distinctly different styles. In summer, there are "sunset" tours on weekdays – so popular that reservations are a must.

Rancho de los Encinos State Historic Park ⓮ (16756 Moorpark Street, Encino), originally the site of a Native American village, later became a ranch belonging to the de la Osa family, who planted vineyards and orchards, and raised cattle. Amidst the 5 acres (2 hectares) of manicured lawns, duck ponds and eucalyptus and citrus groves is the de la Osa Adobe, built in 1849 and restored with period furnishings. Also damaged by the major quake, it too will reopen in 2000. (The grounds are already open to the public, however.) A stone blacksmith shop and a two-story French provincial home, built by the rancho's second owners, are also located here.

Some of LA's major restaurants have branched out into the valley, bringing what's been called "310 food" to the 818 area code. More than anything, though, this is shopping mall country. "You eat, you shop. It's the valley," as one Sher-

BELOW: blazing a trail through the canyons.

man Oaks resident put it. Shopping in the valley is easy. Parking is abundant compared with the rest of Los Angeles, although the burgeoning population, combined with the lack of public transportation, has slowed traffic.

There are mega-malls like the **Sherman Oaks Galleria**, which is in mid-valley about halfway between **Topanga Plaza** to the west and **Glendale Galleria** nearer to LA; also at the western end are **Woodland Hills Promenade**, and **Town and Country Shopping Center** and **Plaza de Oro** in Encino. There's also 21-mile (6-km) long Ventura Boulevard, the valley's upscale artery of restaurants and pricey shops.

Just north of the boulevard, the astonishing **Encino Oak** ⓰, located within the Town and Country Shopping Center and Plaza de Oro (17200 Ventura Boulevard, Encino) is estimated to be over 1,000 years old. The branches spread 150 feet (46 meters) and the trunk is over 25 feet (8 meters) around.

In parts, Ventura Boulevard is beginning to resemble a mini-Wilshire Corridor, while a half-mile strip near Van Nuys Boulevard has taken on the aura of Melrose Avenue. Here is Antique Row comprising over 28 shops on Sherman Way specializing in Americana, from memorabilia and collectables to bric-a-brac and very good furniture for the home.

Pasadena

To the east of the San Fernando Valley and bordering almost on the San Gabriel Mountains, **Pasadena** ⓰ comes fully alive once a year during the Rose Bowl football game and the famous Tournament of Roses Parade. A couple of famous houses are well worth inspecting, but note that they close early.

Near the freeway is the 18-room **Fenyes Mansion** (1905), home of the **Pasadena Historical Museum**, where DW Griffith shot one of his first films (open some afternoons only; admission fee). Half a block away is the impressive **Gamble House**, built for David Gamble (of Procter & Gamble, America's biggest soap company) in 1908. Technically a California-style "bungalow," the terraced wood-tiled house is a product of the turn of the century Arts and Crafts Movement of which the Greene brothers, Charles Sumner and Henry Mather were noted members. Impressive from the outside (and therefore worth seeing even when the house is closed), its interior is a knockout, but to see this you must reserve a place on a tour.

Just before the freeway is the **Norton Simon Museum** (411 W Colorado at Orange Grove, tel: 626 449 6840, open Thursday–Sunday noon–6pm; admission charge), with its major collection of Asian art.

Pasadena's main attraction, however, is the **Huntington Library, Art Collections and Gardens** ⓱ (tel: 626-405 2141, open Tuesday–Friday noon–4.30pm Saturday–Sunday 10.30am–4.30pm; admission charge). Just past the California Institute of Technology on California Street near Allen Street, walk down to Orlando to enter the former gardens and library of multi-millionare railroad magnate Henry Edwards Huntington. With his wife Arabella, Huntington assembled one of the most important collections of art and rare books in the country.

BELOW:
Descanso Gardens.

Because the gardens occupy more than 100 acres (40 hectares), it's not difficult to find yourself in some tranquil spot with nothing but the sound of birds for company. Beyond the lily pond are the colorful Subtropical Garden, the Australian Garden, and the Japanese and Zen gardens flanking a delightful 19th-century Japanese house.

After crossing the little red bridge over the carp-filled lake and climbing the steps, you'll find yourself in the Rose Garden just in time for tea. Reservations are required at the charming **Rose Garden Room**, which shuts its doors mid-afternoon. Admission to the Huntington is free, under the terms of the railroad magnate's will, but donations are invited and you have to pay for parking. The main building has an excellent bookshop with interesting toys.

North of Pasadena, off the Angel's Crest Highway exit on Interstate 210 is **Descanso Gardens** ⓱ (1418 Descanso Drive, La Canada, tel: 626-952 4400, daily 9am–4.30pm; admission charge), which cover what remains of a 30,000-acre (12,140-hectare) ranch. The 165-acre (67-hectare) gardens take a good couple of hours to explore. The oak and camellia woodlands, with more than 600 varieties, constitute one of the largest camellia collections in the world. The woodlands began as carefully planned landscaping along the private drive leading to a magnificent 22-room house built in 1938 by *Daily News* publisher E Manchester Boddy.

This beautiful collection is augmented by winding, shady trails, a lilac garden, the Descanso Rose History Garden (a timeline of roses from Cleopatra's day to ours) and the Japanese Garden and Teahouse, which serves tea and cookies (admission fee). The gardens are cleverly organized so that something is always blooming whenever you arrive. ❑

Map, page 282

ABOVE: Pasadena is a city of gardens. **BELOW:** Pasadena Historical Society.

THE CENTRAL COAST

*Even a century ago, the Santa Barbara area was lauded for
"the beauty of its surroundings, the excellence of its bathing beach
and its pleasant society." Not much has changed*

Map,
page 242

San Francisco
California
Los Angeles

alifornia's coast north of Los Angeles, between Ojai and San Luis Obispo, is a pleasant, easy drive. On the way, consider a side trip off the Pacific Coast Highway along State Route 150 to **Ojai ❶**, hidden away on the edge of the Los Padres National Forest. It's one of those sleepy artists-and-writers' colonies that's somehow remained still unspoiled. The 1926 movie *Lost Horizon* was filmed around here, and Shangri-la is the way some residents think of it. The town itself is centered around its main street on which a graceful tower offsets a row of unpretentious shops under a covered veranda.

The predominantly Spanish-style architecture owes its origins to a glass tycoon, Edward Drummond Libby, who in 1917 built the elegant **Oaks Hotel** opposite the library. Artifacts in the **Ojai Valley Museum** (130 W Ojai Avenue, tel: 805-640 1390, Wednesday–Sunday 1–4pm) include those from Chumash Indian times (baskets, tools, etc) through to the present. Located in the newly-renovated St Thomas Aquinas Chapel (*circa* 1918), permanent and changing exhibits focus on the environmental, cultural and historical factors that shaped the Ojai valley.

The Oaks (tel: 805-646 5573), a 46-room spa hotel, is owned by Sheila Cluff, a fitness buff who has written a syndicated column, and where brisk, pre-breakfast walks are the norm. Nearby is what is probably the friendliest bookstore in California, **Bart's Corner**. There are over 100,000 volumes, and a giant, 200-year-old oak tree grows through the patio. The local winery on Old Creek Road has wine tastings on weekend afternoons. Ojai stages a tennis tournament every spring, an arts festival in October, and a classical music festival in June. West of town, State 150 winds along some 60 miles (97 km) of the shoreline of **Lake Casitas**, but the scenery is even better along the coast.

**PRECEDING PAGES
AND LEFT:** Mission
Santa Barbara.
BELOW: the long
arm of the law.

Ventura and Santa Barbara Island

The town of **Ventura ❷** is dominated by an ostentatious city hall perched on the hillside, but this is much outshone in style and grace by the over 200-year-old **Mission San Buenaventura** with its pretty garden, founded by the redoubtable Father Junípero Serra *(see page 26)*. It sits on the edge of a restored "**Olde Towne**" area which won't detain you.

Trips are made from near Ventura to beautiful, desolate **Santa Barbara Island ❸**, whose 640 acres (259 hectares) are a haven for birds, sea lions and 10,000 breeding seals. None of these islands, part of isolated **Channel Islands National Park**, are inhabited, but most of them can be visited on tours conducted by park rangers (for information, telelephone 805-985 4852). There are flights to **Santa Rosa Island** from Camarillo airport (tel: 805-967 1301).

Near Ventura you can catch a boat or an airplane to visit one of the five Channel Islands. Telephone 805-58 5700 for details on camping and guided tours.

Just on the southern outskirts of Santa Barbara, the charming **Montecito Inn** (tel: 805-969 7854) was popular with refugees from Hollywood in the 1920s when one of its original owners was Charlie Chaplin. The more popular elite retreat today is the **Four Seasons Biltmore** (tel: 805-969 2261). Montecito's other legendary hotel is **San Ysidro Ranch** (tel: 805-969 5046), where John F. Kennedy honeymooned with his wife, Jackie; where Lauren Bacall says she fell in love with Humphrey Bogart, and the site of a midnight wedding in 1940 between Laurence Olivier and Vivien Leigh.

The area around Santa Barbara is the jumping off point for the emerging and increasingly well-regarded **Santa Ynez Valley wineries**, most of which welcome visitors. Included among the 30-plus wineries are the interesting and high-profile **Firestone Vineyard** (tel: 805-688 3940), and the **Fess Parker Winery** (tel: 805-688 1545), run by the ex-actor. For an up-to-date list of wineries and their tour times, contact the Santa Barbara County Vintners' Association, 3669 Sagunto Street, Unit 103, Santa Ynez, tel: 805-688 0881.

Santa Barbara

The town of **Santa Barbara** ❹ itself, which got its start as a health resort after glowing articles by New York journalist Charles Nordhoff touted its mineral spings, is an attractive place whose architecture is almost entirely in idealized colonial Spanish style. Following a disastrous earthquake in 1925, a mandatory building code prohibited anything unharmonious in the flood of designs for replacement buildings. Before the earthquake, one author observed, it was "a wasteland of western junk that had spread over the original Spanish architecture like a smothering fungus."

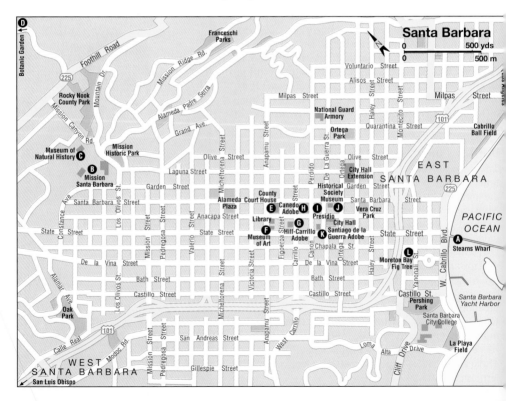

But, its architecture notwithstanding, the city has long been admired. Today, its palm-lined beaches stretch for 5 miles (8 km), and despite the fact that much of its society is not only affluent but aging ("the place where old people go to visit their parents," jokes author Barnaby Conrad), the city's residents have included author and TV cook Julia Child and such movie stars as Fess (Davy Crockett) Parker, Steve Martin, Karl Malden, Cher, Bo Derek, Jonathan Winters, Eva Marie Saint and Jane Russell.

Most of Santa Barbara's activities can be found along its main thoroughfare, **State Street**, particularly where it terminates at century-old **Stearns Wharf Ⓐ**, the oldest on the West Coast. This pier offers everything – seafood stands, restaurants, wine tasting, a marine museum and aquarium, fishing – and is the starting point for whale-watching boat trips which set off most days to catch glimpses of the heavyweight mammals returning north with their offspring after a trip to the Baja coast.

A waterfront shuttle tram operates between the wharf, downtown and the zoo, connecting the beaches which line the shore both sides of the pier with the volleyball courts and the more expensive hotels at the eastern end. A multi-colored 21-feet (6-meter) high **Chromatic Gate** stands on the waterfront near here. It was the work of Herbert Byer, last survivor of the seminal Bauhaus school who spent the years before his death in the town.

After checking out the pier, head north up State Street and turn right for three or four blocks to the **Mission Santa Barbara Ⓑ** (Laguna and Olivos Streets, tel: 805-682 4713, daily 9am–5pm; admission charge), which, with its twin bell towers, is generally regarded as the most beautiful of the remaining missions. Founded in 1786, it was damaged in both of the area's major earthquakes (1812,

Maps,
page 242
& 292

BELOW:
rebuilt in 1925,
Santa Barbara's
architecture is an
idealized colonial
Spanish style.

1925) but lovingly restored and is still in use as a parish church *(see page 26)*. The museum displays relics from the days when Chumash Indians lived at the mission while being "trained" to undertake useful tasks by their Spanish overlords. More about Indian life preceding the occupation can be studied two blocks to the north in the **Museum of Natural History** ☉, with its array of inanimate animals, birds, reptiles and fish. There's one other attraction in this area, although it's more than a mile to the north up Mission Canyon Road: the attraction is the **Botanic Garden** ☉ (tel: 805-682 4726) with trails through 60 acres (24 hectares) of native flowers, shrubs and cacti.

Two blocks from the Greyhound bus station in the center of Santa Barbara is the handsome 1929 Spanish-Moorish **Court House** ☉ (1100 Anacapa Street, Monday–Friday 8.30am–4.30pm, Saturday–Sunday 10am–4pm). Its lobby is lined with mosaics and murals and there's a lovely view from the top of gently-sloping roofs and the multi-level lawn below.

Walk past the library to State Street, passing (or inspecting) the **Museum of Art** ☉, and turning left along Carrillo to visit the **Hill-Carrillo Adobe** ☉, built by Daniel Hill in 1826 for his Spanish bride for whom he constructed the city's first home with a wooden floor. Continue down Anacapa Street to Canon Perdido Street. The block to the left, bordered by the **Canedo Adobe** ☉ (*circa* 1782), is where the city began, centered around the **Presidio** ☉ with its chapel and parade grounds, more restored adobes and the **Historical Society Museum** ☉.

Head back one block towards State Street to admire the **Santiago de la Guerra Adobe** ☉ (1827), the original home of the Presidio's commander and his family. The plaza here is where the city council first met in 1850, an event still celebrated every August with a fiesta. Here also is the enticing cobbled area, **El Paseo** (or "the street in Spain" as tourist officials call it). It is by far the most attractive place in town to shop and sip a coffee at one of the outdoor cafés around the fountain. Half a century ago, the El Paseo theater used to feature on its stage a group of Spanish dancers which included Rita Cansino, better known as Rita Hayworth.

Heading back down State Street to the pier, you might want to make a short diversion to Chapala and Montecito streets to admire what's said to be the largest tree of its kind in America. It's a **Moreton Bay fig tree** ☉, native to Australia and planted here in 1877. Since then, its branches have grown to cover an area of 160 feet (48 meters) and often shade the city's dramatically down-and-out homeless community.

North of Santa Barbara

Leaving Santa Barbara and still traveling north on US 101, the highway passes through **Goleta**, home of a branch of the University of California, and skirts the shore past some gorgeous beaches before offering another sidetrip at **Solvang** ☉, a campily amusing replica of a Scandinavian town with horse-drawn streetcar, windmills and Danish bakeries. On nearby **Cachuma Lake**, there are guided cruises in winter to view a rare flock of migrating bald eagles.

Make a point, if time permits, of leaving US 101 at the **Los Alamos** ☉ turnoff to view this virtually one-block town with its antique stores, frontier-style build-

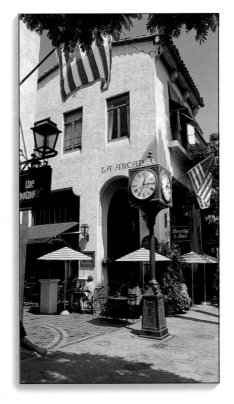

BELOW: El Paseo, a Santa Barbara shopping area.

ings and, especially, the **Victorian Mansion** and adjoining **Union Hotel** (tel: 805-344 2744). The latter has a wonderful saloon and poolroom as well as bedrooms and restaurant furnished completely in the style of a century ago. The first thought that comes to mind is how much honeymoon couples must love it; indeed, the area seems to be romantically attuned to that notion with similarly exotic theme rooms offered by the famously pink **Madonna Inn** (tel: 805-543-3000) which can be admired from US 101 just before San Luis Obispo and old-fashioned wedding ceremonies being promoted at the nearby town of **Nipono** in its 19th-century Victorian Wedding Bells Chapel or the Kaleidoscope Inn's beautiful garden gazebo.

Further north up 101 is **Pismo Beach** ❼, the only shore community actually on that road between Santa Barbara and San Francisco. There's a wide range of places to stay and the usual attractions of a seaside community. The famous Pismo clam, which grows almost to the size of a dinner plate, has almost disappeared, but there's an annual clam festival held in October. Almost as many come from late November through February to see the hordes of colorful Monarch butterflies which winter in a grove of eucalyptus and Monterey pines.

San Luis Obispo ❽, roughly halfway between Los Angeles and San Francisco, owes its beginnings to the 1772 mission, now a parish church. Its development was due to the arrival of the Southern Pacific Railroad in 1894. It's a pleasant town, which offers attractive historic strolls from the restored adobe on **Monterey Street**. The Victorian homes in the **Old Town** neighborhood around Buchon and Broad streets are worth exploring, and there's a regular Thursday night farmers' market downtown that turns into a street festival with entertainment and some great barbecues. ❑

Maps, page 242 & 292

ABOVE: fountain in Santa Barbara.
BELOW: San Luis Obispo's famously tacky Madonna Inn.

ANAHEIM

Despite the great popularity of newer theme parks,
there's nothing quite like the original Disneyland,
or the other family attractions around Anaheim

Map,
page 242

A naheim is best known for its amusement parks and similar attractions, of which Disneyland is by far the most famous. MTA bus 460 travels all the way to Disneyland from Los Angeles, but if you have a car (and ery limited time), you could just squeeze Disneyland and a visit to the archi-cturally fascinating **Crystal Cathedral** (12141 Lewis Street, Garden rove, tel: 714-971 4000, Monday–Saturday 9am–3.30pm, Sunday 6am–pm) of evangelist Robert Schuller at Garden Grove into the same day, and ill have dinner while watching the jousting at Medieval Times.

Another alternative is to stay in the **Anaheim** area overnight. There's not great deal to see locally, but it will save traveling to and from the parks very day. Disneyland itself has two fairly pricey if amusing hotels (with ver 1,800 rooms) conveniently on the grounds, but there are cheaper motels n West and Ball roads; most branches of major hotel chains operate free uttle buses to the park. Needless to say, you're still going to do a lot of alking even if you get there by car.

he Magic Kingdom

isneyland ❾ (1313 Harbor Boulevard, tel: 714-781 4000, hours vary; dmission charge. By mail: Disneyland Guest Rela-ons, PO Box 3232, Anaheim CA 92803) first pened with the tagline "Magic Kingdom" in 1955. Valt Disney once said that Disneyland grew out of is search for a clean, safe, friendly park where he ould take his own daughters.

One of Disney's early designers, John Hench, eferred to Walt's knack for putting "little touches of umanity" in everything he did. Hench said that lickey Mouse's appeal has something to do with his ody shape – all circles, all round, harmless and non-reatening. In fact, because of a height restriction – ou can't have Mickey towering too much over his ins – most of the besuited Mouse persons in Dis-eyland are actually girls.

There's still no successful way to avoid the crowds nd the lengthy line-ups, however, especially in sum-ertime. Obviously it helps to get there as soon as e gates open and head straight for the most popular des. If you want to be truly organized, write ahead or a map in order to plot your Disney strategy onths in advance, but do note: Disneyland is almost lways undergoing major expansions.

To avoid backtracking, it's probably wise to cover e park logically, one "land" at a time. A recent ttraction is the wild Indiana Jones ride, which as xpected, is pulling in the same huge numbers of eople as the ever-pleasing and hugely ambitious

PRECEDING PAGES:
dressed to thrill.
LEFT: introducing
Mr Michael Mouse.
BELOW: just
kidding around.

worlds of **Fantasyland**, **Adventureland**, **Frontierland**, **Critter Country** and jazzy **New Orleans Square**. **Tomorrowland**, always popular but a slave to the advances of technology, has recently undergone a major renovation. Pointing the way to the "land" is **Astro Orbitor**, which has colorful rockets circling a series of moving planets. People pilot their own spaceships as they soar through an animated "astronomical model" of constellations. Favorite thrill rides **Space Mountain** and **Star Tours** are still here, but with updated effects and new technology. As the most popular things to do always seem to be located in Tomorrowland, it makes sense to position yourself at the top of Main Street to maximize your time.

Main Street is the place to get information and maps (City Hall), exchange foreign currency and get credit card advances (Bank of America), rent a camera or camcorder (Kodak), hire a stroller or wheelchair (just inside the main entrance), stash your surplus items in a locker (adjoining Disney Clothiers) and attend to your infant (Baby Center, near the Magic Castle).

ABOVE:
'ere's Mickey.
BELOW: Disney's
nitetime Fantasmic.

Fantasyland will probably be the kids' favorite, but some of the rides there, such as Peter Pan's Flight, Mr Toad's Wild Ride, Alice in Wonderland and Snow White's Scary Adventure, seem to be aimed as much at adults. The first two are especially interesting, demonstrating how much illusion owes to darkness and luminous paint. From the **Sleeping Beauty Castle** and the steam train to the **Mark Twain Steamboat** (⅝th scale), most structures in Disneyland are scaled down from full size. Movie set designers are experts at using tricks of scale to make buildings seem taller or further away. The first floors of the buildings on Main Street, for example, are 90 percent of full size, the second floor 80 percent and so on.

Another interesting point concerns the 147-foot **Matterhorn**. After its 00-ton steel framework was in place, the mountain – ¹⁄₁₀₀th the size of the eal thing – was built from the top down. This was to stop the subsequent ement droppings spoiling the appearance of the slopes below. A ride called 'lying Saucers, based on air cushion technology developed by the space rogram, had a short, five-year life, being abandoned in 1966 after continu-ng maintenance problems. But another aspect of the space program resulted n the triumph of audio-animatronics, of which the moving, speaking fig-ıre of Abraham Lincoln is the earliest example of this technology in the park.

This process culminated in the 225 talking, moving birds, flowers and fig-ıres of the **Enchanted Tiki Room**. The room was first visualized as a res-aurant, but grew into a major attraction. Lincoln had been planned as but ıne element in a grand Hall of Presidents stretching along Liberty Street, ıut this scheme never came to fruition.

How much time you have available will pretty much decide your itinerary. The amusingly hokey **Big Thunder Mountain Railroad**, **Jungle Cruise** ınd the aforementioned Enchanted Tiki Room and Mark Twain Steamboat ıre all good fun, and the seasonal night-time spectacular **Fantasmic** is such ı sensation that crowds start jostling for good viewpoints two hours' ahead. There's sure to be a line-up, too, for Tomorrowland's attraction based on the ınovie "Honey, I Shrunk the Audience", which includes 3D effects.

But try not to miss **New Orleans Square**, with its **Haunted Mansion** and ıearby **Pirates of the Caribbean**. Talking about his cast of 64 humans and ›5 animals in Pirates, sculptor Blaine Gibson explained: "In a ride system 'ou have only a few seconds to say something about a figure through your

**Map,
page 242**

TIP

Disneyland's Main
Street opens half an
hour earlier than the
rest of the park, so you
can get your maps,
film and souvenir
shopping done first.

BELOW: Movieland
Wax Museum.

Map, page 242

art. So we exaggerate their features, especially their facial features, so the can be quickly and easily understood from a distance… we have to instant communicate 'good guy' or 'bad guy.' We try to provide the illusion of life

The same might be said of the guy who started it all. "The way I see Disneyland will never be finished," reflected Walt a long time ago. "I've a ways wanted to work on something alive, something that keeps growin We've got that at Disneyland."

Anaheim's other attractions

A few miles north is **Knott's Berry Farm** (8039 Beach Boulevard, Bue Park, tel: 714-220 5200, hours vary; admission charge), a recreated 19t century gold town, which grew out of a roadside snack bar operated t farmer Walter Knotts and his wife, Cordelia, whose reputation spread f and wide for tasty chicken dinners and slabs of boysenberry pie (served c the couple's wedding china). The place actually predates its bigger rival t a few years and is just as interesting, but a little funkier.

The characters are more primitive than high-tech and the staff char tourists with individual attention. At the town hall, for example, a "hor thief" will chat with strangers; visitors to the jail are always amazed to ha an unseen jailer call them by their first name and make remarks about wh they are wearing. The Ghost Town offers panning for gold, a stagecoa ride, a watery log ride, and stunt and vaudeville shows. In the contemp rary side of the park, the various other theme areas include stomach-dro ping rides such as the 20-story-freefall, the Sky Tower.

Recent additions are also for thrill-seekers, like the tributes to Southe California's beach culture: the 13-acre water par Soak City and the surf-inspired dual roller coaste Windjammer. Kids love the cartoon-themed Can Snoopy with its miniature train and other rides. T Kingdom of the Dinosaurs – a trip through Earth prehistoric era – became fashionable all over aga with the success of the movie *Jurassic Park*.

BELOW: a thirsty business. **RIGHT:** Knott's Berry Farm.

The **Movieland Wax Museum** (7711 Bea Boulevard, CA 39, Buena Park, tel: 714-522 115 daily; admission fee), one block north of Knott's c Beach Boulevard, is easily the most captivati example of its kind, and that includes more famo counterparts like Madame Tussaud's in Londo Maybe it's the glamor of those old Hollywood mo ies, and the delight of finally seeing what Jean Ha low and Mary Pickford look like close up. B whatever, it will occupy you for at least a couple hours, even if you skip the corny Chamber of Ho rors (most kids' favorite) or the shop selling so venirs of you as a super-simulated superstar.

And speaking of corny, what could be sillier th paying to eat a so-so meal without plates with yo bare hands in a fake castle, bowing to a fake king a queen and egging on some pretend-knights in a ba tle whose outcome is already fixed? Well, hundre of enthusiastic customers do it at **Medieval Tim** every night and enjoy themselves enormously. Wh the heck, you have to eat dinner somewhere.

SOUTH BAY AND ORANGE COUNTY

Map, page 242

*Beaches, coves, ecological preserves
and a surfer's Walk of Fame are just a few of the
coastal attractions south of Los Angeles*

I t takes a little longer to drive down the coast from Los Angeles towards San Diego than whizzing down the freeway, but the route is much more interesting because it passes through the various seaside resorts of the **South Bay**. All this area is still in Los Angeles County; the Orange County border begins after you reach Long Beach.

If you have time after passing through the South Bay communities, you could make a short diversion around the **Palos Verdes ⓿** peninsula to see the magnificent seaside homes (buses from the LAX Transit Center cover most of this route, connecting with another bus going into Long Beach). **Abalone Cove** beach, west of Narcissa Drive, is an ecological preserve at the end of a steep path and is perfect for divers and lovers of tidepools.

Just past the Golden Cove shopping center is a lighthouse beside which, at the **Point Vicente Interpretive Center** (31501 Palos Verdes Drive West, tel: 310-377 5370, daily 10am–5pm; admission charge), are telescopes to look for passing whales (December to spring); plus a small exhibit which includes an informative whale-watching video, as well as earphones to hear the mournful voices of these lovable mammals and a relief map of the peninsula showing how mountainous is the terrain. There are nice grassy grounds suitable for picnicking (bring your own food and drink) and leaflets identifying the various plants to be found on the (free) Botanic Trail.

About a mile further on is the wood and glass **Wayfarers Chapel** (tel: 310-377 1650), designed by Frank Lloyd Wright's son, Lloyd, whose inspiration is said to have been Northern California's majestic redwood trees. It was built in 1951 as a memorial to the 18th-century Swedish theologian Emmanuel Swedenborg. Walking around the peaceful gardens to the sound of songbirds, a fountain and the gurgling stream is a very tranquilizing experience. There are services in the chapel every Sunday.

San Pedro

Westwards along the coast is **San Pedro**, headquarters of Southern California's fishing fleet, which once distinguished this town as a genuine fishing port. All the genuine old parts of what aeons ago was a little fishing town are gone, of course, replaced by a pseudo construction, called **Ports O'Call Village**. It is surprisingly imaginative: several blocks of saltbox-type New England, apparently weathered shops – all in appealing, matching styles that are a pleasure to walk around. Harbor tours and fishing trips can

PRECEDING PAGES:
Long Beach and the
Queen Mary.
LEFT: sun & shades.
BELOW: child's play.

The Queen Mary *was built in 1936. One of the most stylish ships to sail the seas, royals and celebrities were regularly among her passengers. During World War II, and painted gray, she transported 800,000 soldiers in a series of daring cloak-and-dagger missions.*

BELOW: Naples.

be taken from here, as well as a classic sailing ship and the *Catalina Express,* (tel: 1-800-833 6685), which sails to Santa Catalina Island (*see page 313*). There's free parking space beside which a heroic fisherman statue proclaims. "Lo, the fisherman, for his harpoon, hook and net have long harvested the endless sea…" etc, etc.

A few miles south is San Pedro's **Cabrillo Beach**, which has earned a reputation as one of the best places in the area to windsurf. Beginners especially favor the sheltered waters inside the harbor breakwater. Palos Verdes Drive segues into 25th Street, from which a left turn on Gaffey (State Highway 110) and up to Highway 47 over the **Vincent Thomas Bridge** takes you straight ahead through Long Beach on Ocean Avenue.

Out in the bay take a close look at the palm-fringed island with the tall towers: it's actually one of four man-made islands created by a consortium of oil companies to hold (and conceal) all the working oil derricks which for 25 years have been tapping one of the richest offshore fields in the United States. The towers are illuminated at night.

The most famous attraction in the town of **Long Beach** ⓫ is the wonderful, historic *Queen Mary* ocean vessel (tel: 562-435 3511), whose Art Deco halls, restaurants and lounges have been beautifully restored. Tours are available, as is dinner or hotel rooms on the ship itself.

The local **Museum of Art** is an active one, and Long Beach is well known in particular for its video art and **street murals**. One of the most attractive suburbs of Long Beach is **Naples**, with its winding streets, waterside houses and one-hour **gondola tours** on boats that cruise elegantly along a series of canals. The tours are very popular, however, so call ahead on 562-433 959! to book. The **Long Beach Aquarium of the Pacifi** (tel: 562-590 3100) is said to be one of the top three in the United States.

The Orange Coast

The Pacific Coast Highway bypasses the sleepy tow of Seal Beach and runs beside the ecological wet lands preserve just before Bolsa Chica state beach At **Huntington Beach**, slow down to avoid the surfers carrying their boards across the road. Many of the communities around here are in dispute about which most deserves the title "Surf City," but Huntington Beach claims to have the best case. In fact, **Surfers Walk of Fame** commemorates legendar surfers on Main Street at the Pacific Coast Highway

At **Newport Beach** ⓬, the Balboa peninsula with its 6 miles of sandy shore encloses a harbor popula with yacht owners. On Main Street, it's hard to mis the **Balboa Pavilion**, built in 1905 as a railroad ter minal, with its distinctive but totally unnecessar steeple. Behind it you'll find fishing boats unload ing their catch if you get here early enough.

Almost as old is the ferry which makes the 3 minute trip from Palm Street to **Balboa Island** wit its million-dollar homes, and classy shops and café On your way back you can see the former homes c John Wayne and cowboy star Roy Rogers on nearb islands. From **Balboa Pier** you can admire the kite

Map, page 242

lyers, frisbee-throwers, body-surfers and just plain sunbathers. Check out
ne restaurant at the end of the pier before finishing up at the Balboa Fun
one, with its rides and video arcades. Beyond **Newport Bay**, at the inter-
ection of Poppy Avenue in Corona del Mar, a red English phone booth
tands outside the ivy-covered Five Crowns, an ersatz English pub.

Pelicans can sometimes be spotted at El Moro beach. Not far away in
aguna Beach ⑬ the annual **Pageant of the Masters** (tel: 949-464 4282)
resents tableaux of famous paintings with costumed participants. About
alfway between here and Corona del Mar, tiny **Crystal Cove** provides a
ranquil hideaway for the crowd-weary traveler. Before turning inland, the
arbor at **Dana Point** ⑭ is worth a stop to browse in the shops and have a
rink in the upstairs bar of the Jolly Roger. Then it's off on Del Obispo Street
o Camino Capistrano on which sits the **San Juan Capistrano Mission** ⑮
Ortega Highway, CA 74, tel: 949-248 2048, daily 8.30am–5pm; admission
harge), seventh in the chain of 21 missions established by Franciscan padres
n the 18th century *(see page 26)*.

Oldest building

ather Junípero Serra founded several of the missions, this one included,
nd his statue stands beside the Great Stone Church to the right as we enter,
vhich is currently being restored. The Serra chapel behind the church is the
ldest still-in-use building in California. Pick up a free map which identi-
es and dates everything, including the bells to the left of the church. The
nap also tells where the swallows' nests can be found during their residence.

At the mission's far-left corner, where the tanning vats, metal furnaces

BELOW: surf's
up in Newport.

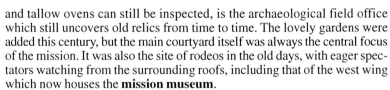

Map,
page242

and tallow ovens can still be inspected, is the archaeological field office which still uncovers old relics from time to time. The lovely gardens were added this century, but the main courtyard itself was always the central focus of the mission. It was also the site of rodeos in the old days, with eager spectators watching from the surrounding roofs, including that of the west wing which now houses the **mission museum**.

Just north of the controversial San Onofre Nuclear Power Plant is the town of **San Clemente**. The **Richard Nixon Library and Birthplace** (18001 Yorba Linda Boulevard, tel: 949-933 3393, Monday to Saturday 10am–5pm, Sunday 11am–5pm; admission charge) chronicles the life and times of the former US president, who operated his Western White House from San Clemente. San Clemente and Doheny beaches allow camping for a small fee. Doheny, Dana Point, Laguna Niguel, Irvine Coast and Newport Beach all have **marine life preserves** which are open to the public.

From Oceanside, boats run across to Santa Catalina Island, but an interesting drive inland is along Route 76 to the village of **Pala** ⑯. The village is notable for the Mission San Antonio de Pala, an *asistancia* (extension mission) built in 1816. Located on the Pala Indian Reservation, it is the only California mission still serving Indians and has celebrated its Corpus Christi Festival with an open-air mass, dances and games, on the first Sunday of every June since 1816.

The road continues southeast to **Rincom Springs**, a community to the north of Escondido on Road S6, and the gateway to **Palomar Mountain**. Rising 5,500 feet (1,859 meters) above sea level and stretching for some 20 miles (32 km), Palomar is the home of the Hale Telescope, contained inside **Mount Palomar Observatory** ⑰ (Palomar Mountain at the end of 56 Road, tel: 760-742 2119, daily 9am–4pm), which is now owned and operated by the **California Institute of Technology**. Open daily with scheduled tours, it includes the **Greenway Museum**, which has photographs of important sightings. Off Route 76 you can catch Route 15 south towards the town of San Diego and pass right by the **San Diego Wild Animal Park** (15500 San Pasqual Valley Road, Escondido, tel: 619-234 6541, daily, hours vary by season; admission charge), a huge park with multi-species exhibits, including giraffes, rhinos, antelopes, oryx, zebras, primates, and lions and tigers. Guests travel around the animal exhibits via monorail. There's also a popular walking safari.

BELOW: a pretty fishy business.
RIGHT: gliding along the coast.

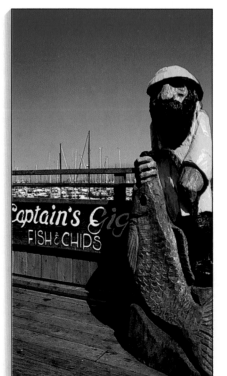

Host for horse lovers

Del Mar, a beautiful spot with a sweeping hillside view of the Pacific, is the site of the Southern California Exposition (a county fair) and national horse show in June and July at the Thoroughbred Club racetrack. This was rescued from collapse in the 1930s by actor Pat O'Brien and singer Bing Crosby, both racing fans, who pumped a huge amount of money into the facility, turning it into one of America's most popular circuit venues. The season begins in July, a week after the big fair ends, and continues to run until well into September. ❑

SANTA CATALINA ISLAND

With two-thirds of its scenic interior protected by an island conservancy council, Santa Catalina is calm, quiet and car-free

Map, page 242

This temperate outcrop 26 miles (42 km) off the coast makes for a lovely weekend excursion, but with a bit of a rush it can also all be squeezed into one day. With its steep and rugged canyons, 54 miles (87 km) of coastline and charming capital of Avalon, **Santa Catalina Island ⓲** (for information, tel: 310-510 1520) seduces even the most jaded traveler who has come to regard Southern California as the capital of Automania. Here, there are no rental cars and the environmentally-oriented island authority has guaranteed that almost two-thirds of the island will always remain in its natural state. The first steamship service began in 1888, at a time when pigeons were still being used to carry messages to and from the mainland.

Begin early in the day by taking the *Catalina Express* (tel: 800-833 6685) in Long Beach, zipping across to **Avalon** in one hour and, with extreme luck, spotting a whale en route. Ferries also run from San Pedro and Newport Beach. The 5-minute walk into town passes a couple of places which rent bicycles or the ubiquitous golf carts which are the main personal transportation: residents here wait 10 years before being allowed to own a car. Stop at one of the four companies on the pier to book for an island tour before thinking of anything else.

The first thing to do is the 45-minute inspection of the **Casino** at the far end of the harbor. It achieved national fame more than half a century ago with broadcasts of such famous bands as Count Basie or Kay Kyser playing in the Art Deco ballroom for as many as 6,000 dancers at a time. Built in 1929 at a cost of $2 million, the casino's ground floor theater with a full-size organ was the first in America to be built especially for the new talking pictures.

LEFT: sailing towards Avalon Bay.
BELOW: Catalina's famous casino was built in 1929.

Dancing to hidden music

Walking back into town past the Victorian hotels among the varied shops of **El Encanto Market Place**, across from the Via Casino archway is a souvenir shop displaying products from the long-defunct Catalina Pottery and other memorabilia.

A 40-minute trip in a glass-bottomed boat from the **Pleasure Pier** traverses shallow waters filled with multi-colored fish (mostly olive or blue with the occasional orange garibaldi) darting in and out of a seaweed "garden." The fronds of kelp, swaying to the motion of the glass-bottomed boat, seem to be dancing to a hidden music with the little fish acting as random soloists. At night, says the guide, nocturnal creatures take over, including "wimpy" lobsters which lack the formidable (but so-edible) claws of their Maine cousins.

This mural in Catalina's casino shows how elegant a building it is; Count Basie and his orchestra played for up to 6,000 people in the Art Deco ballroom.

BELOW: bison graze in Catalina's rural interior.

To really appreciate Catalina and all its attractions, plan to devote the afternoon to the 4-hour **inland motor tour** which heads up through the mountains to the island's airport. The tour makes a stop at **El Rancho Escondido**, the Wrigley-owned ranch where Arabian horses are reared. Immaculately-trained horses are put through their paces to demonstrate skill and intelligence. The tour continues onwards along the old stagecoach route across the island to various ancient Indian sites or secluded bays. The best parts of Catalina are these wilderness areas, popular with campers and hikers, some of whom find accommodation at the mountainous **Blackjack Campsite**.

Early developers

Descendants of General Phineas Banning, who operated the earliest legendary stagecoach routes across the West, once owned most of Catalina Island and began the process of turning it into the tourist resort it eventually became. William Wrigley, the chewing gum tycoon, continued this development when he acquired the island after the great fire of 1919.

He built the 1,000-bed luxury **Hotel St Catherine** at **Descanso Beach** west of town, a magnificent mansion on **Mount Ada** (now a bed and breakfast called the Inn on Mount Ada) and started the Catalina Pottery to provide tiles for other projects. The Wrigley family still owns about 15 percent of the island, donating the remainder to the non-profit Island Conservancy, which takes its responsibilities very seriously.

Although "discovered" by the Portuguese navigator Don Juan Rodriguez Cabrillo in 1542, and claimed for Spain as a safe anchorage for its Europe-bound galleons 60 years later, Catalina had actually been inhabited by Native Ameri

Map, page 242

cans for thousands of years. Two centuries after the Spaniards arrived, they were pretty much eliminated by Russian hunters in their search for sea otter pelts.

In the 1860s there were almost 30,000 grazing animals, mostly goats or sheep which between them de-vegetated most of the terrain. Later visitors, mostly American, included traders, pirates, smugglers and even miners who mistakenly believed the area to be rich in gold and other mineral deposits. All contributed to the devastation of the island by chopping down trees indiscriminately.

Since the Conservancy took over, much of this damage has been repaired. Fauna, such as the bald eagle, fox and wild boar, have been protected and their numbers expanded. Passengers on the bus tour invariably spot a couple of bison – descendants of a herd brought here when the movie of Zane Grey's *The Vanishing American* was shot on the island in 1925, and never taken away again. The Catalina grey fox is local only to the island. The house that Grey once owned ("Avalon… is the most delightful and comfortable place I ever visited") is now the **Zane Grey Pueblo Hotel**. Like the 40 or so other hotels on the island, it tends to be booked up early in summer, so call ahead for reservations.

At the airport, 1,620 feet (494 meters) above sea level, a small display includes historical pictures and a diorama featuring local animals. The Buffalo Springs Station sells buffalo burgers. Apart from some flights to San Diego – which offer probably the most spectacular views of the island – there is no longer a scheduled service from the airport, which is now used mostly by a freight company and a few private plane owners. Negotiating a flight is an alternative way to get into the mountains, landing at the romantically-named Airport-in-the-Sky.

The island's highest point is **Mount Orizaba** (2,069 feet/630 meters); the second is **Black Jack Mountain** at just over 2,000 feet/610 meters. ❑

Songs about the island include: "Catalina Is Calling Me," "When Roses Bloom in Avalon," and the sing-along melody "Catalina Aloha-Oe."

BELOW: Little Harbor is on Catalina's windward side.

PALM SPRINGS AND THE DESERT

Upscale resorts, natural history museums and Joshua Tree National Park are just some of the sites in the desert

Map, page 242

The San Bernadino freeway, then Interstate10, will bring you to Palm Springs (population 43,000) in just under three hours, but you might like to take an alternative route, the Pomona Freeway (continuation of the Santa Monica Freeway) to pass through **Riverside ⑲** with its famous **Mission Inn**. Architect Charles Moore observed that if you could see only one building in Southern California, this ought to be it.

Built by a local eccentric in 1902, the block-long hotel (tel: 909-784 0300), complete with gargoyles, flying buttresses and spiral staircases, was reopened in 1992 after a seven-year renovation that preserved its Tiffany stained-glass windows, the gold-leaf altar from a 17th-century Mexican church, a 120-year-old Steinway piano and the special chair built to accommodate one overweight visitor, President William Howard Taft. Other celebrated visitors have been Richard Nixon and Pat, who held their wedding party in the hotel, and Ronald Reagan and Nancy, who chose it for their honeymoon. Riverside's tourism, however, has declined precipitously since the local movie theater hosted the West Coast premiere of *Gone With the Wind* in 1939. A half-hour southeast of Riverside, between US 215, **Parris Valley Airport** is a favorite lift-off point for hot-air balloonists, and at **Perris Valley Skydiving** would-be parachutists can take a training course that concludes with an actual jump.

Giant dinosaurs

Highway 60 joins US 10 a few miles east of Riverside. Just beyond that, your attention will be caught while passing the truckstop at **Cabazon ⑳**. Many travelers stop off at the **Wheel Inn** (on the left of the freeway) to get a closer look at the giant model dinosaurs towering 30 feet (9 meters) above the highway. From this point, there are views of spectacular hillsides covered with row after row of steel windmills generating electric power. This country is the world's biggest producer of windpower which comes from state-of-the-art machines like these that operate in winds averaging about 16 mph (25 kph). Turn right onto State 111 to drive straight into the town of **Palm Springs, ㉑** and then down along **Palm Canyon Drive**, one of the two parallel main streets around which the town is structured. The classy **Desert Fashion Plaza** on this palm-lined thoroughfare is as upscale as it looks, while a block or two further down you'll come to what passes for an "old town" area that might be of interest.

The tiny **Village Green Heritage Center** consists of a restored adobe, a handful of 1800s buildings and a re-created general store from the 1930s with genuine

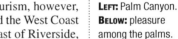

PRECEDING PAGES:
Joshua Tree
National Park.
LEFT: Palm Canyon.
BELOW: pleasure
among the palms.

*Palm Springs'
Moorten Botanical
Garden is a "living
museum" of cacti,
flowers and trees.*

BELOW: the Joshua
Tree in this national
park was named by
Mormons in 1851.

canned and packaged goods bearing their old labels. In this wealthy, ultra-chic, ultra-modern town, this is more interesting than almost anything else except the **Palm Springs Desert Museum** (101 Museum Drive, tel: 760-325 7186, Tuesday–Saturday noon–5pm; admission charge), behind the Fashion Plaza, with its dioramas of the desert and old Native American artifacts. The city has recently attempted to shuck off its image as a college mecca during "spring break" by sponsoring events aimed at the more mature visitor. Street fairs are sometimes held on Village Green. At the lower end of **South Palm Canyon Drive** is **Moorten's Botanical Garden**, an attractive "living museum" with giant cacti, flowers and trees lining shaded nature trails. It is open daily until the afternoon, and there is a small admission charge.

One block east, **Indian Avenue** is the other main street. It heads north, the route to Desert Hot Springs and, eventually, if you drive for 45-minutes, to **Joshua Tree National Park ㉒** (tel: 760-367 7511; admission charge). Joshua Tree is a vast parkland established in 1936 filled with strange rocks, fascinating flora and fauna, and the tall, fibrous plants after which it is named (Mormon explorers named the plant itself in 1851, who thought its twisted branches were like the upraised arms of Joshua). It's unlikely you'll see any of the mostly nocturnal animals – kangaroo rats, rattlesnakes – other than the occasional coyote and lizard, unless you stay overnight in one of the camping grounds. It was near here that an earthquake measuring 7.0 on the Richter Scale struck in October, 1999. Although an Amtrak train was knocked off its rails, no one was killed.

The easiest way to visit this area, the similarly unspoiled Santa Rosa Mountains and the Indian Canyons with their cool palm oases, is with one of the local adventure tour companies. Among the places they visit, **Indian Canyons** (tel:

Map, page 242

760-323 8297; admission charge) are rich in flora and fauna. Hawks and bald eagles circle overhead; tiny kangaroo rats and fleet-footed bighorn sheep can occasionally be seen on the slopes. **Palm** and **Andreas canyons** have the largest stands of palm trees in the world. "Leave nothing but your footprints, take nothing but photographs," reads a cautionary sign in this highly-protected area.

If you don't have time to explore all or even some of the wilderness, be sure to visit **The Living Desert** (47-900 Portola Avenue, tel: 760-346 5694, daily 9am–5pm; admission charge), a nature park 15 miles (24 km) southeast of Palm Springs filled with eagles, irresistible animals such as zebras and gazelles (don't overlook the lovable meerkats), and desert shrubs, flowers and cacti. Just north of town is the **Aerial Tramway** (Tramway Road, tel: 760-323 1391, Monday–Friday 10am–8pm, Saturday–Sunday 8am–8pm; admission charge) which during an awesome 14-minute ride, climbs to an 8,516-foot (2,959-meter) peak of the **San Jacinto Mountains**. From the top there's a magnificent view. (Take a jacket, especially if you want to explore the trails.)

A swimming lizard

The 200-sq.-mile (322-sq.-km) valley is huge enough to enclose completely 10 cities and a wildlife preserve. The preserve's star is a rare lizard whose "fringe toes" allow it to swim through the sand as readily as a fish in water.

In Palm Springs itself, the younger crowd flock to the **Oasis Water Park** (off 1–10 south on Gene Autry Trail, tel: 760-325 7873, open daily 11am–6pm, mid-March through Labor Day, plus weekends through October; admission charge) east of town, into whose 21 acres (8 hectares) are packed a health club, a big swimming pool, volley ball courts and seven water slides that kids love.

BELOW: trekking in the desert.

Medicine Men

The richest Native Americans in the country have been in the news because they want to operate a full-scale gambling casino on their tribal land, several hundred acres of which happen to be in the chic heart of downtown Palm Springs. It took the tireless efforts of dozens of legal friends before the Agua Caliente band of the Cahuila Indians were able to break a legal deadlock, allowing them to use their land at all. The exploitation of their terrain in the last three decades has put them on a par with – or maybe better than – many other American landowners.

Although the acquisition of a minor fortune is applauded, it has also resulted in the dilution of centuries-old wisdom and skills that enabled our earliest Native Americans to survive in totally inhospitable desert.

According to Temalpakh ("from the earth"), a seminal documentation about Indian knowledge and usage of plants, many of the Cahuila themselves regret the loss of a more tradi-

tional way of life whose well-balanced diet produced longevity, mental alertness and good eyesight. "They believe that adopted foods have brought about a general physical weakness, shortened lifespan, a tendency to obesity and proneness to such diseases as diabetes," write the authors, anthropologist Lowell John Bean and tribal authority Katherine Siva Sobel. "When Cahuila speak of their grievances against the white man, they frequently mention the loss of traditional foods."

The Cahuila survived in the hostile desert region, not only because of their knowledge of desert plants and animals, but also because of the curing techniques of their shamans (witch doctors), who used natural substances that have enriched medicine ever since. Bean and Sobel say the shamans, because they employed both plant remedies and sacred power, occupied a more prominent place in the community than doctors.

"It is interesting to note that most of the prescribed drugs in use today trace their roots back to medicine plants known for centuries by indigenous culture and their shamans," writes author Lynn V Andrews. In her book *Jaguar Woman*, she says that the one rift between shamanism and modern medicine that she would like to see bridged "is the one caused by modern medicine's elitism and refusal to communicate."

Among the Cahuila, as with other Native Americans, shamans – "technicians of the sacred" because they mediate between the world of mortals and the world of spirits, according to ethnologist Mircea Eliade – were believed to possess supernatural powers. They gave advice on political decisions, cured diseases and searched nature for signs from the spirit world. The origin and meaning of the word Cahuila is unknown: "master" (in both mental and physical strength) has been suggested. Territory ranges from valleys as high as 5,000 feet (1,525 meters) in the Santa Rosa Mountains, to the desert around the Salton Sea, 200 feet (60 meters) below sea level.

South of Palm Springs, the tribe still owns the five Indian Canyons in which their villages used to sit. There are still some traces of house foundations, ditches and dams. ❑

LEFT: portrait of a brave drawn by George Catlin, one of the first artist/explorers of the 1830s.

As might be imagined, the area abounds in luxury resorts, many of whose guest registers are a litany of famous names. The **La Quinta Resort and Club** (tel: 760-564 4111), for example, is where Frank Capra checked in to polish the movie script of *Lost Horizon* and Irving Berlin composed *White Christmas*. Renovations uncovered sketches by artist Diego Rivera on the high ceilings of the lobby, as well as bringing the number of rooms and suites up to 640 (there were originally 56). Other resorts have also moved in – even foreigners, like the elegant French-owned **Givenchy Hotel and Spa**, tel: 760-324 7280.

A couple of miles from the Salton Sea, whose salt waters provide a habitat for game, fish and a recreation area with campsites, is the state's largest park, the 600,000-acre (243,000-hectare **Anza-Borrego State Park** ㉓ (tel: 760-767 5311), its numerous canyons and gullies easily accessible by car. Camping is permitted in the park, which is populated by jackrabbits, coyotes, kangaroo rats and lizards, as well as hundreds of bird species. Frank Sinatra lived a few miles down State Highway 111 in **Rancho Mirage** until recently, a bedroom community of country clubs, golf courses and tennis courts. Former US President Gerald Ford and Mrs Leonard Firestone, the widow of the industrialist and former ambassador to Belgium, reside there, side by side on a fairway at Thunderbird Country Club.

The little town of **Indio** ㉔ (population 42,500), on US 10 about 10 miles (32 km) east, has been popular with tourists since 1921 when it began staging its annual National Date Festival. The week-long celebration in February includes an Arabian Nights pageant, and ostrich and camel racing. South of Indio and north of the Salton Sea is **Lake Cahuilla** (tel: 760-564 4712; admission charge). The lake is stocked with rainbow trout, striped bass and catfish. For non-anglers,

Map, page 242

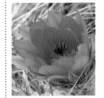

ABOVE: this is not a mirage.
BELOW: looking out over Anza-Borrego Desert State Park.

Map,
page 242

there are hiking and equestrian trails, shady picnic spots, campsites and a children's play area on the sandy beach – away from fishermen. The **Salton Sea** ㉕ was, in fact, all a big mistake. When engineers attempted in 1905 to divert Colorado River water to the Imperial Valley, the river changed course and reflooded the ancient Salton Basin, 235 feet (72 meters) below sea level. This formed a sea of 360 sq. miles (968 sq. km) with royal blue water filling the area where the Coachella and Imperial valleys merge. The sea's saltiness creates a buoyancy popular with water skiers and swimmers. It also provides a habitat for saltwater game-fish. Adjoining marshlands are a refuge for bird-watchers.

The **Salton Sea State Recreation Area** (tel: 760-393 3059) is an 18,000-acre (about 7,300-hectare) park with both developed and primitive campsites. There is a large boat basin at **Varner Harbor** (26 miles away on Highway 86) where geology buffs have a field day with ancient shorelines and layers of marine fossils visible along the base of the Santa Rosa Mountains. The Salton Sea, 35 miles (56 km) long and 9 to 15 miles (14 to 24 km) wide, is flanked by State 111 on the east and State 86 on the west.

Sanctuary for birds

More than 150 species of bird have been sighted in Anza-Borrego park. The vegetation is equally varied, ranging from junipers and pines growing at the 5,000-feet (1,500-meters) level to palm trees at sea level. A 3-mile (5-km) hike from Campfire Center to Palm Grove reveals plants used by the Cahuilla Indians for medicines, dyes and food. About 58 miles (93 km) due east of El Centro is **Yuma**, Arizona, a desert town built on the banks of the Colorado River where it enters Mexican territory. The Colorado forms the entire eastern border of Southern California from Mexico to Nevada. Several dams built across it have created reservoirs while also providing hydroelectric power for the metropolises of Los Angeles and San Diego.

BELOW: French refinement in Palm Springs. **RIGHT:** sunset in the sands.

Lake Havasu ㉖ (tel: 520-855 4115), 46 miles (74 km) long, and no more than 3 miles (5 km) wide, is the reservoir trapped behind the dam. Those who don't want to drink the water enjoy playing in it. Along Arizona State Highway 95 between Parker and Lake Havasu City are recreational-vehicle parks, marinas and campgrounds with room for tens of thousands of visitors. Everyone from water sportsmen and outboard boaters to yachtsmen, water skiers and sail-boarders, love the lake. There's fishing for bass, bluegills and crappies. Small game populates the rugged southeastern (Arizona) shore of the lake that constitutes Lake Havasu State Park. Birds are everywhere, as the entire body of water is contained within the **Lake Havasu National Wildlife Refuge**.

Lake Havasu City, nonexistent as recently as the late 1960s, has exploded into a resort center of 40,000 residents. This has become the new preferred vacation spot for collegiate types at spring break. Developed by the late millionaire Robert P McCulloch Sr, its most famous landmark is the original **London Bridge**. McCulloch had it shipped piece by piece to Long Beach, then trucked to the lakefront "British" community he single-handedly created. ❑

ABOVE: Sin City hype for hopefuls.
BELOW: Fremont Street's glitter.

LAS VEGAS

*Created as a playground strictly for grown-ups,
Las Vegas has transformed itself into a fantasy world
for the whole family. It's a big gamble*

There is only one surefire way to win in "Sin City" and that rule is simple – don't gamble. And although that may seem like a negation of what the place is all about, it makes sense when you realize that what's on offer is virtually everything available elsewhere – only for less money. **Las Vegas ㉗** is a phenomenon, changing and evolving so continuously that it seems there's a grand new theme hotel every year: New York, Egypt, Monte Carlo, ancient Rome, the Wild West, and recently, Venice and Paris.

Imaginative architecture and neon lights have been the making of Vegas, but this recent transformation has come about in the 1990s. Gambling began here in the 1940s, but it took another quarter of a century before the town fully embraced the showbiz element at which it now excels. The policy is "anything goes," with exploding volcanoes, mock sea battles on Main Street, trapeze acts high above the slot machines, a giant sphinx with laser-beam eyes, even legal prostitution not far out of town. In an *LA Times Magazine* story titled "Future World," writer Aaron Betsky said he was convinced that Las Vegas's "mammoth apparitions" were offering a new kind of urban center, " transforming a real city into a realm of fantasy and conversely building a set of fantasies into a real city.... collectively creating a metropolis whose huge scale is bound by lights and set design rather than by walls and streets."

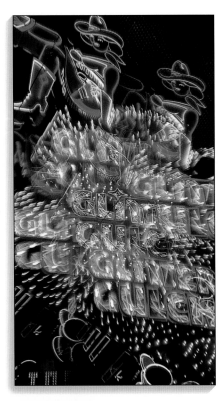

The Strip

Such as it is, Las Vegas's geography is a simple one. The best-known hotels and casinos are located on the bullet-straight **Las Vegas Boulevard**, otherwise known as **The Strip**. These fantasy palaces include **New York, New York**, the **Monte Carlo**, the **Tropicana**, and the **MGM Grand** – all at one busy intersection called the "Crossroads of the World." Heading north along The Strip towards **Downtown**, where the other casinos are congregated, are the **Bellagio**, the **Venetian**, **Paris**, **Caesars Palace**, and the **Mirage**, among others.

The Strip is crammed with family-type attractions, a popular one being the museum-quality **Imperial Palace Auto Collection** at 3535 Las Vegas Boulevard. Its classic cars include those previously owned by Marilyn Monroe, Hitler and Elvis.

About a mile before arriving Downtown, you cannot help but notice the **Stratosphere Tower**, at 1,825 feet (550 meters) one of the tallest buildings in the West. Topped by a revolving restaurant and observation decks, the view from this marvel is the best one in town and worth the admission fee.

Downtown's casinos include the **Golden Nugget** and **Lady Luck**, among many others. Staying Downtown is not as glitzy as being on The Strip, but does put you in line for the single best free show in America. This is the

Fremont Street Experience (on the hour, 6pm–11pm each night) which gathers wildly enthusiastic audiences to watch a six-minute show 100 feet (30 meters) above their heads. Five entire blocks have been covered with a metallic mesh screen across which race herds of giant buffalo, country and western dancers, screaming jet fighter planes trailing smoke and teams of undulating maidens. Downtown merchants heavily subsidized this $70 million project to entice visitors back to an area that was becoming moribund – and it's worked. Local casinos will validate a ticket for five hours of free parking.

Further information

Write to the **Las Vegas Convention and Visitors Bureau** (3150 Paradise Road, LV, Nevada 89109, tel: 702-892 7575) before your trip and request a copy of its comprehensive guide which lists just about everything you need to know. The travel pages of the Sunday edition of the *Los Angeles Times* are also full of Las Vegas offers. Unless you're a high roller, you're not going to find tremendous bargains at the famous hotels (although rates will likely be about half what you'd pay for digs elsewhere), but some Strip hotels such as **Circus Circus** are aggressively marketed with rates often surprisingly low.

Getting around town can be pricey because taxi rides aren't cheap and you'll need to take a lot of them if you plan to see everything. One suggestion is to rent a car at the airport (car rentals are a bargain) and drive along **Tropicana Avenue** to The Strip when, if you turn left (south), you'll find several budget motels. There are other inexpensive motels Downtown on **Ogden Avenue** and around Fremont and **Main Street**.

Of course, you're going to gamble aren't you? Stick to the nickel slots. ❑

Map, page 242

TIP

For hotel addresses, see the Travel Tips section at the back of the book.

BELOW: Las Vegas' neon Strip of dreams.

SAN DIEGO AREA

San Diego is California's second largest city. It is also the oldest, near to pine-tree reserves, glorious beaches and a famous, movie-star hotel

Map, page 332

San Francisco

California
Los Angeles

San Diego

C alifornia began at San Diego's Presidio Hill on July 16, 1769, when Father Junípero Serra conducted a mass dedicating first the Mission San Diego de Alcalá and then the military settlement which surrounded and protected it. The mission was moved from the hill to its present site in Mission Valley only a few years later. Because of these events, the busy, elegant harbor town claims as one of its many attributes a history unsurpassed in the state.

If you're heading down Interstate 5 from Los Angeles, you might want to break up your journey to San Diego by stopping off first for a walk through the groves of strangely-twisted trees at **Torrey Pines State Reserve A** and watch daredevil hang-gliders soar off the 300-foot (90-meter) cliffs. If that seems a little strenuous, try stopping for lunch in the charming town of **La Jolla**, the home of the San Diego campus of the University of California; the highly-regarded **Salk Institute**; and the clifftop **Stephen Birch Aquarium**. Snorklers should head for the **La Jolla Caves B** after lunch.

Then it's onwards towards San Diego itself. Flanked by Interstates 5 and 8 to the west and north, **Presidio Hill**, with its peaceful, sprawling park, is an oasis in a sea of traffic. If you take the curving road east of the Old Town, you'll see, dominating the hillside, the elegant **Junípero Serra Museum C** (tel: 619-297 2727, closed Mondays) which looks like a mission but was actually built in 1929. There are documents of early California life and a seven-minute historical video, but the original records in Father Serra's own handwriting are displayed in the **Mission San Diego de Alcalá** (10818 San Diego Mission Road, tel: 619-283 7319, daily; donations accepted), which since 1774 has stood on a site now to the east of US 15.

PRECEDING PAGES:
Horton Plaza.
LEFT: San
Diego Bay.
BELOW: Mission San
Diego de Alcalá.

Old Town

In the six-block area known as **Old Town D** at the bottom of Presidio Hill – now San Diego's most popular nightlife section – are old adobes and restored Vic-torian homes, shops, museums and charming patio restaurants. One of these, the Casa de Bandini, is located in an 1829 hacienda. *Mariachi* groups entertain in the **Bazaar del Mundo**, a Spanish-style plaza flanked by craft shops and Mexican restaurants. The **Whalley House**, probably Southern California's first two-story brick home, and the **Wells Fargo Museum** (free) are of special interest. The visitor center has guide maps.

Across the freeway is the 4,600-acre (1,860-hectare) **Mission Bay** area, combining parkland, beaches and inner lagoons with extensive outdoor leisure activities. Located here is **Sea World E** (1720 South Shores Road, tel: 619-226 3901, daily, hours vary by season; admission charge), a 150-acre (60-hectare) marine zoological park whose "killer" whales are as famous as

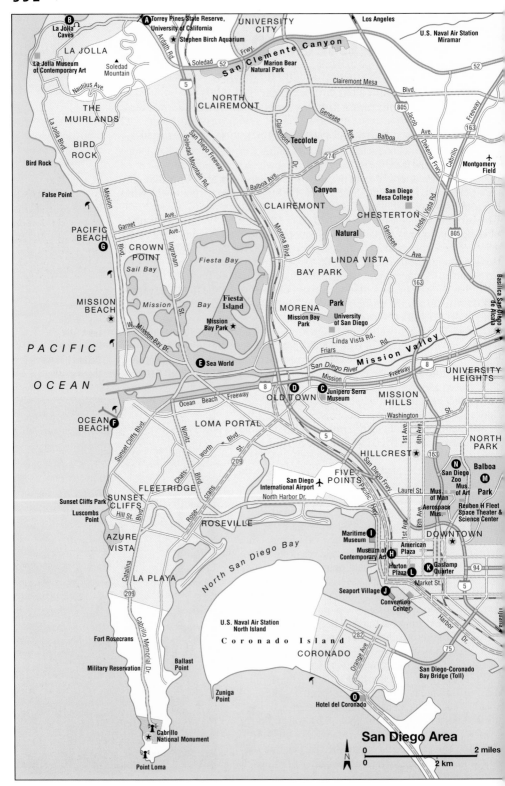

San Diego Area

some movie stars and whose appearances can pack a 5,000-seat stadium. Seals, dolphins, otters and 400 penguins also draw admiring crowds.

South of the channel leading into Mission Bay is **Ocean Beach ❻**; to the north of Mission Beach is **Pacific Beach ❼**, where activities center around Crystal Pier and in the area along Mission Boulevard and up Garnet Avenue. This is where most of the locals shop and dine. The beaches are a great draw most of the year, but there are wonderful beaches along most of this coast – 25 miles (40 km) of them in an unbroken line between Del Mar and Oceanside.

Map, page 332

Downtown San Diego

Towards the top end of the vast bay discovered by Cabrillo is downtown San Diego. A complex adjoining what was formerly the Santa Fe railroad station now consists of the 34-story **American Plaza Tower**, a hotel and a sleek satellite branch of La Jolla's **Museum of Contemporary Art ❽** (700 Prospect Street, tel: 619-454 3541, Tuesday–Saturday 10am–5pm, Sunday noon–5pm; admission charge). Along the Embarcadero just north of the station is the large **Maritime Museum ❾**, which encompasses three ships built prior to 1904, among them the 1863 *Star of India* which is one of the last steel-hulled merchant sailing ships still afloat. San Diego has always been a big naval town and taking a **harbor cruise** will confirm that there is still plenty of activity on the water. In winter, whale-watching tours start from here.

Much of the harbor is centered around attractive **Seaport Village ❿**, with its cafés and century-old carousel. Adjoining this carefully landscaped "village" is the spiffy-looking **Convention Center** right opposite **Gaslamp Quarter ⓚ**, a several-block area of brick-paved sidewalks flanked by restored Victorian build-

ABOVE: taking the plunge.
BELOW: Old Town street scene.

Map, page 332

ings now occupied by galleries, trendy boutiques and cafés. This refurbished section, with a demonstrable appeal to artists and young entrepreneurs, has also become the breeding ground of a flourishing theater movement. Almost next door is **Horton Plaza** ◗, a multi-level collection of stores, eateries, cinemas and a deluxe hotel. Named after a visionary local developer called Alonso Horton, the plaza has a stylish design, layout and omnipresent street performers.

At the northeast edge of town, 1,400-acre (655-hectare) **Balboa Park** ◗ contains seven of the city's museums in Moorish- and Spanish-style buildings, many of which date back to international expositions held here in 1915 and 1935. A pass available at the park's centrally-located **Hospitality Center** allows admission to up to four of the museums. Your choices include the **Aerospace Historical Center** (with a replica of *The Spirit of St Louis* in which Charles Lindbergh crossed the Atlantic; the **House of Champions Sports Museum**; the **Model Railroad Museum**; the **San Diego Museum of Art**; the **Museum of Man**; the **Natural History Museum**; and the **San Diego Museum of Man**. Many people take pleasure in just strolling or picnicking in the park (on Saturdays, there are musical performances and free samples of food from various cuisines), but Balboa Park is really an activity "city" all on its own, attractions including a small Space Center, an arts center and a couple of theaters.

Occupying the western side of the park is the **San Diego Zoo** ◗ (tel: 619-231 1515, gates open daily 9am–4pm, grounds open until 6pm; admission charge), one of the largest and most famous in America with over 800 different animal species. The zoo has a policy of eschewing cages in favor of moats wherever possible, in an attempt to recreate the natural conditions of the wild. Admission to the zoo includes a ride on Skyfari, an aerial tramway from which you can admire all the uncaged elephants, lions, tigers, giraffes and bears in their canyon habitats. North of the city is the **Wild Animal Park** (tel: 619-231 1515).

Coronado

A string of communities surround the lower end of San Diego Bay. **Coronado**, with stately Victorian homes among the cottages and condos, is the most popular and weathiest. Access is either off US 5 on the mainland to the west or by the 2-mile **San Diego-Coronado Bridge** (There are also buses from downtown.)

The community is best known for the superlative **Hotel del Coronado** ◗ (tel: 619-435 6611), a perfect example of elegant Victorian architecture (1888) with all its geegaws and eccentricities. A dozen presidents have stayed here since Thomas Edison personally installed the electric lighting: Britain's future Edward VIII met his future wife here, the notorious Mrs Simpson, who lived in a bungalow on the grounds (the bungalow is still there); Charles Lindbergh dropped by for dinner before and after making the first trans-Atlantic flight; and author J Frank Baum is said to have used it as an inspiration for *The Wizard of Oz*.

Such milestones are memorialized in a history corridor lined with giant photographs. And the hotel itself just has to be seen. So eye-catching is the Coronado that it almost upstaged Tony Curtis and Marilyn Monroe in the movie *Some Like It Hot* – no mean feat.

TIJUANA AND NORTHERN BAJA

Just a few miles to the south of San Diego is another world and another country – Mexico – where the living is easy and the crossing even easier

Map, page 242

Baja, California, the slender, arid peninsula that stretches for about 1,075 miles (1,733 km) south of the California border comprises two states of the Republic of Mexico – the northern state, Baja California, and the southern state, Baja California Sur. Both were largely unexplored land until the completion of the Transpeninsula highway (Mexico Highway 1) in 1973.

Now there are airstrips here and there, plus big towns largely dependent on tourism, as well as sizable trailer colonies of retired Americans living inexpensively beside the beaches. But its mountain ranges and deserts have enabled Baja to retain much of its unspoiled character. It is also highly accessible. The major part of both coastlines can be reached not only by car, but via daily buses that operate all the way to Cabo San Lucas at the southern tip. Crossing from San Diego is easy; US citizens are not required to have a passport unless they're visiting for more than 72 hours, or plan to go beyond the State Highway 1 checkpoint below Baja's town of Ensenada. Non-US citizens, however, should travel with a passport or Green Card.

Just under a mile from the border crossing is the tourist zone of **Tijuana** ㉘ which stretches for seven blocks along Avenida Revolucion. There are tourist information offices at the border but the main State Tourist Department is in the **Plaza Patria** along Boulevard Diaz Ordaz,which is the continuation of Boulevard Agua Caliente.

LEFT: critter on a cactus.
BELOW: Mexitlan in Tijuana.

Downtown Tijuana

The first stop in Tijuana, a building topped with a glass piñata visible from the pedestrian bridge, is **Mexitlan**, an intriguing $23 million theme park containing enormous relief maps of all of Mexico with 150 of its major landmarks reproduced to scale on 20-feet (6-meter) square platforms. Juan O'Gorman's bold mural on the wall of the University of Mexico library is reproduced, along with the copper-domed Olympic Sports Palace, 18th-century Chapultepec castle and the capital's Mayan sites, such as Uxmal and Chichen Itza, and the pyramids at Tenochitlan, all seen in miniature.

The entire project, illuminated at night, was created under the supervision of Mexico's top architect, Pedro Ramirez Vasquez, who earned worldwide renown with his bold design for Mexico City's Museum of Anthropology, a scale model of which is also displayed here. If driving across the border, take the Downtown-Calle 3a Centro exit and enter the parking lot on the right at 2nd or 3rd Street.

There's an arts and crafts market behind Mexitlan, but a greater variety of shops along the city's main drag,

Avenida Revolucion, just to the west. It has lost some of its former tawdry flavor, but is still by far the liveliest street, lined with bars, nightclubs, craft stores, and clothing and jewelry shops mixed up along with the sarapes and leather sandals.

Behind the Plaza Revolucion is the **Wax Museum** whose eclectic subjects range from Madonna, Gandhi and the Pope to Cortéz and an Aztec priest holding the bloody heart of a prostrate victim. Mexican Revolutionary heroes are cheek by jowl with Ayatollah Khomeini, Laurel and Hardy, JFK, and Fidel Castro. Mexico is also represented by various ranchera entertainers, the 17th-century explorer Juan Cabrillo and a grey-haired lady known as Tia Juana ("Aunt Jane"), the legendary cantina owner around whom the city was founded.

History and culture

ABOVE: USA today.
BELOW: leather to go.

A few blocks down Revolucion, past the stylish old **Jai Alai Fronton**, turn left on 10th Street to head towards the river. The main street continues south, seguing onto the Boulevard Agua Caliente and running past the city's old bullring, most of its best hotels, Agua Caliente Racetrack and the Sports Arena where concerts and most big events take place. But that's for another time. Head eastwards along 10th Street, watch for the giant globe (indicating a "world of culture") housing the concert hall and the 85-foot (26-meter) high **Omnitheater** in which is shown daily on a gigantic screen the English-language version of a film about Mexico's history and culture.

Adjoining is the ultra-modern **Tijuana Cultural Center**, whose historical survey embraces Olmec stone heads, Aztec charts showing the god of the hour, a meticulous model of the 16th-century Aztec capital, Tenochtitlan plus skilfully embroidered Indian costumes. Displayed on both sides of a long, wide ramp, they are interspersed with the silk flag of short-term French emperor Maximilian, a presidential chair bearing a gold Aztec eagle, and portraits of Emilio Zapata and Pancho Villa who once almost shared it.

Here also by the river is the **Plaza Rio Tijuana** shopping mall (open till 9pm) with over 100 stores. It is the largest shopping center in northwestern Mexico, and Baja California being a free port, most goods cost less than in San Diego. Shoppers should remember, however, that US Customs demands receipts to be produced for any daily purchases exceeding $400 per person.

The distinctive red **Tijuana Trolley** runs continuously between the city's main sightseeing attractions, but it's a pleasant stroll back northwards along **Via Poniente** which adjoins the river. It will bring you to an older, funkier shopping center, **Puebla Amigo**, which comes alive at night. As well as many restaurants, there's a disco, a theater/concert hall and an ingenious mural offering different pictures from different angles.

The famous old **Agua Caliente Racetrack** still has its marble floors, ornate decoration, mirrored elevators and lobby filled with sculptured *charros*, caged birds and an incongruous pair of playful anteaters, but retains little of the glamor which once caused it to be regarded as the American Monte Carlo. In the days when the track's regular clientele included Charlie Chaplin, Jean Harlow and heavyweight champion Jack Dempsey, fortunes were won and lost at dice, blackjack and roulette.

Map, page 242

its decline began with the repeal of Prohibition in 1933 and the outlawing of gambling two years later. The tracks still host greyhound racing some nights.

The highway west of Tijuana leads to the **Monumental Bullring**, 6 miles (10 km) away beside the sea. Bullfights take place on various Sundays from May to September. The season is split between the oceanside bullring and the older one downtown on the Boulevard Agua Caliente. Tickets are on sale at the bullrings and at tourist agencies. There are inexpensive motels along the seashore road and stalls selling coconut drinks and seafood. The *Cuota* toll road, on the way to Baja's Ensenada, has some fine ocean scenery. It is recommended over the *Libre* free road, which parallels the Cuota as far as Rosarito, then dips inland.

About 17 miles (27 km) south of the border is **Rosarito**, an over-commercialized beach town which gained popularity in 1927 when the newly-opened **Rosarito Beach Hotel** began to attract the movie crowd as well as other celebrities, including heads of state. The hotel features glorious indoor murals by Matias Santoyo and a large swimming pool and bar area above the gray, sandy beach. Lobster is a favorite in the town's numerous restaurants and there is a so-called "Lobster Village," – **Puerto Nuevo**, 6 miles to the south, where the **New Port Beach Hotel** promises an ocean view from each room.

At **El Sauzal**, just before Ensenada, Highway 3 heads across to the east coast, its northbound section bound for the beer-making town of **Tecate**, close to the border. On the way it passes through vineyards on the boulder-strewn hills bordering the **Guadalupe Valley**, which is the center of Mexico's fast-growing wine business. The most interesting town is **Francisco Zara**, with its cemetery and museum both devoted to the history of the Russian immigrants who colonized the area at the turn of the century. About 19 miles (31 km) south of the border, another free road curves inland off the toll road to head up through the tiny village of **La Mision** where there are crumbling ruins of the San Miguel mission. A cross marks the spot once established as the boundary line between the Dominican missions of Baja and the Franciscan missions in Upper California.

Ensenada

Entering the big city of **Ensenada** (population 230,000) almost 70 miles (113 km) south of the border, it is a good idea to turn right off Highway 1 and drive up Avenida Aleman into the Chapultepec hills, a high-rent district which offers a magnificent view of the city. A busy port, Ensenada is a regular stop for cruise ships and the furthest south that the vast majority of tourists penetrate. Popular with fishermen, it tags itself "the yellowtail capital of the world" with surf fishing along the rocky shoreline and organized trips from the sportfishing piers off Boulevard Lazaro Cardenas. There are winery tours every day but Monday at the Bodegas de Santo Tomas and occasional bullfights.

The main tourist shopping zone is along **Avenida Lopez Mateos**, a few blocks from the bay, but prices are lower in the "non-tourist" part of town off Avenida Ruiz. Along here also, just east of Avenida Mateos, is the popular Hussong's, a wooden-frame cantina which has been in business for exactly a century. There are many other restaurants, some with outdoor patios. ❑

BELOW: painting pottery, Tijuana.

DEATH VALLEY AND THE MOJAVE

The name says it all. Most people who travel to the desert do so in order to experience some of the most desolate, challenging landscapes in the Americas

Map, page 242

San Francisco

California

Los Angeles

he Mojave Desert (named after a southwestern native tribe, pronounced "mo-hahv-ee") lies between US Highway 395 and Interstate 40, adjoining the Nevada state border. It has come to mean different things to different people: a battleground of conflicting interests between backpackers, miners, ranchers, scientists, environmentalists and off-road vehicle groups. The first settlers who had the misfortune to wander into Death Valley in 1849 on their way to the Gold Rush found the name to be unfortunately true, but travel these days is infinitely easier and safer, with well-supervised roads and accommodations which, in Death Valley, include two inns and a luxury hotel. The climate between November and April is ideal for outdoor travel, while May through October burn with heat like the North African Sahara.

The *WPA Guide*, published in 1939, reported that August travelers found "intense heat" even while still 1,500 feet (457 meters) above the valley. Apparently experienced travelers could estimate the temperature by putting their hand outside the car and checking how long it took the sunlight "to cause a sharp pain at the base of the nails."

From Los Angeles through the Mojave to Death Valley and back makes for a fascinating two- or three-day trip. Perhaps the best route is to set out from the San Fernando Valley on State Highway 14 through Lancaster to Lone Pine and crossing the mountains into Death Valley via State Route 190.

PRECEDING PAGES: the Devil's Golf Course. **LEFT:** Calico Ghost Town. **BELOW:** documenting the dunes.

Borax to B-bombers

At the junction of State Highways 14 and 58 is the small town of Mohave, gateway to the **Mojave Desert ㉙**. From borax to the B-1 bomber, it has seen more history than places many times its size. Near Edwards Air Force Base, Mojave was part of the Antelope Valley aerospace boom, serving as a temporary community for the aerospace workers, as well as those employed in agriculture and railroads. The winter season is its busiest time, when weekend skiers, heading to and from Sierra slopes, pack the motels and roadside cafés.

About 25 miles (40 km) north of Mojave along State 14 is **Red Rock Canyon State Park ㉚** (tel: 805-942 0662), an unusual camping and picnic spot which despite its geological importance has remained relatively little-explored. Great, brightly-colored columns of sandstone rise off the desert floor on either side of the highway, sculpted towers in the foothills of the eastern Sierras that were once the home of a desert tribe now known only as "the old ones." Much later, about the middle of last century, traffic picked up considerably when desert prospectors began discovering gold nuggets on the surface of dry stream beds. A mini-boom followed, and subsequently about $16 million worth of ore was removed, including one 5-lb (2.27-kg) nugget. On weekends, state rangers give guided nature walks. Picnic tables and about 50 primitive camp-sites are provided for tents and recreational vehicles. Visitors must bring their own food and water, however, as there are no concessions at the park.

An interesting detour for amateur archaeologists lies down Highway 58, east of Mohave and near the town of **Barstow ③**. Paleontologists are still carrying on the work of the late Dr Louis Leakey, the leader of a team of eminent scientists who believed they had found a prehistoric "tool factory" estimated to be some 200,000 years old. The so-called **Calico Early Man Site** is open for public viewing, with guided tours some days of the week. Arrangements can be made with the Federal Bureau of Land Management office in Barstow, a bustling desert town which is largely the suburb of a military community. Situated at the junction of Interstates 15 and 40, it has a 5-mile (8-km) stretch of motels, gas stations and grocery stores that makes it a very good base for stocking up.

Calico Ghost Town, tel: 610-254 2122 was restored by LA's Walter Knott of Knott's Berry Farm fame. Part authentic mining town, part theme park, it's fun to discover which is real and which is whimsy.

Ghost towns

Calico ② itself was established by silver miners in the 1880s, whose boomtown has been imaginatively restored as the **Calico Ghost Town**. Half history and half Hollywood, Calico is an amusement park where visitors can explore mining tunnels, ride the ore train, and browse in old-fashioned dry-goods shops.

BELOW: descent from the peaks.

Back then, towards **Randsburg ③**, a 19th-century ghost town that is actually still a thriving hilltop mining community, which is about 20 miles (32 km) east of Red Rock Canyon on US 395. Named after one of the gold towns of

SURVIVAL IN THE DESERT

The Mohave Desert covers an enormous amount of land – roughly that of the states of Massachusetts, Rhode Island and Connecticut combined. It's easy to get lost and, with conventional vehicles, even to get stranded off the main roads. Water can usually be found if you are equipped to dig deep enough, as the native Shoshone tribe knew very well, but few visitors know anything about survival techniques in such a primitive land.

It is quite literally life-theatening to remain under the desert sun for too long a time. Take adequate provisions, and adequate precautions. Have your car checked out thoroughly before setting off, paying particular attention to the tires and any problems concerning overheating. Pack food, water and sunscreen, for use even while in the car (do not make the journey in a convertible).

Once there, don't panic if trouble arises. If you have car trouble, rangers suggest you wait where you are: do not wander off to look for help. Fever from excessive heat can cause delirium and loss of thirst, and people have been known to die with a full canteen of water beside them. Centuries ago, explorer Juan Bautista de Anza experienced the Mohave's natural furnace and referred to the region as Tierra del Muertos, literally "Land of the Dead." Be warned.

Map, page 242

South Africa, Randsburg struck it rich three times between 1895 and 1947, first with gold, then with silver, and finally with tungsten. After its discovery late in the 19th century, its Yellow Aster mine yielded $20 million in gold before it was exhausted. Turn-of-the-century Randsburg was as wild and woolly as any Western boomtown, with saloons and dance halls, scoundrels and rogues.

Among the ramshackle remains of the original wood-and-corrugated iron buildings on Randsburg's main street today is the **Desert Museum** (open weekends only), with its collection of mining and geological artifacts. Also open are the town saloon, dance hall and barber shop, which have been quaintly converted into shops offering rocks, bottles and mining curios. At the **Randsburg General Store**, wayfarers can sip a chocolate soda at the same swivel-chaired soda fountain that was hauled into town by mules a century ago.

China Lake ❸ is a dry basin near Ridgecrest off US 395. It is best known as the focus of the important China Lake Naval Weapons Center. Near the main gate of the naval station is the small **Maturango Museum** (tel: 760-375 6900, Wednesday–Sunday 10am–5pm), open weekend afternoons. The museum occasionally conducts field trips to study aboriginal rock inscriptions found nearby, possibly the best such collection in the state. As a result of the discoveries made at China Lake, some scientists are tempted to say that humans migrated from Asia at least 40,000 years ago, perhaps even 100,000 years ago.

Not far from China Lake, near the banks of the equally dry Searles Lake, are the **Trona Pinnacles ❺**. This great pincushion of ancient limestone columns in the middle of the Mojave Desert is both rare and bizarre. The spooky stone spires are "national natural landmarks," probably the most outstanding examples of tufa formations in North America, and a challenging moonscape to explore for

BELOW: Lone Pine Peak.

Alternate Energy

California, as well known for its climate as for its automobile culture, is leaping ahead in researching alternate forms of energy. Three of the state's utilities – Southern California Edison, the Los Angeles Department of Water & Power and the Sacramento Municipal Utility District – joined forces with financial help from the US Energy Department to construct a $39 million plant in the Mojave Desert that they hope will provide a feasible alternative to fossil fuels.

The initial 10-megawatt plant will produce a meager 10 percent or less of the current output of fuel-driven plants, but if it is successful, facilities will be built that are 10 or 20 times the size of the proposed plant. The *Los Angeles Times* commented that California was once again on the cutting edge of technology that would change the way the entire world lived.

At a plant known as Solar Two, hundreds of giant mirrors concentrate the sun's rays on

a 300-feet (90-meter) tower, heating to a temperature of 1,050 degrees molten nitrate salt stored in an insulated tank. When needed, the molten salt – a yellowish syrup which retains heat better than water or oil – will convert water into the steam required to power a turbine generator.

Earlier experimentation with solar energy has proved economically impractical partly because of the need for a lot of land and a consistently warm and sunny climate. The largest existing plant is one of nine owned by Luz International, which use the sun's rays to heat water rather than salt.

Although these generate enough light for 350,000 households in Southern California, Luz filed for bankruptcy due, the company claims, to confused Federal policies and "hidden subsidies" to utilities which use regular fossil fuels.

Similar problems have been faced by the pioneers of windpower in which California has also taken the lead, currently producing about 75 percent of the world's supply. Nine-tenths of the US's windpower potential is located in the dozen Western states, where ranching and grain production are major industries and where ranchers have welcomed the royalties that are paid for use of their land for such projects.

US Windpower Co of Livermore, California, the nation's largest builder and operator of these machines, reports that its 3,700 turbines in the northern part of the state have accumulated 40 million operating hours in winds averaging 16 miles (26 km) an hour, driving the blades at almost ten times that speed. Now, with the development of new turbines, 75 feet (23 meters) high with 54-feet (16-meter) blades, the industry's future looks brighter than ever.

Government investment in windpower could make it cheap enough to compete successfully with "dirty" (and diminishing) fossil fuels, so that it would become more significant than nuclear power within the next 25 years. According to one expert in the field, it could provide up to 20 percent of US electricity needs, compared with the 1 percent it presently supplies. ❑

LEFT: alternate energy from the desert is one hope for California's future fuel consumption.

Map, page 242

hikers and rock climbers. The Trona Pinnacles are situated on the west side of bleakly awesome **Searles Lake**, access to which is via State 178 north from Johannesburg. Camping is permitted at the Pinnacles. Ninety-four miles (151 km) north of Johannesburg on US 395 is **Lone Pine** ㊱, a picturesque village that has been a popular location for Hollywood Westerns.

Mount Whitney

From here, **Mount Whitney** ㊲ – at 14,494 feet (4,418 meters) the highest peak in the continental United States – is accessible, although it's an 11-mile (18-km) challenge from the end of Whitney Portal Road to reach the summit *(also see page 204)*. After the climb, a good place for a break is **Keeler**, a ghost town about 10 miles (16 km) from Lone Pine. About 50 miles to the east, beyond Towne's Pass, State Route 190 runs into the Panamint Mountains, some of whose rugged canyons bustled with people and activity in 1873. The town of **Panamint**, now abandoned, came into being when the robbers of a Wells Fargo express discovered silver while hiding out in **Surprise Canyon**.

Persuading two state senators to make a deal with the express company in return for part ownership of the lode, they presided over an instant boomtown with stores, saloons, boarding houses and banks – all along a main street that occupied the entire width of the narrow canyon. Within a year the boom was over, but the canny miners cast their silver in the form of 700-lb (317-kg) cannon balls, a burden too heavy for robbers to carry away.

Indian Ranch Road, an unpaved track off the Trona-Wildrose road and which forks off up Surprise Canyon, continues down to **Ballarat** ㊳. Only crumbling adobe walls and ruined shacks remain here of what was once an important supply town for the miners, to which the stagecoach used to run all the way from Johannesburg.

Another deserted mining town, off Emigrant Canyon Road, was **Skidoo**. Its name was derived from the phrase "23 Skidoo," it having been 23 miles (37 km) from Telescope Peak. Skidoo is famous for its "million-dollar slope," from which $1 million in gold ore was taken early in the century – "it could be scraped out in wheelbarrows," boasted its former owner.

But Skidoo has gone down in legend more than this as "the town that hanged its killer twice," after an incident in which a drunken saloon keeper killed a popular town banker. Skidoo's citizens were wary of what kind of justice might be administered from the nearest lawmen at Lone Pine, so they took it upon themselves to promptly hang the killer. The next day, when a reporter from the big-city *Los Angeles Herald* arrived, they dug up the body and hanged it again so the newsman could get a picture.

Lowest spot on earth

State Route 190 is the main artery through **Death Valley National Park** ㊴, first established as a national monument in 1933. Its fearsome reputation seems to attract as many as it intimidates. Winter or summer sightseers, hikers and amateur naturalists come to scramble up the sand dunes near **Stovepipe Wells**. They also want to marvel at the view from Zabriskie Point, gasp at ancient

ABOVE: land sailors.
BELOW: abandoned mine shaft at Twenty Mule Team Canyon.

Ubehebe Crater, study old mines and abandoned charcoal kilns, explore old ghost towns and snap scores of both color and black and white pictures at humble **Badwater ⓭**, 282 feet (86 meters) below sea level, the lowest spot on earth. Death Valley's summer temperatures are exceeded only in the Libyan Sahara. Autumn through spring, the climate is ideal for exploring Death Valley, with daytime temperatures in the 60s and 70s Fahrenheit (about 15–25°C), although it is chillier at night. Skies are usually bright and free of rain.

Summers are another story. The average daily high in July for the past half-century has been 116°F (47°C). It commonly soars past 120°F (49°C), and once hit a national high of 134°F (57°C). In short, May to October is one continuous heat wave.

ABOVE: only 6 miles to a bathtub.
BELOW: Furnace Creek.

Desert facts

This 120-mile long (193-km) valley is the result of a geological phenomenon. At least 5 million years ago, the deep gap between the Panamint and Funeral mountains was formed by earthquakes and the folding of the earth's crust. This created, technically, not a valley, but what geologists tend to call a graben rock.

Debris eroded from the mountains, filling a plateau which the Ice Ages flattened and swathed in a vast cool sea. This evaporated, leaving alternating layers of mud and salt. Cut off from cooling breezes by the surrounding mountains, this basin (4–16 miles wide) was left to parch with an annual rainfall of less than 2 inches (50 mm).

Despite the harshness of Death Valley's environment, about 900 different species of plant grow in the national park, some throwing down roots 10 times the height of a man. In many ways, Death Valley's human population of 200 or

so seems just as indomitable, enduring terrific heat and isolation. However the growth of Las Vegas, Nevada, 140 miles (225 km) away, inspired the development of the town of Pahrump. It's now only a 60-mile (96-km) drive to the grocery store (the nearest used to be in Vegas).

Years ago, it was traditional for all concessions to close down in the summer, but the tourists kept on coming. Nowadays, in the town of **Furnace Creek ④**, the **Furnace Creek Ranch** and the **Stovepipe Wells Motel** complex stay open throughout the year, and neither is ever empty.

Furnace Creek is a good focal point for a visit to Death Valley. Located not far from Badwater, its **Visitor Center** (tel: 760-786 2331) is open daily all year round. Although Furnace Creek Ranch's 18-hole golf course is said to be the lowest course on earth, nobody would hire a caddy for the valley's other links, the so-called **Devil's Golf Course**, an otherworldly expanse of rugged salt crystals that point to the sky in jagged little edges. It lies between the former sites of the Eagle Borax mill, southwest of Badwater, and the Harmony Borax Works, just north of Furnace Creek, which was developed into a resort from the former workers' quarters. At the **Harmony Borax Works**, an old cleanser-processing plant has been stabilized to show interested visitors the now-very-primitive 19th-century manufacturing methods.

Beginning in 1873, borax – a white, crystalline substance used as a flux, cleansing agent and antiseptic – was a major product of the valley, transported by wagons hauled by 20-mule teams 165 miles (265 km) to the town of Mojave. The company set up resting stations with water tanks and feedboxes every 16 miles (26 km). Eventually the price of borax was undercut by producers in Italy, and the Death Valley companies suspended operations entirely.

Map, page 242

BELOW:
Scotty's Castle.

Overlooking Badwater to the east is **Dante's View** (5,475 feet/1,669 meters) and, in the west, **Telescope Peak**, the highest point in the Panamint Range (11,049 feet/3,368 meters).

Among Death Valley's other natural beauty spots are **Zabriskie Point**, made famous by a 1960s movie and located southeast of Furnace Creek in the Black Mountains near interesting **Twenty Mule Team Canyon**; **Artists Drive** and the **Golden Canyon**, with its vivid displays of color among old outcroppings; and empty **Ubehebe Crater**, an extinct volcano nearly 2,000 years old at the north end of the national monument.

Death's big attraction

Near Ubehebe Crater is the 25-room **Scotty's Castle** ⓫ (tel: 760-786 2392), a $2 million Spanish palace that is Death Valley's biggest visitor attraction. It is operated by the National Park Service which runs hourly tours. Work on the castle began in 1926, at the foot of a natural spring-fed canyon at an elevation of 3,000 feet (about 900 meters). About 2,000 workmen assembled the castle, completing it in 1931, all at the vast expense of a young Chicago millionaire by the name of Albert Johnson.

Earlier, he had been charmed into investing thousands of dollars in a fruitless search for gold by an affable roustabout named Walter Scott, popularly known as "Death Valley Scott." After years of waiting for Scott to strike his fortune, Johnson's patience ran out – but not before he had grown so fond of Death Valley that he decided to build a summer retreat there.

A facsimile of a Spanish-Mediterranean villa, Scotty's Castle contains beautiful continental furnishings and *objets d'art*. The Chicago financier and his wife lived on and off at the castle for many years until his death in 1948. "Death Valley Scotty," the good-natured rogue, also lived there. He died in 1954, and his grave lies along a trail just behind the castle. ❏

RIGHT: the endless, sandy dunes of Stovepipe Wells, Death Valley.

INSIGHT GUIDES

TRAVEL TIPS

New Insight Maps

Maps in Insight Guides are tailored to complement the text. But when you're on the road you sometimes need the big picture that only a large-scale map can provide. This new range of durable Insight Fleximaps has been designed to meet just that need.

Detailed, clear cartography
makes the comprehensive route and city maps easy to follow, highlights all the major tourist sites and provides valuable motoring information plus a full index.

Informative and easy to use
with additional text and photographs covering a destination's top 10 essential sites, plus useful addresses, facts about the destination and handy tips on getting around.

Laminated finish
allows you to mark your route on the map using a non-permanent marker pen, and wipe it off. It makes the maps more durable and easier to fold than traditional maps.

The first titles
cover many popular destinations. They include Algarve, Amsterdam, Bangkok, California, Cyprus, Dominican Republic, Florence, Hong Kong, Ireland, London, Mallorca, Paris, Prague, Rome, San Francisco, Sydney, Thailand, Tuscany, USA Southwest, Venice, and Vienna.

𝕏 INSIGHT GUIDES
The world's largest collection of visual travel guides

CONTENTS

Getting Acquainted

Area: 156,260 sq. miles (404,815 sq. km)
Capital: Sacramento
Population: approximately 30 million
Time zone: GMT minus 8 hours
Currency: US dollars (US$)
Weights and measures: Imperial
Electricity: 110 volts
International dialing code: 00 1

Climate

Northern California: San Francisco's climate is typical of the Northern California coast. Daytime temperatures average in the mid-50s Fahrenheit (10-15° Celsius) and drop as much as 10° at night. Average temperatures are significantly higher in the South Bay and inland valleys. In fact, in the Sacramento and San Joaquin valleys, summer temperatures often reach the 90s. Summers tend to be warm and dry. Winters are generally rainy; temperatures rarely go below freezing along the coast.
Southern California: one of the few places in the world where you can ski in the morning and surf in the afternoon. It is not uncommon for the temperature to vary by 30–40°F (17–22°C) as you travel from mountains to deserts to the beach. The change of seasons is not as dramatic as it is elsewhere. The winters are mild, with a rainy season that lasts from January through March. In the summer months, the humidity is usually low, so discomfort is rare. The famous LA smog is at its worst in August and September.

Language & Culture

The native language is English, but as more than one third of Los Angeles' population is of Latino origin, Spanish is commonly spoken in many parts of that town.
The culture and customs of Southern California especially are influenced by its Mexican heritage. It is not uncommon to go downtown at night and hear Mexican mariachis in the restaurants and on the streets. Some of the best restaurants around are Mexican and many residents consider Mexican food to be the local cuisine.

Population

California, as the most populous state (30 million people) and the physically largest except for Texas and Alaska, has an economy that, if it were a country, would be large enough to rank it among the world's top 10 nations. Although the country's top producer of fruits, nuts and vegetables (mostly from the 450-mile/724-km long Central Valley), California agriculture accounts for only two percent of the gross state product, greatly exceeded by the manufacturing sector (aircraft, spacecraft, missiles, autos) which accounts for 17 percent.

The state has four of the country's largest cities (Los Angeles, San Francisco, San Jose and San Diego) and claims such superlatives as the country's highest peak (Mt Whitney: 14,405 ft/4,418 meters) and its lowest point (Death Valley: 282 ft/86 meters below sea level.)

Government and Economy

With a conventional legislature consisting of a Senate of 40 members and an Assembly of 80 members, the former elected to four-year terms and the latter to two-year terms, California is one of the few states whose citizens possess additional representation in the form of the ballot initiative. Citizens can initiate legislation by collecting the signatures of five percent of the people who voted in the previous elections for governor in support of a particular measure, which will then be put to popular vote in the next election.

Geography

State Tourist officials divide California into the following regions: **San Diego**, with **Orange County** and the **Inland Empire** respectively to the northeast and northwest of it; the **Deserts** and **High Sierras** eastwards to the Nevada border; the **Central Valley** and **Gold Country** between them and the coast, along which are the **Los Angeles** region, the **Central Coast** and the **North Coast** running up to the Oregon border. The most northeastern part is categorized as **Shasta-Cascade**.

Time Zones

California is situated entirely in the Pacific Time Zone, which is two hours behind Chicago, three hours behind New York and eight hours behind Greenwich Mean Time. On the first Sunday in April, the clock is moved ahead one hour for Daylight Savings Time. On the last Sunday in October, the clock is moved back one hour to return to Standard Time.

Planning the Trip

What to Bring

Northern California: With the exception of the finer restaurants, jackets, ties and formal dresses are unnecessary. San Francisco is famous for its breezy hilltops and fog, so bring along a sweater or jacket, even if it is warm and sunny elsewhere.

Southern California: Dress in Southern California is decidedly casual. Relatively few restaurants require jackets and ties for men. Unless you are visiting the mountain areas, the moderate climate makes heavy clothing unnecessary. Wool sweaters or lightweight overcoats are sufficient for winter evenings, and a light jacket is adequate for summer evenings. Expect rain in winter and springtime.

If you are planning to go to the mountains or desert, pack accordingly.

Visas & Passports

Most foreign travelers to the US must have a passport, visa and, depending on where you are coming from, a health record. Prior arrangements must be made to leave the country. Exempt from these rules are: Canadian citizens; certain British nationals; and certain government officials.

Any person who enters the US can visit Mexico or Canada for a period of less than 30 days and still be readmitted to the States without needing a new US visa.

Visas can be obtained from any US embassy. If a visitor loses their visa while in the country, a new one may be obtained from the embassy of the visitor's home country. Extensions are granted by the US Immigration and Naturalization Service, 425 I Street, Washington DC 20536, tel: 202-514 2000.

Extension to Stay: All visitors are given a six-month visa. If you wish to stay longer, contact the immigration office. Obtaining a six-month extension is usually only a formality.

Customs

Whether or not they have anything to declare, all people entering the country must go through US Customs. It can be a time-consuming process, but in order to speed things up, be prepared to open your luggage for inspection and try to keep the following restrictions in mind:

• There is no limit to the amount of money you can bring in with you. If the amount exceeds $10,000, however, you must fill out a report.

• Anything you have for your own personal use may be brought in duty- and tax-free.

• Adults are allowed to bring in one quart of alcohol for personal use.

• You can bring in gifts valued at less than $400 duty- and tax-free. Anything over $400 is subject to duty charges and taxes.

• Dogs, cats and other animals may be brought into the country with certain restrictions. For details contact the US consulate nearest you or write to the Department of Agriculture.

• Automobiles may be driven into the US if they are for the personal use of the visitor, family and guests.

US Customs, 1301 Constitution Ave. NW, Washington DC, tel: 202-566 8195.

Getting There

By Air

In addition to the international airports listed below, there are smaller, regional airports in several locations throughout the state, including Palm Springs, Ontario, Hollywood-Burbank, Fresno, Sacramento, San Jose and Orange County. Shuttle flights are usually available at all of the larger air terminals.

San Francisco International Airport: Known as "SFO," the airport is 14 miles (22 km) south of downtown San Francisco near the town of San Mateo. For public transportation to and from the city, call the Airport Transportation Information line, tel: 1-800-736 2008. Several private shuttles go to most of the bay area. Call SuperShuttle (tel: 415-558 9593 or 1-800-258 3826) or look around the pedestrian island outside the baggage claim areas for departing vans. For airport information, tel: 650-876 7809.

Oakland International Airport: Much smaller and less crowded than SFO, Oakland Airport is well-served by public transportation and much closer to East Bay destinations. Shuttles link the airport with the BART subway system and SFO. General airport information, tel: 510-577 4245.

Los Angeles International Airport: Among the world's busiest airports, handling the majority of the international, domestic and regional air traffic. Information booths just outside the terminal for buses of the Metropolitan Transit Authority, tel: 213-626 4455. For general airport information, telelephone 310-646 5252.

San Diego International Airport: Known as Lindbergh Field, flights arrive from most major American cities. Transportation information, tel: 619-2333004. General airport information, tel: 619-231 7361.

Airlines

Airlines that fly regularly into California include:
Alaska Airlines; America West; American Airlines; Continental Air; Delta Airlines; Northwest; Sky West Airlines; Southwest; TWA; United Airlines; USAir.

By Rail

Amtrak (tel: 800-872 7245) is the major rail passenger carrier in the US. Though the system is little used and little appreciated by Californians, it can be a pleasant way to get around the state, provided you are not in too much of a hurry. The California Zephyr is the main rail line into Northern California, stopping at Sacramento, Colfax, Davis, Martinez and Richmond before reaching Oakland's 16th Street Station, where there is a free bus service to San Francisco.

Southern Pacific Railroad also runs passengers between San Francisco and San Jose, with several stops along the peninsula. Commonly called Caltrain, this rail service operates from the terminal located at Fourth and Townsend streets in San Francisco.

Amtrak offers several major rail lines in Southern California. The Sunset Limited from New Orleans stops at Indio, Ontario and Pomona before it finally reaches Los Angeles. The San Diegan runs between Los Angeles and San Diego, with stops at Santa Ana, San Juan Capistrano, Oceanside and Delmar.

The state is tied together by the Coast Starlight, which travels north from Los Angeles all the way to Seattle, stopping at Glendale, Simi Valley, Oxnard, Santa Barbara, San Luis Obispo, San Jose, Oakland (from here there's a bus transfer to San Francisco before the route continues), Martinez, Davis, Sacramento, Marysville, Richmond, Chico, Reading and across the Oregon border. Amtrak offers some local services also. Contact Amtrak directly for details, tel: 1-800-872 7245 or 215-628 1846. 1-800-523 6590.

By Bus

The national bus line, Greyhound/Trailways (tel: 800-231 2222), as well as a number of smaller charter companies provide an impressive network of ground travel throughout California, offering daily service to major towns and cities. Routes and schedules are subject to change; it is a good idea to check all arrangements with local stations – in advance. San Francisco, Oakland, Los Angeles, San Diego and other large towns also have municipal bus systems.

Bus service information numbers within major cities include: San Francisco, tel: MUNI at 415-673 6864; East Bay AC

Speed limits

Keep in mind that the national speed limit on all interstate highways is now 65 miles per hour, and 55 miles per hour on most other local highways. California law requires that every passenger wears a seat belt, that small children and babies be secured in youth or infant seats, and that drivers carry a valid license. There is also a state law that requires all motorcycle riders to wear helmets.

Transit at 510-839 2882; Los Angeles Metropolitan Transit Authority at 213-626 4455; San Diego Transit Company at 619-233 3004.

By Road
The best way to see California is, of course, by car. Gasoline is relatively inexpensive, and the road system generally well-maintained and clearly marked. Of primary importance is a good map and some patience – Californian cities have major traffic jams. Local radio stations give road condition updates and traffic alerts. For road condition information in Northern California, tel: 916-445 1534.

The principal north-south byways in California are listed below:
Interstate 5 (the Golden State and Santa Ana freeways), which covers the distance from Canada to Mexico via Seattle, Sacramento, Los Angeles and San Diego.
Interstate 15, which transits San Bernardino and San Diego after a long passage from Montana's Canadian border, via Salt Lake City and Las Vegas.
US Highway 101 (the Ventura and Hollywood freeways), which proceeds south down the Pacific coast from Washington state, crosses San Francisco's Golden Gate Bridge, and ends in downtown Los Angeles.

More colour
for the world.

HDCplus. New perspectives in colour photography.

AGFA

Probably the <u>most</u> <u>important</u> TRAVEL TIP you will ever receive

Before you travel abroad, make sure that you and your family are protected from diseases that can cause serious health problems.

For instance, you can pick up *hepatitis A* which infects 10 million people worldwide every year (it's not just a disease of poorer countries) simply through consuming contaminated food or water!

What's more, in many countries if you have an accident needing medical treatment, or even dental treatment, you could also be at risk of infection from *hepatitis B* which is 100 times more infectious than AIDS, and can lead to liver cancer.

The good news is, you can be protected by vaccination against these and other serious diseases, such as *typhoid, meningitis* and *yellow fever*.

Travel safely! Check with your doctor at least 8 weeks before you go, to discover whether or not you need protection.

Consult your doctor before you go... not when you return!

SB

SmithKline Beecham

V A C C I N E S

Produced as a service to public health

State Highway 1 (the Pacific Coast Highway), which hugs the coast from San Diego to San Francisco and further north. The principal east-west byways in California are:
Interstate 8, which departs from Interstate 10 at Casa Grande, Arizona and ends in San Diego.
Interstate 10 (the San Bernardino and Santa Monica freeways), which begins on the East coast in Jacksonville, Florida, and continues through New Orleans, Houston, El Paso, Tucson and Phoenix before cutting through Los Angeles, then ending at the coast in Santa Monica.
Interstate 40, which connects Knoxville, Tennessee, with Barstow, California, via Memphis, Oklahoma City and Albuquerque.

Special Information

Children
Because of the large number of world-famous playgrounds, such as Disneyland, Knott's Berry Farm and Magic Mountain, the state is a good place to vacation with kids. Hotels and motels are usually accommodating, allowing children to stay in parents' rooms with only a nominal charge for extra beds. Chronicle Books of San Francisco has published two useful guides: *Places to Go With Kids in Northern California* and its Southern Californian equivalent.

Disabled
For more than a decade California has had legislation requiring public buildings to be accessible to the disabled. There are also some special concessions: Greyhound buses allow a disabled person plus a companion to travel for one fare and the railway system, Amtrak, offers a free booklet, called *Travel Planner*, from the National Railroad Corporation, 400 N Capital Street NW, Washington DC 20001.

Practical Tips

Business Hours

Standard business hours are from 9am–5pm weekdays. Most department stores open at 10am and many stores, especially those in shopping malls, stay open until 9pm. Los Angeles and San Francisco have a number of 24-hour restaurants. A few supermarkets and convenience stores also open around the clock. Bank hours usually run from 9am-5pm, although some stay open until 6pm. Some branch offices keep Saturday morning hours. However, most banks are equipped with 24-hour automated tellers on the outside of their buildings, and if you have an ATM card you can use these machines for simple transactions at your convenience. Be careful at night.

Keep in mind that during the public holidays, post offices, banks, government offices and many private businesses are closed.

Media

Television & Radio
Television and radio are invaluable sources of up-to-the-minute information about weather, road conditions and current events. It is now almost standard for decent hotels and motels to include televisions in the price of a room, although you may have to pay extra for cable service. Television and radio listings are published in local newspapers. Sunday papers usually have a detailed weekly guide.

Newspapers & Magazines
San Francisco has two major daily newspapers, the *San Francisco Chronicle* in the morning and the *San Francisco Examiner* in the afternoon. The two papers combine into one edition on Sunday. This weekend paper includes special sections, such as the "Pink Pages," which highlight the area's sports, entertainment and cultural events. Other papers in Northern California include the *Sacramento Bee*, the *San Jose Mercury-News* and the *San Francisco Bay Guardian*.

The *Los Angeles Times* is one of the most widely-read papers in the country. There are several editions, and there is probably no better entertainment section than the *Times*' Sunday "Calendar" section. Other large daily papers are San Fernando Valley's *The Daily News*, *The San Diego Union-Tribune* and the *Orange County Register*.

Los Angeles Magazine, *Palm Springs Life*, *San Diego* and *Orange Coast* are monthly regional magazines that carry feature articles on Southern California culture, as well as listings of restaurants and current events. The *Los Angeles Reader*, a free weekly, lists most local events.

Some of the free local weekly newspapers are excellent sources of up-to-the-minute information on what's going on in a particular town. Check out the *LA Weekly* in Los Angeles, the *East Bay Express* in the East Bay, and the *San Francisco Bay Guardian* in San Francisco.

Telephone & Faxes

Telephone
Coin-operated telephones are ubiquitous – in hotels, restaurants, shopping centers, gas stations and often in lighted booths on street corners. To place a long-distance call, dial 1+area code+local number. Be

Postal Services

Post offices open between 7 and 9am and usually close at 5pm, Monday–Friday. Many of them are also open for a few hours on Saturday morning. All post offices are closed on Sunday. If you don't know where you will be staying in any particular town, you can receive mail by having it addressed to General Delivery at the main post office in that town. You must pick up General Delivery mail in person and show proper identification. In LA, the Worldway Postal Center, 800 W Century Boulevard, tel: 310-337 8845, is open 24 hours.

sure to have plenty of change with you to deposit on the operator's prompting.

If you are having problems, dial "0" for the operator from any phone. Another indispensable number is for information assistance, which can provide telephone listings if you do not have a phone book handy. For local information dial 411; for long distance dial 1+area code+555-1212. For a toll-free number directory dial 1-800-555-1212. Make use of toll-free numbers when possible (toll-free telephone numbers within the US are indicated by 1-800 or 888). For personal calls, take advantage of lower long-distance rates after 5pm on weekdays and during weekends.

Telegrams & Faxes
Western Union, (tel: 1-800-325 6000), and International Telephone and Telegraph (ITT) will take telegram and telex messages as well as orders to

Telephone Codes

With the proliferation of fax lines, modems and portable telephones, California has been forced to divide, then sub-divide its existing telephone exchanges. Although every effort has been made to keep the telephone prefixes listed here up to date, it's always a good idea to check with the operator if you're in doubt.

wire money over the phone. Fax machines can be found in most hotels and convenience stores.

Weights & Measures

The US uses the Imperial system of weights and measures. Metric is rarely used. Below is a conversion chart:

1 inch	=	2.54 centimeters
1 foot	=	30.48 centimeters
1 mile	=	1.609 kilometers
1 quart	=	1.136 liters
1 ounce	=	28.40 grams
1 pound	=	0.453 kilograms
1 yard	=	0.9144 meters

Reservations

Make reservations at hotels and popular restaurants, especially May–September. Not all restaurants take bookings, but if you call ahead, the staff will tell you how long the wait will be.

Tipping

Just as in other parts of the country, service personnel in California rely on tips for a large part of their income. In most cases, 15–20 percent is the going rate for waiters, and bartenders, 15 percent for taxi drivers. The accepted rate for baggage handlers at airports and hotels is around $1 per bag. For overnight stays it is not necessary to tip the chambermaid. For longer stays the rule of thumb is to leave a minimum tip of one or two dollars per day. A doorman expects to be tipped for helping unload your car or for other services; 50¢ to one dollar should cover it.

Visitor Information

General information on visiting California is available from the **State Office of Tourism**, 801 K St Suite 1600, Sacramento, CA 95812 Tel: 1-800-862 2543.

Visitors' Bureaus:
Local Visitors' Bureaus will send maps and information about hotels, attractions and events.

Anaheim Area Visitors' and Convention Bureau,
800 W Katella Ave., Anaheim, CA 92802, Tel: 714-999 8999.
Berkeley Convention and Visitors' Bureau,
2015 Center St, Berkeley, CA 94704
Tel: 510-549 7040; 1-800-847 4823.
Beverly Hills Visitors' and Convention Bureau,
239 South Beverly Drive, Beverly Hills, CA 90212 Tel: 310-271 8174; 1-800-345 2210.
Buena Park Convention and Visitors' Bureau,
6280 Manchester Blvd., Suite 102, Buena Park, CA 90621 Tel: 714-521 0261. *Also:* 7711 Beach Blvd. # 100 Buena Park 92628
Tel: 714-562 3569.
Long Beach Area Convention and Visitors' Council,
1 World Trade Center, Suite 300, Long Beach, CA 90831 Tel: 562-436 3645; 1-800-452 7829.
Los Angeles Convention and Visitors' Bureau,
633 W 5th St., Suite 6000, Los Angeles, CA 90071 Tel: 213-624 7300.
Los Angeles Chamber of Commerce,
404 South Bixel, Los Angeles,

Insight Guides portray destinations in depth, providing the complete picture and the top photography

Insight Pocket Guides *focus on the best choices for places to see and things to do and include large fold-out maps*

Insight Compact Guides' *portability makes them the perfect books to carry with you for on-the-spot reference*

Three types of guide for all types of travel

INSIGHT GUIDES Different people need different kinds of information. Some want *background information* to help them prepare for the trip. Others seek *personal recommendations* from someone who knows the destination well. And others look for *compactly presented data* for on-the-spot reference. With three carefully designed series, Insight Guides offer readers the perfect choice. Insight Guides will turn your visit into an experience.

The world's largest collection of visual travel guides

When you're
bitten by the travel bug,
make sure you're protected.

Check into a British Airways Travel Clinic.

British Airways Travel Clinics provide travellers with:
- A complete vaccination service and essential travel health-care items
- Up-dated travel health information and advice

Call **01276 685040** for details of your nearest Travel Clinic.

**BRITISH AIRWAYS
TRAVEL CLINICS**

Ca 90017. Mail: PO Box 3696, Los Angeles, CA 90051
Tel: 213-580 7500.

Monterey Peninsula Visitors' and Convention Bureau,
380 Alvarado St.
Tel: 408-649 1770.

Napa Valley Conference and Visitors' Bureau,
1310 Napa Town Center, Napa, CA 94559
Tel: 707-226 7459.

North Lake Tahoe Chamber of Commerce,
245 North Lake Blvd., Tahoe City
Tel: 530-581 6900
1-800-824 6348.

Palm Springs Desert Resorts Convention and Visitors' Bureau,
69-930 Highway 111, Suite 201, Rancho Mirage, CA 92270
Tel: 760-770 9000;
1-800-417 3529.

Sacramento Visitor Center,
1104 Front St.
Tel: 916-442 7644.

San Diego International Visitors Information Center,
11 Horton Plaza.
Tel: 619-236 1212.

San Diego North County Convention and Visitors' Bureau,
720 N Broadway, Escondido, CA 92025.
Tel: 760-745 4741
1-800-848 3336.

San Francisco Visitor Information Center,
900 Market St.,
San Francisco, CA 94101.
Tel: 415-391 2000.

San Francisco Convention & Visitors' Bureau
PO Box 429097
San Francisco
CA 94142-9097
Tel: 415-391 2000;
1-888-782 9673.
201 3rd St., Suite. 900,
CA 94103.

San Francisco Chamber of Commerce,
465 California St.,
San Francisco, CA 94104.
Tel: 415-392 4511.

San Luis Obispo County Visitors' and Conference Bureau,
1041 Chorro St., Suite E, San Luis Obispo, CA 93401
Tel: 805-541 8000;
1-800-634 1414

San Jose Visitor Information
Tel: 1-888-847 4875.

Consulates

Foreign visitors looking for home country representatives can find consulates in San Francisco and Los Angeles. Check in the *Yellow Pages* of local telephone books, available in libraries and post offices, or call "Information" (411 if calling within town; 1 + area code of city + 555-1212 if calling from out of town).

Santa Barbara Visitor Information Center,
1 Santa Barbara St.,
Santa Barbara, CA 93101
Tel: 805-965 3021/966 9222.
1-800-927 4688/676 1266

Santa Catalina Visitor's Bureau,
PO Box 217, Avalon, CA 90704.
Tel: 310-510 1520.

Santa Cruz County Convention and Visitors' Bureau,
701 Front St., CA 95060
Tel: 1-800-833 3494.

Sonoma County Convention & Visitor's Bureau
5000 Roberts Lake Rd, Suite A, Rohnert Park, CA 94928.
Tel: 707-586 8100;
1-800-326 7666.

South Lake Tahoe Visitors Authority,
1156 Ski Run Blvd..
Tel: 800-288 2463.

Ventura Visitors' and Convention Bureau,
89C South California St.,
Ventura, CA 93001.
Tel: 805-648 2075.

Yosemite and Sierra Visitor's Bureau
Tel: 559-683 4636

Emergencies

Security & Crime
Like big cities all over the world, California's cities have dangerous neighborhoods. Common sense is your most effective weapon. Do not walk alone at night. Keep a careful eye on your belongings – lock valuable possessions in a hotel safe. Never leave your car unlocked. Never leave small children by themselves.

If you are driving, never pick up anyone you don't know, especially if you are alone. Always be wary of who is around you. If you have trouble on the road, stay in the car and lock the doors, turn on your hazard lights and leave the hood up in order to increase your visibility and alert passing police cars.

Hotels usually warn that they do not guarantee the safety of belongings left in the rooms. If you have any valuables, you may want to lock them in the hotel safe.

Health & Emergencies
In the case of an emergency, dial 911 from any telephone for the police, fire department or ambulance service.

In the event you need medical assistance, consult the local *Yellow Pages* for the physician or pharmacist nearest you. In large cities, there is usually a physician referral service number listed. If you need immediate attention, go directly to a hospital emergency room.

There is nothing cheap about being sick in the United States. It is essential to have adequate medical insurance and to carry an identification card or policy number at all times.

Getting Around

San Francisco: San Francisco is served by an excellent public transportation system. The city's MUNI (tel: 415-673 6864, open 6am–midnight, with some night service) network of buses, street cars and historic cable cars makes getting around a snap. In addition, the Bay Area Rapid Transit (known locally as BART) subway system (tel: 415-922 2278, open 4am–midnight) connects San Francisco with the East Bay via a tube that goes under the bay.

The Bay Area Rapid Transit (BART) is one of the most efficient and modern rail lines in the US. Often compared to the super-subways of Europe and The Far East, BART serves 34 stations in three counties, from San Francisco to Daly City and throughout the East Bay. Hours are: Monday–Friday 4am–midnight; Saturday 6am–midnight and Sunday, 8am–midnight.

A new-ish bus service with headquarters in San Francisco, the Adventure Network for Travelers (ANT) offers inexpensive transport between the northern city and Los Angeles with side routes to Las Vegas and the Grand Canyon. Stops at scenic spots en route, as well as at Monterey, Santa Barbara, Stanta Cruz and San Luis Obispo. For information, tel: 800-336 6049.

Los Angeles: The only public transportation available is the Southern California Metropolitan Transit Agency bus company, which everyone calls the MTA. MTA offers a discount of about 10 percent if you buy booklets of 10 tickets or more. For information and schedules, tel: 213-626 4455. Visitors can buy an MTA pass good for use on Metro bus and rail lines for seven days (call 1-800-COMMUTE to find out the nearest location to buy).

Southern California is still in the early stages of implementing its most ambitious public transit plans for half a century, which, when completed, will link areas as far apart as Long Beach and Palmdale, 50 miles north of LA. The 400-mile system of light rail, subway and other transportation facilities will not be fully in place until 2010, although a few lines in central LA have opened already. The county's Metropolitan Transit Authority, or MTA (tel: 213-626 4455), oversees the extensive bus system, as well as the new Metro and light rail system.

Ameribus Tours offers a daily loop-type tour between Anaheim, Los Angeles, Santa Barbara, San Simeon, Monterey, San Francisco, Merced and Yosemite. Travelers can either take the full guided tour or buy a monthly pass enabling them to hop on and off at different destinations. Make reservations through travel agents or through Ameribus (tel: 954-923 1480).

Archtours
Tel: 323-294 5821
Various Los Angeles tours visit work by Frank Lloyd Wright and Richard Neutra, as well as restaurants and other facilities.
Off 'n' Running Tours
Tel: 1-800-523 8687
Walking and running tours in the Los Angeles area
Angel City Tours
Tel: 310-470 4463
Two-hour strolls and Metro rides in downtown Los Angeles.

Driving is by far the most flexible and convenient means of travel in California, although newcomers are often confused by the many freeways. Roads are well-maintained throughout the state, and gasoline is relatively inexpensive. Before you set out, however, there are some important things to keep in mind.

Seagull signs in blue and white mark the 49 Mile Scenic Drive. A free map from the San Francisco Visitor Center at Powell and Market streets details the route.

Drivers who seek to explore the old US Route 66 in the south of the state can get a free map charting 29 points of interest along 62 miles (100 km) of the route from the LA Visitors Center, 633 W 5th St, tel: 213-689 8822.

Motoring Advisories
If you plan on driving any distance, it's a good idea to join the American Automobile Association (811 Gatehouse Road, Falls Church, VA 22047, tel: 703-222 6334) or through any of their affiliate offices throughout California (the Automobile Club of Southern California at 4512 Sepulveda Boulevard, Culver City, CA 90230-4833 is not far from Los Angeles International Airport; in San Francisco, contact AAA, 150 Van Ness Avenue, tel: 415-565 2012). In addition to emergency road service, AAA offers maps, guidebooks, insurance, bail bond protection and an arrest certificate to its members.

Travelers should check local listings for the AAA office. There are reciprocal arrangements with many international AAA organizations, such as those in

Germany, Great Britain, Australia, etc.

Desert & Mountain Travel

A word of caution for desert travelers: the single most important precaution you can take is to tell someone your destination, route and expected time of arrival. Check tires carefully before long stretches of desert driving. Heat builds pressure, so have them at slightly below normal air pressure. The desert's arid climate makes carrying extra water – both for passengers and vehicles – essential. Carry at least one gallon per person. Keep an eye on the gas gauge. It's a good idea to have more than you think you need. Remember, if you should have car trouble or become lost, do not strike out on foot. A car, visible from the air and presumably on a road, is easier to spot than a person, and it affords shelter from the weather. Wait to be found.

Mountain drivers are advised to be equally vigilant. Winter storms in the Sierras occasionally close major roads, and at times chains are required on tires. Phone ahead for road conditions before you depart.

Traveling to Tijuana/Baja

Non US citizens should bring.their passports or green cards. US citizens don't need a passport unless they're visiting for more than 72 hours, or plan to go beyond the State Highway 1 checkpoint below Baja's Ensenada. If so, they must acquire a tourist visa in San Diego from any travel agent, the Mexican Consulate General, the Mexico Government Tourism Office or the Automobile Club of Southern California. Proof of nationality must accompany the visa.

US insurance is not valid in Mexico and it is definitely a wise move to obtain short-term insurance, obtainable at innumerable sales offices just

Car Rental

National car rental companies are located at all airports and large towns. The best rates are usually available by booking in advance on the toll-free line. In most cases, you must be at least 21 years old to rent a car (often 25), and you must have a valid driver's license and at least one major credit card. Foreign travelers may need to produce an international driver's license or a license from their home country. Always take out collision and liability insurance, which may not always be included in the base price of the rental. It is also a good idea to inquire about an unlimited mileage package, especially on a long trip. If not, you may be charged 5-25¢ per mile in addition to your rental fee, and considering the vast area of California, your vacation miles add up quickly.

Alamo	1-800-327 9633
Avis	1-800-331 1212
Budget	1-800-527 0700
Dollar	1-800-800 4000
Enterprise	1-800-325 8007
Hertz	1-800-654 3131
National	1-800-227 7368
Thrifty	1-800-367 2277

north of the border.

Crossing into Mexico is easy, with immigration officers at both sides usually just waving you along. There are three major crossings: at busy **San Ysidro**, 18 miles (29km) south of downtown San Diego, which is the gateway to Tijuana; at **Tecate** off State 94, where there is rarely a wait, although the solitary customs officer tends to close the border in early evening; and at **Mexicali** (Baja's capital), a dreary industrial city opposite the California town of Calexico, which is about 90 miles (144 km) to the east.

Because driving is not easy in Tijuana for those unfamiliar with the city (and the Spanish language), many drivers park in San Diego's San Ysidro, crossing into Tijuana via the elevated pedestrian walkway. Avoid leaving your car in the parking places of merchants unless you want to have it towed away by police.

There's an all-day secure lot off the "Last Exit US parking" ramp – turn right at the stop sign to the Tijuana side. Cheap taxis and buses are available.

Crossing Back: The return to California can be a bit more tense than the entry into

Mexico, as US Border Patrol officers take far more interest in who's coming into the country. During busy American holiday periods, such as Independence Day (July 4) and Labor Day (early September), waiting up to two hours to cross is not uncommon.

Hitchhiking

In California, as elsewhere in the US, hitchhiking is dangerous and unpredictable. In general, well-meaning hitchers in California won't stop for hitchhikers as they might have 20 years ago because of fear – a fear the hitchhiker might do well to have of people who pick up hitchers.

Hitchhiking is illegal on all highways and interstates and on many secondary roads as well, and, because traffic is sparse in some regions, it can also be quite difficult.

However, if you do decide to hitch, it is best to do it from an exit ramp (if legal) or a highway rest stop rather than on the road itself. For long distances it is advisable to make a sign clearly stating your destination. To find the safest situations, it is worth checking ride services and college campus bulletin boards for posted ride shares.

Where to Stay

California offers the complete spectrum of accommodation - from elegant European-style hotels to inexpensive motels rented by the week.

In Los Angeles, the most expensive hotels are situated downtown and in Beverly Hills, and have the best access to shopping and public transportation. In San Francisco, they are generally located on Nob Hill, the Financial District and Union Square. These grand hotels are particularly well-suited to the international traveler, and many are attractive landmarks in their own right.

The concierge at most finer hotels will arrange theater tickets, tours, telexes, limousines with bilingual drivers and airline reservations. Rates average anywhere from $150–$500 per night, double occupancy.

There are also a large number of smaller hotels and hotel chains for you to chose from. These establishments usually offer all of the essential comforts without the high prices of the grand hotels.

The price guide indicates approximate rates for a standard double room:

Northern California

SAN FRANCISCO

Hotel reservations may be made through services including San Francisco Reservations, 22 Second Street, San Francisco, CA 94102 or by telephone (415-227 1500). The Convention and Visitors' Bureau can advise you regarding special needs or general information about their member hotels, motels and inns, Tel: 415-391 2000/800-220 5747. Hotel chains like Hilton, Hyatt and Marriott offer toll-free telephone numbers for reservations.

Abigail Hotel
246 McAllister St.
CA 94102
Tel: 415-861 9728;
1-800-243 6510;
Fax: 415-861 5848.
Fine little hotel with antiques and eccentric touches. $

Adelaide Inn
Isadora Duncan Pl. (off Taylor between Geary and Post)
CA 94102
Tel: 415-441 2474;
Fax: 415-441 0161.
Small, casual hotel popular with Europeans. $

Hotel Bedford
761 Post St., CA 94109
Tel: 415-673 6040;
1-800-327 5642;
Fax: 415-563 6739.
Reasonable and popular; Café Bedford. Recently renovated. $$

Best Western Grosvenor Hotel
380 South Airport Blvd., South San Francisco, CA 94080
Tel: 415-650-873 3200;
1-800-528 1234;
Fax: 650-589 3495.
Close to the airport. Renovated in 1996. $$

Campton Place
340 Stockton off Union Square, CA 94108
Tel: 415-781 5555;
1-800-235 4300 (in California);
Fax: 415-955 5536.
Known for personal service. Renovated in 1996. $$–$$$

Cathedral Hill Hotel
1101 Van Ness Ave.
CA 94109
Tel: 415-776 8200;
Fax: 415-441 2841.
Roof-top pool and garden patio. Recently renovated. $–$$

Hotel Chancellor
433 Powell St., CA 94102 Tel: 415-362 2004;
1-800-428-4748;
Fax: 415-362 1403.
A good-value hotel on Union Square, first opened in the 1920s. $–$$

Clift Hotel
495 Geary, CA 94102
Tel: 415-775 4700;
1-800-652-5438;
Fax: 415-441 4621.
Just west of Union Square downtown; this hotel is old, conservative and has an understated elegance. $$$

Embassy Suites
150 Anza Blvd., Burlingame, CA 94010
Tel: 650-342 4600;
1-800 362 2779;
Fax: 650-343 8137.
Situated on the bay, many of the rooms have excellent views. $

Doubletree Hotel
San Francisco Airport
835 Airport Blvd., Burlingame, CA 94010
Tel: 650-344 5500;
1-800 362 2779;
Fax: 650-340 8851.
Many rooms with a bay view. Exercise room. Airport transportation. $

Fairmont Hotel
950 Mason St., CA 94108
Tel: 415-772 5000;
1-800-527-4727;
Fax: 415-837 0587.
A San Francisco landmark, and one reason many people come to Nob Hill. Fine rooms, an elegant atmosphere, and very good city views. $$$

Grand Hyatt
345 Stockton St., CA 94108 Tel: 415-398 1234;
1-800-233-1234;
Fax: 415-391 1780.
Overlooking Union Square and a lovely fountain in the garden, this hotel was formerly known as the Hyatt on Union Square. $$$

Hotel Griffon
155 Steuart St.
Tel: 415-495 2100
1-800 321 2201;
Fax: 415-495 3922.
Charming brownstone; attentive service; near Ferry Building.

San Francisco Airport Hilton
670 Gateway Blvd., CA 94080
Tel: 650-872 1515;
1-800-445-8667;
Fax: 415-589 1096.

San Francisco Hilton & Towers
333 O'Farrell, CA 94128
Tel: 415-771 1400;
1-800-445-8667;
Fax: 415-771 6807. $$
Pool, exercise room, five
restaurants. One of the largest
hotels in the city. $$

Holiday Inns
Tel: 1-800-465-4329
central reservations. Five large
hotels; amenities vary according
to property; all but Union Square
have swimming pools; $–$$
depending on the property:

Civic Center
50 Eighth St., CA 94103
Tel: 415-626 6103.

Financial District
750 Kearny, CA 94108
Tel: 415-433 6600.

Fisherman's Wharf
1300 Columbus, CA 94133
Tel: 415-771 9000.

Golden Gateway
1500 Van Ness, CA 94109
Tel: 415-441 4000.
A last resort on a busy
thoroughfare.

Union Square
480 Sutter At Powell, CA 94108
Tel: 415-398 8900.
The best of the bunch. $$

Holiday Inn Airport
275 South Airport Blvd.,
CA 94080
Tel: 650-873 3550;
1-800-465 4329;
Fax: 650-873 4524.
224 units, saunas, whirlpool and
exercise room. Near airport. $$

Huntington Hotel
1075 California St.,
CA 94108
Tel: 415-474 5400;
1-800-227-4683;
Fax: 415-474 6227.
Popular with opera stars and
other celebrities who request
their favorite, individually
furnished rooms. $$$

Hyatt Regency Embarcadeo
5 Embarcadero Center

Tel: 415-788 1234;
1-800-233-1234;
Fax: 415-398 2567.
Spectacular architecture: don't
miss the lobby atrium that soars
for several floors. $$$

Inn at the Opera
333 Fulton St., CA 94102
Tel: 415-863 8400;
1-800-325-2708;
Fax: 415-861 0821.
A favorite resting spot for the
performing artists who appear
nightly in San Francisco's nearby
arts centers. $$$

King George Hotel
334 Mason St., CA 94102
Tel: 415-781 5050;
1-800-288-6005;
Fax: 415-391 6976.
Small, traditional rooms and
afternoon tea, a favorite with the
British traveler. Renovated in
1997. $$$

Price Guide

Standard Double Room
$ under $150
$$ $150–$225
$$$ over $225

The Mansion
2220 Sacramento St.,
CA 94115
Tel: 415-929 9444;
1-800-826-9398;
Fax: 415-567 9391.
A twin-towered Victorian house
(1887) which has been turned
into a hotel of unusual
distinction: each room is
individually and eccentrically
decorated. Restaurant serves
Victorian-style dinner. $$

Mark Hopkins Intercontinental,
No 1 Nob Hill, CA 94108
Tel: 415-392 3434;
1-800-327-0200;
Fax: 415-421 3302.
Along with the Fairmont, Nob
Hill's most famous hotel. The
"Top of the Mark" restaurant and
many rooms offer panoramic
views. Neoclassical touches and
lavish bathrooms are only two of
the other attractions. $$$

Marina Inn
3110 Octavia St.
(at Lombard St.), CA 94123
Tel: 415-928 1000;
1-800-274-1420;
Fax: 415-928 5909.
Lombard Street-area hotel that
has more the feel of a
countrified B&B than a city
establishment. $

The Maxwell Hotel
386 Geary St., CA 94102
Tel: 415-986 2000;
888-734-6299;
Fax: 415-986 2193.
Well-located and within most
people's budgets, new owners
have given this pleasant, well-
located hotel a pretty, Art Deco
look. $$

Miyako
1625 Post St., CA 94115
Tel: 415-922 3200;
1-800-533-4567;
Fax: 415-921 0417.
Attractive, tasty Japanese
decor. $$

Monticello Inn
127 Ellis St., CA 94102
Tel: 415-392 8800;
1-800-669-7777;
Fax: 415-398-2650.
Colonial-style flair right in the
heart of downtown, with a
popular grill room. $

The Palace
2 New Montgomery St.,
CA 94105
Tel: 415-512 1111;
Fax: 415-243 8363.
A historical landmark; the
famous Garden Court
Restaurant. $$$

Parc 55 Renaissance
55 Cyril Magnin St.,
CA 94102
Tel: 415-392 8000;
1-800-650-7272;
Fax: 415-403 6602.
Excellent views. Restaurant,
health club. $$

The Prescott Hotel
545 Post St., CA 94115
Tel: 415-563 0303;
1-800-283-7322;
Fax: 415-563 6831.
A fine hotel recently renovated,
with emphasis on personal

service and famed California chef Wolfgang Puck's Postrio restaurant. $$

Queen Anne Hotel
1590 Sutter St., CA 94109 Tel: 415-441 2828;
1-800-227-3970;
Fax: 415-775 5212.
Individually appointed rooms in a restored Victorian building. $

Ramada Plaza
1231 Market St., CA 94103
Tel: 415-626 8000;
1-800-227-4747;
Fax: 415-487 4436.
A San Franciscan landmark, one block from Civic Auditorium. Public and guest rooms renovated in 1997. $$

Ritz-Carlton San Francisco
600 Stockton St., CA 94108
Tel: 415-296 7465;
1-800-241-3333;
Fax: 415-291 0288.
Oil paintings and crystal chandeliers are two of the innovations that were added when a major hotel chain took over San Francisco's neoclassical Metropolitan Life Insurance Company to create an "instant" landmark hotel. $$$

Renaissance Standford Court,
905 California St., CA 94108
Tel: 415-989 3500;
1-800-468-3571;
Fax: 415-391 0513.
Located near Nob Hill, the Renaissance has a stained-glass dome, an elegant lobby and one of San Francisco's best-known restaurants. $$$

Royal Pacific Motor Inn
661 Broadway near Chinatown,
CA 94133
Tel: 415-781 6661;
Fax: 415-781 6688.
Sauna, exercise room. $

San Francisco Fisherman's Wharf Marriott
1250 Columbus Ave.
CA 94133
Tel: 415-775 7555;
Fax: 415-474 2099.
Sauna, exercise room. Three blocks from Fisherman's Wharf.
$$

Sherman House
2160 Green St., CA 94123 Tel: 415-563 3600;
Fax: 415-563 1882.
Absolute luxury, very expensive, Golden Gate views and fireplaces. $$$

Sir Francis Drake
450 Power St., CA 94102
Tel: 415-392 7755;
1-800-227-5480;
Fax: 415-395 8559.
Doormen are decked out in Beefeater costumes, and rooms styled as if from an English country home. $$–$$$

Stanyan Park Hotel
750 Stanyan St., CA 94117
Tel: 415-751 1000;
Fax: 415-668 5454.
Listed on the National Register of Historic Places, near Golden Gate Park, Haight-Ashbury district and the UC Medical Center. $

The Tuscan Inn at Fisherman's Wharf
425 North Point St., CA 94133
Tel:415-561 1100;
800-578 7878
Fax: 415-561 1199.
Just two blocks west of Pier 39, many of the rooms offer a spectacular view of the bay. $$

Warwick Regis Hotel,
490 Geary St., CA 94108
Tel: 415-928 7900;
1-800-827-3447;
Fax: 415-441 8788.
Antiques and canopy beds are the features of this small, refurbished hotel. $–$$

Westin St Francis
335 Powell St., CA 94102
Tel: 415-397 7000;
1-800 228 3000;
Fax: 415-774 0124.
A city landmarks. Choose rooms in the original 1904 building or the modern tower. $$–$$$

ALBION
Albion River Inn
3790 Highway 1
PO Box 100, 95410
Tel: 707-937 1919;
Fax: 707-937 2604.
A romantic setting by the sea for

both dining out and staying in.
$$–$$$

ANAHEIM
Days Inn
1604 S. Harbor Blvd.
Tel: 714-635 3630
1-800-624 3940.
Near Disney, Pool, spa and restaurant. $

Disneyland Hotel
1313 Harbor Blvd.
Tel: 714-956 6582
800-624 5391.
Pools, spa, tennis courts, restaurants and a new Peter Pan "relaxing" area. $$$

Peter Pan Motor Lodge
2029 S. Harbor Blvd.
Tel: 714-750 0232.
Pool, spa and kitchenettes. $

BIG SUR
Big Sur Lodge
State Route 1, Big Sur, 93920
Tel: 831-667 3100;
Fax: 831-667 3110.
Big Sur architect Mickey Muenning used the sea and the mountains as a backdrop to this lush, plush resort. $–$$

Ventana Inn
Highway 1, Big Sur, CA 93920
Tel: 831-667 2331;
Fax: 831-667 2419.
Quoted as America's most romantic resort, by an *LA Times*' writer. $$$

Price Guide	
Standard Double Room	
$	under $150
$$	$150–$225
$$$	over $225

PASO ROBLES
The Paso Robles Inn
1003 Spring St., Paso Robles,
CA 93446
Tel: 805-238 2660;
Fax: 805-238 4707.
Downtown; bungalows and lovely garden. $

SAN SIMEON

San Simeon Lodge
9520 Castillo Dr.
San Simeon, CA 93452
Tel: 805-927 4601
Fax: 805-927 2374. $
Silver Surf Motel
9390 Castillo Dr.
San Simeon, CA 93452
Tel: (805) 927-4661;
1-800-621 3999
Fax: 805-977 3225. $
Whitewater Inn
San Simeon, CA 93452
Tel: 805-927 1066;
Fax: 805-927 0921.
Very small and pretty, some
rooms with hot tubs. $$

YOSEMITE NATIONAL PARK

The Ahwanee
Yosemite Valley, 95389.
Write to: Yosemite Reservations,
5410 East Home St., Fresno,
CA 98727
Tel: 559-252 4848;
Fax: 559-456 0542.
Spectacular, historic lodge with
equally spectacular views.
Booking is up to a year in
advance. $$–$$$
Yosemite Lodge
Yosemite Valley, CA 95389
Tel: as above.
Cabins and motel rooms in
lovely country; near the Falls.
Booking up to six months in
advance during the summer
season. $

SEQUOIA NATIONAL PARK

The Wuksachi Lodge
Tel: 1-888-252 5757
102-room lodge at 7,200ft in
sight of Mt Whitney. $$$

Southern California
LOS ANGELES

**Best Western Executive
Motor Inn**
603 S New Hampshire Ave.,
CA 90005
Tel: 213-385 4444;
Fax: 213-380 5413.
Downtown; all the facilities of a
chain motel including pool,
jacuzzi, free parking. $

Chancellor Hotel
3191 West 7th Street,
CA 90005
Tel: 213-383 1183;
Fax: 213-385 6657.
Downtown; pool, laundromat,
free parking, free breakfast. $
Figueroa Hotel
939 S Figueroa St., CA 90015
Tel: 213-627 8971;
Fax: 213-689 0305.
Pool, jacuzzi, restaurants. $
Holiday Inn Downtown
750 Garland Ave., CA 90017
Tel: 213-628 5242;
Fax: 213-628 1201.
Downtown; pool, laundromat,
free parking. Completely
renovated. $
Metro Plaza Hotel
711 N Main St., CA 90012
Tel: 213-680 0200;
Fax: 213-620 0200.
Downtown; laundromat, sauna,
whirlpool, restaurant. $
Miyako Inn
328 East 1st St., CA 90012
Tel: 213-617 2000;
Fax: 213-617 2700.
Downtown; laundromat,
whirlpool, sauna, restaurant. $
New Otani
120 S Los Angeles St.,
CA 90012
Tel: 213-629 1200;
Fax: 213-622 0980.
Downtown (beside Little Tokyo);
two shopping levels, delightful
Japanese garden. $
Wilshire Grand
930 Wilshire Blvd.
CA 90017
Tel: 213-629 4321;
Fax: 213-612 3989.
Downtown; pool, exercise room,
coffee shop and four
restaurants. $–$$
Regal Biltmore
506 S Grand Ave., CA 90071,
Tel: 213-624 1011;
Fax: 213-612 1545.
Downtown; restaurants, pool,
jacuzzi, luxurious decor. $$
Marriott Downtown
333 S Figueroa St., CA 90071
Tel: 213-617 1133;
Fax: 213-613 0291.
Downtown on landscaped

grounds with pool near Music
Center; luxurious. $$
Westin Bonaventura
404 S Figueroa St., CA 90071
Tel: 213-624 1000;
Fax: 213-612 4800.
Downtown; very distinctive
interior and exterior, pool,
rooftop restaurant. Has installed
a Hollywood Poster Gallery along
the walk from the lower level
parking garage and guests can
ride the glass elevators that
appeared in *True Lies* and *Line
of Fire*. $$

LOS ANGELES (WESTSIDE)
Holiday Inn Century City Inn,
10330 W Olympic Blvd., Century
City, CA 90064
Tel: 310-553 1000;
Fax: 310-277 1633.
All rooms with whirlpool. $$
Beverly Inn
7701 Beverly Blvd., Hollywood,
CA 90036
Tel: 323-931 8108;
Near Farmers' Market, pool
free parking. $
Doubletree Hotel
10740 Wilshire Blvd.,
CA 90024
Tel: 310-475 8711;
Fax: 310-475 5220.
Pool, sauna, whirlpool, exercise
room. $$
Hollywood Roosevelt Hotel,
7000 Hollywood Blvd.,
CA 90028
Tel: 323-466 7000;
Fax: 323-462 8056.
Legendary landmark with Art
Deco trimmings, palm-shaded
pool, mezzanine museum. $
Hotel Bel Air
701 Stone Canyon Road
Bel Air, CA 90077
Tel: 3100472 1211;
Fax: 310-476 5890.
Deluxe, in landscaped grounds
and secluded canyon, elegant
suites. Offers eight guests the
opportunity to sit at Table One,
from which they can view their
meal being prepared in the
adjacent kitchen. $$$
Hyatt on Sunset
8401 Sunset Blvd.,

West Hollywood, CA 90069
1-800-233 1234
Tel: 323-656 1234:
Fax: 323-650 7024.
Restaurant, rooftop pool.
$$–$$$
Ramada Plaza Hotel
6333 Bristol Pkwy
Culver City, CA 90230
Tel: 310-670 3200;
Fax: 310-484 7073.
Pool, whirlpool, exercise room
and 24-hour room service. $
Summerfield Suites
1000 Westmount Dr.,
West Hollywood, CA 90069
Tel: 310-657 7400;
Fax: 310-854 6744.
Suites, kitchens, rooftop pool
and jacuzzi, sauna, laundromat,
exercise room. $$
Wyndham Bel Age
1020 N San Vicente Blvd., West
Hollywood, CA 90069
Tel: 310-854 1111;
Fax: 310-854 0926.
Deluxe, all suites, phones and
TVs in bathrooms. $$$

LOS **A**NGELES **(C**OASTAL**)**
Cadillac Hotel
8 Dudley Ave., Venice,
CA 90291;
Tel: 310-399 8876;
Fax: 310-399 4536.
Art Deco spot on the boardwalk
with a roof sundeck. $$
Comfort Inn
2815 Santa Monica Blvd., Santa
Monica, CA 90404
Tel: 310-828 5517;
Fax: 310-829 6084.
A mile and a half from beach,
pool. $
Foghorn Hotel
4140 Via Marina
Marina del Rey, CA 90292
Tel: 310-823 4626;
Fax: 310-578 1964.
Near beach. $
Loew's Santa Monica
Beach Hotel
1700 Ocean Ave.
Santa Monica, CA 90401
Tel: 310-458 6700;
1-800-235-6397;
Fax: 310-458 6761.
Pool, whirlpool, health club. $$$

Malibu Beach Inn
22878 Pacific Coast Highway,
Malibu, CA 90265
Tel: 310-456 6444;
Fax: 310-456 1499.
Near the pier; rooms with
fireplaces, VCRs. $$
Malibu Country Hotel
6506 Westward Beach Road,
Malibu, CA 90265
Tel: 310-457 9622;
1-800-386-6787;
Fax: 310-457-1349.
Overlooking the ocean; pool,
baby-sitting. $$
Miramar Sheraton Hotel
101 Wilshire Blvd., Santa
Monica, CA 90401
Tel: 310-576 7777;
Fax: 310-458-7912.
Landscaped grounds, pool,
health club, coffee shop. $$$
Oceana Suites
849 Ocean Ave.,
Santa Monica, CA 90403
Tel: 310-393 0486;
1-800-777 0758;
Fax: 310-458 1182.
Pool, laundromat, ocean views.
$$$
Pacific Shore Hotel
1819 Ocean Ave.
Santa Monica, CA 90401
Tel: 310-451 8711;
1-800-622-8711;
Fax: 310-394 6657.
Pool, sauna, whirlpool,
laundromat. $$
Ramada Limited Hotel
3130 Washington Blvd., Venice,
CA 90291
Tel: 310-821 5086;
Fax: 310-821 6167.
A few blocks from the beach
and boardwalk. $
Santa Monica Pico
Travel Lodge
3102 Pico Blvd.
Santa Monica, CA 90405
Tel: 310-450 5766;
Fax: 310-450 8843.
Kitchenettes, laundromat, and a
pretty good free breakfast. A
bargain. $
Shangri La Hotel
1301 Ocean Ave.
Santa Monica, CA 90401
Tel: 310-394 2791;

1-800-345 7829;
Fax: 310-451 3351.
Art Deco landmark opposite
Palisades Park; kitchenettes. $$
Shutters
1 Pico Blvd., Santa Monica, CA
90405
Tel: 310-458 0030;
1-800-334 9000;
Fax: 310-458 4589.
On the beach; pool, whirlpool,
restaurants. $$$
Venice Beach House
15 30th Ave CA 90291
Tel: 310-823 1966;
Fax: 310-823 1842.
A tranquil nine-room B&B with
garden that was once the home of
Venice founder Abbot Kinney. $$

LOS **A**NGELES **(U**NIVERSAL **C**ITY**)**
Sheraton Universal Hotel
333 Universal Terrace
Pkwy, CA 91608
Tel: 818-980 1212;
1-800-325 3535;
Fax: 818-985 4980.
Actually located on Universal
Studios; whirlpool, exercise
room. $$$

Price Guide	
Standard Double Room	
$	under $150
$$	$150–$225
$$$	over $225

Universal City Hilton
and Towers
555 Universal Terrace Pkwy,
CA 91608
Tel: 818-506 2500;
1-800-445 8667;
Fax: 818-509 2031.
Near Universal Studios; pool,
whirlpool, exercise room. $$

LONG **B**EACH
Comfort Inn
3201 E Pacific Coast Highway
CA 90804
Tel: 562-597 3374;
1-800-228 5150
Fax: 562-985 3142.
Pool, whirlpool, laundromat. $

Guest House Hotel
5325 E Pacific Coast Highway,
CA 90804
Tel: 562-597 1341;
1-800-990 9991;
Fax: 562-597 1664.
Pool, deli-restaurant. $

Long Beach Airport Marriott,
4700 Airport Plaza Dr.,
CA 90815
Tel: 562-425 5210;
1-800-228 9290;
Fax: 562-425 2744.
Pools, sauna, whirlpool
exercise room. $$

Los Alamos
**Victorian Mansion and
Union Hotel**
362 Bell St., Box 616,
Los Alamos, CA 93440
Tel: 805-344 2744;
Fax: 805-344 3125.
Unique theme rooms in two
elegant Victorian structures; well
worth the trip. $$–$$$

Nipomo
Kaleidoscope Inn
130 East Dana St., CA 93444
Tel: 805-929 5444.
Century-old Victorian mansion
with gazebo, popular with
wedding couples. $$

Palm Springs
Casa Cody
175 S Cahuila Road,
Palm Springs, CA 92262
Tel: 760-320 9346;
1-800-231-2639;
Fax: 760-325 8610.
Founded by Buffalo Bill's niece;
airy suites around pool. $$

Ingleside Inn
2000 Ramon, Palm Springs,
CA 92264
Tel: 760-325 0046;
Fax: 760-325 0710.
Greta Garbo slept here; garden,
antiques, pool, restaurant. $$$

La Mancha Inn
444 Avenida Caballeros,
CA 92262
Tel: 760-323 1773;
1-800-255 1773;
Fax: 760-323 5928.
Attractively furnished villas, pool,

sauna, putting green, lighted
tennis courts, croquet. $$$

La Quinta Hotel and Resort
49–499 Eisenhower Dr.,
LA Quinta, CA 92253
Tel: 760-564 4111;
1-800-598 3828;
Fax: 760-564 5718.
Twenty miles (32 km) from Palm
Springs; numerous swimming
pools and spas, tennis courts
and five restaurants. $$$

Orchid Tree Inn
261 S Belardo Road
CA 92262
Tel: 760-325 2791;
1-800-7333435;
Fax: 760-325 3855.
Landscaped grounds, pool,
whirlpool, kitchenettes. $$

Quality Inn
1269 E Palm Canyon Dr.,
CA 92264
Tel: 760-323 2775;
1-800-228 5151
Fax: 760-323 4238.
Large grounds, pool, whirlpool,
laundromat. $

Ramada Hotel Resort
1800 E Palm Canyon Dr.
Tel: 760-323 1711;
Fax: 760-327 6941.
Pool, sauna, coffee shop and
laundromat. $$

Riviera Resort
1600 N Indian Canyon Road,
CA 92262
Tel: 760-327 8311;
Fax: 760-327 4323.
Near Aerial Tramway; tennis
courts, pools, supervised
children's camp. $$$

Royal Sun Hotel
1700 S Palm Canyon Dr.,
CA 92264
Tel: 760-327 1564;
1-800-619 4786
Fax: 760-323 9092.
Pool, sauna, adjoining
restaurants, free breakfast. $

Shadow Inn
1875 N Palm Canyon Dr.
CA 92262
Tel: 760-320 7676;
Fax: 760-320 9543.
Landscaped grounds, pool,
sauna, exercise room. $

Vagabond Inn
1699 S Palm Canyon Dr.
CA 92264
Tel: 760-325 7211;
1-800-522 1555;
Fax: 760-322 9269.
Pool, saunas, coffee shop. $

**Villa Royale Bed and
Breakfast Inn**
1620 Indian Trail,
Palm Springs, CA 92264
Tel: 760-327 2314;
Fax: 760-322 3794.
Suites decorated in styles of
different countries, charming
courtyards, pool. $$

Pismo Beach
Sandcastle Inn
100 Stimson Ave.,
CA 93449
Tel: 805-773 2422;
1-800-822 6606;
Fax: 805-773 0771.
On beach, whirlpool. $$

Roseview Garden Inn
230 Five Cities Dr.,
CA 93449
Tel: 805-773 1841;
Fax: 805-773 1944.
Just off US 101. $

Riverside
The Mission Inn
3649 Seventh St., Riverside,
CA 92505
Tel: 909-784 0300;
Fax: 909-683 1342.
Historic hostelry popular with
presidents and movie stars.
Unique pastiche of architectural
styles. $

San Diego
Balboa Park Inn
3402 Park Blvd., CA 92103
Tel: 619-298 0823;
Fax: 619-294 8070.
Near the zoo; bar, in-room
jacuzzi, free breakfast. $

Clarion Hotel Bay View
660 K St., CA 92101
Tel: (619) 696-0234;
Fax: (619) 231-8199.
Sauna, whirlpool, exercise room,
laundromat. $$

Comfort Inn and Suites
2485 Hotel Circle, CA 92108,

Tel: 619-291 7700;
Fax: 619-297 6179.
Just off Interstate 8; completely
refurbished with pool, whirlpool,
laundromat and free shuttle to
the zoo. $
Holiday Inn-Harbor View
1617 1st Ave., CA 92101
Tel: 619-239 9600;
Fax: 619-233 6228.
Close to Interstate 5; pool,
laundromat. Remodeled in
1997. $$
Hotel del Coronado
150 Orange Ave. Coronado,
CA 92118
Tel: 619-435 6611;
Fax: 619-522 8238.
World-famous Victorian-era
landmark; tennis court, pool,
restaurants. $$$
Hyatt Regency
Harbor Dr. and Market Pl., CA
92101
Tel: 619-232 1234;
1-800-233 1234;
Fax: 619-239 6464.
Pool, sauna, tennis courts,
exercise room. $$$
La Jolla Beach Travelodge,
6750 La Jolla Blvd., CA 92037
Tel: 619-454 0716;
1-800-255 3050
Fax: 619-454 1075
Jacuzzi and new swimming pool.
Good restaurant opposite. $
Mission Valley Hilton
901 Camino del Rio S,
CA 92108
Tel: 619-543-9000;
1-800-445 8667;
Fax: 619-543 9358.
Pool, whirlpool, exercise room.
$$
Quality Inn
2901 Nimitz Blvd., CA 92106
Tel: 619-224 3655;
1-800-228 5151;
Fax: 619-224 4025.
Near airport, zoo and Seaworld;
pool, coffee shop. $
Ramada Inn and Suites
830 Sixth Ave., CA 92101
Tel: 619-531 8877;
Fax: 619-231 8307.
Near Gaslamp Quarter; harbor
view rooftop, lobby bar and grill. $
Ramada Plaza Hotel-Old Town,

2435 Jefferson St.,
CA 92110
Tel: 619-299 7400;
Fax: 619-299 1619.
Near historic attractions; pool
and spa, free breakfast. $
San Diego Paradise Pt. Resorts
1404 W Vacation Road,
CA 92109
Tel: 619-274 4630;
1-800-344 3370;
Fax: 619-581 5929.
Bungalows in spacious
landscaped grounds on Mission
Bay; pools, tennis courts, boat
rentals, jogging track. $$
The Inn at La Jolla
5440 La Jolla Blvd., CA 92037
Tel: 858-454 6121;
Fax: 858-459 1377.
Close to beach, pool, whirlpool,
putting green. $
Town and Country Hotel
500 Hotel Circle N, CA 92108
Tel: 619-291 7131;
Fax: 619-291 3584.
Landscaped grounds; pools,
restaurants, coffee shops. $
US Grant Hotel
326 Broadway, CA 92101
Tel: 619-232 3121;
Fax: 619-232 3626.
Historic downtown hotel near
shopping; exercise room,
restaurant. $$
The Westin Horton Plaza
910 Broadway, CA 92101
Tel: 619-239 2200;
Fax: 619-239 0509.
Pool, saunas, lighted tennis
courts, health club. $$
The Westgate
1055 2nd Ave., CA 92101
Tel: 619-238 1818;
Fax: 619-557 3737.
Lovely interiors and furnishings,
exercise room, restaurant. $$
Wyndham Garden Hotel
5975 Lusk Blvd., CA 92121
Tel: 619-558 1818;
Fax: 619-558 0421.
North of town; pool, whirlpool,
exercise room, restaurant. $

Travelodge Downtown
345 Marsh St., CA 93401
Tel: 805-543 6443;

Fax: 805-545 0951.
Near downtown; pool,
laundromat. $
Madonna Inn
100 Madonna Road, CA 93405
Tel: 805-543 3000;
Fax: 805-543 1800.
Hotel well known for its
eccentricity and bizarre decor.
Rooms come dressed up in
Western, Hawaiian, Austrian
styles. $$

SANTA BARBARA
The Cheshire Cat Inn
38 W Valerio St., CA 93101
Tel: 805-569 1610;
Fax: 805-682 1876.
Century-old house in suburbs;
rooms with fireplaces, whirlpool.
$$
El Encanto
1900 Lasuen St., CA 93101
Tel: 805-687 5000;
Fax: 805-687 3903.
In town; restaurant, pool
tennis courts. $$$
Franciscan Inn
109 Bath St., CA 93101
Tel: 805-963 8845;
Fax: 805-564 3295.
At the beach; health club
pool, tennis courts. $
Harbor View Inn
28 W Cabrillo Blvd., CA 93101
Tel: 805-963 0780;
Fax: 805-963 7967.
On the beach opposite Stearns
Wharf; pool, whirlpool, adjacent
restaurant. $$–$$$
Inn by the Harbor
433 W Montecito, CA 93101
Tel: 805-963 7851;
Fax: 805-962 9428.
Close to the beach; pool,
kitchenettes, laundromat. $
Secret Garden Inn
1908 Bath St., CA 93101
Tel: 805-687 2300;
Fax: 805-687 4576.
Main house and cottages in
pleasantly landscaped grounds,
some rooms with hot tubs. $$
San Ysidro Ranch
900 San Ysidro Lane,
Montecito, CA 98108
Tel: (805) 969-5046;
1-800-368 6788

Fax: 805-565 1995.
Luxury resort with a celebrated
history. $$$
Sandpiper Lodge
3525 State St., CA 93105
Tel: 805-687 5326;
Fax: 805-687 2270.
North end of midtown; pool,
jacuzzi, nearby coffee shop. $
Radisson Santa Barbara Hotel,
1111 E Cabrillo Blvd., CA 93101
Tel: 805-963 0744;
Fax: 805-962 0985.
Across from beach; pool,
whirlpool, health club. $$
**Tess Oarker's
Doubletree Resort**
633 E Cabrillo Blvd., CA 93103
Tel: 805-564 4333;
Fax: 805-564 4964.
Across from beach in spacious
grounds; pool, sauna, putting
green. $$$
The Upham
1404 De La Vina, CA 93101
Tel: 805-962 0058;
Fax: 805-963 2825.
Last of the great, old SB hotels
(founded 1872) with all the
charm and style you'd expect.
Beautifully furnished garden
bungalows. $$$
Villa Rosa
15 Chapala Ave., CA 93101
Tel: 805-966 0851;
Fax: 805-962 7159.
At the beach; pool, spa. $$

The Santa Catalina Island
Company offers various bargain
packages (round-trip
transportation, two nights'
accommodation, three tours).
Other hotels range from
inexpensive to luxury. Relatively
inexpensive are:
El Terado Terrace
230 Marilla Ave., CA 90704
Tel: 310-510-0831;
Fax: 310-510 1495.
A B&B near the bottom of Marilla
Avenue. On a hill above the
harbor. Some rooms have views.
$$.
La Paloma Cottages
Tel: 310-510 0737;
Fax: 310-510 2424.

Self-contained properties at the
top of Metropole near the golf
course. $$
Pacific Isle Apartments
Tel: 310-510 1148;
Weekly rates for apartments.
$–$$
Snug Harbor Inn
Crescent Ave
Tel: 310-510 8400.
Six luxurious bay view rooms in
the century-old former Hotel
Monterey. $$$

SOLVANG
Royal Scandinavian Inn
400 Alisal Road, Box 31
CA 93464
Tel: 805-688 8000;
Fax: 805-688 0761.
Pool, whirlpool, restaurant. $
Svendsgaards Danish Lodge
1711 Mission Dr.,
CA 93463
Tel/Fax: 805-688 3277.
Pool, whirlpool, kitchenettes. $

Price Guide

Standard Double Room

$	under $150
$$	$150–$225
$$$	over $225

VENTURA
Bella Maggiore Inn
67 S California St., CA 93001
Tel: 805-652 0277;
Fax: 805-648 5670.
Architectural landmark from
1925, downtown, near beach. $
Vagabond Inn
756 E Thompson Blvd.,
CA 93001
Tel: 805-648 5371;
1-800-522 1555;
Fax: 805-648 5613.
Pool, whirlpool, coffee shop. $

Nevada
LAS VEGAS
Algiers
2845 Las Vegas Blvd.
Tel: 702-735 3311;
1-800-732 3361.
Fax: 702-792 2112

Centrally located between Circus
Circus and Convention Center
Drive with a pleasant patio café
beside a huge swimming pool.
The Bellagio
3600 Las Vegas Blvd.
Tel: 702-693 7111
1-888-987 6667
Fax: 702-792 7646
Modeled after the lakeshore
village of that name in Northern
Italy, this 3,000-room luxury
resort has indoor gardens,
fountains, waterfalls, a $10 art
gallery and a Cirque de Soleil
show on its premises. $$$
Bally's Las Vegas
3645 Las Vegas Blvd. S
Tel: 702-739 4111;
1-800-634 3434;
Fax: 702-739 4405/967-4405.
2,814 rooms and suites. One of
the world's largest luxury
resorts. Rooms range from kings
and doubles to Royal Penthouse
suites. Honeymoon suites are
particularly popular. Events
center, spa, shopping mall, six
restaurants, casino. $$$
Barbary Coast Hotel & Casino,
3595 Las Vegas S,
(at Flamingo),
Tel: 702-737 7111;
1-800-634 6755;
Fax: 702-737 6304.
196 rooms including 12 suites;
casino, three restaurants, dining
room specializing in Chinese
food, cable TV. $$$
Best Western Mardi Gras Inn,
3500 Paradise Road
Tel: 702-731 2020;
1-800-634 6501;
Fax: 702-733 6994.
Over 300 decorated mini-suites;
wet bar, refrigerator, TV and in-
room movies; free shuttle to
airport and Strip, casino.
Caesars Palace
3570 Las Vegas Blvd. S
Tel: 702-731 7110;
1-800-634 6661;
Fax: 702-731 6636.
1,518 rooms; three spacious
casinos; nine restaurants;
health spa; various sports
facilities; Appian Way & Forum
shops and much more. $$$

California Hotel
12 Ogden
Tel: 702-385 1222;
1-800-634 6255;
Fax: 702-386 4463.
Rents rooms for around $40 from Sunday to Thursday; this increases at weekends.

Circus Circus Hotel & Casino
2880 Las Vegas Blvd. S
Tel: 702-734 0410;
1-800-444-CIRCUS;
Fax: 702-737 2268.
Unique family-oriented gaming resort; 2,880 rooms; three dining areas; free circus; wedding chapel. $$$

Days Inn-Town Hall Casino,
4155 Koval Lane
Tel: 702-731 2111;
1-800-329 7466;
Fax: 702-731 1113.
360 rooms; restaurant; heated pool and spa; walking distance to Strip. $$

Excalibur Hotel & Casino
3850 Las Vegas Blvd. S
Tel: 702-597 7777;
1-800-937 7777;
Fax: 702-597 7009.
A magical white castle, complete with moat and drawbridge. 4,032 rooms; two pools; six restaurants. **$$$**

Fairfield Inn by Marriott
3850 Paradise Road
Tel: 702-791 0899;
1-800-228 2800;
Fax: 702-791 2705.
129 rooms; located near area attractions; cable TV; outdoor pool; airport shuttle. $

Flamingo Hilton
3555 Las Vegas Blvd. S
Tel: 702-733 3111;
1-800-732 2111;
Fax: 702-733 3353.
Located on the four corners of the Las Vegas Strip; 3,530 rooms and suites; casino; restaurants; pool. $$$

Four Queens
202 E. Fremont St.
Tel: 702-385 4011;
1-800-634 6045;
Fax: 702-387 5123.
Offers competitive rates. $–$$

Golden Nugget Hotel & Casino
129 E Fremont St.
Tel: 702-385 7111;
1-800-634 3403;
Fax: 702-386 8362.
1,907 rooms; lavish European elegance; crystal chandeliers and Grecian marble; five restaurants; Olympic-size heated pool. $$$

Harrah's Casino Hotel Las Vegas
3475 Las Vegas Blvd. S
Tel: 702-369 5000;
1-800-HARRAHS;
Fax: 702-369 6014.
1,711 rooms and suites; located center Strip; complete casino; five restaurants; entertainment; pool and health club. $$$

Howard Johnson Plaza Hotels & Lodges
3111 W Tropicana Ave.
Tel: 702-798 1111;
1-800-300 7339;
Fax: 702-798-7138.
150 rooms. $

Imperial Palace Hotel & Casino,
3535 Las Vegas Blvd. S
Tel: 702-731 3311;
1-800-634 6441;
Fax: 702-735 8578.
2,700-room resort in the heart of Las Vegas Strip. Home of the famous Imperial Palace Auto Collection. Casino; restaurants; bars, health center; wedding chapel; Olympic pool. $$$

Las Vegas Hilton
3000 Paradise Road
Tel: 702-732-5111;
1-800-732 7117;
Fax: 702-794 3611.
3,174 luxurious rooms and suites; one of the world's largest resort and convention complexes; 13 distinctive restaurants. $$$

Luxor Las Vegas Hotel and Casino
3900 Las Vegas Blvd. S
Tel: 702-262 4000;
NV 1-800-262 4444;
US 1-800-288 1000;
Fax: 702-262 4405.
A 30-story bronze pyramid housing 2,526 rooms, including 14 suites and 236 jacuzzi

suites. Features the world's largest atrium, seven themed restaurants and a full-size replica of King Tut's Tomb.$$$

Mandalay Bay
3950 Las Vegas Blvd.
Tel: 702-632 7777;
Fax: 702-632 7190.
Museum of rare coins, boxing events, 3,300 rooms and all the usual luxurious amenities.$$

MGM Grand Hotel
3799 Las Vegas Blvd. S
Tel: 702-891 1111;
1-800-929 1111;
Fax: 702-891 1030.
A $1 billion mega-resort with 5,005 rooms, four casinos and a 33-acre MGM Grand Adventures Theme Park.$$$

Paris Las Vegas
3645 Las Vegas Blvd.
Tel: 702-967 4611;
1-888- BONJOUR;
Fax: 702-967 4288.
Halfsize, 50-story Eiffel Tower, other evocations of the city of lights, plus good shopping and eating and 2,900 luxurious rooms.$$$

Plaza Hotel
1 Main St.
Tel: 702-386 2110;
Fax: 702-386 8281.
Located next to the Greyhound bus station, with Amtrak station directly behind, is good value and very friendly.$

Quality Inn Hotel & Casino
377 E Flamingo Road
Tel: 702-733 7777;
1-800-634 6617;
Fax: 702-734 5071.
370 mini-suites with wet bar, jacuzzi; laundry; restaurant; full casino; shuttle service to the Strip. $$

Residence Inn by Marriot
3225 Paradise Road
Tel: 702-796 9300;
1-800-331 3131;
Fax: 702-796 9562.
192 studio or penthouse accommodations; complimentary breakfast, lite dinner (Monday–Friday) and grocery shopping service. $$

Sheraton Desert Inn
3145 Las Vegas Blvd. S
Tel: 702-733 4676;
1-800-634 6906;
Fax: 702-733 4676.
821 rooms on 200 garden-like acres. Facilities for the handicapped. The resort has an 18-hole professional tour golf course, health spa and 24-hour casino. $$$
Treasure Island at The Mirage,
3300 Las Vegas Blvd. S
Tel: 702-894 7111;
1-800-944 7444;
Fax: 702-894 7414.
Each room features floor-to-ceiling glass with a spectacular view of the mountains, Buccaneer Bay and the Strip or the pool area. $$$
The Venetian
3355 Las Vegas Blvd. S
Tel: 702-414 1000
1-888-283 6423
Fax: 702-414 1100
720 rooms and suites in an 18-story tower and outlying buildings. Two pools; nine-hole putting green; health spas; three restaurants.$$
Westward Ho Hotel
2900 Las Vegas Blvd. S
Tel: 702-731 2900;
1-800-634 6803;
Fax: 707-731 3544.
777 rooms; 24-hour restaurant and deli, seven pools and jacuzzis; live entertainment and casino. $$

Bed & Breakfast Inns

Country inns have become extremely popular in the last decade throughout the United States, especially in New England and Northern California. Most cluster in such scenic areas as the Wine Country, Gold Country, North Coast and Monterey Peninsula. Situated in such beautiful rural settings, they do a thriving business with city dwellers in search of a romantic weekend retreat.

Converted from mansions and farmhouses with five to fifteen rooms, these inns offer the traveler a highly individual experience; no two inns are alike, and in most inns, no two rooms are alike. For those accustomed to the strict uniformity of large hotels and motel chains, the inns provide a warm, hospitable and quaint alternative.

Many inns have shared bathrooms and only a few have televisions or telephones situated in the rooms. Most include breakfast with the price of the room, hence the name bed and breakfast inns.

Prices vary greatly, but they do tend to be pricey. Call or write in advance – the inns are particularly popular on weekends and in summer. In fact, they are so popular that small intimate inns are even popping up in large urban cities to compete with the large hotels. Here is an incomplete but wide-ranging (north to south) sampling of the B&Bs in California.

Price Guide

Standard Double Room
$ under $150
$$ $150–$225
$$$ over $225

Northern California
SAN FRANCISCO
Bed and Breakfast Inn
4 Charlton Court, CA 94123
Tel: 415-921 9784;
Fax: 415-921 0544.
A restored Victorian, English-style pension on Union Street. $$
The Mansions Hotel
2220 Sacramento St.,
CA 94115
Tel: 415-929 9444;
1-800-826 9398;
Fax: 415-567 9391.
A unique celebrity favorite with magic shows, nightly concerts and Benjamino Bufano sculptures in Pacific Heights. Breakfast included. $$

Petite Auberge
863 Bush St., CA 94108
Tel: 415-928 6000;
1-800-365 3004;
Fax: 415-775 5717.
Gourmet breakfast buffet. Located near Union Square. $
Washington Square Inn
1660 Stockton St., CA 94133
Tel: 415-981 4220;
1-800-388 0220;
Fax: 415-397 7242.
Within walking distance of Fisherman's Wharf, Chinatown, the Financial District, in North Beach. $$

CAMBRIA
The Blue Whale Inn
6736 Moonstone Beach Dr.,
CA 93428
Tel: 805-927 4647;
Fax: 805-927 3852. $$.

CARMEL
The Pine Inn
Ocean Ave. and Lincoln,
CA 93921
Tel: 831-624 3851;
Fax: 831-624 3030. $$

DANA POINT
Blue Lantern Inn
34343 Street. of the Blue Lantern, CA 92629
Tel: 949-661 1304;
Fax: 949-496 1483. $$

MONTEREY
Old Monterey Inn
500 Martin St., CA 93940
Tel: 831-375 8284;
Fax: 831-375 6730. $$$

NAPA
La Residence Country Inn,
4066 St. Helena Highway North,
CA 94558
Tel: 707-253 0337;
Fax: 707-253 0382. $$

NEWPORT
Doryman's Inn
2102 West Ocean Front,
CA 92663
Tel: 949-675 7300;
Fax: 949-675 7300. $$$

SAN SIMEON
Olallieberry Inn
Tel: 805-927 3222;
Fax: 805-927 0202.
A stylish 1870s home. $$
Whitewater Inn
San Simeon, CA 93452
Tel: 805-927 1066;
Fax: 805-927 0921.
Very small and pretty, hot tub, some rooms with jacuzzi. $$

SONOMA
The Gaige House
13540 Arnold Dr., Glen Ellen
Tel: 707-935 0237
1-800-935 0237
Fax: 707-935 6411
Delightful bed & breakfast inn located in an elegant restored 1890s property in the Valley of the Moon.

Southern California
LA JOLLA
The Bed and Breakfast Inn,
7753 Draper Ave., CA 92037
Tel: 858-456 2066;
1-800-582 2466
Fax: 858-456 1510. $

NORTH HOLLYWOOD
La Maida House and Bungalows
11159 La Maida St.
CA 91601
Tel: 818-769 3857;
Fax: 818-753 9363. $$

SANTA BARBARA
The Mary May Inn
111 West Valerio St.,
CA 93101
Tel: 805-682 3199. $$
SAN LUIS OBISPO
The Garden Street Inn
1212 Garden St., CA 93401
Tel: 805-545 9802;
Fax: 805-781 7469. $-$$

Reservation Services

Bed & Breakfast International,
1181 Solano, Albany, CA 94706
Tel: 510-9525 4569.

Motels

If you're traveling by car and don't plan on spending much time in your room, motels are the best solution. Whether located along busy Sunset Boulevard in Los Angeles or along the river bank in a remote Northern California town, most motels provide parking space, at a premium in most of California, within steps of your room.

Motel quality varies, but you can usually expect clean and simple accommodations. This is especially true for most of the national chains. A restaurant or coffee shop, swimming pool and sauna are often found on the premises. Room facilities generally include a telephone, television and radio, but don't hesitate to ask the motel manager if you may inspect a room before agreeing to take it.

Other than their accessibility by auto, the attraction of motels is their price. Motels in California cities range from $75 to $150 per night, double occupancy. They are less expensive in the outlying areas.

LAS VEGAS
Best Western
(Not in BHI franchise)
1000 N Main St.
Tel: 702-382 3455;
1-800-528 1234. $
Budget Host Inn
3227 Civic Centre Dr.
Tel: 702-399 3297. $
El Cortez
600 E Fremont
Tel: 702-385 5200;
1-800-634 6703. $
Comfort Inn South
5075 Koval Lane
Tel: 702-736 3600;
1-800-228 5150;
Fax: 702-736 0726.
106 rooms; free continental breakfast; kids stay free; free local phone calls. $
Crest Budget Inn
207 N 6th St.
Tel: 702-382 5642;

1-800-777 1817;
Fax: 702-382 8038.
Free breakfast, bacon and eggs; coffee all day; free in-room TV, VCR, free local calls. $
Downtowner
129 N 8th St.
Tel: 702-384 1441
1-800-777 2566;
Fax: 702-384 2308.
Free breakfast, bacon and eggs; coffee all day; free in-room TV, VCR, free local calls. $
Fairfield Inn
3850 Paradise Road
Tel: 702-791 0899;
1-800-228 2800.
Fax: 702-791 2705. $
Golden Inn Motel
120 Las Vegas Blvd. N
Tel: 702-384 8204. $
Las Vegas Inn (Travelodge)
11501 W Sahara
Tel: 702-733 0001;
Fax: 702-733 1571. $
Super 8 Hotel & Casino
4250 Koval Lane
Tel: 702-794 0888;
1-800-800 8000;
Fax: 702-794 3504.
300 rooms; on the Strip. $

Motel chains

Motel chains can be found all around California. Many chains have toll-free numbers available from other countries; check your local telephone directory. Toll-free telephone numbers within the US are indicated by 1-800 or 1-888.

Best Western	1-800-528 1234
Comfort Inn	1-800-228 5150
Doubletree	1-800-222 8733
Hotels	1-800-222 8733
Embassy	1-800-362 2779
Suites	1-800-326 2779
Holiday Inn	1-800-465 4329
La Quinta	1-800-531 5900
Motor Inns	1-800-531 5900
Quality Inns	1-800-228 5151
Motel 6	1-800-466 8536
Ramada	1-800-272 6232
Travelodge	1-800-255 3050
Vagabond	1-800-522 1555

Travelodge Strip
2830 Las Vegas Blvd. S
Tel: 702-735 4222;
1-800-255 3050;
Fax: 702-733 7695.
58 rooms. $
Warren Motel
3965 Las Vegas Blvd.
Tel: 702-736 6235.
Rooms $31–36 weekdays, more
on weekends. $

Hostels

Some travelers may want to take
advantage of California's chain
of hostels. Hostels are clean,
comfortable and, on the
opposite end of the spectrum
from B&Bs, very inexpensive (as
low as $5 per night). Although
suitable for people of all ages,
they are definitely for the young
at heart. Beds are provided in
dormitory-like rooms. Hostelers
carry their own gear (silverware,
sleeping bag, towel, etc) and are
expected to take 15 minutes to
help clean up and perform other
communal tasks. Hostels are
closed from 9.30am–4.30pm,
so most guests fill their days
with nearby outdoor activities.
Reservations recommended.

Northern California has a
chain of more than 20 hostels
up and down the Pacific coast,
from Jedediah Smith Redwood
State Park at the Oregon border
down to John Little State Beach.
All the hostels are along the
shoreline; some are located
inside old lighthouses. For lists
of hostels in both Northern and
Southern California try these
numbers:
Central California Council,
PO Box 3645, Merced,
CA 95344
Tel: 559-383 0686.
Golden Gate Council,
425 Divisadero St., Room 307,
San Francisco, CA 94117
Tel: 415-863 1444.
Los Angeles Council,
3601 South Gaffey St.,
San Pedro, CA 90731-6969
Tel: 310-831 8109.

Campgrounds

Public and private campgrounds
are located in or near the state
and national parks. Most public
campgrounds offer primitive
facilities – a place to park, rest
rooms and outdoor cooking.
Fees are around $5 per site.
Private campgrounds are usually
a little more expensive and offer
additional facilities such as
hook-ups, coin laundries, pools
and restaurants. Most are busy
from mid-June to September and
are allotted on a first-come-first-
served basis. If possible, make
reservations. For information on
camping grounds call or write:
**California Department of
Parks and Recreation**
Angeles District
1928 Las Virgenes Road
Calabasas, CA 91302
Tel: 916-653 6995
National Park Service
Western Regional Office
600 Harrison St., Suite 600
San Francisco, CA 94107-1372
Tel: 415-556 0560
National Park Service
Department of the Interior
Washington DC 20013-7127
Tel: 202-208 4747.
US Forest Service,
Pacific Southwest Regional
Office, 630 Sansome St., San
Francisco, CA 94111
Tel: 415-705 2874.

Santa Catalina
The Santa Catalina Island
Company operates the fully-
equipped campground **Hermit
Gulch** about a mile from town
(shuttle bus), close to the
Botanical Garden and hiking
trails. Reservations are required
(tel: 310-510 3000). Other
campsites around the island are
operated by LA County's
Department of Parks and
Recreation, tel: 310-510 0688
and Catalina Island Camping,
tel: 310-510 0303.

Where to Eat

California is a food-lover's
paradise and has the statistics
to prove it. There are more
restaurants in San Francisco,
per capita, than any other US
city, and it's been estimated that
Southern Californians dine out
on average two or three times a
week. Although the most
prevalent ethnic food you'll
encounter here is Mexican, there
is an endless variety of other
ethnic foods, as well as classic
American cuisine.

The following list is a mere
sampling of some notable
restaurants across the state.
Prices listed include a meal for
two without wine:

Where to Eat

NORTHERN CALIFORNIA

San Francisco
Balboa Cafe,
3199 Fillmore
Tel: 415-921 3944.
The city's finest California
cooking: warm salads, perfect
pasta, hamburgers and fresh
fish. $$
Caffe Sport,
574 Green St.
Tel: 415-981 1251.
Chaotic and crowded at all
hours. Campy decor and superb
shellfish. Closed Sunday–
Monday. $ $
Elizabeth Daniel,
550 Washington St
Tel: 415-397 6129 $$
Fournou's Ovens,
Stanford Court Hotel,
905 California
Tel: 415-989 1910.
Order from the oven - a

succulent roast rack of lamb, fine fowl or other meats. Award-winning wine list. $$$$

Green's,
Fort Mason, Building A
Tel: 415-771 6222.
Gourmet vegetarian restaurant managed by the Zen Center. Only takes reservations two weeks in advance, and they're hard to come by. Closed for Sunday dinner and Monday lunchtime. $$$

Julius Castle,
1541 Montgomery St.
Tel: 415-392 2222.
Contemporary French with an Italian accent and a magnificent view overlooking the bay. $$$

La Rondalla,
901 Valencia St.
Tel: 415-647 7474.
Cheap Mexican food served until 3.30am. Closed Mondays, cash only. $

MacArthur Park,
607 Front St.
Tel: 415-398 5700.
Something to please everyone, including the hopeful singles at the long bar in front. Grilled fresh fish, tender ribs, decent hamburgers. Unfortunately, closed for lunch on weekends. $$

Mal's,
316 Clement
Tel: 415-221 3046.
Great Vietnamese cooking, from the Saigon-style shrimp-and-pork-noodle soup to the Hanoi-style anise-and-lemon-flavor soup. $$

Mama's,
1701 Stockton St.
Tel: 415-362 6421.
Just plain good food. It's jammed on weekends, so try it during the week. Closed Monday. $$

Masa's,
684 Bush St.
Tel: 415-989 7154.
One of the finest French restaurants in town. Smoking is not permitted; coats and ties are required, reservations recommended. Closed Monday. $$$$

Osome,
3145 Fillmore
Tel: 415-346 2311.
Excellent sushi bar plus usual range of cooked Japanese food. Closed for lunch on weekends. $$

Prego,
2000 Union
Tel: 415-563-3305.
The perfect place for elegant pizza pie, baked in a wood-burning brick oven. Open daily, 11.30am–midnight. $

Postrio,
545 Post St.
Tel: 415-776 7825.
If you haven't had a chance to eat in one of renowned chef Wolfgang Puck's restaurants, now is your chance. $$$

Tadich Grill,
240 California
Tel: 415-391 1849.
Fresh fish and hefty drinks in an atmosphere of male conviviality. Long waiting lines. Closed Sunday. $$

Yank Sing,
427 Battery, near Clay
Tel: 415-781 1111.
Classiest dim sum place in the city, serving food unique to Hong Kong and San Francisco. A very San Francisco experience. $$

Zuni,
1658 Market St.
Tel: 415-552 2522.
Simply cooked California cuisine made from fresh local ingredients. Closed Monday. $$

Price Guide

For two without wine

$	under $30
$$	$30–$60
$$$	$60–$100
$$$$	over $100

East Bay

Chez Panisse,
1517 Shattuck Ave. Berkeley,
Tel: 510-548 5525.
One of the most famous restaurants in the country.

Restaurant downstairs. Open Monday–Saturday for dinner with set menu only. $$$$
Café upstairs open for lunch and dinner, Monday–Saturday. Reservations recommended. $$

Hunan,
396 Eleventh St., Oakland Tel: 510-444 1155.
One of the few restaurants in Oakland's Chinatown serving excellent spicy food. Menus are impressive and amazingly inexpensive. Don't forget to ask for the day's specials. You really can't go wrong in any Chinese restaurant in this area. $

O Chame,
1830 Fourth St.
Tel: 510-841 8783.
Reservations required. Closed Sunday. Very smooth, modern Japanese food in a serene restaurant. Highly creative, short menu changes daily. $$$

Oakland Grill,
301 Franklin St, Oakland
Tel: 510-835 1176.
Airy and attractive. Burgers are big and breakfasts are good. $

Santa Fe Bar and Grill,
1310 University Ave., Berkeley
Tel: 510-841 4740.
Restored train station and blues piano provide great atmosphere for California cuisine. $$$

Siam Cuisine,
1181 University Ave., Berkeley
Tel: 510-548 3278.
Exceptional Thai cuisine; spicy and irresistible. $

Monterey/Big Sur

Casanova,
Fifth St. near San Carlos, Carmel
Tel: 831-625 0501.
Emphasis on seafood served with light sauces, but there are also veal, lamb and beef selections. Breakfast, lunch, dinner and Sunday brunch in a French cottage setting. $$

Glen Oaks,
State Highway 1, Big Sur
Tel: 831-667 2264
Rustic exterior belies elegant dining-room filled with fresh flowers and shimmering with fine

music. Large, eclectic menu.
$$$
Grenot's Victorian House,
649 Lighthouse Ave.,
Pacific Grove
Tel: 831-646 1477.
This Victorian home with just 12
tables requires reservations well
in advance. Austrian food and
more, including absolutely divine
desserts. $$$
Nepenthe,
State Hwy 1, Big Sur,
Tel: 831-667 2345. Spectacular
view of waves crashing 800 ft
(244 meters) below, homemade
soups and enormous chef's
salads. Tourists and locals
mingle comfortably. $$
Sierra Mar,
State Hwy 1, Big Sur
Tel: 831-667 2800.
The glass-walled restaurant
overlooking the sea serves up
some of the classiest and
interesting cuisine around. $$$
Ventana,
State Hwy 1, Big Sur
Tel: 831-667 4242.
A luxurious resort set back in the
woods. Save room for the
accomplished desserts. $$$

NORTHERN COAST

Albion River Inn,
State Hwy 1, Albion
Tel: 707-937 4044.
Serves hearty fare at
reasonable prices. $$
Boonville Hotel,
State Hwy 128, Boonville
Tel: 707-895 2210.
California cooking to the core -
fresh, simple and sensitively
prepared. All the food has been
grown or raised right near the
hotel. Closed Tuesday. Dinner
only. $$$$
Café Beaujolais,
961 Ukiah St., Mendocino
Tel: 707-937 5614.
A really cozy atmosphere.
Beautifully-prepared dishes with
fresh ingredients. $$

Ledford House,
7051 State Hwy 1,
Little River
Tel: 707-937 0282.
A rustic little house overlooking
the sea. Locally-grown food is
always cooked to order. Dinner
only; closed Monday and
Tuesday. $$
St Orres
36601 State Hwy 1, in Gualala,
below Mendocino
Tel: 707-884 3303.
A beautiful restaurant
emphasizing North Coast
cuisine in a Russian-style hotel.
Also serves Sunday brunch. $$
Station House Café,
11285 State Hwy 1,
Point Reyes
Tel: 415-663 1515.
Fresh, well-cooked food in a
warm, bustling atmosphere.
Perfect stop after a day's hiking
on Point Reyes Peninsula. $

Price Guide

For two without wine
$ under $30
$$ $30–$60
$$$ $60–$100
$$$$ over $100

Eureka
Café Marina,
Woodley Island at the
Eureka Marina
Tel: 707-443 2233.
Serves very fresh scampi,
scallops and sole. If fish is not
your fare, there are scrumptious
sandwiches and Italian dishes.
Breakfast, lunch and dinner. $
Samoa Cookhouse,
Off Hwy 101 across the Samoa
Bridge
Tel: 707-442 1659.
Breakfast includes orange juice,
scambled eggs, pancakes,
sausages, hash browns and
coffee. Hefty lunches and
dinners start with soup, salad
and plenty of bread, and end
with hot apple pie. $

High Sierra/Yosemite
Ahwahnee,
Yosemite National Park
Tel: 559-372 1488.
The Grande Dame of hotels
nestled in breathtaking Yosemite
Valley serves grand meals in its
cathedral-like dining-room. $$$$
Erna's Elderberry House,
48688 Victoria Lane
(Hwy 41), Oakhurst
Tel: 559-683 6800.
Elegant French country inn hidden
in the forest. Stunning interior
design mingles with superb
classic European cuisine. Far
from cheap but worth the trip.
Reservation recommended. $$$$

Lake Tahoe
Old Post Office Coffee Shop,
5245 North Lake Blvd.,
Carnelian Bay
Tel: 530-546 3205.
Crowded, friendly and
inexpensive. Serves breakfast
and lunch only. $
Le Petit Pier,
2572 North Lake Blvd., Tahoe
Vista
Tel: 530-546 4464.
Classic French cuisine with many
exotic touches. Closed on
Tuesday. $$$

Peninsula/San Jose
Chantilly,
530 Ramona St., Palo Alto
Tel: 650-321 4080.
Wonderful but small European
restaurant; closed all day Sunday
and for lunch on Saturday. $$
El Charro,
2169 Winchester Ave., Campbell
Tel: 408-378 1277.
Mexican fare – excellent
margaritas and chiles colorados
– plus some Argentinian steak
specialties. $
Émile's,
545 S Second St., San Jose
Tel: 408-289 1960.
French contemporary and Swiss
cuisine. Dinner only; closed
Monday. $$$
Henry's Hi-Life,
301 W Saint John St.,
San Jose

Tel: 408-295 5414.
Good barbecued food at reasonable prices. Open for lunch and dinner, closed for lunch Saturday-Monday. $$
La Forêt,
21747 Bertram Road, San Jose
Tel: 408-997 3458.
On the site of the first adobe hotel in California (built in 1848), this charming old house is graced with tuxedo-clad waiters, French-Italian entrées, fresh mussels and clams, and tempting desserts. Dinner and Sunday brunch; closed Monday. $$
La Hacienda Inn,
18890 Saratoga Los Gatos Road, Los Gatos
Tel: 408-354 6669.
Get a full Italian dinner here at moderate prices. $$
Original Joe's,
301 S First St., San Jose
Tel: 408-292 7030.
Home of the famous "Joe's Special" – a tasty sandwich of spinach, ground beef, mushrooms, onions and scrambled eggs. $
Paolo's Continental Restaurant,
333 W San Carlos St.,
No 150, San Jose
Tel: 408-294 2558.
Good service and superb pastas. Closed Sunday. $$

Sacramento
Hong Kong,
501 Broadway
Tel: 916-442 7963.
Good Chinese food from a variety of regions in a converted Western barbecue place that still has the wagon-wheel light fixtures. Closed Wednesday. $$
The Mandarin,
4321 Arden Way
Tel: 916-488 4794.
Excellent Szechuan and Hunan Chinese food. Spicy and tasty. $$
The Water Boy,
2000 Capital
Tel: 916-498 9891.
Seasonal Mediterranean food. $$
Wakano Ura,
2217 10th St.

Tel: 916-448 6231.
An upstairs place in the Japanese district that can be noisy with revelers, although the fun becomes infectious. $$
Zelda's,
1415 21st St.
Tel: 916-447 1400.
Deep-dish pizza is a specialty. $

San Joaquin Valley
The Ripe Tomato
5064 North Palm, Fresno
Tel: 559-225 1850.
Quail and venison are standard menu items; typical specials include duck with apricot-garlic sauce, veal with oysters and mushrooms in vermouth and lamb with pesto sauce. Closed Sunday–Monday. $$$
Vintage Press,
216 North Willis, Visalia
Tel: 559-733 3033.
Fresh food with a European flair. Open Monday–Saturday and Sunday brunch. $$

Wine Country
Auberge du Soleil,
180 Rutherford Hill Road, Rutherford
Tel: 707-963 1211.
Wine country cuisine with fresh food and a view of the vineyards. $$$$
Calistoga Inn and Brewery,
1250 Lincoln Ave., Calistoga
Tel: 707-942 4101.
Casual, friendly service, large portions and excellent food. $$
John Ash and Co,
4330 Barnes Road, Santa Rosa
Tel: 707-527 7687.
Wine country cuisine. Closed Monday lunch. $$
Hydro Bar & Grill
1403 Lincoln St,
Calistoga
Tel: 707-942 9777
Over 20 microbrews and California cuisine in a breezy cafe atmosphere.$$
Showley's at Miramount,
1327 Railroad Ave.,
Saint Helena
Tel: 707-963 1200.
California cuisine with French

and Italian influences. Food looks as good as it tastes. $
The Diner,
6476 Washington St., Yountville
Tel: 707- 944 2626.
Good old American meals. The malts are made with real ice-cream. Open for breakfast, lunch and dinner, closed Monday. $
The French Laundry
6640 Washington St.,
Yountville
Tel: 707-944 2380
A true wine country gem with award-winning cuisine.$$

Price Guide

For two without wine

$	under $30
$$	$30–$60
$$$	$60–$100
$$$$	over $100

SOUTHERN CALIFORNIA

Los Angeles
Aunt Kizzy's Back Porch,
4325 Glencoe Ave.,
Marina del Rey
Tel: 310-578 1005.
Actors and athletes favor the ambience (and fried chicken). $
Barney's Beanery,
8447 Santa Monica Blvd.
Tel: 323-654 2287.
A newspaper-sized menu offering more different beer labels than you can shake a stick at, plus tables for a friendly game of pool, Barney's is casual, funky and fun. $
Café Latte,
6254 Wilshire Blvd.
Tel: 323-936 5213.
California cuisine with fresh sausages. $$
Café Pinot,
700 W 5th St., Downtown
Tel: 213-239 6500.
Delicious food in an unlikely elevated glass box adjoining the Central Library. $$$
Campanile,
624 South La Brea Ave.
Tel: 323-938 1447.
Closed Sunday dinner, open all

day the rest of the week. First rate California-Mediterranean cooking with the best bread in town from the bakery next door. $

California Pizza Kitchen,
207 S Beverly Dr., Beverly Hills
Tel: 310-275 1101.
One of a chain – "the People's Spago" says one critic. $

Canter's Fairfax Restaurant Delicatessen and Bakery,
419 North Fairfax Ave.
Tel: 323-651 2030.
Famous large and lively deli with classic 1950s interior. Open around the clock. $

Checca Italian Cafe,
7321 Santa Monica Blvd.
Tel: 323-850 7471.
A true American bistro with "old Hollywood" ambience and live jazz until 1.30am except Sundays. $$

Cicada
617 S Olive St.
Tel: 213-488 9488.
Classy eatery in the plush surroundings of the downtown Oviatt Building. Northern Italian food for a well-heeled crowd. $$$

Citrus
6703 Melrose Ave.
Tel: 323-857 0034
Arguably the best restaurant in Los Angeles. This crisp white and glass room is the setting for renowned pastry-chef Michel Richard's fabulous dishes. Enjoy, but leave room for dessert. Closed Saturday lunch and Sunday. $$$

Dar Maghreb,
7651 Sunset Blvd.
Tel: 323-876 7651.
Very popular with tourists, this lushly-decorated restaurant offers a solid Moroccan menu. Open for dinner only. $$

Gaucho Grill,
1754 San Vincent Blvd.
Brentwood
Tel: 310-447 7898.
Various mixed grill combinations are good choices at this modestly-priced Argentine hideway. $

The Gumbo Pot,

6333 W 3rd St.
Tel: 323-933 0358.
One of many great eating places in the Farmers' Market. Note: the market closes early evening. Open daily until 6.30pm. $

Kate Mantilini,
9101 Wilshire Blvd.
Tel: 310-278 3699.
In a distinctive-looking building this popular late-night spot serves until 1.30am or later every night but Sunday. Open for breakfast, lunch and dinner. $$

Malibu Inn & Restaurant,
22969 Pacific Coast Hwy
Tel: 310-456 6106.
Attractive, unpretentious eating spot long familiar to Hollywood stars whose pictures line the walls. $

Mandarin Deli,
727 N Broadway
Tel: 213-623 6054.
It's worth going downtown to sample these great Chinese dumplings. $

Original Pantry Café,
877 S Figuero
Tel: 213-972 9279.
Always crowded, inexpensive downtown landmark that's been around even longer than Richard Riordan who owns the place. $

Sidewalk Café,
1401 Ocean Front Walk
Tel: 310-399 5547.
The best place on the Venice boardwalk from which to watch the non-stop action. $

Spago
Horn Ave. in Hollywood 176 N Canon Dr., Beverly Hills
Tel: 310-385 0880;
Fax: 310-385 9690.
Among LA's most famous restaurants. From his renowned pizzas to his delectable desserts, owner and chef Wolfgang Puck delights. Better (and much more expensive) than Disneyland. Reservations required. $$$$

Woody's Bar-B-Que,
3446 W Slanson Ave.
Tel: 323-294 9443.
The best in LA according to some BBQ aficionados. $

Yamishiro,
1999 North Sycamore Ave.
Tel: 323-466 5125.
Some claim it offers the nicest view in LA. Surrounded by Japanese gardens, this is a lovely place for dinner (not open for lunch) or just a drink. $$$

Anaheim

Acapulco Mexican Restaurant,
1410 South Harbor Blvd.,
Anaheim
Tel: 714-956 7380.
Award-winning Mexican food right across the st. from Disneyland. $$

The Catch,
1929 State College Blvd.
Tel: 714-634 1829.
Steak and seafood. $$

The Cellar Restaurant,
305 North Harbor Blvd.,
Fullerton
Tel: 714-525 5682.
Superb French cuisine and expansive wine cellar 4 miles (6 km) from Disneyland. Closed Sunday-Monday. $$$

Home Town Buffet,
1630 W Katella
Tel: 714-539 2234.
Salad and dessert bars along with steam tables offering varied entrées. $

Five Crowns,
3801 East Coast Hwy, Corona del Mar
Tel: 949-760 0331.
Award-winning food served in a beautiful two-story building modeled after Ye Olde Bell, England's oldest inn. $$

Hansa House Smorgasbord,
1840 S Harbor Blvd.
Tel: 714-750 2411.
Smargasbord - Scandinavian decor and cuisine served in buffet style. $

Koisan Japanese Cuisine,
1132 E Katella Ave.
Tel: 714-639 1330.
Traditional Japanese food served with a background of kabuki music. $$$

National Sports Grill,
450 N State College Blvd.,
Orange

Tel: 714-935 0300.
This branch in Orange of a
national chain offers dozens of
TV monitors, four giant screens,
pool tables, 50 different beers
and an extensive menu. $$
Plaza Garibaldi Dinner Theatre,
1490 S Anaheim Blvd.
Tel: 714-758 9014.
Mariachi singers, folklorico and
tango dancers, accordians, Inca
flutes and other entertainment
accompanies the Mexican
cuisine. $$$
Tandoor Cuisine of India,
1132 E Katella Ave.
Tel; 714-538 2234.
70 spiced and tasty dishes with
many ingredients made on the
premises. $$$

Long Beach
Belmont Brewing Co,
25 39th Place
Tel: 562-433 3891.
Brew pub with good drinking
dishes and a view of the Queen
Mary. $
L'Opera,
101 Pine Ave.
Tel: 562-491 0066.
A romantic Italian spot with tasty
veal and fettucine. $$

Newport Beach
Crab Cooker,
2200 Newport Blvd.
Tel: 949-673 0100.
Grilled seafood on paper plates,
reasonable prices but no
reservations. $$
Tutto Mare,
Fashion Island,
545 Newport Center Dr.
Tel: 949-640 6333.
Italian bistro with pasta, fried
fish and view of the open
kitchen. $$

Palm Springs
Banducci's Bit of Italy,
1260 South Palm Canyon Dr.
Tel: 760-325 2537.
Steak, lobster and excellent
homemade cannelloni cooked to
perfection. Open only for dinner,
Piano Bar open Wednesday–
Sunday. $–$$

**Elmer's Pancake and
Steak House**,
1030 East Palm Canyon Dr.
Tel: 760-327 8419.
Can become very crowded on
weekend mornings. 20 varieties
of pancakes and waffles, fine
steaks and seafood for dinner. $
Kobe Japanese Steak House,
Hwy 111 at Frank Sinatra Drive
in Rancho
Tel: 760-324 1717.
Hibachi-style steak and chicken
in a replica of a 300-year-old
Japanese country inn. $$$
Las Casuelas Terraza,
222 South Palm Canyon Dr.
Tel: 760-325 2794.
Mexican-style cuisine on a
pleasant outdoor patio at
reasonable prices. $

Price Guide

For two without wine
$	under $30
$$	$30–$60
$$$	$60–$100
$$$$	over $100

Pasadena / South Bay
El Emperador Major,
1823 S San Gabriel Blvd.
Tel: 626-288 7265.
Spicy food from Yucatan. $

Redondo Beach
Aimee's,
800 S Pacific Coast Hwy
Tel: 310-316 1081.
Shrimp, salmon and tasty
desserts, all prepared in a
French manner. $
Chez Melange,
Palos Verdes Inn,
1716 Pacific Coast Hwy
Tel: 310-540 1222.
A wide variety of cuisines
including Italian, Chinese and
even Cajun are on the extensive
menu. $$

San Diego
**Anthony's Star of
the Sea Room**,
1360 North Harbor Dr.

Tel: 619-232 7408.
Fabulous seafood served with
dramatic flair. Located on the
waterfront. Jackets and
reservations required. Open for
dinner only. $$$
Casa de Pico,
2754 Juan St.
Tel: 619-296 3267.
Located in the Bazaar del Mundo
in Old Town. Reliable Mexican
food and great margaritas. $
Ruben E. Lee
880 East Harbor Island Dr.
Tel: 619-291 1974.
Dine aboard a genuine
Mississippi steamboat with a
great view of the surrounding
harbor. $$
The Marine Room,
2000 Spindrift Dr., La Jolla
Tel: 858-459 7222.
At high tide the waves crash just
outside the windows. $$
North China,
5043 N Harbor Dr.
Tel: 858-224 3568.
Bay views from the patio, Man-
darin and Szechuan cuisine. $$
Old Trieste,
2335 Morena Blvd.
Tel: 858-276 1841.
Justly reputed to be one of the
best Italian restaurants in town.
Closed Sunday-Monday. $$$
Shanghai,
1930 Quivira Way
Tel: 619-297 3110
Mongolian and Mandarin cuisine
and a nice view of the bay. $$

San Fernando Valley
Art's Deli,
12224 Ventura Blvd., between
Laurel Canyon Blvd. and Whitsett
Ave., Studio City
Tel: 818-762 1221.
Where "every sandwich is a work
of art." $
Bamboo,
14010 Ventura Blvd., between
Woodman and Hazeltine
avenues
Tel: 818-788 0202.
A good neighborhood place for
Chinese cuisine. $$
**Dr Hogly Wogly's Tyler
Texas BBQ**,

8136 N Sepulveda Blvd.,
one block south of Roscoe Blvd.,
Van Nuys
Tel: 818-780 6701.
LA's top-rated ribs. $

La Parrilla,
18716 Ventura Blvd.,
between Reseda Blvd. and Van
Alden Ave., Tarzana
Tel: 818-708 7422
Authentic Mexican in a fun
setting. $$

Moonlight Tango Café,
13730 Ventura Blvd., half a
block west of Woodman Ave.,
Sherman Oaks
Tel: 818-788 2000.
A late-night supper club with
singing waiters and a white-
tuxedoed "big band" combo that
inspires conga lines and frivolity.
Closed Monday. $

Mistral,
13422 Ventura Blvd,
between Woodman and
Coldwater Canyon boulevards,
Sherman Oaks
Tel: 818-981 6650.
Good food in the valley's version
of a French bistro. $$

Smoke House,
4420 Lakeside Dr., Burbank
Tel: 818-845 3731.
Ribs, chicken, unforgettable
garlic cheese bread are favorites
of the crowd from the nearby
studios. $$

Sushi Nozawa,
11288 Ventura Blvd., two blocks
west of Vineland Ave., Studio
City
Tel: 818-508 7017.
Japanese and good with it. $$$

The Great Greek,
13362 Ventura Blvd.,
Sherman Oaks
Tel: 818-905 5250.
Boisterous restaurant/club with
Greek cuisine and the familiar
plate-breaking, dancing waiters,
etc. $$

Santa Barbara

Acapulco,
1114 State St.
Tel: 805-963 3469.
Artfully prepared and spiced
Mexican food provided for

almost three decades now. $

Bay Café,
131 Anacapa St.
Tel: 805-963 2215.
Among the best seafood going.
$$

Charlotte,
742 State St.
Tel: 805-966 1221.
Tasty fare from Italy and France.
$–$$

Citronelle,
901 Cabrillo Blvd.
Tel: 805-963 0111.
French food from Michel Richard
of LA's glorious Citrons. $$$

Michael's Waterside,
50 Los Patos Way
Tel: 805-969 0307.
Gourmet cuisine in an elegant
Victorian mansion. $$$

Paradise Café,
702 Anacapa St.
Tel: 805-962 4416.
Always interesting — for the
young, chattering crowd as much
as for the food. $–$$

Playa Azul Café,
914 State St.
Tel: 805-966 2680.
Mexican food near the Presidio.
$$

The Wine Cask,
813 Anacapa St.
Tel: 805-966 9463.
Hundreds of wines from the
adjoining wine shop to accom-
pany delicious California cuisine
served in a lovely room with
painted, beamed ceilings. $$$

NEVADA

Las Vegas

Andres French Restaurant,
401 S. Sixth SV
Tel: 702-385 5016
Chef proprietor Andre Rochal
has won many recent awards for
excellence. $$

Bacchanal's,
at Caesar's Palace
Tel: 702-731 7731.
A Roman feast, including three
wines, for around $70. $$$$

Ben & Jerry's,
In the Santa Fe Hotel Casino

Ice cream store offering lots of
new gambling-theme flavors. $

Boogie's Diner,
The Forum shops at Caesar's,
3500 Las Vegas Blvd. S
Tel: 702-892 0860.
50s nostalgia dining featuring all
homemade items. Famous for
its hot turkey plate, burgers, and
thick shakes and malts. $

Buccaneer Bay Club,
Tel: 702-894 7111.
With windows overlooking the
lagoon where the pirate ship and
frigate do daily battle is not to be
missed. $$$

Celebrity Deli,
4055 S Maryland Pkwy
Tel: 702-733 7827.
Pastrami, smoked fish, corned
beef. 8am–9pm (Sun 'til 8pm) $

Coyote Cafe,
Inside the MGM Grand
Tel: 702-891 7777
Santa Fe style, has partly-tiled
clay walls, marble tables and
staff in denim. Try barbecued
duck quesadilla with chipotle
sauce and cheese or shrimp
diablo with olives, chillies and
scallions. $$$

Drink,
at Harmon Ave. and Koval Lane
near the MGM Grand,
Has 100 microbrew, 25 brands
of vodka and a score of vodka
"infusions." It stores cigars in an
8-foot-tall humidor in Smoke at
Drink, one of the establish-
ment's six concept rooms. $

Mayflower Cuisinier,
4750 W Sahara Ave.
Tel: 702-870 8432.
Contemporary California-style
cuisine. $$

Morton's of Chicago,
Fashion Show Mall,
3200 Las Vegas Blvd. S
Tel: 702-893 0703.
Waiters present enormous
uncooked steaks for inspection.
$$$

The Palace Court,
At Caesar's Palace,
Tel: 702-731 7731.
Under a domed stained glass
ceiling which the *New York Times*
tagged as a "romantic formal

dining room." $$$$
Peppermint Lounge,
2985 Las Vegas Blvd. S.
Tel: 702-735 4177.
The relaxing Fireside Lounge has soft seats by a flaming pool.
Open 24 hours. $$$
The Circus Buffet,
Circus Circus Hotel/Casino,
2880 Las Vegas Blvd. S
Tel: 702-734 0410;
Breakfast 6–11.30am, brunch noon–4pm, dinner 4.30–11pm.
Sundae bar at brunch and dinner. Carved-to-order roast beef and ham at dinner. $$$
Fisherman's Broiler
Palace Station and Boulder Station Hotel & Casinos, 4211 W Sahara, 4111 Boulder Hwy
Tel: 702-367 2411;
1-800-544 2411;
702- 432 7777;
1-800-683 7777.
Open daily 11am–4pm for lunch (noon–4pm Saturday and Sundays). Dinner served between 4pm–11pm. $$
Fog City Diner,
Hughes Center, one mile east of the Maxim on Flamingo
Tel: 702-738 0200.
A chrome, neon and mahogany interior clones the famous flagship. The sirloin and black bean chilli and the horseradish potato pancake are recommended. $$
Golden Steer,
308 W Sahara Ave.
Tel: 702-344 4470.
30 years of serving seafood and steaks. $$
Green Shack Restaurant,
E Fremont St.
Has served its speciality fried chicken since 1930. $$
Guadalajara Bar & Grille,
Palace Station and Boulder Station Hotel & Casino,
2411 W Sahara
Tel: 702-367 2411;
1-800-544 2411.
Traditional. Serves 99 percent margaritas. Open 11am–5pm for lunch and 5pm–11pm for dinner. $$
Iron Horse Café,
Palace Station and Boulder

Station Hotel & Casino, 2411 W Sahara, 4111 Boulder Hwy
Tel: 702-367 2411;
1-800-544 2411;
702-432 7777;
1-800-683 7777.
Serving guests 24 hours a day, 7 days a week. Traditional American fare. $$
Isis
Luxor Hotel,
Tel: 702-262 2773.
Five-star dining at the Luxor $$$$
Rib house
Imperial Palace Hotel & Casino 3535 Las Vegas Blvd. S
Tel: 702-731 3311
1-800-634 6441.
Relaxed Western-style restaurant features BBQ ribs and chicken. Original sauces and down-home flavors. Open Tuesday–Saturday 5–11pm. $
Ruth's Chris Steak House,
3900 Paradise Road;
4561 W Flamingo Road
Tel: 702-248 7011
1-800-544 0808#26
Home of serious steaks! These steaks come only from selected Midwestern beef, corn- fed, aged and never frozen and then served sizzling. $$
Sadie's Southern Dining,
505 E Twain Ave.
Tel: 702-796 4177.
11am–9.45pm Tuesday–Saturday, 11am–7.45pm Sunday. $$
Silver Dragon,
1510 E Flamingo just off Maryland Pkwy
Tel: 702-737 1234.
Award-winning cuisine. $$$
Sir Reginald's,
at MGM
Tel: 702-891 7777.
For English pub-like ambience. $$
Spago,
The Forum Shops at Caesar's, 3500 Las Vegas Blvd. S
Tel: 702-369 6300.
Celebrity Chef Wolfgang Puck's "California Cuisine" which incorporates the cuisines of Europe, the Orient, Latin

America, as well as the United States to create a truly eclectic menu. $$$$
The Steak House at Bally's Casino,
Tel: 702-967 4661.
Offers everything from sushi to prime rib and a complimentary glass of champagne. $$
Teahouse Buffet,
Imperial Palace Hotel & Casino, 3535 Las Vegas Blvd. S,
Tel: 702-731 3311.
A feast for a king. Monday–Friday brunch 7am–2.30pm, Saturday–Sunday champagne brunch 8am–2.30pm, prime rib and champagne dinner buffet. $$$
Vacation Village,
6711 Las Vegas Blvd.
Tel: 702-897 1700.
Offers a beer and free hotdog to bettors who buy $10 worth of chips or slot play. $
The Vineyard,
3630 S Maryland Pky.
Tel: 702-731 1606.
Features its famous "antipasto buffet" as well as traditional Italian entrées. $$
World's Fare Buffet,
Riviera Hotel & Casino, 2901 Las Vegas Blvd. S
Tel: 702-734 5110;
1-800-634 6753;
Fax: 702-794 9451.
Open daily for breakfast, 7–10am, lunch 11am–3pm, and dinner 4.30–11pm. $$$

Price Guide	
For two without wine	
$	under $30
$$	$30–$60
$$$	$60–$100
$$$$	over $100

Culture

Concerts and Operas
Audium,
1616 Bush St. in the Civic
Center area
Tel: 415-771 1616.
Presents contemporary and
precedent-setting kinds of
music. This is the first theater of
sound exploration,
experimenting with 136
speakers which move music
around you in a kind of
sculpture.
**The Bay Area Women's
Philharmonic,**
Tel: 415-543 2297
Performs the works of women
composers. Also other musical
menus from which to choose.
Golden Gate Park Band,
Music Concourse, Golden Gate
Park
Tel: 415-666 7035
Each Sunday April to October,
1pm. Pack a picnic and enjoy a
traditional brass band, free.
The Kronos Quartet,
Tel: 415-731 3533.
Unconventional string quartet;
includes rock, jazz, blues in its
classical repertoire.
**San Francisco Conservatory of
Music,**
1201 Ortega,
Tel: 415-564 8086/759-3477 (a
24-hour tape recording lists
music activities).
Offers professional chamber
music as well as student
recitals. With graduates like
Isaac Stern to its credit, it is
regarded as the best West Coast
music school.
San Francisco Opera,
Grove and Van Ness avenues in

the Civic Center area.
Tel: 415-864 3330.
Features internationally
renowned stars of the opera
world. Having entered its
seventh decade of annual
seasons, ten operas are
presented each year in
repertory. Standing room tickets
can be purchased two hours
before the performance.
San Francisco Symphony,
Davies Symphony Hall, Van Ness
and Grove avenues in the Civic
Center Area,
Tel: 415-864 6000. The San
Francisco Symphony plays a
summer pops series, a
Beethoven Festival and the
Mostly Mozart Festival each year
in addition to its regular season.

Dance
San Francisco Ballet,
Tel: 415-703 9400
Established for over 60 years,
continues to delight audiences.
Well-known for traditional
choreography and consistently
excellent productions, the San
Francisco Ballet was the first in
the country to perform the
Nutcracker Suite as a Christmas
event. Performances at the San
Francisco Opera House, Van
Ness and Grove in the Civic
Center arena. Tickets may be
purchased through BASS or at the
box office for performances at
the Opera house.
San Francisco Dance Theater,
60 Brady St.
Tel: 510-595 8770.
Pioneers of dance.
The Joffrey Ballet,
Tel: 415-703 9400.
American Ballet Theater and
Stuttgart Ballet visit the San
Francisco Opera House stage
regularly.

Theater
Actors' Theatre,
533 Sutter St.
Tel: 415-296 9179.
Often does classics by such
luminaries as Tennessee
Williams and other innovators.

Thursday-Sunday at 8pm. An
intimate, fun setting.
**American Conservatory Theater
(ACT),**
Tel: 415-749 2228.
Every kind of material.
**Asian American Theatre
Company,**
403 Arguello Blvd.
Tel: 415-440 5545.
Thursday–Saturday at 8pm;
Sunday 3.30 and 7.30pm.
Known for innovative Asian
themes and casts.
Curran Theater,
Tel: 415-551 2000.
The Eureka,
2730 16th St.
Tel: 789 SHOW.
Gay/lesbian-oriented material.
Golden Gate Theater,
Tel: 415-551 2000.
Fort Mason, Building B
Experimental Works.
The Magic Theater,
Fort Mason, Building D,
Tel: 415-441 8822.
Innovative and known for
premiering plays by Michael
McClure and Sam Shepard.
**Potrero Hill Neighborhood
House,**
953 De Haro
Tel: 415-826 8080.
Professionals and amateurs
perform together to present
contemporary issues and gritty,
urban themes.
Theater Rhinoceros,
2926 16th St.
Tel: 415-861 5079.
Gay and lesbian works.

Colleges, universities, cultural
centers and churches sponsor
theatrical productions on a
regular basis. Check "Datebook"
listing under Theater for current
information.

Concerts and Operas
The 3,200-seat **Dorothy
Chandler pavillion**, part of the
Music Center complex, is the
home of the Los Angeles
Philharmonic. The June to

September season at the Hollywood Bowl sees nightly concerts: jazz, classical and pops. Park free at specific lots and take the roundtrip bus or take Bowlbus from 14 different locations. For more information and reservations: call the Music Centre line: 213-972 7211. Ask about free morning rehearsals.

Nightlife

Evening diversions in California are as varied and all-encompassing as the state itself. Visitors can entertain themselves with events that range from world-class operas and musicals, theater and symphonies to first-rate comedy and funky live blues, jazz and rock'n'roll.

To track down nightlife, you would do best to refer to the local newspaper as a guide to what's on where. In San Francisco, the *Sunday Chronicle & Examiner*'s "Pink Pages" will appraise you of most of the Bay Area's activities, while the "Calendar" section of Sunday's *Los Angeles Times* will fill you in on action in the Southland. The concierge at many larger hotels can help you in your quest for fun when the sun goes down in the Golden State.

There are also regular concerts at the **Greek Theatre**, (tel: 323-665 1927) in Griffith Park and the venerable **Palace** in Hollywood (1735 N Vine St., tel: 323-462 3000), and performances on summer Sundays in Warner Park, Woodland Hills. Call the Valley Cultural Center (tel: 818-704 1587) for schedule. Santa Clara's summer concerts take place in **Old Orchard Park**, (tel: 661-255 4910); in Thousand Oaks, in **Conejo Community Park** (tel: 818-597 7361).

Dorothy Chandler Pavilion, 135 N Grand Ave., Downtown Tel: 213-972 7211/972 7483 The pavilion showcases the Los Angeles Civic Light Opera. The building is richly appointed with marble walls, sculptured columns, and quite a few crystal chandeliers.
The Wilshire Ebell Theater, 4401 W Eighth St. Tel: 213-939 1128. This Spanish-designed venue was built in 1924, and often hosts the Los Angeles Opera Theater.
Wiltern Theater, Wilshire Blvd. and Western Ave Tel: 213-380 5005. Built in 1930 and now a protected Art Deco landmark, the Wiltern is also venue for the Los Angeles Opera Theater and musical events.

Dance

The Music Center, 135 N Grand Tel: 213-972 7211. The Western home of the Joffrey bi-coastal ballet company, which is most active in the spring.
The Shrine Auditorium, 649 W Jefferson Tel: 213-972 7211 1-800-472 2272. The Shrine hosts the American Ballet Theater in March.
UCLA **Center for the Arts**, 4405 N Hilgard, Westwood Tel: 310-825 2101. Famous ballet companies share this center for the arts with the UCLA Dance Company.
The **Wiltern Theatre**, (tel: 213-380 5005); the **Veterans Wadsworth Theatre** (tel: 310-479 3003); the **Pasadena Civic Theatre**, and **Glendale's Alex Theatre** also stage dance concerts semi-regularly. For specific listings, consult the Sunday Calendar section of the *Los Angeles Times*.

Theater

The Groundlings, 7307 Melrose Ave. (tel: 323-934 9700), is a long-established venue and now under challenge from the breakaway **Acme Comedy Theatre**. But in addition to the dozens of tiny houses there are also the better-known **Shubert Theatre**, (tel: 800-447 7400), in Century City; the **Mark Taper Forum** (tel: 213-972 0700); the **Ahmanson** (tel: 213-972 7401) in the Music Center at 135 N Grand; and the **Geffen Theatre**, (tel: 310-208 6500), on the UCLA campus.

Repertory can be enjoyed at the **Cast Theatre**, 804 N El Centro, Hollywood, (tel: 323-462 0265). Other theaters with a regular schedule include the **Wilshire**, 8440 Wilshire Blvd. (tel: 323-468 1716); the **Pantages**, 6233 Hollywood Blvd. (tel: 323-468 1770); and the **James A Doolittle**, 1615 N Vine (tel: 323-462 6666).

Further afield are the **Back Alley**, 15231 Burbank Blvd., Van Nuys (tel: 818- 780 2240), as well as the **Pasadena Playhouse**, 39 El Molino Ave. (tel: 818-356 7529). Productions at Santa Monica's Highways, the Bilingual Foundation for the Arts north of downtown, the Japan American Theatre and the Vision Complex, 4310 Degnan, Leimert Park, (tel: 213-291 7321), are always worthy of note. Look for listings in the free *LA Weekly*, widely distributed around town or call **Theater LA** at 213-688-ARTS which offers comprehensive listings.

Half price tickets are available from **Times Tix** at Jerry's Famous Deli in West Hollywood (tel: 310-659 3678).

Festivals

For listings of festivals, parades and other celebrations in Southern California, check the "Calendar" section of the *Los Angeles Times* or a current copy of *LA Weekly* or *Los Angeles Magazine*. In Northern California check out the *San Francisco Chronicle* or the *Bay Guardian*. Listings for more specialized events will appear in smaller local papers. Here are just a few of the most popular festivals and events in California.

The Datebook

The "Datebook" section of the *Sunday Examiner & Chronicle* lists events including new music, early music, baroque, band, harpsichord, orchestra, piano, and chamber music under Classical/Opera/Dance. Popular music concerts and festivals are featured with advertisements throughout the Pink Pages section.

JANUARY

Colorado River Country Music Festival, Blythe,
Tel: 619-922 8166.
Sacramento Symphony Pops Series,
Tel: 916-756 0191.
San Diego Open Golf Tournament,
Tel: 619-281 4653.
Tiburon Children's Film Festival,
Tel: 415-435 1234.
Tet Vietnamese New Year,

Santa Clara County Fairgrounds, San Jose
Tel: 408-295 9210.
Tournament of Roses Parade and Rose Bowl Football Game, Pasadena
Tel: 626-795 9311

FEBRUARY

Bok Kai Festival,
Marysville
Tel: 530-742 ARTS.
Festival celebrates the water god with lion dancers, tours of temples and sideshows.
Chinese New Year,
Large celebrations in San Francisco, Los Angeles and San Diego. Call local tourist bureaus for information.
Clam Chowder Cook-Off,
Santa Cruz
Tel: 831-423 5590.
Teams work on their recipes for tasting and prizes.
Mardi Gras Jazz Festival,
Pismo Beach
Tel: 805-773 4811.
Mardi Gras also celebrated in San Luis Obispo
Tel: 805-541 2183.
Monterey County Hot Air Affair,
Monterey
Tel: 831-649 6544.
Balloon racing, skydiving aerobatics.
National Date Festival,
Indio
Tel: 760-863 8245.
Arabian Nights pageant, camel and ostrich races.
San Luis Obispo Mardi Gras,
San Luis Obispo
Tel: 805-541 2183.
Whisky Flat Days,
Kernville
Tel: 619-376 2629.
Parade, rodeo, gunfighters, arts and crafts, food.

MARCH

African Cultural Festival,
Oakland
Tel: 510-763 3962.

Bay Area Music Awards,
San Francisco
Jumping Frog Jubilee,
Angels Camp
Tel: 559-736 2561
Accompanying the amphibians' contest is a carnival, rodeo and county fair.
Saint Patrick's Day.
Parades and celebrations, San Francisco, Los Angeles and San Diego.
San Francisco International Film Festival,
San Francisco
Tel: 415-931-FILM.
Santa Barbara International Film Festival,
Santa Barbara
Tel: 805-963 0023.
Snowfest Winter Carnival,
Tahoe City
Tel: 530-583 7625

APRIL

Apple Blossom Festival,
Sebastopol
Tel: 707-823 3032.
Camellia Festival,
Sacramento
Tel: 916-447 2286.
Parade, flower ball, golf tournament.
Cherry Blossom Festival,
San Francisco
Tel: 415-563 2313.
Easter Sunrise Service,
Hollywood Bowl, Los Angeles
Tel: 323-850 2000
Paderewski Festival,
Paso Robles
Tel: 805-238-0527.
Concert tribute to the famous Polish pianist, tour of Victorian homes.
Santa Barbara Arts Festival,
Santa Barbara
Tel: 805-966 7022.
The Freeway Series,
Los Angeles
Tel: 714-634 2000.
A three-game series between the LA Dodgers and the California Angels.

MAY

Applefest,
Tehachapi
Tel: 805-822 4180.
Arts and crafts, entertainment,
apple dumplings.

Bay to Breakers,
San Francisco
Tel: 415-777 7770.
The world's largest (not longest
at 7½ miles/12 km) footrace.

California Festival of Beers,
San Luis Obispo
Tel: 805-781 2777.
The largest regional beer-tasting
event in the country.

Carlsbad Village Faire,
Carlsbad
Tel: 760-729 9072.
California's largest one-day
street fair.

Cinco de Mayo,
San Francisco, Los Angeles, San
Diego and Santa Barbara

Fiesta de las Artes,
Hermosa Beach
Tel: 310-376 0951.

Jazz Jubilee,
Sacramento
Tel: 916-372 5277.
Largest Dixieland festival.

**Long Beach Lesbian and Gay
Pride Celebration**,
Long Beach
Tel: 562-435 5530.

**Rancho California Balloon and
Wine Festival**,
Temecula
Tel: 714-676 5090.

Sacramento Dixieland Jubilee,
Sacramento
Tel: 916-372 5277.
Known as "America's
International Jazz Festival."

Strawberry Festival,
Garden Grove
Tel: 714-638 0981.

Street Painting Festival,
Santa Barbara Mission
Tel: 805-966 9222.

JUNE

Back to Blue Treasure Hunt,
Tel: 818-789 7866.

For divers and kids on Malibu
beach.

Carnaval San Francisco,
San Francisco
Tel: 415-826 1401.
Mardi Gras parade.

Country Music Festival,
Ojai
Tel: 805-646 8126.
Bluegrass, Cajun, Rockabilly.

Freeport Portuguese Festa,
Sacramento
Tel: 916-935 2327.
Parade and picnic.

Haight Street Fair,
San Francisco

**Lesbian and Gay Freedom Day
Parade**,
San Francisco

Living History Celebration,
San Juan Bautista
Tel: 408-623 4881.
Costumed participants portray
the old days.

National Shakespeare Festival,
San Diego

North Beach Festival,
San Francisco
Tel: 415-989 2220

**Scottish Games and Clan
Gathering**,
Modesto
Tel: 559-577 5757.
Dancing, music, food, sports.

Southern California Exposition,
San Diego
Tel: 619-236 1212.
A miniature world's fair.

Strawberry Festival,
Susanville
Tel: 916-257 4323.
Arts and crafts, music and food.

JULY

Annual Rodeo,
Fortuna
Tel: 707-782 3716.

**Boat Parade and Fireworks
Show**,
Bass Lake
Tel: 559-642 3676.

California Rodeo,
Salinas
Tel: 1-800-771 8807

Fourth of July.
Celebrations and fireworks

throughout the state.

Gilroy Garlic Festival,
Gilroy
Tel: 408-842 6436.

Heritage Quilt Show,
Julian
Tel: 760-765 1857.
Two-hundred-year-old quilts on
display.

Mark Twain Days,
Angels Camp
Tel: 559-754 3521.
Barbecue, beer garden, rodeo.

Mozart Festival,
San Luis Obispo
Tel: 805-781 2777

Sandcastle Days,
Imperial Beach
Tel: 619-424 6663.
Three-day-long sandcastle
building contest for serious
contenders and curious
onlookers.

Sawdust Festival,
Tel: 714-494 3030.
Laguna Beach's traditional arts
and crafts festival.

AUGUST

California State Fair,
Sacramento
Tel: 916-263-FAIR.
Livestock, food, music,
entertainment.

International Surf Festival,
Hermosa, Manhattan and
Redondo beaches.
Exhibition surfing. Call beach
city tourist bureaus for
information.

**Lake Tahoe Starlight Jazz
Festival**,
South Lake Tahoe
Tel: 530-542 4166.

Lambtown USA Festival,
Dixon, Solano County
Tel: 707-678 2650.
Cook-off with entertainment.

Nihonmachi St. Fair,
Japantown, San Francisco
Tel: 415-771 9861.
Lion Dancers, Taiko Drummers,
Japanese arts and crafts.

**Oakland Chinatown Street
Festival**,
Chinese festivities all around the

Oakland area. Good parades.
Tel: 510-893 8979.

Renaissance Pleasure Faire,
Novato
Tel: 415-892 0937
1-800-52-FAIRE.

Sunset Junction Street Fair,
Los Angeles
Tel: 213-661 7771.

SEPTEMBER

A la Carte, A la Park,
San Francisco
Tel: 415-383 9378.
Sample food from the city's fine
restaurants and enjoy live music
in Golden Gate Park.

Fiesta de las Artes,
Hermosa Beach
Tel: 310-376 0951.

Los Angeles County Fair,
Pomona
Tel: 714-623 3111.

Mammoth Cycling Classic,
Mammoth Lakes
Tel: 760-934 2571.
World-class cyclists fill the
streets.

Monterey Jazz Festival,
Monterey
Tel: 831-373 3366.

Oktoberfest,
Big Bear Lake
Tel: 909-866 5634.
Weekends between Labor Day
and the end of October.

Purisima's People Day,
Lompoc
Tel: 805-733 2497.
Costumed volunteers depict old
Mission life.

Sausalito Art Festival,
Sausalito
Tel: 415-332 0505.

Triathlon,
Ventura
Tel: 805-880 4915.
Contestants swim, bike and run
to complete the event.

OCTOBER

Art and Pumpkin Festival,
Half Moon Bay
Tel: 650-726 9652.

Banjo and Fiddle Contest,
Julian
Tel: 760-282 8380.

California Avocado Festival,
Carpinteria
Tel: 805-684 0038.

Columbus Day Celebration,
San Francisco
Tel: 415-434 1492.

Cultural Heritage Festival,
Riverside
Tel: 909-782 5407.
Ethnic food, entertainment and
crafts.

Exotic Erotic Ball,
Cow Palace, Daly City, San
Francisco
Tel: 415-469 6065,
The largest indoor masquerade
ball in the world.

Johnny Appleseed Day,
Paradise
Tel: 530-877 9356.
Arts and crafts, entertainment,
apple pie contest.

Lithuanian Fair,
Los Angeles
Tel: 213-665 4082.
Music, folk art, ethnic food.

Street Festival,
San Bruno
Tel: 415-588 0180.
Arts and crafts, ethnic food,
entertainment.

NOVEMBER

Chocolate Fest,
Ghirardelli Square, San
Franscisco
Desserts from Ghirardelli
Square restaurants, plus an ice-
cream sundae-eating contest.

**Death Valley '49ers
Encampment,**
Death Valley
Tel: 760-786 2345.
Fiddlers contest, art shows,
valley trek.

Fall Flower Tour,
Encinitas
Tel: 619-7533 6270.

Gold Mine Tour,
Friant
Tel: 559-822 2332.
River-boat trip to an old mine.

Golf Cart Parade,
Palm Desert
Tel: 760-346 1204.
Decorated golfcarts, marching
bands, etc.

Village Fair,
Carlsbad
Tel: 760-931 8400.
The state's largest one-day
street fair.

Winterfest,
Solvang
Tel: 805-688 6144.
Carriage rides, entertainment.
There is a similar **Winterfest,**
festival in Sacramento, tel: 916-
442 8575.

DECEMBER

Christmas on the Prado,
San Diego
Tel: 619-232 0512.

Lighted Boat Parades,
Marina del Rey and San Diego.
Call local tourist bureaus for
information.

The Nutcracker,
Performed by the San Francisco
Ballet and Oakland Ballet,
Tel: 415-865 2000

Parade of Lights,
Oxnard
Tel: 805-985 4852.

**Spirit of Christmas Crafts Fair
and Exhibition,**
Santa Rosa
Tel: 707-575 9335.

Outdoor Activities

CALIFORNIA PARKS

California State Department of Parks and Recreation, Los Angeles District,
1928 Las Virgenes Road, Calabasas, CA 91302
Tel: 916-653 6995
1-800-533-PARK.
Free admission.
National Park Service,
Western Regional Office, Western Region Information Office, Fort Mason Building 201, San Francisco, CA 94123,
Tel: 415-556 0560
Fax: 415-561 4610.
National Park Service,
Department of the Interior, PO Box 37127, Washington DC 20013-7127
Tel: 202-208 4621
Fax: 202-208 7889.
US Forest Service,
Pacific Southwest Regional Office, 630 Sansome Street, San Francisco, CA 94111
Tel: 707-562 8737

SOUTHERN CALIFORNIA GARDENS

Earl Burns Miller Japanese Garden,
California State University at Long Beach, Earl Warren Drive, Long Beach
Open 9am-5pm, free admission. This garden has all the traditional Japanese garden components – tea house, stone lanterns, azalea, iris and pine - arranged with eminent and sympathetic grace. Landscape architect Edward R Lovell visited Japan's Imperial Gardens for inspiration and consulted Dr Koichi Kawana of UCLA for authenticity. Dark, still waters filled with koi reflect weeping willows, white-trunked birch trees and two handsomely-detailed wood bridges. A lovely memorial to businessman and philanthropist Earl Burns Miller, this Japanese garden keeps regular opening hours, rendering it more accessible than most. Tours of the home on the tour.

El Pueblo de Los Angeles State Historic Park,
622 N Main St., Los Angeles
Tel: 213-628 1274.
Open Monday-Saturday 10am-3pm. This historical 44-acre (18-hectare) park houses the city's first church, fire-house and theater. Its center is Olivera St., a block-long pedestrian way lined with open-air stalls, cafés, restaurants and gift shops. Free admission.

Exposition Park Rose Garden,
900 Exposition Blvd., Los Angeles.
Open 8am-till dusk. Broad grass walkways firmly edged with white concrete bands define more than 200 rectangular rose beds each filled with plants of a single cultivar. This 7½-acre (3-hectare) sunken garden is bounded by an ageing brick balustrade that offers a perfect perch from which to watch the goings-on below. The simple and straightforward plan affords the perfect backdrop for the wildly prolific and brightly-colored roses. Installed in 1926, this is one of the oldest public gardens in Los Angeles. The magnificent flowering period extends from late April to early November, but peak bloom occurs between June and September. In between the University of Southern California campus and the Rose Bowl, this garden is a delightful stop-over in the middle of a day of sight-seeing. Free admission.

Franklin D Murphy Sculpture Garden,
University of California Los Angeles, Los Angeles.
Adjoins the Wight Art Gallery at the north end of the campus (tel: 310-825 3264). Always open. This well-loved garden lacks many conventional garden elements. It is gateless, with a loosely-defined perimeter and just a simple palette of plants. The layout is more akin to a small park than a museum, and shade is provided by flowering jacaranda and coral trees. There are more than 50 works of art representing the era's foremost sculptors, including August Rodin, Henry Moore and Alexander Calder. Figurative, abstract or constructivist, they make a diverse yet egalitarian assemblage and are further interspersed by UCLA students studying or sunning themselves. Free admission.

Los Angeles State and County Arboretum (LASCA),
301 N Baldwin Ave., Arcadia
Tel: 626-821 3211.
Open 9am– 4.30pm in winter, until 6.30pm Monday–Friday in summer. This 127-acre (51-hectare) county-run arboretum was established to house horticulturalist Dr Samuel Ayres's extensive collection of brilliantly colored plants - he traveled the world collecting and growing plants with which to brighten Southern California. There are some 30,000 permanent plants on the grounds representing 4,000 species, varieties or forms. Half a million people visit LASCA a year – it affords the casual visitor dozens of scenarios to experience and explore by foot or tram. There is a jungle garden, aquatic garden, tropical greenhouse, herb garden, bamboo grove, 3½-acre (1½-hectare) lagoon and on and on; it is impossible to cover in one day. The trees and shrubs are routinely upstaged by peacocks,

descendants of the original three pairs brought from India near the turn of the century. Admission fee.

Rancho Los Alamitos, 6400 Bixby Hill Road, Long Beach Tel: 562-431 3451. Open Wednesday–Sunday 1–5pm. Seven-and-a-half cultivated acres (3 hectares) are scant souvenir of the vast, semi-arid spread of more than 28,000 acres (11,331 hectares) held by John Bixby and his partners in 1881, but the ranch house and other main buildings remain. The grounds are considered the definitive standard of accuracy for reconstructed historic landscapes, and one project is to maintain the robust and fun atmosphere created here by the family-oriented Bixbys in the 1920s and '30s. These gardens were not erected for status or show, but rather reflect the preferences of the owners. There is not a plant sign in sight – visitors experience the garden directly, not as an institution or museum. Free admission.

Sherman Library and Gardens, 2746 E Pacific Coast Hwy, Corona del Mar Tel: 949-673 2261. The garden is open daily from 10.30am–4pm and the library is open Monday–Friday 9am–4.30pm. This modern and tidy series of interlocking rooms, residential in scale, can be covered in a pleasurable afternoon's time. The library and gardens were established in 1958 in memory of industrialist MH Sherman by Sherman's right-hand man and beneficiary, Arnold Haskell, a caring man who incorporated handicapped accessibility decades before its time as well as a Discovery Garden, which recounts a history of herbs in scent and touch for the blind. The library, tucked in the corner of the site, specializes in the Pacific Southwest and features

Sherman's papers. Beginning at the site of Haskell's office, a tiny 1940s adobe cottage in Corona del Mar, the Sherman Foundation came to fill one city block. The horticultural goal at Sherman is to grant glorious color all year long – the Sun and Central gardens feature bedding plants rotated by season. The Tropical Conservatory nurtures orchids; the Specimen Shade garden hosts a spectrum of begonias from July until fall. Admission fee.

UCLA **Hannah Carter Japanese Garden**, 10619 Bellagio Road, Bel Air Tel: 310-825 4574 (UCLA Visitors' Center). Open by reservation only, Tuesday, Wednesday and Friday 11am– 2pm. In this compendium of Japanese garden features, asymmetry, naturalness and the subtlety of seasons prevail. The plan is an ingenious adaptation of Japanese themes to the vertical topography of Bel Air, and compromises have been made for the dry, bright and genial Southern California climate – the pruning is less refined, allowing a variation of forms and a proliferation of intense color. Additionally, the garden is a veritable museum of garden artifacts – Buddha carvings, stone water basins, pagoda, lanterns and more – all transported from Japan. Free admission.

Sport

BASEBALL

California possesses some of the finest teams in professional sports. Baseball season runs from April–October. In Southern California, the Los Angeles Dodgers play at Dodger Stadium; the California Angels play at Anaheim Stadium; and the San Diego Padres play at San Diego Jack Murphy Stadium. In Northern California, the San Francisco Giants play at Candlestick Park, and the Oakland Athletics (known as the A's) play in the Oakland Coliseum.

BASKETBALL

The regular National Basketball Association (NBA) season runs from October through April, with championship playoffs continuing in June. The Los Angeles Lakers, who are almost always a league powerhouse, and the LA Clippers play at the brand new Staples Center downtown, and the Golden State Warriors play at the Oakland Coliseum Arena.

FOOTBALL

The National Football League (NFL) season begins in September and ends in December. There are pre-season games in August and post-season playoffs in January. In Southern California, the LA

Rams play at Anaheim Stadium; LA Raiders at Los Angeles Memorial Coliseum; and San Diego Chargers at San Diego Jack Murphy Stadium. The Rose Bowl is held annually on New Year's Day between the best team in the Pac-10 conference and the best team in the Big Ten. This popular event is held at the Rose Bowl Stadium in Pasadena which seats over 100,000 people, but it is still difficult to get seats. The only professional football team in Northern California, the San Francisco 49ers, play at Candlestick Park.

HOCKEY

California has two professional hockey teams, the LA Kings, who play at the 19,000-seat Staples Center downtown, and the younger San Jose Sharks, who play at the San Jose Arena.

HORSE RACING

For those who prefer the sport of kings, Southern California has three tracks to choose from: Hollywood Park in Inglewood hosts thoroughbred racing from April to July and harness racing in November and December; Santa Anita Park in Arcadia hosts thoroughbred racing from October to mid-November and from December to late April. The season at the Del Mar Track, about 30 miles north of San Diego, runs from mid-July to early September. There are two tracks in the San Francisco Bay Area: Bay Meadows is located on the Peninsula south of San Francisco and is one of the oldest, busiest and most beautiful tracks in the state; Golden Gate Fields is located in the East Bay.

Participant Sports

BALLOONING

Around Monterey call Balloons-by-the-Sea, and for trips over the Sierras contact Sunshore Balloon Adventures (tel: 1-800-829-7238). Temecula in the Wine Country north of San Diego is one of the most popular ballooning areas. Call DAE Flights (tel: 909-302 8080), or Abobe All Balloon Charters (tel: 909-694 6287).

BICYCLING

Organized five-day bicycle adventures which include accommodation operate in San Diego, San Francisco and other parts of the state and cost around $170 from Imagine Tours (tel: 1-800-228-7041). Mammoth Mountain Bike Park (tel: 1-800-228-4947), offers 50 miles of cycling trails and stunt tracks.

FISHING

California's Department of Fish and Game oversees fishing areas at wildlife and ecological reserves in various parts of the state and offers a free copy of its magazine, *Outdoor California* (tel: 1-800-THE-WILD). One day in June and another in September each year are "Free Fishing Days" when a license is not needed to fish.

HIKING/BACKPACKING

Low-cost tours in the surrounding desert are available from Desert Survivors in Oakland (tel: 510-357 6585); in the Eastern High Sierras by Shootin' Star Pack Outfitters of Bishop (tel: 619-873 8877); and in Yosemite National Park by the Yosemite Mountaineering

School (tel: 559-372 8435).
Horses can be rented from Yosemite Stables (tel: 559-372 8348).

GOLF COURSES

SAN FRANCISCO AREA
Half Moon Bay Golf Links, 2000 Fairway Dr, Half Moon Bay, tel: 650-726 4438.
Harding Park Golf Course, Harding Road and Skyline Blvd., San Francisco, tel: 415-664 4690.
Lincoln Park Golf Course, 34th and Clement streets, San Francisco, tel: 415-221 9911.
Pasatiempo Golf Course, 18 Clubhouse Road, Santa Cruz, tel: 831-459 9155.
Tilden Park Golf Course, Grizzly Peak Blvd. and Shasta Road, Berkeley, tel: 510-848 7373.

MONTEREY PENINSULA
Del Monte Golf Course, 1300 Sylvan Road, Monterey, tel: 831-373 2700.
Laguna Seca Golf Club, 10520 York Road, Monterey, tel: 408-373 3701.
The Links at Spanish Bay, 2700 17-Mile Dr., Pacific Grove, tel: 831-624 6611, ext. 66.
Pacific Grove Municipal Golf Links, 77 Asilomar Blvd., Pacific Grove, tel: 831-648 3177.
Pebble Beach Golf Links, 17-Mile Dr., Pebble Beach, tel: 408-624 3811, ext. 228.
Poppy Hills Golf Course, 3200 Lopez Road, Pebble Beach, tel: 831-625 2035.
Rancho Canada Golf Course, 1 mile east of State 1 on Carmel Valley Road, Carmel, tel: 831-624 0111.
Spyglass Hill Golf Course, Stevenson Dr. and Spyglass Hill Road, Pebble Beach, tel: 831-625-8563.

SIERRAS
La Contenta Lakes Golf and Country Club, 1635 State 26, Valley Springs, telephone 559-

Whale Watching

The American Cetacean Society is among the many groups that organize trips to see some of the thousands of 40-ton California gray whales that start their 10,000-mile (17,700-km) migration from Alaska to South America in the fall, and back in the spring. Traveling 80–100 miles (130–160 km) per day, some of these mammals can be seen from high spots along the coast – particularly from the Palos Verdes Peninsula – and around the Channel Islands.

Some other whalewatching cruise options are: Point Reyes Lighthouse at the Point Reyes National Seashore, north of San Francisco; boats go out from Santa Cruz Harbor (tel: 831-475 6161); Sea Landing in Santa Barbara (tel: 805-963 3564); and Redondo Sport Fishing (tel: 310-372 2111) in Redondo Beach. Seals and sea lions are also plentiful in the islands to which Island Packers (tel: 805-642 1393), run trips and about which the Channel

Islands National Park (tel: 805-658 5730), can provide a wealth of information. In addition, snowy plovers and cormorants are found on San Miguel; kestrels, larks and owls on Santa Barbara; and brown pelicans, who nest between May and August, on Anacapa, the closest island to the mainland. For information about Santa Cruz, the largest island of the group, call the Nature Conservancy (tel: 805-962 9111).

772 1081 for information.
Lake Tahoe Golf Course, State 50 West, South Lake Tahoe, tel: 530-577 0788.
Northstar-at-Tahoe Golf Course, Basque Dr. off State 267, Truckee, tel: 530-562 2490.
Tahoe Donner Golf Course, Northwoods Blvd., Truckee, tel: 530-587 9440.
Tahoe Paradise Golf Course, State 50, Tahoe Paradise, tel: 530-577 2121.

WINE COUNTRY
Napa Municipal Golf Course, 2295 Streblow Dr., Napa, tel: 707-255 4333.
Silverado Country Club and Resort, 1600 Atlas Peak Road, Napa, tel: 707-257 0200.
Sonoma Golf Club, 17700 Arnold Dr., Sonoma, tel: 707-996 0300.

GREATER LOS ANGELES AREA
Brookside Golf Course, 1133 N Rosemont Ave., Pasadena, tel: 626-796 0177.
Griffith Golf Courses, 4730 Crystal Springs Dr., Los Angeles, tel: 323-663 2555.
Industry Hills Golf Club, 1 Industry Hills Pkwy, City of Industry, tel: 626-810 4653.
Rancho Park Golf Course, 10460 W Pico Blvd., Beverly Hills, tel: 310-838 7373.

ORANGE COUNTY
Costa Mesa Golf Course, 1701 Golf Course Dr., Costa Mesa, tel: 714-754 5267
Newport Beach Golf Course, 3100 Irvine Ave., Newport Beach, tel: 949-852 8681.

SAN DIEGO AREA
Balboa Park Municipal Golf Course, Golf Course Dr., San Diego, tel: 619-239 1632.
Mission Bay Golf Center, 2702 N Mission Bay Dr., San Diego, tel: 619-490 3370.
Pala Mesa Resort, 2001 State 395, Fallbrook, tel: 760-728 5881.
Rancho Bernardo Inn and Country Club, 17550 Bernardo Oaks Dr., Rancho Bernardo, tel: 619-487 0700.

SANTA BARBARA AREA
Alisal Golf Course, 1054 Alisal Road, Solvang, tel: 805-688 4215.
La Purisima Golf Course, 3455 State 246, Lompoc, tel: 805-735 8395.
Ojai Valley Inn and Country Club, 1203 Country Club Road, Ojai, tel: 805-646 5511.
Sandpiper Golf Course, 7925 Hollister Ave., Santa Barbara, tel: 805-968 1541.

PALM SPRINGS AREA
Indian Wells Golf Resort, Grand

Champions Hotel, Indian Wells, tel: 760-346-GOLF.
La Quinta Hotel Golf and Tennis Resort, La Quinta, tel: 760-564 7610.
Mission Hills Resort Hotel and Golf Club, Rancho Mirage, tel: 760-770 9496.
Palm Springs Municipal Golf Course, 1885 Golf Club Dr., Palm Springs, tel: 760-328 1956.
PGA West, 56150 PGA Blvd., La Quinta, tel: 760-564 7170.

SKIING

LAKE TAHOE AREA
Alpine Meadows, Alpine Meadows Road off State 89 between Truckee and Tahoe City, tel: 530-581 8225.
Boreal Ridge, Castle Peak exit off Interstate 80 at Soda Springs, tel: 530-426 3666.
Heavenly Valley, Ski Run Blvd. off US 50, South Lake Tahoe, tel: 530-541 1330.
Homewood, State 89, 6 miles south of Tahoe City, tel: 530-525 2992.
Northstar-at-Tahoe, State 267 Between Truckee and Kings Beach, tel: 530-562 1010.
Squaw Valley USA, Squaw Valley Road off State 89, 5 miles north of Tahoe City, tel: 530-583 6985.

CENTRAL SIERRA

Badger Pass, Glacier Point Road in Yosemite National Park off State 41, tel: 530-372 8344.
Dodge Ridge, Off State 108, 32 miles east of Sonora, tel: 530-965 3474.
Kirkwood, State 88 at Carson Pass, 35 miles south of South Lake Tahoe, tel: 530-258 6000.
Mount Reba/Bear Valley, State 4, 52 miles east of Angels Camp, tel: 530-753 2301.
Sierra Ski Ranch, off US 50, 12 miles west of South Lake Tahoe, tel: 530-659 7475.
Sierra Summit, State 168, 64 miles northeast of Fresno at Huntington Lake, Big Creek, tel: 559-893 3311.

WATER ACTIVITIES

Whitewater rafting expeditions are organized in the Gold Country near Yosemite and Tahoe and throughout the Sierras by many companies including: Arta River Trips (tel: 1-800-323-2782); Earthtrek Whitewater Expeditions (tel: 1-800-229-8735); Whitewater Voyages (tel: 1-800-488-7238).

Kern River Tours (tel: 760-379 4616, operates out of Lake Isabella, three hours north of Los Angeles. Aqua Adventures Kayak School in San Diego and Paddle Power Inc (tel: 949-729 DUNE, of Newport Beach offer kayak lessons and rentals. Cass' Sailing School and Charters (tel: 1-800-4SAIL95) in Sausalito organizes sailing and yachting in the San Francisco Bay area.

Shopping

Shopping Areas

Northern California

From elegant malls to farmers' markets, Northern California offers a wide array of shopping opportunities. In San Francisco alone, there are 20 distinct shopping areas. The most famous is probably **Union Square**, where most of the large, prestigious department stores are located, including Neiman-Marcus, Macy's and Saks. A block away is **Maiden Lane**, a cute pedestrian street with boutiques, stationery stores and an outdoor café. **The Galleria**, a collection of specialty shops, restaurants and services housed under a vaulting glass dome, modeled after Milan's Galleria Vittorio Emmanuelle, is nearby, as is the **San Francisco Centre**. In SoMa, look for good souvenirs in the galleries and art shops, plus check out Sony's **Metreon Center**.

Visitors will find an abundance of shopping in the **Fisherman's Wharf** area. The shopping area extends from **Pier 39** to **Ghirardelli Square** and includes the Cannery, the Anchorage and a host of street vendors. Once a cargo wharf, Pier 39 now offers two levels of shops, restaurants, amusements and free outdoor entertainment by some of the city's best street performers. Both the Cannery and Ghirardelli Square are converted factories. The Cannery was once a Del Monte peach canning plant, and Ghirardelli once housed a chocolate factory. The Anchorage, a colorful, modern

shopping complex, is also located along the Northern Waterfront. Along with specialty shops and galleries, each complex offers unique land-scaping, live entertainment, open-air walkways and breath-taking views across to Alcatraz, the Golden Gate Bridge and the bay.

The **Embarcadero Center** is also located on the waterfront, east of Pier 39 near the Financial District. This is San Francisco's largest mall with numerous shops, restaurants and nightclubs in four complexes between Sacramento and Clay streets.

Other shopping areas in San Francisco tend to reflect the unique character of the neighborhood. They include Columbus Avenue. and Grant Street in North Beach (**Little Italy**), Grant Street in **Chinatown**, **Castro** Street between 20th and Market and between Market and Church, **Haight Street** along the Golden Gate Park Panhandle, **Union Street** at Cow Hollow, and the **Japan Center**.

In the **East Bay**, visitors will find a distinct collegiate shopping atmosphere along vendor-laden Telegraph Avenue in Berkeley, and Berkeley's famous "Gourmet Ghetto" along Shattuck Avenue, as well as a stretch of College Avenue up near the campus. Other locations in the Bay Area boasting boutiques, restaurants and specialty stores include Solano Avenue in Albany, Piedmont Avenue and Jack London Square in Oakland, University Avenue in Palo Alto, Stanford's toned-down "Telegraph Avenue" and the entire business district of Sausalito.

Southern California

For intrepid shoppers, Southern California is right up there with the big guns like Paris, New York and Hong Kong. No matter what your taste or budget, you are bound to find whatever you're looking for.

Of course, the glitziest shopping street is Los Angeles' renowned **Rodeo Drive**. While Rodeo has become quite a tourist trap, with more people window shopping than buying, there are some terrific, world-

Melrose Avenue

A trip down **Melrose Avenue** is a must. Some of Southern California's best people-watching goes on here, and there are plenty of little cafés to serve as rest stops. Those into avant-garde high fashion can go to **Maxfield** near Doheny and Melrose, an austere temple of haute style, where stars like Jack Nicholson, Robin Williams and a host of rock 'n' rollers find labels like Gaultier, Lagerfeld and Katherine Hamnett. For a change of pace you might want to browse among one of the country's largest collections of antique books at the **Heritage Book Store** in the 8500 block of Melrose, where an extensive autograph collection includes those of Mark Twain and Charles Dickens.

class shops along the drive, with names like Chanel, Armani, Ungaro, Alaia and Bottega Veneta.

Rodeo Drive's luxurious amenities were increased dramatically, by 40 percent, with the ingenious addition of another street, **Two Rodeo** (or **Via Rodeo**), a curving, cobble-stoned walkway lined with top-name stores like Tiffany, Christian Dior and Cartier, whose classy emporiums feature granite colonnades and copper-toned roofs. Developer Douglas Stitzel and his Japanese

Clothing Sizes

This table gives a comparison of American, Continental and British clothing sizes. It is always best to try on articles before buying, however, as sizes may vary.

Women's Dresses/Suits

American	Continental	British
6	38/34N	8/30
8	40/36N	10/32
10	42/38N	12/34
12	44/40N	14/36
14	46/42N	16/38
16	48/44N	18/40

Women's Shoes

American	Continental	British
4½	36	3
5½	37	4
6½	38	5
7½	39	6
8½	40	7
9½	41	8
10½	42	9

Men's Suits

American	Continental	British
34	44	34
-	46	36
38	48	38
-	50	40
42	52	42
-	54	44
46	56	46

Men's Shirts

American	Continental	British
14	36	14
14½	37	14½
15	38	15
15½	39	15½
16	40	16
16½	41	16½
17	42	17

Men's Shoes

American	Continental	British
6½	39	6
7½	40	7
8½	41	8
9½	42	9
10½	43	10
11½	44	11

partners compare Via Rodeo with its Rome counterpart, Via Condotti. An underground parking lot offering free valet parking feeds shoppers right into the middle of the street.

Although such trendy shopping streets as **La Brea Avenue** off Melrose and Santa Monica's **Montana Avenue** have not lost their luster, there always seems to be a thriving newcomer. A recent one that has had people flocking is Venice's **Abbott Kinney Boulevard** (named after the visionary developer who created Venice at the turn of the century.) Palm trees have been planted and set off art galleries, vintage clothing and jewelry stores. Even more recently the **Silver Lake** district – centered on Vermont Avenue and Sunset Blvd. – has become the trendy area, full of fashion boutiques and street vendors.

It mustn't be forgotten that for mall-lovers, Southern California is a shopper's Valhalla. One of the Southland's most famous landmarks, the outstanding former Uniroyal tire plant beside the Santa Ana Freeway in the City of Commerce, has re-emerged as the **Citadel Outlet Collection**, an enticing shopping plaza whose 42 stores spread around a tree-flanked courtyard. The mind reels at the number of mega-malls dotted throughout the region: **Century City, Beverly Center, Topanga Plaza, Del Amo Fashion Square** and **Fashion Island** among them. But you might want to concentrate your energies on the South Coast Plaza in Costa Mesa (just a stone's throw from Newport in Orange County), a shopping tour-de-force.

South Coast Plaza is huge and all the shops are first-rate: J Crew (of mail-order fame), Armani, a Museum of Modern Art giftstore, Joan and David, Yves Saint-Laurent and the West Coast's first Calvin Klein Boutique to name just a few, as well as a wide range of eateries.

Because of its upscale nature, the Palm Springs region is understandably one big shopping area, with the **Desert Fashion Plaza** on Palm Canyon Drive possibly outclassed only by Palm Desert's nearby **Town Center**, where dozens of shops and an outdoor ice-skating rink are flanked by five major department stores. Equally attractive is the charm and ambiance of Santa Barbara's **La Arcada** shopping paseo, a cheerful Spanish-style courtyard adorned with tiles, ornamental ironwork and bright flags.

Yet another era is evoked by San Diego's **Gaslamp Quarter**, a 16-block, 38-acre (16-hectare) district recommended for arts and crafts browsers. In addition to that city's **Seaport Village** and the multilevel **Horton Plaza**, it also allows a short excursion to the Mexican border town of **Tijuana**, where there are different souvenirs and lower prices.

In California there is a sales tax of 7.25 percent on most items (unprepared food, for example, is exempt), which is always assessed at the cash register, so prices never reflect the tax included price (unless indicated – gasoline prices always include the tax). To further complicate matters, various cities and counties levy an additional sales tax, usually approved by the voters to raise money to meet an urgent need. Residents of Los Angeles, for example, voted to increase the local sales tax to 8.25 percent in order to raise money to accelerate repairs after the 1994 earthquake.

Further Reading

General

Back Roads of California, by Earl Thomas. Clarkson N Potter, 1983.

Behind the Mask of Innocence, by Kevin Brownlow. Alfred A Knopf, 1990.

California: A Guide to the Golden State, by the Federal Writers Project. Hastings House, 1939.

California Coastal Access Guide, by the California Coastal Commission.

California: The Golden Coast, by Philip L Fradkin. Viking Press, 1973.

California: Ranch Days, by Helen Bauer. Doubleday, 1953.

California Southern Country, by Carey McWilliams. Duell, Sloan Pearce, 1946.

California's Missions, edited by Ralph B Wright. Hubert A Lowan, 1978.

Coast Walks by John Mckinney Olympus Press, 1999

A Guide to Architecture in Los Angeles and Southern California, by Gebhard and Winter.

Let Me Entertain You, by David Brown. William Morrow, 1990.

Los Angeles A–Z: an Encyclopedia of City & Country, by Dale & Leonard Pitt. University of California Press, 1997.

Los Angeles: A City Apart, by David L Clark. Windsor Publications, 1981.

The Los Angeles Food Guide, by Peggy Mellody. Clarkson Potter, 1992.

The Missions of California, by Melba Levick and Stanley Young. Chronicle Books, 1988.

The Real Oscar, by Peter H Brown. Arlington House, 1991.

Southern California: An Island on the Land, by Carey McWilliams. Peregrine Smith, 1946.

Street Gallery: Guide to 1000 Los Angeles Murals, by Robin J Dunkitz. RJD Enterprise, 1993.

Take Sunset Boulevard, by Barbara and Rudy Marinacci. Presidio Press, 1980.

Tales from the Hollywood Raj, by Sheridan Morley. Viking Press, NY 1983.

Walk Los Angeles: Adventures on the Urban Edge, by John McKinney. Olympus Press, 1992.

People & Places

All the Stars in Heaven: Louis B Mayer's MGM, by Gary Carey. E.P. Dutton, 1981.

The Encyclopedia of Hollywood, by Scott and Barbara Siegel. Facts on File, 1990.

Fantasy by the Sea, by Tom Sewell Moran. Beyond Baroque Foundation, 1979.

The Great Movie Stars: The Golden Years, by David Shipman. Crown, 1970.

Hollywood, Land and Legend, by CC and B Crane. Arlington House, 1980.

Life and Good Times of William Randolph Hearst, by John Tebbel. EP Dutton, 1952.

The Life of Raymond Chandler, by Frank McShane. EP Dutton, 1976.

Los Angeles Stories, Great Writers on the City, edited by John Miller. Chronicle Books, 1991.

Out with the Stars, by Jim Heimann. Abbeville, 1985.

Santa Barbara Architecture, by Noel Young and Herb Andree. Capra Press, 1980.

Santa Barbara Celebrities: Conversations from the American Riviera, by Cork Millner. Santa Barbara Press, 1989.

Day Hikers Guide to California State Parks by John Mckinney Olympus Press, 1998

The Los Angeles Watts Towers, by Bud & Arloa Goldstone. The Getty Institute, 1997.

This is Hollywood, by Ken Schessler. Universal Books, 1989.

Venice of America, by Jeffrey Stanton. Donahue Publications, 1987.

Geography & Natural History

California Patterns: A Geographical and Historical Atlas, by David Hornbeck. Mayfield, 1983.

California Wildlife Map Book, by Vinson Brown and David Hoover. Naturegraph Publishers, 1967.

California: The Geography of Diversity, by Crane Miller and Richard Hyslop. Mayfield, 1983.

California Wildlife Reviewing Guide, by Jeanne L Clarke. Falcon Press, 1996.

The City and the Country, by Harry Ellington Brook. Kingsley, Barnes and Newner, 1987.

Natural Los Angeles, by Bill Thomas. Harper and Row, 1989.

The Natural World of San Francisco, by Harold Gilliam and Michael Bry. Doubleday, 1967.

Spring Wild Flowers of the San Francisco Bay Area, by Helen Sharsmith. University of California Press, 1965.

Walk Los Angeles: Adventures on tbe Urban Ridge, by John McKinney. *Los Angeles Times*, 1992.

History

Berkeley: The Town and Gown of It, by George Pettitt. Howel North Books, 1973.

California: A Bicentennial History, by David Lavender. WW Norton, 1976.

The California Missions: A Pictorial History, by the editors of Sunset Magazine. Lane, 1979.

A Century of Dishonor, by Helen Hunt Jackson. Scholarly Press, 1880.

A Companion to California, by James Hart. (Oxford University Press, 1978.

The Days of the Great Estates, by David F Myrick Trans-Angelo Books, 1990.

History of the San Fernando Valley, by Frank M Keffner. Stillman, 1934.

Hollywood: The First Hundred Years, by Bruce T Torrence. New York Zoetrope, 1982.

Indians of Early Southern California, by Edna B Ziebold. Sapsis, 1969.

Los Angeles, Biography of a City, by John and LaRee Coughey. University of California Press, 1977.

Los Angeles: A Profile, by WW Robinson. University of Oklahoma, 1968.

Los Angeles: From Pueblo to City of the Future, by Andrew Rolls. Boyd and Fraster, 1981.

Los Angeles Two Hundred, by David Lavender. Harry N Abrams, 1980.

Oakland: The Story of a City, by Beth Bagwell. Presidio Press, 1982.

Pictorial History of California, by Paul C Johnson. Bonanza, 1970.

The San Fernando Valley, Past and Present, by Lawrence C Jorgensen. Pacific Rim Research, 1982.

San Francisco Almanac, by Gladys Hansen. Presidio Press, 1980.

A Short History of San Francisco, by Tom Cole. Monte Rosa, 1981.

A Short History of the Movies, by Gerald Mast. University of Chicago Press, 1971.

The Times We Had: Life with William Randolph Hearst, by Marion Davis. Bobbs Merrill, 1975.

Yesterday's Los Angeles, by Norman Dash. EA Seamann Publishing, 1976.

Other Insight Guides

Other Insight Guides highlighting destinations in this region include:

An insider's look at America's most fascinating city, and the beautiful countryside around it.

Capture the energy and glamour of America's movie capital.

Insight Pocket Guides and Compact Guides offer essential information and personal recommendations for visitors in a hurry.

ART & PHOTO CREDITS

A & I 2/3
Bill Bachman/Scoopix 156/157
Bancroft Library 23, 24, 25L, 34, 37, 38, 39, 40, 41, 46, 210T
Bodo Bondzio 30, 220/221, 228/229
California State University 22
Shubroto Chattopadhyay 194/195
City Hotel/Tom Bender 212
The El Capitan Theatre Company 259T
Lee Foster 211
Glyn Genin 1, 120T, 121, 122B, 123, 124B, 125, 131, 133B, 134, 137, 138BL, 140, 141, 147, 151, 153T, 159, 162T, 162B, 172T, 172B, 252, 257, 259B, 265T, 266, 275T, 283, 284, 291, 300T, 307, 308T, 309L, 320T, 324, 326T, 326B, 333B
Allen Grazer 217
D J Hawkins/Bret R Lundberg 311
Kerrick James 8/9, 10/11, 61, 82/83, 84, 91, 93, 118, 119, 130, 138T, 138BR, 139, 184/185, 188T, 198T, 206/207, 288/289, 290, 345, 350/351
Catherine Karnow 4/5, 14, 55, 56/57, 58/59, 63, 66, 69, 86, 96/97, 99, 103, 106/107, 108/109, 120B, 126, 127, 136, 143, 146, 158, 161, 164, 168/169, 170, 174/175, 177, 179T, 179B, 182T, 183, 214/215, 218, 224, 225, 227T, 227B, 231, 232T, 234, 236/237, 240, 250, 253, 254B, 260B, 261, 262, 263B, 267, 273T, 274, 277, 278/279, 280, 281, 287T, 299, 303, 320B
Las Vegas News Bureau 327
Bud Lee 65, 67, 98, 223, 245, 258, 285, 295B, 302, 306
Lewis Kemper 343, 347B, 348T
Melba Levick 104/105, 238/239, 247, 275B, 296/297
Bret R. Lundberg 6/7, 12/13, 62, 122T, 135, 142, 144/145, 153B, 160, 173, 196, 205, 208, 209, 233, 255, 270, 271, 312, 313, 314, 315, 316/317, 323B, 330, 331, 335, 336, 339, 340/341, 344, 347T, 348B
Jim Mendenhall/Los Angeles Convention & Visitors Bureau 263T, 265B
Movieland Wax Museum 301
Palm Springs Tourism 319, 321, 346

Carole Pearlman 80
Petersen Automotive Museum 101
David Ryan 154
San Diego Convention & Visitors Bureau 334
San Diego Zoo 333T
San Francisco Museum of Modern Art (SFMOMA) 133T
John Sanford 28, 132, 202B
Santa Barbara Conference and Visitors Bureau 293
Seaver Center for Western History 43, 44, 47, 72/73
Sunkist Growers Inc. 42
Thomas Gilcrease Institute of American History & Art, Tulsa, Oklahoma 18/19
Tom Till 349
Topham Picturepoint 50, 52L, 52R, 53, 54
Doug Traverso 60, 64, 68, 87, 88, 89, 90, 92, 102, 110, 114, 115, 122T, 149B, 150T, 155, 163, 171, 181T, 181B, 182B, 186, 187, 188B, 189, 197, 199R, 200, 201, 202T, 204, 213, 216, 244, 246, 251, 254T, 264, 272, 273B, 276, 286, 287B, 292T, 294, 309R, 310, 314T, 325, 352
Tom Tuttle/Santa Barbara Conference and Visitors Bureau 295T
Universal Studios 282
Vautier de Nanxe 31, 85, 100, 191, 192B, 193, 256, 318, 323T, 342
© Walt Disney Company 298, 300B
Michael Webb 304/305, 328/329
Wells Fargo History Museum 33
Jan Whiting 150B, 165, 176, 180, 190, 196, 199L, 203, 219, 222, 226, 230, 232B, 235
Marcus Wilson Smith 337
Marcus Wilson Smith/APA 338T, 338B

Maps Polyglott Kartographie, Berndtson & Berndtson

Publications, Elsner & Schichor
Cartographic Editor Zoë Goodwin
Production Mohammed Dar
Design Consultant Klaus Geisler
Picture Research Hilary Genin, Monica Allende

Index

The World of Insight Guides

400 books in three complementary series cover every major destination in every continent.

Insight Guides

Alaska
Alsace
Amazon Wildlife
American Southwest
Amsterdam
Argentina
Atlanta
Athens
Australia
Austria
Bahamas
Bali
Baltic States
Bangkok
Barbados
Barcelona
Bay of Naples
Beijing
Belgium
Belize
Berlin
Bermuda
Boston
Brazil
Brittany
Brussels
Budapest
Buenos Aires
Burgundy
Burma (Myanmar)
Cairo
Calcutta
California
Canada
Caribbean
Catalonia
Channel Islands
Chicago
Chile
China
Cologne
Continental Europe
Corsica
Costa Rica
Crete
Crossing America
Cuba
Cyprus
Czech & Slovak Republics
Delhi, Jaipur, Agra
Denmark
Dresden
Dublin
Düsseldorf
East African Wildlife
East Asia
Eastern Europe
Ecuador
Edinburgh
Egypt
Finland
Florence
Florida
France
Frankfurt
French Riviera
Gambia & Senegal
Germany
Glasgow

Gran Canaria
Great Barrier Reef
Great Britain
Greece
Greek Islands
Hamburg
Hawaii
Hong Kong
Hungary
Iceland
India
India's Western Himalaya
Indian Wildlife
Indonesia
Ireland
Israel
Istanbul
Italy
Jamaica
Japan
Java
Jerusalem
Jordan
Kathmandu
Kenya
Korea
Lisbon
Loire Valley
London
Los Angeles
Madeira
Madrid
Malaysia
Mallorca & Ibiza
Malta
Marine Life in the South
    China Sea
Melbourne
Mexico
Mexico City
Miami
Montreal
Morocco
Moscow
Munich
Namibia
Native America
Nepal
Netherlands
New England
New Orleans
New York City
New York State
New Zealand
Nile
Normandy
Northern California
Northern Spain
Norway
Oman & the UAE
Oxford
Old South
Pacific Northwest
Pakistan
Paris
Peru
Philadelphia
Philippines
Poland
Portugal
Prague

Provence
Puerto Rico
Rajasthan
Rhine
Rio de Janeiro
Rockies
Rome
Russia
St Petersburg
San Francisco
Sardinia
Scotland
Seattle
Sicily
Singapore
South Africa
South America
South Asia
South India
South Tyrol
Southeast Asia
Southeast Asia Wildlife
Southern California
Southern Spain
Spain
Sri Lanka
Sweden
Switzerland
Sydney
Taiwan
Tenerife
Texas
Thailand
Tokyo
Trinidad & Tobago
Tunisia
Turkey
Turkish Coast
Tuscany
Umbria
US National Parks East
US National Parks West
Vancouver
Venezuela
Venice
Vienna
Vietnam
Wales
Washington DC
Waterways of Europe
Wild West
Yemen

Insight Pocket Guides

Aegean Islands★
Algarve★
Alsace
Amsterdam★
Athens★
Atlanta★
Bahamas★
Baja Peninsula★
Bali★
Bali Bird Walks
Bangkok★
Barbados★
Barcelona★
Bavaria★
Beijing★
Berlin★

Bermuda★
Bhutan★
Boston★
British Columbia★
Brittany★
Brussels★
Budapest &
    Surroundings★
Canton★
Chiang Mai★
Chicago★
Corsica★
Costa Blanca★
Costa Brava★
Costa del Sol/Marbella★
Costa Rica★
Crete★
Denmark★
Fiji★
Florence★
Florida★
Florida Keys★
French Riviera★
Gran Canaria★
Hawaii★
Hong Kong★
Hungary
Ibiza★
Ireland★
Ireland's Southwest★
Israel★
Istanbul★
Jakarta★
Jamaica★
Kathmandu Bikes &
    Hikes★
Kenya★
Kuala Lumpur★
Lisbon★
Loire Valley★
London★
Macau
Madrid★
Malacca
Maldives
Mallorca★
Malta★
Mexico City★
Miami★
Milan★
Montreal★
Morocco★
Moscow
Munich★
Nepal★
New Delhi
New Orleans★
New York City★
New Zealand★
Northern California★
Oslo/Bergen★
Paris★
Penang★
Phuket★
Prague★
Provence★
Puerto Rico★
Quebec★
Rhodes★
Rome★
Sabah★

St Petersburg★
San Francisco★
Sardinia
Scotland★
Seville★
Seychelles★
Sicily★
Sikkim
Singapore★
Southeast England
Southern California★
Southern Spain★
Sri Lanka★
Sydney★
Tenerife★
Thailand★
Tibet★
Toronto★
Tunisia★
Turkish Coast★
Tuscany★
Venice★
Vienna★
Vietnam★
Yogyakarta
Yucatan Peninsula★

★ = Insight Pocket Guides
with Pull out Maps

Insight Compact Guides

Algarve
Amsterdam
Bahamas
Bali
Bangkok
Barbados
Barcelona
Beijing
Belgium
Berlin
Brittany
Brussels
Budapest
Burgundy
Copenhagen
Costa Brava
Costa Rica
Crete
Cyprus
Czech Republic
Denmark
Dominican Republic
Dublin
Egypt
Finland
Florence
Gran Canaria
Greece
Holland
Hong Kong
Ireland
Israel
Italian Lakes
Italian Riviera
Jamaica
Jerusalem
Lisbon
Madeira
Mallorca
Malta

Milan
Moscow
Munich
Normandy
Norway
Paris
Poland
Portugal
Prague
Provence
Rhodes
Rome
St Petersburg
Salzburg
Singapore
Switzerland
Sydney
Tenerife
Thailand
Turkey
Turkish Coast
Tuscany
UK regional titles:
    Bath & Surroundings
    Cambridge & East
        Anglia
    Cornwall
    Cotswolds
    Devon & Exmoor
    Edinburgh
    Lake District
    London
    New Forest
    North York Moors
    Northumbria
    Oxford
    Peak District
    Scotland
    Scottish Highlands
    Shakespeare Country
    Snowdonia
    South Downs
    York
    Yorkshire Dales
USA regional titles:
    Boston
    Cape Cod
    Chicago
    Florida
    Florida Keys
    Hawaii: Maui
    Hawaii: Oahu
    Las Vegas
    Los Angeles
    Martha's Vineyard &
        Nantucket
    New York
    San Francisco
    Washington D.C.
    Venice
    Vienna
    West of Ireland